PRAISE FOR *TO BEGIN WHERE I AM*

"Milosz's vigorous and sinewy prose is that of a man of a particular historical moment ... [*To Begin Where I Am*] draws not only on the twelve books of prose already available in English but also on writings unpublished in English and newly translated for this volume by the admirable editors (who offer, in their introduction, the best brief summary in English of Milosz's importance). The reader will find, in both the expository essays and the incomparable portraits of his contemporaries, Milosz's characteristic intensity, momentum, and savage intelligence."

—HELEN VENDLER, *Harper's Magazine*

"[This collection] could not have hit the bookstores at a better time. Perhaps now, more than ever, we can appreciate Milosz's penetrating sense of the transience of butterflies, books, trees, people, civilizations. A *Weltanschauung* that only a few months ago would have seemed absurdly remote and exotic to the American experience—vanished cities and empires; criminal mass destruction and the psychic demolition it entails—is suddenly urgent and palpable ... A remarkable body of work ... Enlightening."　　—CYNTHIA L. HAVEN, *San Francisco Chronicle*

"Beguiling ... [*To Begin Where I Am*] grants privileged access to a singular literary mind ... [Milosz] displays his genius for wedding palpable, personal loss to larger themes."

—CARLIN ROMANO, *The Philadelphia Inquirer*

"A man of uncommon clearheadedness."

—CHARLES SIMIC, *The New York Review of Books*

Beginning with My Streets: Essays and Recollections

Bells in Winter

A Book of Luminous Things:
An International Anthology of Poetry

The Captive Mind

The Collected Poems, 1931–1987

Conversations with Czeslaw Milosz
(by Ewa Czarnecka and Aleksander Fiut)

Emperor of the Earth: Modes of Eccentric Vision

Facing the River

The History of Polish Literature

The Issa Valley

The Land of Ulro

Milosz's ABC's

Native Realm

Nobel Lecture

Postwar Polish Poetry: An Anthology

Provinces

Road-side Dog

The Seizure of Power

The Separate Notebooks

Striving Towards Being:
The Letters of Thomas Merton and Czeslaw Milosz

Talking to My Body: Poems by Anna Swir
(translated by Czeslaw Milosz and Leonard Nathan)

Unattainable Earth

Visions from San Francisco Bay

With the Skin: The Poems of Aleksander Wat
(introduction by Czeslaw Milosz)

The Witness of Poetry

A Year of the Hunter

TO BEGIN
WHERE
I AM

CZESLAW MILOSZ

TO BEGIN
WHERE
I AM

·

SELECTED ESSAYS

·

EDITED AND WITH AN INTRODUCTION BY

BOGDANA CARPENTER AND MADELINE G. LEVINE

·

FARRAR, STRAUS AND GIROUX

NEW YORK

Farrar, Straus and Giroux
19 Union Square West, New York 10003

Grateful acknowledgment is made for permission to reprint the following previously published material: "In Warsaw" from The Collected Poems, 1931–1987 by Czeslaw Milosz, translated by Robert Hass. Copyright © Czeslaw Milosz Royalties, Inc. Reprinted by permission of HarperCollins Publishers, Inc. "The Pebble" from Selected Poems of Zbigniew Herbert, edited and translated by Czeslaw Milosz and Peter Scott. English translation copyright © 1968 by Czeslaw Milosz and Peter Scott. Introduction copyright © 1968 by A. Alvarez. Reprinted by permission of HarperCollins Publishers, Inc. "The Most of It" by Robert Frost from The Poetry of Robert Frost, edited by Edward Connery Lathem. Copyright 1942 by Robert Frost, © 1970 by Lesley Frost Ballantine, © 1969 by Henry Holt and Co. Reprinted by permission of Henry Holt and Company, LLC. "Continent's End" from The Selected Poems of Robinson Jeffers. Copyright © 1924 and renewed 1952 by Robinson Jeffers. Used by permission of Random House, Inc. "A Ballad of Going Down to the Store" from A Memoir of the Warsaw Uprising by Miron Białoszewski, edited and translated by Madeline G. Levine. Copyright © 1977 by Ardis Publishers. Reprinted by permission of Ardis Publishers. "Alpha the Moralist" from The Captive Mind used by permission of Alfred A. Knopf, a division of Random House, Inc. "Ruins and Poetry" reprinted by permission of the publishers from The Witness of Poetry by Czeslaw Milosz, pp. 77–98, Cambridge, Mass.: Harvard University Press. Copyright © 1983 by the President and fellows of Harvard College. "Building the Barricade" and "A Woman Said to Her Neighbor" from Building the Barricade by Anna Świrszczyńska. Reprinted by permission of Ludmiła Admaska-Orłoneska.

The Library of Congress has cataloged the hardcover edition as follows:
Milosz, Czeslaw.
    [Prose works. English. Selections]
    To begin where I am : selected essays / edited and with an introduction by Bogdana Carpenter and Madeline G. Levine.— 1st. ed.
        p.   cm.
    ISBN 0-374-25890-2
    1. Milosz, Czeslaw—Translations into English.   I. Carpenter, Bogdana.   II. Levine, Madeline G.   III. Title.

PG7158.M553 A23 2001
891.8'58709—dc21

                                                                                2001033356

Paperback ISBN: 0-374-52859-4

CONTENTS

INTRODUCTION

RECOGNIZED AS ONE of the greatest twentieth-century poets, Czeslaw Milosz is equally admired as a prose writer. Among his most widely read works are *The Issa Valley*, a hauntingly beautiful novel about his native Lithuania, and *The Captive Mind*, a political treatise on Communism that is by now a classic of the genre. But Milosz's prose includes many more titles, with different rhetorical strategies and narrative devices. It embraces the most diverse genres and styles: sketches, reminiscences, philosophical essays, social and political commentaries, literary analyses, polemical articles, poetic manifestos, diaries, letters, and aphorisms, as well as two novels and a comprehensive history of Polish literature. Like his poetry, Milosz's prose expresses the desire for a "more spacious form." Sometimes, the demarcation line between poetry and prose is blurred. Thematically, Milosz's prose writings can be divided into at least four broad categories: essays on poetry and poets, philosophical and religious meditations, works of political analysis and engagement, and biographical and autobiographical sketches.

Despite the many pages he has written in praise of contradictions—including his own contradictions of spirit, to which he has repeatedly confessed—Milosz is a surprisingly consistent writer. Indifferent to intellectual and literary fashions, he has centered his writings on a few fundamental philosophical questions: the meaning of history; the existence of evil and suffering; the transience of all life; the ascendance of a scientific worldview and the decline of the religious imagination. These themes occur time and again, whether addressed directly or in the guise of an autobiographical reminiscence or historical anecdote. Although Milosz engages these fundamental questions from varied perspectives, depending on the impulse that gave rise to a particular essay or the circumstances in which it was written, and although the tone may be light, whimsical, or gravely serious, these same philosophical and metaphysical problems underlie all his work.

A reactive as well as reflective writer, Milosz responds to external stimuli that are both intellectual and purely physical. His response may be evoked by a landscape or a chance encounter, by events he has witnessed or heard about, by an artist's drawing, often by something he has read—a philosophical treatise, a poem, a memoir. He is a voracious reader, combining a scholar's intensity with a breadth of interest to match his insatiable curiosity. Like few other writers, Milosz is deeply attuned to the world around him. He has extremely sensitive antennae and is passionately engaged in all aspects of the reality that defines us as people of a certain place and time. "I am experiencing this second half of the twentieth century so intensely—kinetic sculpture, new music, fashions, the streetscapes of great cities, social mores," he declares in "Notebook."

Milosz's thought is defined by two opposite qualities: stability and movement. The first has an ethical system at its core—belief in values, hierarchy, good and evil, the ugly and the beautiful. The second arises from Milosz's perception of man's duality: "Atrocity has always lurked just below the surface of our daily hustle and bustle, our habits, social organizations, phrases, smiles." There is a constant tension in Milosz's thought between these two opposing impulses; his mind operates in contradictions which spur his thought on and account for its dynamics. His writings can be compared to concentric circles which widen with the passage of time to encompass an ever greater area. Each new experience feeds reflection, and in so doing adds another element to the intellectual architecture of his oeuvre.

Certain of Milosz's life experiences were pivotal, and triggered a need for self-redefinition as well as a fundamental revision of attitudes. Among these, two seem particularly critical: his experience of World War II and the Holocaust, and his experience of exile. The first of these caused a spiritual crisis that led to a re-evaluation of his own era and the entire European cultural heritage. Letters written in 1942–1943, in the midst of the Nazi occupation, to his fellow writer Jerzy Andrzejewski—one of which is included in this anthology—offer a dramatic testimony of Milosz's spiritual crisis. A twentieth-century version of Musset's *Confession of a Child of the Century,* they express his moral outrage at the brutality of this all-out war against "inferior" peoples and his anger toward a culture that made such brutality possible. Milosz's rebellion is directed not only at the two totalitarian ideologies, fascist and communist, but also at Western liberalism, which proved to be complacent and spiritually vacuous when confronted with totalitarian evil. Milosz's rage at this time recalls that of his younger compatriot Tadeusz Borowski, author of *This Way for the Gas, Ladies and Gentlemen,* one of the grimmest accounts of Auschwitz ever published and a bitter indictment of traditional liberalism. But there is an essential difference between Milosz and Borowski: whereas Borowski begins and ends with a gesture of disgust and with rejection of this world, Milosz goes beyond rejection and, despite the odds, pins his hopes on the tiny grain of human decency which he believes resides in each of us and which has been called, at various times, "reason, *daimo-*

nion, common sense, the categorical imperative, the moral instinct."

The letters to Andrzejewski, published in Polish in their entirety only in 1996, reveal how crucial the war years were in Milosz's spiritual evolution. They contain the nuclei of ideas he would develop later in *The Captive Mind* and *Native Realm,* in the long poems *A Treatise on Morals* and *A Treatise on Poetry,* and in many essays and shorter poems. Because of their spontaneity, because he can "loosen the reins a bit" and allow himself to "pontificate in the manner of a prophet or a preacher," the letters—like few of his other writings—reveal Milosz without any disguise. More open and closer to a personal journal than *A Year of the Hunter,* his carefully constructed "diary" of 1987–1988, the letters are a precious document of a time of profound crisis from which Milosz would draw both religious and creative strength.

The exile that began in 1951—most particularly his American exile, which started a decade later—was a cultural experience. Unlike the war, it had a spatial rather than a temporal dimension; if the axis of Milosz's wartime experience was vertical—metaphysical and ethical—his writings of exile have a horizontal axis, with "here" opposed to "there," the land of exile opposed to the native realm. America revealed to Milosz the importance of space as an ontological category, both as distance (exile) and expanse (nature). This is not to say that exile had no temporal quality; "here" and "there" implicitly assume a "now" and a "then." But Milosz's American exile, which began in 1960 with his appointment to the faculty of the University of California at Berkeley, was not just a relocation or loss. On the most immediate and emotional level, it was an encounter with North American nature, with the continent's vast expanses and elemental "inhuman" quality, so alien to a European sensibility. Intellectually, it was a confrontation with the American spiritual tradition. Milosz confronted both nature and America's spiritual tradition through the poetry and philosphy of the California poet Robinson Jeffers.

In his prose, Milosz is a master storyteller as well as a master portrait painter able to turn even the most ordinary people into vibrant characters. Personal stories are often projected against a broad historical and social background, resembling a vast canvas. These stories reflect Milosz's conception of history as the sum of an infinite number of individual lives, whether lived in the glare of fame or in total obscurity. Thus the prevalence of biographical sketches in his prose: the analytical studies of four Polish writers at the core of *The Captive Mind*; the vivid depictions of friends and colleagues in *Native Realm*; the tender obituaries commemorating dear friends; the novelistic portrayals of a host of people who return to haunt his memory in the year following his wife Janina's death in *A Year of the Hunter*; the mini-portraits painted with just a few brush strokes that combine to lend *Milosz's ABC's* the weight of a collective history. Always guarding his privacy, averse to confessional writings of a personal nature, Milosz has discovered that biography can be a form of, and a surrogate for, autobiography. Milosz's most self-revealing pages are not those where he speaks of himself, but those where he speaks of others. The portraits of Alpha in *The Captive Mind* and Tiger in *Native Realm* serve Milosz as foils, as a way to confront himself. For decades he has been writing—in a number of prose genres—the story of his life and times. It is as if he has created through the totality of his prose writings the capacious novel of the twentieth century, analogous to *The Magic Mountain*, that he describes in *A Year of the Hunter*.

Milosz's cumulative "novel" is an even grander enterprise than the one he projected. It encompasses, and rescues from oblivion, scores of individuals who lived and died without anyone taking particular notice of them. Having experienced in his lifetime all the major convulsions of twentieth-century Europe, Milosz has taken upon himself the duty to bear witness, to counter the voices that would obscure the historical facts as he knows them, and simultaneously to challenge the omnipotence of death. For Milosz, it would seem, everyone who survives in his memory has a claim on his pen. In 1945, in the poem "In Warsaw," the poet voiced his fear of the demands of the dead: "I cannot / Write anything; five hands / Seize my pen and order me to write / The story of their lives and deaths." The dead have been tugging at Milosz's sleeve for over half a century. He has found in their stories a key to his own, and in taking note of their lives (because "no one but me remembers their names anymore") he has accomplished that most important of obligations: taking his stand on the side of man, against the "humiliation" that is death.

Other people serve as interlocutors in Milosz's philosophical writings; they are adversaries in a debate and allies in an argument. Milosz's temperament is "dialogical," and his ideas develop most forcefully in the process of writing polemics. Among those with whom he polemicizes are Jeffers, Dostoevsky, Frost, and Pasternak. The intellectual challenge of Jeffers's "inhumanism" or Dostoevsky's Russian messianism has been particularly poignant for Milosz because of the admiration—and, in the case of Jeffers, the deep affinity—he feels for them as writers. Equally important is Milosz's need for teachers and kindred souls: "I met Tiger in the way a river, hollowing out a bed for itself on a plain, meets a second river; it had been inevitable." The image captures the importance of intellectual friendships in Milosz's life and his need for partners against whom he can try out his ideas or with whom he shares common values. These partners can be friends, but they can also be writers or philosophers from other eras. His essays on Simone Weil, Lev Shestov, William Blake, and Oscar Milosz are good examples of dialogues conducted across time and space. Milosz constructs a private pantheon of philosophers, poets, and thinkers who share his preoccupations and come close to his own solutions, whether it be Shestov's protest against necessity and reason, Weil's praise of contradictions and her unorthodox Catholicism, or Blake's vision of the land of Ulro. They are "other voices," but they accord with his own.

As in all his writings, Milosz's views on poetry and literature as expressed in his essays are rooted in historical experience and philosophical meditation. His opinions are often at odds with major literary trends of the twentieth century. For instance, the experience of World War II did not lead Milosz to despair and nihilism. Believing that affirmation is more important than negation for human survival, Milosz defends the "arcadian myth" and the need for beauty and poetry in the face of destruction, and thus indirectly rejects Adorno's famous adage about the impossibility of writing lyric poetry after Auschwitz. His defense is carried out on behalf of man: "Sometimes the world loses its face," he writes in "A Semi-Private Letter About Poetry." "It becomes too base. The task of the poet is to restore its face, because otherwise man is lost in doubt and despair." This is the path followed by the best Polish postwar poets, whom Milosz discusses in his Norton lecture "Ruins and Poetry," delivered at Harvard University in 1981. The poetry of Zbigniew Herbert, Anna Świrszczyńska and Miron Białoszewski becomes for Milosz an example of what poetry can be in the twentieth century: a poetry in which the individual and the historical are fused and in which "events burdening a whole community are perceived by a poet as touching him in a most personal manner."

Milosz's conception of poetry is fundamentally teleological, and rooted in a deep respect for reality. The description of external reality implies more than mimesis; it is "a revelation of reality" because it requires "intense observation, so intense that the veil of everyday habit falls away and what we paid no attention to, because it struck us as so ordinary, is revealed as miraculous." Poetry thus conceived becomes an instrument of knowledge, and at the same time a metaphysical experience that affords instants of epiphany.

There is a striking consistency throughout Milosz's life in his approach to poetry and to reality. In his childhood love of the world of nature, and in his early passion for naming plants, birds, and insects, one can already see his future insistence on the superiority of reality to art. Naming, for the young boy and for the mature poet, is a means of appropriating the world: "I was an unrequited romantic lover, until I found the way to dispel that inva-

sion of desires, to make the desired object mine—by naming it."
Milosz's poems, like his childhood notebook entries, teem with
names of people, places, trees, rivers: Polish, Lithuanian, American. Naming is an act of appropriation, but also an act of sal-
vaging reality from oblivion and nonexistence by placing it
outside time in an ideal place—a poem. Much the same impulse
governs his prose.

Thematically consistent in his writing, Milosz has a protean
ability to reach for, and just as often to create, ever-new forms.
The sheer diversity of the genres he commands is astonishing.
Yet it would be inaccurate to describe the evolution of his prose
in terms of simple linear progression. Certain forms, such as portraits or sketches, characterize many of his works—from *The
Captive Mind*, written in 1951, to his most recent, the *ABC's*. At
best, it is possible to point to a few general tendencies. The earlier
pieces, usually inspired by a specific experience, found their most
appropriate forms in letters, manifestos, polemics. Their tone, as
in the letters to Andrzejewski and Wyka, is personal and passionate. The 1950s, 1960s, and 1970s, marked by double exile and a
need for self-redefinition, required distance and objectivity;
whether Milosz speaks of himself directly—as in the openly autobiographical *Native Realm*—or indirectly—as in the biographies of his Polish fellow writers in *The Captive Mind*—the tone
is detached and analytical. At the same time, self-redefinition implies taking a stance, often polemical, toward the new experience.
The essays written in the 1980s and 1990s are no longer closely
connected to a particular experience, but become general reflections on man, history, culture, and religion. They are reflective
rather than reactive; their tone is calmer and meditative, rarely
critical or argumentative.

Milosz is one of the most accomplished essayists in Polish
postwar literature, which abounds in excellent writers of essays.
The free, unregulated form of the essay is attractive because it
adapts to different subjects and personal styles. Under Milosz's

pen, the essay, while retaining its formal suppleness, becomes an instrument of rigorous intellectual inquiry. Many of Milosz's earlier essays are parts of carefully constructed and thematically cohesive projects such as *The Captive Mind, Visions from San Francisco Bay,* and *The Land of Ulro.* Milosz's prose of the past ten years tends toward shorter and shorter forms; it is often digressive, less concerned with an overall structure, and organized by an arbitrarily adopted order—chronological in *The Year of the Hunter,* alphabetical in *Milosz's ABC's.* This looser form allows forays into many more topics, places, and times, and is particularly well suited to reflection. As Milosz approaches ninety, it becomes harder and harder for him to enclose his vast experience within a single structure, and only a calendar or an alphabet can impose upon it some order, however limited and imperfect.

The present volume gathers together a sampling of Czeslaw Milosz's nonfiction prose writings. It spans a period of five decades. The earliest piece, "Letter to Jerzy Andrzejewski," was written in occupied Warsaw in the autumn of 1942; the most recent essay, "Happiness," appeared in 1998. Seven of the essays were translated specifically for inclusion in this volume. They reveal aspects of Milosz's spiritual development and his responses to contemporary poetry that have hitherto been accessible only to his Polish readers.

The selection of essays here was guided by a desire to represent Milosz's extraordinary thematic breadth as well as the diversity of the genres and styles he commands. The essays are grouped into three sections. Part I, "These Guests of Mine," introduces Milosz through autobiographical accounts and biographical sketches of people who were representative of the historical currents that shaped his life. Part II, "On the Side of Man," presents Milosz as the profoundly serious religious thinker he has always been. Part III, "Against Incomprehensible Poetry," gathers together Milosz's most significant writings on the obligations of poetry and concludes with his assessments of four major poets of the twentieth century. Part IV, "In Constant Amazement," containing the excerpts from "Notebook" with which this volume concludes, serves as a reprise of the themes that have dominated Milosz's writing, and thus this book.

BOGDANA CARPENTER
MADELINE G. LEVINE
APRIL 2001

The editors gratefully acknowledge the assistance of Svetlana Krylova and Carla Stec, doctoral students in the Department of Slavic Languages and Literatures at the University of North Carolina, Chapel Hill.

MY INTENTION

I AM HERE. Those three words contain all that can be said—
you begin with those words and you return to them. Here
means on this earth, on this continent and no other, in this
city and no other, in this epoch I call mine, this century, this year.
I was given no other place, no other time, and I touch my desk to
defend myself against the feeling that my own body is transient.
This is all very fundamental, but, after all, the science of life depends on the gradual discovery of fundamental truths.

I have written on various subjects, and not, for the most part,
as I would have wished. Nor will I realize my long-standing intention this time. But I am always aware that what I want is impossible to achieve. I would need the ability to communicate my
full amazement at "being here" in one unattainable sentence
which would simultaneously transmit the smell and texture of
my skin, everything stored in my memory, and all I now assent to,
dissent from. However, in pursuing the impossible, I did learn
something. Each of us is so ashamed of his own helplessness and
ignorance that he considers it appropriate to communicate only
what he thinks others will understand. There are, however, times

when somehow we slowly divest ourselves of that shame and begin to speak openly about all the things we do not understand. If I am not wise, then why must I pretend to be? If I am lost, why must I pretend to have ready counsel for my contemporaries? But perhaps the value of communication depends on the acknowledgment of one's own limits, which, mysteriously, are also limits common to many others; and aren't these the same limits of a hundred or a thousand years ago? And when the air is filled with the clamor of analysis and conclusion, would it be entirely useless to admit you do not understand?

I have read many books, but to place all those volumes on top of one another and stand on them would not add a cubit to my stature. Their learned terms are of little use when I attempt to seize naked experience, which eludes all accepted ideas. To borrow their language can be helpful in many ways, but it also leads imperceptibly into a self-contained labyrinth, leaving us in alien corridors which allow no exit. And so I must offer resistance, check every moment to be sure I am not departing from what I have actually experienced on my own, what I myself have touched. I cannot invent a new language and I use the one I was first taught, but I can distinguish, I hope, between what is mine and what is merely fashionable. I cannot expel from memory the books I have read, their contending theories and philosophies, but I am free to be suspicious and to ask naïve questions instead of joining the chorus which affirms and denies.

Intimidation. I am brave and undaunted in the certainty of having something important to say to the world, something no one else will be called to say. Then the feeling of individuality and a unique role begins to weaken and the thought of all the people who ever were, are, and ever will be—aspiring, doubting, believing—people superior to me in strength of feeling and depth of mind, robs me of confidence in what I call my "I." The words of a prayer two millennia old, the celestial music created by a composer in a wig and jabot make me ask why I, too, am here, why me? Shouldn't one evaluate his chances beforehand—

either equal the best or say nothing? Right at this moment, as I put these marks to paper, countless others are doing the same, and our books in their brightly colored jackets will be added to that mass of things in which names and titles sink and vanish. No doubt, also at this very moment, someone is standing in a bookstore and, faced with the sight of those splendid and vain ambitions, is making his decision—silence is better. That single phrase which, were it truly weighed, would suffice as a life's work. However, here, now, I have the courage to speak, a sort of secondary courage, not blind. Perhaps it is my stubbornness in pursuit of that single sentence. Or perhaps it is my old fearlessness, temperament, fate, a search for a new dodge. In any case, my consolation lies not so much in the role I have been called on to play as in the great mosaic-like whole which is composed of the fragments of various people's efforts, whether successful or not. I am here— and everyone is in some "here"—and the only thing we can do is try to communicate with one another.

PART ONE

THESE GUESTS
OF MINE

WHO WAS I?

1

W HO WAS I? Who am I now, years later, here on Griz-
zly Peak, in my study overlooking the Pacific? I have
long deferred the telling of certain spiritual adventures, alluding to them until now only discreetly and grudgingly.
Until I noticed that it was getting late—in the history of our
shrinking Earth, in the history of a life—and that it was time to
overcome my long-abiding distrust of the reader. That distrust
can be traced back to my literary origins, to the distant thirties.
Even in those days, as one who sensed the general drift of things,
as a "Catastrophist" who nonetheless pined for an age of "faith
and fortitude"—as one of my early poems had it—there were
few in whom to confide my hopes and fears. No doubt I was inhibited by certain class-inherited prejudices, resident in me as
well, of the Polish intelligentsia, so that I was everywhere confronted by forbidden territory. The label "a young avant-garde
poet" was, again, a significant source of misunderstanding: by
and large, the avant-garde shunned those things with which I

was, secretly, engaged. But since I had to belong somewhere, I conformed, often to the point of dissimulating. Thus was I given to many defense strategies, all the more as my attitude toward those monuments of wisdom towering in the universities and literary columns was one of sacred awe mixed with suspicion (maybe they were foundering, too), and nothing so favors arrogance and disdain as such an ambivalence. Not that I would condemn arrogance; it can be a protection.

This partially explains my obsession with silence, the fear that if I spoke, no sound would escape from my mouth. One can well imagine the effect, on one so inhibited, of having one's gravest forebodings borne out; of wartime Warsaw and that postwar spectacle when suffering, by then routine, was to be experienced in even stronger doses, and how solitude and academic work could be a blessing. My work for foreigners has been of a practical, even pedagogic nature—I do not believe in the possibility of communing outside a shared language, a shared history—while my work in Polish has been addressed to readers transcending a specific time and place, otherwise known as "writing for the Muses."

I do not understand my life (who does?). Nor my books, and I shall not pretend to understand them. All bespeak a strenuous self-discipline—of which it can be said that those who lack it yearn for it, while those who have it to spare know how much is lost through it and long to be released from it, to proceed by impulse and the hand's own free momentum.

But to gain that freedom is to commune with a reader, hoping for some flicker of understanding in his eyes, believing that he is really communing with us, that we are joined by the same belief or at least by the same hope. I shall now assume such a reader; that a new audience, however few in number, is there. Among the readers of books, one in a thousand will suffice. If I idealize that audience slightly, it is to rid myself of old habits.

2

To begin, then. At the age of sixty-five, after a month's stay in Holland and France, I returned to Berkeley in mid-July, where I settled down to gardening and reading, mainly works from around the year 1800. These were Goethe's *Wilhelm Meister* and *Elective Affinities*, both in English translation, and a volume of German Romantics in the Pléiade series. At the same time, I became distracted, or rather consumed, by the sort of thoughts inspired by my every trip to Paris—after Wilno, the second site of my ill-fated youth. Thirty years after the war, to Leśmian's question "Can economic well-being be achieved in a world of nonbeing?" Paris was answering unequivocally, without a quibble: "Yes, it can." But how did that affect me, I who had nothing to say to any Frenchman?

We are born on earth only once and we indulge in much mimicking and posing, dimly aware of the truth, but with pen in hand it is difficult to escape that awareness: then, at least, one wants to keep one's self-respect. As a young man I was struck by the magnitude of what was occurring in my century, a magnitude equaling, perhaps even surpassing the decline and fall of antiquity, so that I remained oblivious to, almost unconscious of, disputes over poetics, whether those of Skamander or the Avant-Garde; to the political comedies of the late thirties; and to the sort of literary debates promoted by Karol Irzykowski. How, then, at a later date, as a witness to what was under way, could I seriously have pursued a literary career, either in the People's Republic of Poland or abroad among the émigrés, as if nothing had happened? To whom, about what, was I to speak? Even after I had surfaced from my meditations on History, now investing them with a new tone and sense, and brought my thoughts to bear on language, on Polish poetry, and on individual poets, I was against narrowing the argument to questions of craft and thus ignoring the great paramount theme. Yet I lacked the tools to handle that theme, nor am I much better equipped now. Today I am awed by the violence of my prewar poetry, a violence of tone born of a disproportion between the matter conveyed and the imagery to match it. To have pursued a "literary career" would have signaled a retreat from far more dramatic urgencies. Even my switching of careers—from diplomat to a professorship in Berkeley—may have been a way of escaping literature. If I was to evade that highest calling, which only in a handful of poems I had managed not to betray, then let it be to a minimum, which consideration, along with my disdain for the laws of the marketplace, saved me from the frantic pursuit of fame and money. If my earlier conflicts with the literary profession had been ambivalent, condemning myself to the agonies of a civil servant had proved calamitous. My conflict with the market in the West, on the other hand, was clear and decisive, my arrogance blatant; and my persistence was rewarded, quite providentially, for, unlike the tedium of bureaucracy, working with young people can be meaningful and of mutual benefit. From the moment I became a "professor of Slavic literatures," I was relieved of having to attend to the success of my literary work; that is, I was again denied a writer's vocation, and this time happily so.

Those readings from around the year 1800 which occupied me during July and August of 1975 were in preparation for a fall course on Dostoevsky; but not only. Their choice alone testified to the gradual nurturing of this book's undertaking, one in which the Romantic era will rear its head more than once.

3

To obey the freely moving hand . . . Is that possible? To forget that there may be other readers, not just Polish, and yet to write only in Polish, for an exclusively Polish audience? One of the most serious and frustrating dilemmas resulting from prolonged residence abroad is having to repress the constantly intruding thought: How would this sound in English? How construed by a foreign reader? I cannot stand writing in a foreign language; I am incapable of it. There was a time when I dreamed of an international role for myself, of world renown—guiltily, hesitantly so—and though my fantasies never took any definite shape, they were no less real. True, I did get a taste of that fame, even my share of foreign reviews, like those in Germany comparing me to Faulkner (?), or those in the United States acknowledging my influence on American poets of the younger generation, but seldom were they written with intelligence and even more seldom were they willing to grant me any originality. The din of the marketplace, I could not help thinking—part of the general clamor of voices and names that are quickly forgotten the next day. How glad I am now that I clung to my native language (for the simple reason that I was a Polish poet and could not have been otherwise); that I did not emulate those émigrés in France and the United States who shed one skin and language for another. I would not deny that my Polish served my pride by erecting a protective barrier between myself and a civilization in the throes of puerility (*qui sombre dans l'idiotie*), just as my "Westernness," my "universality," served me as a faithful ally in my revolt against "Polishness"—both when the word "Nation" was enthroned with a capital "N," and later, following its dethronement, when it was restored to full honors. Let my case stand as a lesson: behold the enduring image of a poet, ill at ease in one place, ill at ease in the other—"always and everywhere ill at ease"—who managed to distance himself by spinning, cocoon-like, his incomprehensible language. Sartre once wrote to Camus that in view of his distaste for political systems, he saw only one place for him: the Galápagos Islands. How often I have recalled those words, here, in California, which has been—for me, a Polish poet—my Galápagos; and how I grieved, even suffered guilt, over the forfeiture, until I accepted it and stopped feeling ashamed. What did I have to be ashamed of? That I was made of this very clay?

Nonetheless, I belong to the estate of Polish literature and to no other. What American writer feels himself a part of an

American literary estate, especially when, in light of the different service to which the word is put here, the reality of that
estate remains something tenuous? While the estate of Polish,
Russian, and Czech literature is for me something visible, even
palpable, I am not so sure but that the estate of French literature—notwithstanding its Academy, its annual awarding of
prizes and honors (more reminiscent of some tribal contest)—has
not gone to seed amid all the furor.

One would like to astound the world, to save the world, but
one can do neither. We are summoned to deeds that are of moment only to our village, our Catalonias, our Waleses, and our
Slovenias. Not that in defying Alfred Jarry's "Debraining Machine" I would now try to uphold a belief in Slavic idylls. But if I
am to nourish the hope of writing with a free hand, with gaiety,
and not under pressure, then I must proceed by keeping only a
few Polish readers in mind.

NOTES ON EXILE

*He did not find happiness, for there
was no happiness in his country*
ADAM MICKIEWICZ

USAGE

Exile accepted as a destiny, in the way we accept an incurable illness, should help us see through our self-delusions.

PARADIGM

He was aware of his task and people were waiting for his words,
but he was forbidden to speak. Now where he lives he is free to
speak but nobody listens and, moreover, he forgot what he had to
say.

COMMENTARY ON THE ABOVE

Censorship may be tolerant of various avant-garde antics, since they keep writers busy and make literature an innocent pastime for a very restricted elite. But as soon as a writer shows signs of being attentive to reality, censorship clamps down. If, as a result of banishment or his own decision, he finds himself in exile, he blurts out his dammed-up feelings of anger, his observations and reflections, considering this as his duty and mission. Yet that which in his country is regarded with seriousness as a matter of life or death is of nobody's concern abroad or provokes interest for incidental reasons. Thus a writer notices that he is unable to address those who care and is able to address only those who do not care. He himself gradually becomes used to the society in which he lives, and his knowledge of everyday life in the country of his origin changes from tangible to theoretical. If he continues to deal with the same problems as before, his work will lose the directness of captured experience. Therefore he must either condemn himself to sterility or undergo a total transformation.

NEW EYES

New eyes, new thought, new distance: that a writer in exile needs all this is obvious, but whether he overcomes his old self depends upon resources which he only dimly perceived before.

One possibility offered him is to change his language, either literally, by writing in the tongue of the country of his residence, or to use his native tongue in such a manner that what he writes will be understandable and acceptable to a new audience. Then, however, he ceases to be an exile.

Another, much more difficult choice consists of preserving his postulated and imagined presence in the country he comes from. Imagined: for he must visualize the history and literature of his country as one organism developing in time and assign to his work a function in a movement which leads from the past to the future. This implies a constant reassessment of tradition in search for vital roots as well as critical observation of the present. Certain literary genres (the realistic novel, for instance) and certain styles cannot, by definition, be practiced in exile. On the other hand, the condition of exile, by enforcing upon a writer several perspectives, favors other genres and styles, especially those which are related to a symbolic transposition of reality.

DESPAIR

Despair, inseparable from the first stage of exile, can be analyzed, and then it would probably appear as resulting more from one's personal shortcomings than from external circumstances. There are three main causes of such despair: loss of name, fear of failure, and moral torment.

A writer acquires a name through a complex interchange with his readers, whether he appeals to a large audience or to a narrow circle of sympathizers. He elaborates an image of himself as reflected in the eyes of those who react to his writings. When he emigrates, that image is suddenly annihilated and he makes up an anonymous member of the mass. He no longer even exists as a person whose virtues and faults were known to his friends. Nobody knows who he is, and if he reads about himself in the press, he finds that the data concerning him are grotesquely distorted. Then his humiliation is proportionate to his pride, and that is perhaps a just punishment.

He has good reasons to fear failure, for only a few possess the resilience necessary to oppose the corroding effects of isolation. He belonged to a community of writers committed to a certain ritual and occupied with distributing praise and blame to one another. Now, no community, no ritual, no sweet games of satisfied ambition. He suffers because he has contracted collectivistic habits, which means perhaps that he has never learned to stand on his own feet. He may win, but not before he agrees to lose.

Exile is morally suspect because it breaks one's solidarity with a group, i.e., it sets apart an individual who ceases to share the experience of colleagues left behind. His moral torment reflects his attachment to a heroic image of himself and he must, step by step, come to the painful conclusion that to do morally valid work and to preserve an untarnished image of himself is rarely possible.

ACCLIMATIZATION

After many years in exile one tries to imagine what it is like not living in exile.

SPACE

Imagination, always spatial, points north, south, east, and west of some central, privileged place, which is probably a village from one's childhood or native region. As long as a writer lives in his country, the privileged place, by centrifugally enlarging itself, becomes more or less identified with his country as a whole. Exile displaces that center or rather creates two centers. Imagination relates everything in one's surroundings to "over there"——in my case, somewhere on the European continent. It even continues to designate the four cardinal points, as if I still stood there. At the same time the north, south, east, and west are determined by the place in which I write these words.

Imagination tending toward the distant region of one's childhood is typical of literature of nostalgia (a distance in space often serves as a disguise for a Proustian distance in time). Although quite common, literature of nostalgia is only one among many modes of coping with estrangement from one's native land. The new point which orients space in respect to itself cannot be eliminated, i.e., one cannot abstract from one's physical presence in a definite spot on the Earth. That is why a curious phenomenon appears: the two centers and the two spaces arranged around them interfere with each other or—and this is a happy solution—coalesce.

SHADOWS ON THE WALL

It is being said that our planet is slowly but inexorably entering an era of unification brought about by technology, hygiene, and literacy. And yet the opposite opinion may be advanced as well, and only in exile can its validity be fully understood. A writer who lives in a foreign country brings a thorough knowledge of the geographical area from which he comes—its history, economy, politics, et cetera. He is sensitive to any information about what he knows so well, whether it is provided by books, newspapers, or television. This leads him to discover how new divisions between men come about. A hundred years ago average people not familiar with remote regions of the globe quietly relegated them to the realm of the legendary or at least the exotic. Today, however, they feel they are offered the means to embrace places and events of the whole Earth simultaneously. But when confronted with a newcomer's firsthand knowledge, news and reports on the land of his origin prove to be completely misleading. Multiplied, the sum of similar disparities between the message and the fact reaches astronomical proportions. Plato's parable of the cave, which until now has been discussed only in philosophy classes, acquires a more practical meaning as well. As we remember, the prisoners chained there cannot move their necks and are able to see only the wall facing them. Shadows are projected on that wall and they take them for reality. An outsider wonders whether he could convince newspaper readers and television viewers that they are in error, but arrives at the conclusion that he neither could nor should. Were deception due merely to ignorance or political bias, the predicament of modern cave dwellers would offer some hope. But what if—and this should not be excluded in advance—deception resides in the very nature of the media, i.e., of mediation?

SELF-EXAMINATION

Here is a draft of a speech which may be addressed by a writer in exile to himself. "Are you certain that your colleagues here who move in a world familiar to them from childhood fare better than you do? It is true that they write in their own tongue. But do art and literature correspond to what we have learned about them in school and at the university? Couldn't they have changed so rapidly in these last decades that their names are now no more than empty shells? Don't they perhaps become an exercise in solitude, a signal sent forth by the disinherited? How many of these people are rewarded by love and respect in their hometowns, the only kind of love and respect that is really worth seeking? They share the same language with their audience, but do they see a gleam of comprehension on the faces of their listeners? Isn't the same tongue just an illusion where uncountable individual languages fill space with a jamming noise? Are your colleagues listened to or read by the public at large, or do they read only each other? Can you even be sure that they read each other? After all, it is possible that you are better off: your exile is legitimized.

"You have always believed that the true goal of writing is to reach all the people of the world and to change their lives. And what if such a goal is unattainable? Does it cease to be valid? Don't you believe that every one of your colleagues here has in his heart remained faithful to that, yes, childish dream? Yet haven't you witnessed their defeat?

"And if you cannot save the world, why should you care whether you have a large or a small audience?"

LANGUAGE

A writer living among people who speak a language different from his own discovers after a while that he senses his native tongue in a new manner. It is not true that a long stay abroad leads to withering of styles, even though the vivifying influence of everyday speech is lacking. What is true, however, is that new aspects and tonalities of the native tongue are discovered, for they stand out against the background of the language spoken in the new milieu. Thus the narrowing down in some areas (street idioms, slang) is compensated for by a widening in others (purity of vocabulary, rhythmic expressiveness, syntactic balance). Rivalry between two languages is not necessarily typical of literature written in exile. For a couple of centuries in several European countries the literati were bilingual, their vernacular being modified by their Latin and vice versa.

HAPPINESS

ETWEEN THE AGES of seven and ten I lived in perfect happiness on the farm of my grandparents in Lithuania. The localities of our valley are mentioned for the first time around 1350 by the chronicles of the Teutonic Knights, who invaded the region while fighting my still-pagan ancestors. My grandparents' farm, where I was born, had belonged to my mother's family for several centuries, during which its landscape gradually changed, and I now know that I should be especially grateful to my great-grandfather, who, on a grassy slope descending to the river, planted many trees, creating a grovelike park. And he established orchards, two by the house, the third a little farther, beyond the old white-walled granary. It was long ago, and huge oaks and lindens made my fairyland, while orchards allowed me to discover the taste of apples and pears of many species.

I do not know the date when a new house replaced the wooden one. Probably it was in the middle of the nineteenth century. The white walls hid not a brick structure but a wooden scaffolding covered with mortar. The inside was cool in summer and difficult to heat in winter by stoves that burned mostly birch logs. Many years later I found in Dutch paintings the images of interiors just like those in my childhood house.

I lived without yesterday or tomorrow, in the eternal present. This is, precisely, the definition of happiness. I ask myself whether I now mythologize that period of my life. We all build myths when speaking of the past, for a faithful reconstruction of fleeting moments is impossible. The question, however, remains: Why do some people speak of their childhoods as happy, others, as miserable? The extreme vividness and intensity of my experience forces me to believe in its authenticity. It was, I do not hesitate to say, an experience of enchantment with earth as a Paradise.

To tell about one's childhood usually is to tell about one's family, yet in this respect I must confess that for me adults resided in a hazy world, not my own. I was a lone child in a magic kingdom that I explored from early morning till dusk. My younger brother was then a baby, and I paid no attention to him, nor did I have any companions of my age. Thus I was a little Adam, running all day in a garden under trees that seemed to me even bigger than they were in reality, with my perceptions and fantasies unhampered by the sarcastic jeer of a demon.

What seems strange to me today is that at the age of seven I had already lived a story of adventures that could have provided memories for a whole lifetime. There were travels in military trains through Russia during World War I, when my father, a civil engineer, was drafted to build bridges for the czarist army; there was the Bolshevik revolution, with its perquisitions, escapes, fears, which I lived through in a town on the Volga. All that must have somehow persisted in me, yet it did not bring more awareness; on the contrary, it receded, perhaps thanks to self-protection's peculiar mechanism. I remained innocent, which means that I had not formed any judgment on the cruelty of the world.

Particular events that would have sufficed to impose such a

judgment did not coagulate into any whole; rather, each one existed in my mind separately. Neither did the routine of life on a farm, with its unavoidable knowledge of the pain and death of animals, affect me much. When fishing, I concentrated on the goal of my action—to catch a fish—and did not reflect on the worm squirming at the hook's end, or on the pain of a little perch that, a hook placed in its body through an incision in its skin, served as bait for a pike. And yet, who knows? Perhaps my future pessimism could be traced back to moments in my tender age, a pessimism reaching so far that as an adult I was to really value one philosopher only, the bitter Schopenhauer.

My happiness came, it seems, from, as William Blake would say, cleansing the gates of perception, in avidly seeing and hearing. A path in the shade of oaks led down to the river, and my river was never to abandon me throughout my life, wherever fate carried me, even during my years on the far shores of the Pacific. Its slow current allowed the growth of water lilies, and in certain places their pads covered the whole surface. Its banks, with their rim of calamus, were shaded by bushes and alder trees. I spent hours watching sunlight on water, movements of little water creatures and flights of dragonflies and . . . I am ready to call it daydreaming, yet it would not be correct, for this would suggest passivity, while my imagination was vividly active.

Thus as a child I was primarily a discoverer of the world, not as suffering but as beauty. The trees of the park, the orchards, and the river founded a separate realm of intensified, radiant reality more true than anything situated outside.

We often become aware of the harshness of the world through struggle with others, frequently with other children. On the farm I had nobody to compete with, nobody who would try to submit me to his or her will. Of course I often cried, for instance, when my mother would force me to abandon my playing and sit down to the impossible task of learning how to write the letters of the alphabet. Yet it was not a real pressure—this ordinarily comes from our peers, as I later had the occasion to convince myself, when I went to school in town.

Happiness experienced in childhood does not pass without a trace: the memory of ecstasy dwells in our body and possesses a strong curative power. As a young man I was somber and tormented; I showed a considerable talent for gathering wounds and bruises. Perhaps this was simply my line of fate, yet time and place might have had something to do with my depressive predisposition. In the thirties the Central European–Baltic area carried in its air premonitions of the crimes to be perpetrated. To the east, in Soviet Russia, millions of "class enemies" were toiling and dying in the so-called corrective labor camps. I was twenty-two when neighboring Germany voted Hitler into the position of absolute ruler. A few years later the mass murder committed at his orders horrified humanity.

My religion and philosophy were marked by a dark vision, and I was inclined to believe that the universe was created as a result of a cosmic catastrophe, perhaps by Satan himself. Brought up a Roman Catholic, I felt the attraction of the old Manichaean heresy. It suited the time when, to use the expression of Emmanuel Lévinas, "God left in 1941." The poetry I wrote before the war and later in Nazi-occupied Poland would have been utterly without hope if not for my awareness of the beauty of the things of this earth, and that beauty was incomprehensible, as it coexisted with horror.

Many years later, at the age of eighty, I returned to the place of my birth and childhood. The landscape had changed, and probably those changes were more radical than any made there by man since the Middle Ages. Lithuania, an independent country before World War II, was occupied in 1940 by the Soviet Union, and the collectivization of agriculture was enforced by the Communist government. Whole villages, with their houses, yards, barns, stables, gardens, were erased. In their place stretched the open space of huge fields cultivated by tractors. I stood at the edge of a plateau above my river's canyonlike valley and saw only a plain without a trace of the clumps of trees that once marked the emplacement of every village. Among the many definitions of Communism, perhaps one would be the most apt: enemy of orchards. For the disappearance of villages and the remodeling of the terrain necessitated cutting down the orchards once surrounding every house and hut. The idea of collective farming—grain factories instead of little peasant lots—was rational, but with a vengeance, and a similar vengeance lurking in practically every project of the planned economy brought about the downfall of the Soviet system.

Orchards under Communism had no chance, but in all fairness let us concede they are antique by their very nature. Only the passion of a gardener can delight in growing a great variety of trees, each producing a small crop of fruit whose taste pleases the gardener himself and a few connoisseurs. Market laws favor a few species that are easy to preserve and correspond to basic standards. In the orchards planted by my great-grandfather and renewed by his successors, I knew the kinds of apples and pears whose very names pronounced by me later sounded exotic.

I found myself in the spot, now marked by a clump of weeds, where the house once stood. It was taken apart in the fifties, and instead of a round lawn before it, a tangled forest of young trees, mostly maples, began, sloping down to the river. The lawn was nearly impassable, as the old paths had disappeared in the wild outgrowth. Here and there an aged oak or elm survived. The orchards were gone, just of their old age, to judge by the few dry stumps remaining. Everything here had been abandoned for years, and nobody seemed to make use of the land. In a haphazardly put together hut an old couple lived a squatters' life, and the only profit they drew from the estate was, I guess, the abundance of dry wood to feed their stove during the long northern winters.

I did not feel any regret, or anger, or even sadness. I was confronted not by the history of my century but by time itself. All the human beings who once walked here were dead, as were most of those anywhere on the earth born the same year as I. Granted the privilege of return, I was aware that it was only possible because a certain big empire had fallen, but what was most important at the moment was the tangible element of flowing time. I went down to my river. It had no lily pads and no calamus, and its reddish color confirmed the presence of chemical plants operated in its upper run. A lonely wild swan kept itself immobile in the middle of oily water, an incongruous sight, suggesting illness or the bird's suicidal intent.

The sky was clear, vegetation lush on that June day. I tried to grasp and name my feelings. My memory recognized the outline of hills on the other side of the river, the slope of the park, a meadow by the road, a dark shaded patch of greenery where once there was a pond. In spite of all the changes, the configuration of the terrain persisted, and it seemed to me I could have found my way even with closed eyes, for my feet would have carried me everywhere themselves.

Much was going on inside me, and I was stunned by the strength of that current for which no name seemed adequate. It was like waking up from a long dream and becoming again the person whom I have never ceased to be. Long life, narrow escapes, my two marriages, children, my failures and triumphs, all flickered as if telescoped into a film running at a great speed. No, this is not a proper description, for all that existed in a big lump separated from me, placed in its own dimension of the past, while I was recovering my continuity from myself as a child to myself as an old man.

In a world dominated by technology and mass mobility, most of us are first- or second-generation immigrants from the country to big cities. The theme of homeland, the whole nostalgic rhetoric of *patria* fed by literature since Odysseus journeyed to Ithaca, has been weakened if not forgotten. Returning to my river valley, I carried with me my heritage of these venerable clichés, already grown somewhat pale, and I was rather impervious to their sentimental appeal. Then something happened—and I must recognize that the myth of Ithaca stems from profound layers of human sensibility. I was looking at a meadow. Suddenly the realization came that during my years of wandering I had searched in vain for such a combination of leaves and flowers as was here and that I have been always yearning to return. Or, to be precise, I understood this after a huge wave of emotion had overwhelmed me, and the only name I can give it now would be—bliss.

DICTIONARY
OF WILNO STREETS

Why should that city, defenseless and pure as the wedding
  necklace of a forgotten tribe, keep offering itself to me?

Like blue and red-brown seeds beaded in Tuzigoot in the copper
  desert seven centuries ago.

Where ocher rubbed into stone still waits for the brow and
  cheekbone it would adorn, though for all that time there has
  been no one.

What evil in me, what pity, has made me deserve this offering?

It stands before me, ready, not even the smoke from one
  chimney is lacking, not one echo, when I step across the rivers
  that separate us.

Perhaps Anna and Dora Drużyno have called to me, three
  hundred miles inside Arizona, because except for me no one
  else knows that they ever lived.

*They trot before me on Embankment Street, two gently born
parakeets from Samogitia, and at night they unravel for me
their spinster tresses of gray hair.*

*Here there is no earlier and no later; the seasons of the year and
of the day are simultaneous.*

*At dawn shit-wagons leave town in long rows, and municipal
employees at the gate collect the turnpike toll in leather bags.*

Rattling their wheels, Courier *and* Speedy *move against the
current to Werki, and an oarsman shot down over England
skiffs past, spread-eagled by his oars.*

*At St. Peter and Paul's the angels lower their thick eyelids in a
smile over a man who has indecent thoughts.*

*Bearded, in a wig, Mrs. Sora Kłok sits at the counter, instructing
her twelve shopgirls.*

*And all of German Street tosses into the air unfurled bolts of
fabric, preparing itself for death and the conquest of
Jerusalem.*

*Black and princely, an underground river knocks at cellars of
the cathedral under the tomb of St. Casimir the Young and
under the half-charred oak logs in the hearth.*

*Carrying her servant's-basket on her shoulder, Barbara, dressed
in mourning, returns from the Lithuanian Mass at
St. Nicholas to the Romers' house on Bakszta Street.*

*How it glitters! the snow on Three Crosses Hill and Bekiesz
Hill, not to be melted by the breath of these brief lives.*

*And what do I know now, when I turn into Arsenal Street and
open my eyes once more on a useless end of the world?*

*I was running, as the silks rustled, through room after room
without stopping, for I believed in the existence of a last door.*

*But the shape of lips and an apple and a flower pinned to a dress
were all that one was permitted to know and take away.*

*The Earth, neither compassionate nor evil, neither beautiful nor
atrocious, persisted, innocent, open to pain and desire.*

*And the gift was useless, if, later on, in the flarings of distant
nights, there was not less bitterness but more.*

*If I cannot so exhaust my life and their life that the bygone
crying is transformed, at last, into a harmony.*

Like a Noble Jan Dęboróg *in Straszun's secondhand bookshop, I
am put to rest forever between two familiar names.*

*The castle tower above the leafy tumulus grows small and there
is still a hardly audible—is it Mozart's* Requiem?—*music.*

*In the immobile light I move my lips and perhaps I am even
glad not to find the desired word.*

ANTOKOL

First one passed the dock. Iron barriers along the sidewalk polished to a shine by the touch of hands; you could lean against
them, or sit and watch. If I am to speak now about what one
could see there, I should first explain that I am there simultane-

ously as a small boy and an adolescent and a young man, so that many years of watching are concentrated in a single moment. So, what one saw first of all was a boat preparing for departure or, rather, the public boarding by means of a gangplank, the pressing of fingers into ears as the whistle sounds once and then again, the untying of the ropes with Józiuk shouting at Antuk and Antuk at Józiuk; or, a boat approaching, still far away when the shimmering of its wheels is first discerned. The boats were named *Courier*, possibly *Express* (although I am not sure about that); later on there was a third one, *Speedy*, a wonderful boat with a real deck. A lot depended on which one you happened to take during school outings to Werki. They went upstream, to Werki and even farther, to Niemenczyn—never downstream. There was also a dock for the small boats painted with stripes of many colors along their sides, from the slightly elevated prow to the stern. The ferryman would seat five or six people and cross over to the other shore, to the Pióromont district, using a long oar, also painted, punting, unless the water, in spring or late autumn, was high. One also watched the "flats" floating by, long trains of floating timber, mainly pine, with a hut and a fire on the last raft, which also had an enormously long and heavy steering oar. The sawmills where the "flats" tied up, so that sometimes the Wilia would be completely covered by them, were somewhat farther downstream, past the Green Bridge, across from St. Jacob's.

I also knew larger boats—they were on the Niemen, not the Wilia—from my visits to Kaunas. Almost like illustrations in travel books, they had decks loaded with crates and barrels; sometimes there were cows and horses, too. They went to distant places, as far as Jurbork. To tell the truth, the one I used to take was not large, because it went up the Niemen for only part of its route, to the mouth of the Niewiaża, and then it sailed up the Niewiaża to the town of Bobty. The Niewiaża is quite deep but very narrow and tortuous; it is navigable to that point, but not farther upstream. For some reason, I thought of the local boats as something official, like the post office, and I was surprised that their crews spoke among themselves in exactly the same sort of Polish as the crews of the *Speedy* and the *Courier.*

One always walked past the dock on the way to Antokol; that is why I'm speaking of it now. Then the bridge or, rather, the bridge across the Wilenka where it flows into the Wilia. Antokol itself is, first of all, the boredom of a long, only partly built-up street, a muscular memory in the legs, about a space "in between": between the Wilia on the left and the hills on the right. Only the slopes of Castle Hill, in the angle formed by the Wilia and the Wilenka, were luxuriantly green, with the foliage of a deciduous forest. Three Crosses Hill and the other hills were sandy inclines sparsely dotted with pines. We often went climbing there, for the view and the solitude, but basically it was too windswept a place, and the somewhat more distant, hilly Antokol, beyond St. Peter and Paul's, was more interesting. I knew the Baroque statues of that church from photographs, and even from the postage stamps of Central Lithuania, but when I toured the interior I was disenchanted: a host of details obscured by whitewash, details so minuscule that they could be seen only with a magnifying glass. Beyond the church, deeply rutted, sandy roads wound through the forest; they had street names: Sunshine, Springtime, Forest, etc., with a few wooden houses concealed in the thickets, more like dachas than villas. In one of them lived Leopold Pac-Pomarnacki, my schoolmate and partner in my naturalist's passions: a phlegmatic elderly gentleman with a protruding belly, fourteen years of age. I was in awe of his collections of rare ornithological books and stuffed birds. An only child, the son of rather elderly parents, I think, he had his very own shotguns. An expedition with him to the country, to visit Nowicki, another schoolmate, whose face I remember but not his first name, remains in my memory as something exceptionally enigmatic, a tormenting darkness from which I am able to retrieve only one or another fragment that immediately disappears. It took place on All Souls' Day, somewhere on the southern boundary of the Rudnicka Wilderness, because it seems we got off the train at Stasily, beyond Jaszuny. Frozen earth, sunsets and sunrises that mixed reds and blues, hoarfrost, a hamlet, fried bliny at dawn, conversations in Belorussian, hunting, and staying by ourselves in a house that was, I think, the residuary part of an estate. There were four of us, one a girl, a student at a Wilno *gymnasium* or technical school—her black eyes, pallor, throaty laugh (but I have no image of her face)—and although Pac and I were complete outsiders here, Nowicki and she kept getting into ominous erotic brawls that excluded me, a mere puppy, from their partnership. During that same school year, in early spring, she was found dead in Zakret, in the German military cemetery—it was suicide, poison or a revolver, but not connected with Nowicki.

Next to St. Peter and Paul's there were also some trails leading up to the ski slopes. An absolutely undeveloped highland, called Antokol Grove and Altaria on the city maps, extended all the way to the outskirts of Zarzecze and Belmont; the runs were mostly short and headlong. I skied like a cow, but for a brief period at the beginning of my university career and my ardent participation in the Vagabonds' Club, I did so stubbornly. It was the period of my friendship with Robespierre, who used to ski wearing a red flannel shirt, so for me the snow of the Antokol hills is fused with that shirt in a single image. But I remember the outskirts of Antokol, where the city ended and the highway to Niemenczyn began, because that is where as a child I observed the panic of the 1920 retreat.

Nevertheless, Antokol remains for me not so much streets which one walks on as a shore along which one sails: just beyond the bridge on the Wilenka were the rowing clubs, among them the AZS [Academic Sport Union], from whose landing we would push off in a kayak or canoe. The Wilia is a swift river and though we paddled energetically against the current, we could only glide quite slowly along the Antokol shore. Across from the AZS, on the opposite shore of the Wilia, was Pronaszko's Mickiewicz, a gigantic Cubist bloated figure, exiled there by the town fathers, who were probably right not to want to place it in the center of town among the old stones. There, too, all of a sudden, was the first sandy beach: Tuskulany. We were drawn to more distant places, so I was at that beach only once, while I was still a high school student playing hooky. It happens that, for no obvious reason, particular hours in my life have been preserved with absolute clarity about their details, so I can see the naked people lying there beside me. One of them is a future electrical engineer and officer in the Royal Air Force: Staś. Many years later (it is painful to count them), in 1967, the two of us camped on the shores of big Eagle Lake in the California Sierras, and when we headed straight from our tent to the water the moment we woke up, or went kayaking along its wild forested shores, we didn't look the way we did in Tuskulany; yet it was difficult for me to grasp how our bodies had changed—only perhaps that his wedge-shaped, Russian czar's beard had begun to turn gray.

In the names of the settlements along the Wilia one could discover amalgams of familiar and foreign words. Tuskulany, I assume, was named by enlightened readers of Latin literature who perceived similarities between this region and Tusculum, the country retreat of wealthy Romans. Wołokumpie is less refined. Trynopol, actually only a white church on a bluff, a sign to oarsmen that they can relax because the most treacherous currents are behind them, makes one think of Trinitas and thus has a derivation similar to that of nearby Kalwaria. Charming forested Werki reminds one of German Werk, but according to legend the name is derived from crying eagle chicks—in Lithuanian, *verkti* means to cry.

The Wilia alongside Antokol and all the way to Werki was our city's *freeway*, a word I learned much later, substituting it for the dubiously Polish word *autostrada*. Although I would prefer to say *gościniec*—highroad. So, a highroad, down which the Wilno population would travel on a Sunday outing—the native population that had been living there for generations, which was neither gentry nor working-class but rather petit bourgeois and thus employed for the most part as artisans. On passenger ships or in small boats, in family groups: shirts, suspenders, taking turns at the oars, the women's colorful dresses, and a jar of pickles for a snack. Another popular amusement was the sauna. At the end of the week one could hear all sorts of idiosyncrasies of "local" speech there, which would have been a treasure for linguists, although I doubt that linguists ever frequent public saunas.

Upstream from Werki, and almost never frequented by people on excursions, the Wilia remained virtually untouched by "civilization." I have preserved it in my memory from the point where the Żejmiana emptied into it. Absolute silence, only the splashing of water against the hull, in the sunshine the brilliant whiteness of the steep sandy bluffs with holes drilled into them by cliff swallows, the dangling roots of the pines. Occasionally, a long string of floating log rafts with smoke rising from a stove. There is a particular majesty in the slow turning of these "flats" along the bend of a river. A steering oar in front, a steering oar in back, often plied by two people, a man and a woman, the long train of rafts gliding slowly into a new current. Occasionally a fishing boat would flash by in the other direction, toward the bank; sometimes there would be a naked lad in a kayak, who was probably spending his school vacation somewhere nearby, unaware of the devilish traps that History had already set for him.

In the summer the Wilia across from Antokol became shallow; sometimes it was possible to wander downstream for a couple of kilometers, swimming some of the time, but mostly touching the bottom. I associate the Wilia with Antokol because the sawmills beyond the Green Bridge signaled its end as a highroad. Farther on, the river headed for the closed Lithuanian border; besides which, it probably wasn't navigable, considering that in at least one spot it had whirlpools and rapids that were difficult to negotiate. The city's sewage, especially from the hospital in Zwierzyniec, made one loath to swim in the river near Zwierzyniec and also near the opposite shore, by the Zakret forest. Excursions downriver exposed one to an arduous return trip against the current and therefore were rarely organized. We took the train to the settlements of the Students' Union in Legaciszki, which were right on the Lithuanian border.

ARSENAL STREET

This is a short street, stretching from the corner of Embankment Street, just beside the boat dock, to Cathedral Square. In the olden days, it seems, it was simply the continuation of Antokol Street, its extension. A handful of houses along a single sidewalk; in place of a second sidewalk, the iron curves of a low palisade enclosing a garden (at the rear of the cathedral) that was called the Calf Pen. The corner of Embankment Street was occupied by a large, rather ugly building, the Tyszkiewicz Palace, which was always locked; later on, I learned that it housed the Wróblewski Library; its function derived from the fact that it existed and I never asked myself why. A few years before the war it was taken over to house the Institute for the Study of Eastern Europe and then I often had occasion to go to this building. On the other hand, from the time I was in the lowest *gymnasium* classes I paid regular visits to the house in the middle of Arsenal Street, at number 6, because my relatives lived there, distant relatives, to be sure: the Pawlikowskis. The blood tie was with her, Cesia Pawlikowska, *née* Sławińska, I think; she insisted that I call her aunt. The man of the house, Przemysław Pawlikowski, was an ex-colonel of the czarist army; on the walls hung photographs from Bessarabia, where they had lived for a long time and apparently once owned an estate. Tall, swarthy, lean, taciturn, he walked about in a patterned bathrobe, sat on the balcony staring at the green of the garden, or played patience. He also worked on his stamp albums, which tantalized me, because of course I was caught up in this mania, and he would give me rare specimens as a gift. Of their two sons, I have no recollection of the first, Danek, who committed suicide as a young man; the second, an engineer, went to Soviet Turkestan after the war to work there as a specialist (a "spets"), returned with a Russian wife, bought a car, and became one of the first taxi drivers in Wilno, an avant-garde profession—for who ever heard of a well-born man taking tips from a guest? His Russian wife wore Oriental *sharovary* at home and smoked cigarettes in a long cigarette holder. Wacek's sister, Marysia, worked in an office, and so that peaceful family collective (they all lived together) could serve as an illustration of the sociological changes that were taking place at the time. I met Marysia when I was a very young boy, because she stayed with my grandparents for a while in Szetejnie, in Kaunas, Lithuania, and it was she who read *With Fire and Sword* to me on the oil-cloth couch near the window in the dining room, where you had to curl up in a hollow and guard the spot you had warmed up, not letting your bare feet protrude onto the cold oilcloth beside you. Marysia, as I think the old folks told me, was somewhat "man-nered"; for me, she was simply mysterious, introspective, pensive, swaying at the hips, tall; she wore a black velvet ribbon around her white neck. She belonged to the generation that came to ma-turity on the threshold of the First World War, which is why there were volumes of poetry and literary journals from that pe-riod in the house on Arsenal Street. If I had not examined the contents of those shelves, I would never have known, for exam-ple, that an almanac, *Żórawce*, was published in 1914 or 1915, filled with poetry and prose of late-period Young Poland. In gen-eral, my relatives, who were already grown-up young ladies, af-fected me somewhat erotically in my childhood, furnished me with an insight into an epoch that I could not remember; their style of living itself had preserved something from it. Today it strikes me as laughable to call those times, which then were only ten years in the past, another "epoch," for if those who were fa-miliar with it seemed to me to have emerged from murky dark-ness, probably a general law was at work: for every generation the events, styles, and fashions that are just barely in the past are ex-tremely distant. However, it is impossible to determine if that is always so and if, for example, the 1950s are another geological era for young people today. Certainly, the First World War and the independence of Poland were a watershed for Marysia and her generation, but not as significant a one as I thought them to be.

Marysia lived an office life, which meant not only work but also friendships, picnics with colleagues, even office excursions abroad. During those years when I used to visit them, first as a *gymnasium* student, then as a university student, she was beginning to age and I would think about how it is that women become old maids. At 6 Arsenal Street I felt at home, and because it would have been hard to find a more central location in the city, sometimes I dropped in there simply to stretch out on the sofa. I wrote a couple of poems there that I like to this day. Also, I spent my last night in Wilno in that apartment, before my journey, which was more risky than I wanted to admit to myself, to Warsaw across the green border in 1940. This was shortly after the occupation of the city by Soviet troops, which was barely noticed by the family, because Uncle Pawlikowski was dying and their main worry was buying bottles of oxygen.

The Institute for the Study of Eastern Europe, housed in the rebuilt or added-on part of the large corner building, was modernity, lots of light, brightly painted walls, furniture made from light-colored woods. Usually I would wait patiently while Dorek Bujnicki attended to the students at his little window, after which we showed each other our poems and dreamed up literary pranks. There was a Lithuanian who also used to hang around there— Pranas Ancewicz. We were close friends and there was a time when we saw each other every day, because we both lived in the Student House on Bouffałowa Hill. Now that I've mentioned his name, I cannot refrain from remarking that I know of very few people who have been slandered the way that wise and good man was. And no one knows better than I that it was all barefaced lies.

The Institute is for me the period just before my departure for Paris and immediately after my return, 1934 and 1935, a period of dramas and intoxications, also of travels. Perhaps, aside from strictly personal causes, one might detect in this some sort of short-lived opening up in the whole country, between the chaos of the economic crisis and the gathering darkness of the end of the thirties, a soaring, along with, to be sure, a presentiment of the approaching terror. I received a literary fellowship to Paris. Nika, a woman I had met in the Institute and had become friendly with, went to Moscow on a fellowship. The first book of poems by Boris Pasternak that I read, *Vtoroe rozhdenie* [*Second Birth*], was a gift from her. Just about that time Pasternak traveled abroad for the last time, to Paris, to the Congress in Defense of Culture, but he was in a tenuous position and was no longer being published.

The entrance to the Calf Pen was directly across from Arsenal Street. I had all sorts of experiences along the boulevard that led to Royal Street, but there are no sentimental memories associated with this garden. Open to passersby like a public square, it was not considered a congenial place for conversation or for holding hands, because the sight of all the nannies and the soldiers crowded together on its benches cast something of a pall on the splendid repetitiveness of such occupations. Probably my most detailed memories of the garden's recesses are from my childhood, from daytime games, when it was still neglected and practically empty.

BAKSZTA STREET

Never in my Wilno years did I stop to consider why this street bore this name. The word was vaguely associated with *baszta*, or tower, which is correct. Bakszta was a very old, dark, narrow street, with horrible ruts in the roadway, no wider than two or three meters in some spots, and with deep open gutters. As a child I was rather afraid to venture into it because it had a bad reputation: right after you turned onto Bakszta from Grand

Street you passed a multistory building with white-painted windows—the hospital for venereal diseases. At the upper windows sat whores who were there for a compulsory cure, mocking the passersby and screaming ugly words. It is not because it was so widespread that prostitution in Wilno is worth paying attention to; this oldest of human professions shows no signs of disappearing anywhere, it just changes its form. In Wilno, prostitution maintained completely nineteenth-century forms or, rather, nineteenth-century-Russian forms, just as in Dostoevsky's novels. That is, the drinking bouts of officers and students in exclusively masculine company would end with trips "to the girls," to the numerous little brothels whose addresses were known by every cabby. On certain streets (especially those below Bakszta on the Wilenka River, such as Łotoczki Street, Safjaniki, etc.) creatures of the female sex would stand in front of the gates for hours, adapting to the rigors of the climate, so that in winter they wrapped themselves up in woolen scarves, wore thick felt boots or tall leather boots, and stamped their feet in the snow to keep warm. The reservoir for this working force, just as for servant girls, was the countryside or the wooden outskirts of the city, which were not too different from the village.

But, more than anything, Bakszta was Barbara. Here and there, especially from the direction of the hillsides and bluffs near the Wilenka, a pedestrian looking in through the gates would see large courtyards and gardens; one of these sprawling estates was the Romer House. If I am not mistaken, my first journey from Niewiaża to Wilno ended there, because we used horses, and the Romers' courtyard, outfitted with a stable and a carriage house, made a good stopping place. The journey was a long one, 120 kilometers, and its significance is not in the least diminished by the fact that later I learned to drive that same distance by car in an hour. That is why we stopped at the Romers'; I don't know what social ties there were between us. In any event, later, throughout my entire stay at the *gymnasium*, the Romer House was managed by Barbara, a major domo and a housekeeper. Barbara came from my part of the country, even somewhat deeper into Samogitia, from the environs of Krakinów, and she had once served as my grandfather's senior housekeeper; we preserved a certain intimacy on the basis of these ties, and Barbara frequently visited us on Foothills Street. Tall, erect, severe, thin-lipped, she looked like so many of those numerous dark-haired and dark-eyed Lithuanians. An old maid, a pious woman, and a fanatical Lithuanian—the older people in our household used to make fun of these traits of hers, but gently. In all of Wilno only one church, St. Nicholas's, held Lithuanian Masses (that is, sermons and singing in that language) and naturally Barbara went to Mass only at St. Nicholas's. Anyway, most of the faithful there were servants. I used to smile when, many years later, I would listen to my Viennese-Parisian friends' stories about Czech towns under the Habsburg monarchy. Naturally, German was spoken there, and Czech was considered the language of the household servants. I knew that only too well, except that in our eastern region Polish took the place of German.

From what I am saying about Barbara it is not easy to make any inferences about the strength of my emotional attachment. However, her image has accompanied me on my wanderings across a couple of continents. There must be a reason for someone surviving this firmly in our imagination. I remember Barbara's "lodgings" in Szetejnie, which were as severe as she was, and this undoubtedly long-dead person has remained for me one of the most important figures from my early childhood.

Since it was so close to the university, almost directly across from the corner of Grand and St. John's Streets, Bakszta played an important role in the students' lives, because that is where the Mensa was located. Not a dining room, not a cheap restaurant, not a cafeteria, not a canteen, not "a place of collective eating," but precisely: a *Mensa*. It was one of the Students' Union's chief undertakings; the free or reduced-priced dinner coupons served as a stake in the political struggles for power. A rather dingy, dark building, it apparently housed the seminarists' dormitory at one time; for many years it was the only dormitory in Wilno—before the second one, very modern, was built on Bouffałowa Hill. I never lived on Bakszta, but every now and then I ventured into its corridors, with their blackened and well-worn wooden floors, in order to visit my classmates. The smell of lye, naphtha, soapsuds, tobacco. A similar corridor, on the ground floor, led to the Mensa. I have only a hazy recollection of its tables, covered with stained tablecloths (or was it oilcloth?), but I can see very clearly the small cashier's table at the entrance where one bought tickets for individual dishes. Almost always they were sold by a little gnome with a withered face, wearing a fantastic floppy black bow instead of a tie: Gasiulis.* An "eternal student," an already legendary personality, because he was active in student organizations in prehistoric times, perhaps even in 1922 or 1923. In the Vagabonds' Club he was respected as an elder, as one of the founders; it was from his era that certain songs dated, quite obviously inspired by Kipling's *Jungle Book*, which was idolized at that time. ("On a high hill the baboons were dancing their wild dance.") Today I think that Gasiulis, like all the members of the Vagabonds' Club, was very much a *hippie*. Our wide black berets with colorful tassels made fun of the generally accepted head coverings. On the other hand, his black ascot came straight out of the bohemia of Young Poland, as did the cape of the popular city scoutmaster: skinny, sad-faced Puciata. Despite his pure Lithuanian surname, I don't think that Gasiulis knew Lithuanian. At one time he had wandered through various distant regions; perhaps he had even lived for a while in Cracow or Poznań—I could never find this out because the difference in generations precluded familiarity with such a celebrated, even if somewhat comic, figure.

---

*Executed by the Soviet authorities for tearing down official posters

FOUNDRY STREET

Foundry Street means walking downhill. Many a time, innumerable times, over the course of many years, because I usually lived in the newest part of the city, beyond Zawalna and Wileńska Streets, and it was Foundry Street that led from there to Napoleon Square and beyond, to the university or to bustling Grand Street. A triumphal descent, the ecstasy of physical exertion, the happiness of long, almost dancing steps, or absolute despair, or else, probably most often, that spiritual state when the young organism rejoices in its own way, despite the delusions of its tormented imagination. The descent began at the building on the corner of Wileńska, where the meeting halls of the Professional Unions and other similar institutions were located. A colorful array of notices was posted there, announcing lectures and boxing matches; fans of these performances, mainly young Jews, used to gather in groups on the sidewalk. A little farther down, on the right, but not as far as the corner of Tatar Street, were a couple of apartment houses with balconies that meant nothing to me until the moment when I began to spend my spring evenings on one of them with Stanisław Stomma, abandoning myself to intellectual disputes accompanied by rosy sunsets. It was 1929, I was a student in the eighth class at the *gymnasium*; Stomma, I think, was a second-year student in the law faculty and also an older brother in our lodge—the conspiratorial group "Pet." "Lodge" is an exaggeration, but I cannot think of our group or of the Vagabonds' Club, which I joined shortly afterward, other than as the peculiar creations of Wilno, the city of Freemasonry. Just as during the period of Wilno University's preeminence, prior to 1830, when many of our city's luminaries belonged to the Masonic lodges and rumors about this circulated freely, although I found out how numerous were the Masons among us only many years later. Unfortunately, the right-wing press erred in ascribing to Masonry a decisive influence on the course of historical events.

So, with Stomma on a balcony above a ravine of a street that descended toward tree-lined squares. We argued about Petra-życki, into whose theory of law and morality Stomma was being initiated by a young professor, a fanatic Petrażyckyist, a certain Lande. Having heard about Petrażycki, I, in turn, began reading some of his writings. We also argued about Henri de Massis's book, which was quite popular then—*La Défense de l'Occident.* At the time I was devoting myself wholeheartedly to studying French in order to read French authors in the original. It was probably Stomma from whom I borrowed the Massis, and still, over thirty years later, in California, I appreciate his lending me that book. This does not mean that I was ever, then or now, attracted to the French nationalists, the heirs of the monarchy. One must admit, however, that they were the first to sound the alarm, alerting people to the presence of ergot, the black discoloration that had begun to contaminate thought and language. According to them, this disease would arise in Asia and spread to the European mentality through the intermediary of Germany in particular; after 1918, through Weimar Germany—Schopenhauerism, Hinduism, Buddhism, Spengler, Keyserling, etc. Massis and other defenders of the Cartesian trenches were unable to ward off the growing opaqueness of the French language under the influence of German philosophy, which, by the way, was not necessarily an import from the Orient. Who knows, perhaps my distaste for the "wisdom of the East" that is sweeping California can be explained by the fact that I read those early warnings when I was seventeen years old.

Past the corner of Tatar Street, on the right, there was the open space of a plaza; on the left, some small shops, unremembered, and a restaurant or cafeteria that opened during the second half of my time at the university, where one got good-tasting dinners for 60 groszy. The owner was a Warsaw Jew, the clientele was made up of students, but for the most part they were not the same students whom one saw in the Mensa. Here I met my Jewish classmates from the law faculty, who came mainly from War-

saw; Lithuanians and Belorussians also gathered here. I do not
know why my memory has preserved only a few faces and names.
One of them: my colleague Lerner.

A few more steps took one past the Church of the Bonifraters
(the Brothers of the Order of St. John the Divine). It was the
lowest church in Wilno, and the church itself, plus the monastery
buildings, which were also low, formed a kind of miniature
fortress on a small square that was full of trees—lindens, I think.
The Brothers ran some sort of charitable enterprise; at one time,
they had an institution for the mentally ill, which is why if someone talked nonsense, we would say that he was fit for the Brothers. The church had two little towers, but in keeping with the
nature of the whole building, they were mere curves, just two
breasts on the building. The interior was like a crypt or grotto
decorated in Baroque style, with a small spring-fed well more or
less in the center of its elongated rectangular space. Miraculous
healing properties were ascribed to the water from this spring; although its fame did not extend even to other parts of the city, its
reputation continued to be useful within the parish. What was
special about the Church of the Bonifraters was the way it gave
one a sense of security, of the homeliness of divine-human affairs, of an impregnable shelter from the world. Later—after
Poland— I had occasion to visit Eastern Orthodox churches,
which are like little chests made of gold, or cells of beeswax,
where the warm radiance of the walls, the smell of incense, and
the liturgical songs have a hypnotic effect. No doubt this fulfills a
human need for an enclosed, delineated space, subject to its own
laws and fenced off from that other, limitless space. That was
why I loved the Brothers; particularly at Easter, when people visited the "tombs," it would not do to pass by that church. If in the
other churches Christ's tomb, displayed with more or less ingenuity, vanished beneath the high vaulted ceilings, was diminished
in comparison with the altar and the columns, in the Church of
the Brothers of the Order of St. John the Divine it was the central place, because everything there was practically on the same

level as the floor. I almost forgot to add that Foundry Street turned into the Street of the Bonifraters near that small square.

GERMAN STREET

Narrow and not too long, German Street was the most cosmopolitan of Wilno's streets, because the street that was supposed to be the main street was definitely not cosmopolitan. It was officially named St. George Boulevard at first, then Mickiewicz Boulevard; less officially, it was known as St. George Street, or Georgie for short. This thoroughfare, laid out with a straight edge and bordered by rows of apartment houses from the second half of the nineteenth century, did not elevate Wilno any higher than a provincial town, a Rennes or an Elizavetgrad, as I imagine it, where there must also have been a "boulevard" for the officers' and students' *gulianie* [Russian for "rowdy strolling," i.e., carousing]. By contrast, German Street's cosmopolitan aspect was not diminished by its cobblestone roadway, which was repaved with bricks (as were all the important streets) only in the 1930s. As one approached German Street one left the underpopulated area behind and penetrated into a region of sudden density. Sidewalks, gates, doors, windows all sprouted multitudes of faces and seemed to bulge from the crowds. It seemed that on German Street every house concealed an infinite number of inhabitants who engaged in every possible trade. Beneath enormous painted signs, shop after shop fronted on the street, but the faces of lions, the pictures of stockings of monstrous proportions, of gloves and corsets, also advertised shops inside the courtyards, while the signs inside the gates gave information about dentists, seamstresses, hosiers, pleaters, shoemakers, and so forth. Trade also overflowed from the buildings into the roadway; it seethed around the pushcarts and the stalls erected at intervals in recesses along the sidewalks. Loaded carts, pulled by straining horses, thundered past. Touts circulated among the passersby; their job was to spot potential customers, praise their goods, and conduct those people they had managed to corral to a shop that often was located somewhere in a distant inner courtyard. I am positive that I never connected German Street with the illustrations in my French school texts that depicted nineteenth-century Paris; I arrived at that comparison slowly, only when I was already a resident of France. In the second half of our century, when it no longer exists, I have often thought about German Street, particularly when I wander about in the Marais district, staring at the signboards, especially since several of them practically beg to be remembered. For example, the one from the rue de Turenne on which to this day Monsieur Szatan recommends his tailoring establishment for men's suits.

German Street was exclusively Jewish, but it was significantly different from Warsaw's Nalewki, for example. More old-fashioned, more settled, it acted as the representative of a whole labyrinth of twisting, astonishingly narrow medieval alleys, and I never felt that hidden background in Warsaw. With its stones that bore the patina of time, Wilno's cosmopolitan fragments were probably closer to Paris than to Warsaw.

I visited German Street at various stages of my life, above all as a little boy accompanying Grandmother Milosz. We were living in an apartment house at 5 Foothills Street, so we would walk down Foothills to the corner of Sierakowski Street, then along Port Street to Wileńska. Sierakowski Street demands a digression. At that time one could still see veterans of the 1863 Uprising; they wore uniforms and cornered hats, which were navy blue with a raspberry-colored rim. They received a modest pension, and even the widows of these veterans were not excluded, although of course it only amounted to pennies. Grandmother Milosz also received such a pension. The street named after Sierakowski led to the Łukiszki district, to the square where the leader of the Uprising in Lithuania was hanged. My grandfather fought under Sierakowski in 1863, as his adjutant or officer for special commissions, I am not absolutely certain. In any event, he was a close collaborator and was saved, because in Serbiny, his family estate near Wędziagoła (north of Kaunas), he had as neighbors a village of Old Believers who liked him very much. The elders gathered and debated for an entire night over a by no means trivial problem: does a Christian have the right to swear a false oath in order to save a life? And they swore under oath that he had never left home throughout 1863.

From Foothills, across Sierakowski, then down Port Street to Wileńska and German Streets—always to Sora Kłok's store. The store was in the courtyard, but it didn't need signs or touts; it was famous in the city and had a faithful clientele. It was well known that buttons, linings, wadding, and similar items such as no other shop carried could always be found there. I was fascinated by Mrs. Sora Kłok herself—hideously ugly, fat, a faded redhead in a wig, with her goiter and her obviously shaved chin. She only commanded the troop of salesgirls; she was very imperious. From her store came the so-called tailor's supplements for my suits, which were either continually made over or sewn from homespun to leave room for growing. Shall I reveal the secret of habits I acquired in childhood? To this day a conditioned reflex takes over whenever I buy a suit: I'd better get it one size larger, because what if I should outgrow it?

After my boyhood years there is a big gap in my relations with German Street; I passed by there from time to time, and that's all. Only toward the end of my stay at the university did I begin to establish contact with it, attending guest performances of a Yiddish theater or visiting the little restaurants on its side streets with Pranas Ancewicz. The taste of chilled vodka and marvelous herring, but also the sensation of human warmth, dimly preserved in memory, guaranteed that I would always like Jewish restaurants. The jumble of side streets near German Street is worth mentioning, too, because that is where I sought out a rabbi in order to fulfill a certain errand. Namely, in 1933 or 1934 Oscar Milosz sent me three copies of his little book from Paris; he had published it privately in a very small number of copies. Considering its contents, it is not at all surprising that he did not intend this work for sale. *L'Apocalypse de St. Jean déchiffrée*—the book I'm talking about—prophesied catastrophes of cosmic dimensions that were supposed to strike humanity around the year 1944. It is possible, after all, that there were two pamphlets, not one—the other essay (either bound together with the first or separate) proposed the hypothesis that the most ancient fatherland of the Jews was located on the Iberian peninsula; and only there, and nowhere else, should one look for the biblical Eden. From this work, *Les Origines ibériques du peuple juif,* it appeared that the Jews are, most likely, the oldest autochthonous people of Europe. So, one copy was for me, and the others I was supposed to give to the (in my opinion) two most appropriate individuals— one a Christian and the other a Jew, if possible one of the "illustrious rabbis." I selected Professor Marian Zdziechowski, because his pessimism about the future of Europe seemed to make him relatively open to gloomy prophecies. But I did not know Zdziechowski personally. As luck would have it, I approached him, stammering and blushing, on the steps of the university library, without having been properly introduced, and met with such an unresponsive welcome that it seems I didn't hand him the copy. Who the most famous rabbi was and on what grounds I selected him, I do not recall. I gave the copy to his secretary. I shall never know if it was read and if the author's intention—to issue a warning—was fulfilled.

L'Apocalypse de St. Jean déchiffrée is a bibliophilic rarity, and my next adventure connected with this text took place many years after the death of Oscar Milosz, in 1952, in the vicinity of the rue Vaugirard, where I was living at the time. I had run into Henry Miller in a small restaurant; I was astounded when I heard that he had been searching for this text for a long time. I promised to get him a copy, which wasn't at all difficult, since the Collection Doucet collects Milosziana. I did not keep my promise and Miller excoriated me for that. Why didn't I keep it? It simply slipped my mind, but I suspect that the causes must have gone deeper than that and Miller rightly saw in it a reason to take of-

fense. In my conversation with him I found his California catastrophism terribly distasteful: that's all we need, as if we don't
have enough problems coping with the heritage of our European
catastrophism. I detected intellectual chaos in what he said, and
in his greediness for apocalyptic texts I saw a lust for sensational-
ism. So it cannot be ruled out that my resistance had a sacral
character to it: I did not consider Miller to be one of the chosen to
whom Oscar Milosz had once wanted to issue his warning.

WILEŃSKA

A street with a strange name, not homogeneous, changing form
every dozen or so steps, ecumenical to boot, Catholic-Jewish. At
its beginning (or end) at the Green Bridge, it was wide, lacking a
distinctive consistency, for there were no more than a couple of
apartment houses at the outlets of the various side streets; it con-
stricted into a narrow throat beyond the intersection with St.
George (or Mickiewicz) Boulevard. When I was a child, the foundations of an unfinished building sat there for a long time, until
at last a huge edifice was erected, a department store owned by
the Jabłkowski brothers, the first more or less "universal" store in
Wilno, several stories high.

Not far from the Jabłkowskis', across from the Helios movie
theater, was an amazing haberdashery, the likes of which I never
saw anywhere else in the city. Its owners were not Jews but Poles
from somewhere far away in Galicia, distinguished from ordinary
people by their speech and their exaggerated politeness. The
family: two women and a man, a family triangle, it seems. The
man smelled of eau de cologne, his slightly curled hair was
parted and combed smooth, his hands were white and puffy.
They said, "I kiss your hand." And the shop did not remind one
at all of what was normally meant by a "shop"; the gleaming
parquet floor was polished so that there wasn't a speck of dust on
it; the goods were in glass cases.

Next door to this shop was a small bookstore, where every year on the first of September I experienced strong emotions, jostling against the other pupils and buying my new schoolbooks. Without a doubt, one of the most powerful experiences is to only look and touch for a moment, without knowing what is hidden under the colorful dust jackets.

Across the street, as I said before, was the Helios movie theater, remembered along with various films seen there, among them Pudovkin's *Storm Over Asia*, which made a powerful impression on me. But this theater also has remained in my memory as a symbol that evokes a vague feeling of disgust and shame that has been pushed away to a level deeper than consciousness. Among Witold's many unsuccessful careers (before he died of tuberculosis at age thirty-six)—his service in the Borderland Defense Corps, for example, his participation in a Jewish fur-trading cooperative, etc.—there was also an attempt at founding a cabaret review. The premiere took place in the hall of the Helios, and I, a fourteen-year-old boy at the time, was unable to defend myself with rational judgment against the bawdy vulgarity of this show; hence the shame—because of Witold, who, like it or not, belonged to the family, and also because of my parents, who even laughed—remained undiminished, spreading like a greasy stain.

On the same side of the street, right behind the movie theater, Rutski's bookstore was to serve as a kind of counterweight much later on. The son of the dignified, dour Mr. Rutski was my colleague at the university and was married to Sitka Danecka; my relations with Sitka, before then, testify optimistically to the diversity of human relationships and the freedom from Form that is possible every now and then. We used to go on kayaking trips together, and we felt so comfortable with each other that we forgot about the difference in our sex. We were not, however, just "colleagues"; we were linked by a much warmer mutual heartfelt caring. Nonetheless, no Form compelled us into erotic intimacies; friendship was more precious.

Beyond Halpern's shop (I think that was his name), where

there was dust, semi-darkness, a wealth of dyes, pencils, paper in many colors, notebooks, Wileńska Street, now even narrower, turned into a street of Christian harness makers, cobblers, tailors; there was even a Turkish bakery. From it, or perhaps from another, came my *gymnasium* colleague Czebi-Ogły, who was a Muslim. Next, the façades of the buildings became subdivided into a multitude of little Jewish shops, and after a momentary rise in dignity across from the little square near the Church of St. Catherine (there was a beautiful old store there that carried hunting guns), Wileńska was dominated by impoverished trade all the way to the intersection of Trocka, Dominican, and German Streets.

From a courtyard on Wileńska, in its "artisan" section, one entered a lending library to which Grandmother Milosz had a subscription paid for out of her modest pension. I often turned up there, either delegated by her or to borrow books for myself, when I was twelve, thirteen. Mostly Żeromski, Rodziewiczówna, Szpyrkówna, that is to say, bad literature, and it seems to me that a tolerable intelligence in someone who received such training should not be underrated, with a few points added for the obstacles that he must have had to overcome. In all languages, *belles lettres* are predominantly kitsch and melodrama; however, the accidents of Polish history decreed that fiction had an exceptionally powerful effect on people's minds, as a language and as a sensibility, so that I suspect there is in the so-called Polish soul an exceptionally rich underpinning of kitsch. As for me—let's be frank: in the books that I borrowed from the library I was enchanted by such scenes as the death of the beautiful Helen in *Ashes*, who threw herself into a ravine, and perhaps even more so by the ending of a certain story that was translated from the French about the Chouans, or the counter-revolutionaries in the Vendée. The hero's head is sliced off on the guillotine, but that does not put an end to his highly emotional adventures. To this day I can remember the last sentence: "But his head, still rolling, whispered, 'Amélie!' "

AFTER ALL . . .

AFTER ALL, I've done quite a lot of traveling. Partly of my own volition, but mainly as a result of circumstances which carried me about the world. Already as a high school student in Wilno I was trying to make order out of images of war and revolution in Russia; beyond that, everything was the future and a pledge that would never be redeemed. How many emotions I must have experienced, both good and bad, to have been, one after the other, in France, Italy, Switzerland, Belgium, Holland, Denmark, Sweden—I can't even count them, and then there's North and Central America. So I fulfilled, and then some, my adventurer father's dreams, although despite my romantic desires I never succeeded in assuming the role of a collector of places and countries, because life made too many demands on me. In any event, what at the beginning of the century might have seemed exotic was transformed with the passage of time into something universally familiar, in accord with an era of increasing motion.

My ancestors only rarely crossed the borders of their native

Kiejdany district to visit one of our cities, either Wilno or Riga, but my father, even before Krasnoyarsk, had brought back from a journey through the Baltic region something of Europe in 1910, and leafing through the album about Holland, I would study the Amsterdam canals. Just as I studied his photograph, from 1913, taken on the deck of Fridtjof Nansen's steamship at the mouth of the Yenisei River.

There weren't many photographs in my childhood, and my imaginings about foreign countries were fed by a drawing or a woodcut—for example, the illustrations to Jules Verne's and Mayne Reid's books. But cinema had already come into play.

Many cities, many countries, and no habits of the cosmopolite; on the contrary, the timidity of a provincial. Once I had settled down in a city, I didn't like to venture beyond my own district and had to have the same view in front of my eyes every day. What this expressed was my fear of being broken down into my constituent parts, fear of losing my center, my spiritual home. But I would define this somewhat differently. We construct our private mythologies throughout our lives and those from the earliest years last the longest. The farther afield I was carried (and California, I'd say, is quite far), the more I sought a link with my former self, the one from Szetejnie and Wilno. That is how I explain my bond with the Polish language. That option seems lovely, patriotic, but in truth I was locking myself inside my own fortress and raising the drawbridges: let those others rage outside. My need for recognition—and who doesn't need it?—was not strong enough to lure me out of there and incline me to write in English. I felt called to something else.

My return after more than half a century to my birthplace and to Wilno was like a closing of the circle. I could appreciate the good fortune that had brought me such a rare encounter with my past, although the power and complexity of that experience were beyond my linguistic abilities. Perhaps I simply fell mute from an excess of emotion, and that is why I went back to expressing myself indirectly; that is, instead of speaking about myself, I started assembling a registry, as it were, of biographical sketches and events.

MISS ANNA
AND MISS DORA

Miss ANNA was short, almost a dwarf, with a huge head and a very ugly face in which the enormous wart on her nose was the most prominent feature. She carried out her profession as a teacher proudly and sternly; in her youth, it was a patriotic activity to teach the language which was looked at askance by the czars and to spread knowledge about the Polish Romantic poets. Many manor houses in Lithuania and Samogitia employed such teachers and the respect for Miss Anna in our family derived from her having been my father's teacher once upon a time. When independent Lithuania was formed in 1918, for a while Miss Anna carried out the duties of director of the Polish *gymnasium* in Poniewież. Later, however, during my student years, that is, she lived with her sister in Wilno, subsisting (poorly) on her meager savings.

She came from a backwater gentry family; she did not find a husband and became a teacher because there were very few ways for a single woman to earn money in those days. Miss Anna's spinsterhood embittered her and hardened her character traits, her resoluteness taken to the point of dictatorial rages, her easily triggered anger. She had no one, however, on whom to unload that anger other than her sister, Dora. Dora, who was certainly born to be married, also remained an old maid and had no one in the world other than Anna, whom she obeyed in every detail; she never insisted on her own opinion. Rather stupid, almost retarded, she fussed about her sister, doing the marketing, cooking, and cleaning.

They rented a room on Embankment Street and I used to visit them there, not quite sure why. It was one of my family obligations, like visiting relatives. These visits never took place without conflicting emotions: the sisters were from a long-past era, they were old, poor, and helpless; my twentieth century, my youth, and my education made me superior, and from that came pity, empathy, and something like sorrow for the world, because human fates could turn out like that. I have never stopped seeing those two old women, defenseless against historical time, and simply time itself. No one but me remembers their names anymore.

JOURNEY TO THE WEST

THIS HAPPENED in the year 1931. There were three of us, and the sum of our ages made sixty years. Robespierre, whom we, like the majority of Vagabonds' Club members, tacitly recognized as our leader, marched along, arms churning like a windmill, his sinuous, knobby figure bent forward under the weight of his knapsack. He never indulged his fatigue, and to show that he despised it he turned his body into a mileage-eating machine. His severe face with its arched nose resembled the faces of monks in old German woodcuts. Elephant waddled like a tall, plump drake. I could have recognized him in the dark simply by touch. His shaggy body was pleasant to grab and pinch, and his woolly head of black hair used to provide a convenient fingerhold when we wrestled in the school corridors, for our friendship dated that far back. He had the gentleness and solicitude of a *yiddische mammeh,* which he probably got from his Jewish mother. He was cultivating a beard and encouraged its growth with caresses; besides that, his trousers were always falling down. Robespierre and I used to say that only the will of

God held them up. I looked at the most fifteen, and my childishly round cheeks caused me a great deal of embarrassment.

We represented three kinds of humor: Robespierre's was dry and sarcastic, Elephant's ironic but gentle, and mine noisy. Our humor came in handy when we wanted to abuse the owners of dishonest means of communication. If a car (and there were few in our region) passed us, stirring up clouds of dust, we sang our cursing song after it, wishing it the soonest possible disaster ("She broke down, oh that proud automobile," went the refrain).

During June 1931, however, after our spring exams in law, we were setting off for regions beyond our own and we had to take advantage of an equally dishonest means of locomotion: the train. Our plan was to take the train from Wilno to Prague, buy a used Canadian canoe there (because sporting goods were half as expensive in Czechoslovakia as in Poland), transport the canoe to Lindau in Bavaria on Lake Constance, and from there paddle down the Rhine and its tributaries as near as we could get to Paris, to which we had been lured by the Colonial Exposition. Our love for maps was responsible for this plan. Though surely Vasco da Gama, starting out on his journey to India, knew more about the seas through which he was to sail than we did about our route.

The first Western European type of small town we happened to explore was Litomyśl in Czechoslovakia, where we were hospitably entertained by a haberdasher whom we met quite by accident. In the western part of Poland I would have encountered similar small towns, but where I was from, in the east, usually such clusters of houses and streets were no more than "trading posts" for the manors and hamlets, where old-fashioned Jews carried on all the trading. Their bad paving, dust, dirt, straw, and horse manure were viewed with contempt by the inhabitants of larger towns or the countryside. My admiration for Czech tidiness and for our friend the haberdasher's standard of living is a good example of the "Western complex" that is found in all people from the East. It does not have the same intensity everywhere, of course. I was to remember Litomyśl again in 1940 on a Russian train as, pretending to be asleep, I overheard two commissars talking about the territory the Soviet Union had acquired as a result of the Molotov-Ribbentrop pact. About even the poorest counties they talked like two Alices in Wonderland. But their wonder was not friendly. There was envy in it and anger.

Prague, the first Western European capital I saw, intoxicated us with its effervescent air of laughter and music, its taverns in the narrow streets near Hradčany Castle, its crowds in Baťa tennis shoes, wandering outside the city on Sundays, walking or riding with balls, javelins, discuses. My first modern crowd. Everywhere posters announced *Hikers and Lovers*—I do not know whether it was a movie or a play; in other words, tourism as a sport (unmotorized as yet) was already part of mass culture.

I spent two weeks in Czechoslovakia. Robespierre and Elephant went on to walk across the Bavarian Alps, and I remained to carry through the purchase and transport of the canoe we had tested on the Moldau. In the parks of Prague a familiar hunger assailed me. That feeling can be compared to physical hunger except that it is insatiable. The tree-lined gravel paths grated under my feet; I passed couples kissing; there was music, whispers through the foliage—a carnival of hot, jostling, embracing humanity. I was an outsider, yet at the same time so avid for their reality I was ready to devour them all, whole and entire. Had I been sitting on a bench with my own girl, I would have been part of them, but I would only have deceived my hunger. My timidity drove me into solitude, but it was not only that. My erotic desire went further than any object, my pansexuality included the whole world and, not able to be a god or an ogre who swallows the world, tastes it with his tongue, bites, I could only take it in an embrace with my eyes. Besides, like all hungers, this one disperses, too, at the limit of words.

(I would have been unable to guess then what my next visit to Prague would be like—predestined, waiting within these walls. The passage of time, love affairs, nothing was to slow my chase

after that unattainable feast of a pansexual image-devourer. My
plane from London was to land at an empty white airport. Snow
was falling. It was December 1950. A huge fellow with the face of
a hoodlum, wearing the uniform of the Czech Security Police,
opened the door to the cabin and asked for passports. The waiting
room was empty. My footsteps echoed back at me. In one corner a
handful of people in dark, ill-fitting suits stood whispering
among themselves—some sort of delegation waiting for a digni-
tary. At the front entrance to the waiting room were three snow-
covered cars and a boringly deserted square. I took a taxi. The
tribe of taxi-drivers has a gift for discerning whom one can or
cannot speak freely to; for half an hour my driver spilled out his
laments and reproaches against "them." I did not answer. From
Prague I took the train to Warsaw, where a portly Robespierre
was now a high-ranking Stalinist bureaucrat. Colorless streets in
the twilight. From some building high over the city shone a huge
red star. Pedestrians walked quickly, with downcast eyes.)

Summer. From the train taking me to Bavaria I jumped out in
Pilsen. To kill a superphysical hunger, the best thing is a hike. So
I walked, buying only a bit of sausage and bread in the villages.
Out of frugality I refused to eat dinner in a restaurant, allowing
myself at the most only a glass of beer. The things I remember
from that hike: the white highway, the taste of dust in my mouth,
the mileage, the farm where I helped with work in the fields
and the pleasant country girl—some of her teeth were missing.
Then the train again, and a feeling of strangeness as I passed over
the German frontier—all around me people were speaking a language I did not understand. Furious with myself, I made an act of
will and entered, for the first time in my life, the dining car.
There I was greeted by a spectacle for which even now I still try
to imagine an explanation. Beside me sat a raw-boned man who
looked like an officer in civilian clothes. He ordered a steak and
absorbedly tied a napkin under his chin; then, with eyes glued to
the steak, he rubbed his hands. He did not really eat the contents
on his plate but, rather, engulfed them; chomping and grunting

to himself, he immediately ordered a new portion. It was the same thing all over again: the ritual of rubbing his hands, the rapt gazing at the plate in anticipation of its delights, and that same speed. Most surprising of all, his speed did not diminish with each successive steak. Who was he? Where was he coming from? I have no idea why, but it seemed as if he were returning from the trenches, or from a POW camp of the last war, or that he had spent thirteen years somewhere frozen in a block of ice.

I arrived in Lindau at four in the morning. A fine drizzle was coming down, and the sailboats moored at the docks near the station were rocking to and fro, their masts touching because the lake was stormy. As I stood on the shore, getting sprinkled by the waves, I did not see the Alps on the other side. Every form, even the feel of the air, was new and astonished me. What I did next shows that I was a real savage: I adjusted the straps of my knapsack and headed through the empty streets, where a milk horse was clip-clopping along the asphalt, to a "safe place." That meant the forest. For a long time I forced my way through a thicket on the mountainside, to find a place as far off the path as possible. I cut off some branches, prepared a place to sleep under a low-hanging spruce tree, and rolled up in a blanket. In the middle of a foreign country I could now sleep as if I were in my own home.

The meeting with Robespierre and Elephant took place in the afternoon. They related their adventures while soaking their callused feet. We chose to spend the night in a Deutsche Jugend Herberge, and the next morning we began our trip. The plan had to be fulfilled; to wait for the weather to clear would have been beneath our dignity. At the station we picked up our Canadian canoe, carried it to the lake, and here were seized by alarm, but we put on a good face in front of each other. A group of people on the pier were staring at the madmen; no doubt they were making bets: will they get off or not? Wind, rain, waves battering against the cement. We rowed desperately for a quarter of an hour, rising and falling like a cork, almost in the same spot. Finally the port began to grow distant. Elephant, who was sitting in the middle, was chattering from the cold and from the torrents of rain pouring down his collar. Such was our start. Not too charming. But we were not interested in passive pleasures. On the map we had divided our route into segments, and each segment had a date. By evening of that day we were supposed to be in Constance, on the other side of the lake.

For me the narrow streets of the little shoreline towns, the asphalt, the quiet, the cleanliness, the waiter's green apron in the tavern, the children in raincoats, the checkered shopping bag of a *Frau* passing by were all enveloped in a dreamy majesty. I actually believed that those who participated in this order and wealth should be spiritually superior to the rest of mankind, which was slightly soiled, impulsive, and easier to understand; they should know a higher kind of love and carry on conversations of a loftier nature. A pile of horse manure in the street provoked the mental exclamation: so even here! . . . It was not easy to bring myself to accept the fact that here, at the foot of the Alps (how romantic!), a wave obeyed the same laws as waves everywhere, and that the oarsman's effort to steer the prow of his boat into it brought the same results.

We passed Friedrichshafen, the base for hydroplanes. Toward evening the lake calmed and we stuck to our paddles as dusk fell, then rowed in darkness. An oncoming ship could have crushed us, but it passed alongside, cabin lights glowing. Our goal was already close. With relief we listened to the faint lapping of water against the boardwalk on the edge of the long gulf beside which the town of Constance lies. Our boots rapped on the paving of the square and we stood in the presence of the history of the Church: before us loomed the gilded wooden structure in which the Council of Constance had been held between the years 1414 and 1418. Here we found a link with Western Europe other than through natural elements, which are the same everywhere. We had only to think back on our schooldays and the pages of the textbook devoted to the Council of Constance, which was important because it condemned the teachings of Jan Hus.

The ensuing days of our trip took us from ecstasy to ecstasy. The lake as it narrowed changed into a taut sheet, almost bulging from the pressure of a current that was already the Rhine. With every thrust of the paddle our canoe fairly leaped into the air. And our physical joy was undiminished by the almost constant downpour. Further on, the Rhine carried us so fast that all we had to do was steer. Warnings of rocks or tree stumps passed incessantly from prow to stern. Yet our joy was not only physical. Every bend in the river concealed a secret which, when disclosed, took away our breath. If anywhere, it was here we could have said that we had penetrated into an enchanted land. From the steep slopes branches hung out over the green water, making grottoes which were surely apartments for nymphs. In those branches Delaware warriors from the novels of Fenimore Cooper could have been crouching. Higher up the slopes vineyards rolled by, and castles. Our glances were all the more avid because we glimpsed all that luxuriance only from the corner of our eyes, as we wiped the sweat from our faces. Sometimes, when the river's treacherousness demanded less of our attention, we rested the paddles on our knees, knowing that what was passing before our eyes would not be given us again—ever.

We flew on under wooden covered bridges that seemed like tunnels on posts. A world like the old-fashioned engravings I had loved to look at as a child. Our passion for discovery drove us onward, and we would put off choosing a town to spend the night in if the current favored us. Once it favored us to such an extent that we found ourselves plunging ahead with the speed of an express train. Some vague misgiving whispered in us that we had better start thinking about what this meant. The waterfall at Schaffhausen had for a long time been considered a wonder of nature, and my grandfather, like other tourists, must certainly have visited it— the grandfather who died in the train crash near Baden-Baden and whose album of engravings had been left behind in the house where I was born in Lithuania. Our reflex came just in time, for we stopped within six hundred feet of the abyss that

sucked down a white column of foaming water. In Schaffhausen
there was no cheap Deutsche Jugend Herberge, so we spent the
night beneath the patchwork quilts of the local Salvation Army.
The next morning we transported our canoe around the European Niagara in a rented auto.

Disaster struck further on. Near the Swiss town of Koblenz
the Rhine has a few miles of rapids, and one needs to be familiar
with the current. But even that helps very little, and accidents are
frequent. A special police patrol on the German side of the river
had the job of fishing out those who capsized. But all that we
found out too late. Robespierre was in charge of the map and he
guided us along the Rhine, but since he treated obstacles lightly,
he looked into it rarely. We had not even tied down our knapsacks. In this seething and frothing water it did not do much good
to strain our attention, because our oar strokes remained behind
the river's rush. We struck, without knowing it, an underwater
rock which tore open a hole the size of a fist in the bottom of our
canoe. It may also have been that a patch had simply come loose
in our used boat. In any case, I did not understand why the prow
of the canoe had lifted so high, was getting higher and higher,
and finally why something cast me out like a frog, head first.
Everything changed then. I was spitting water, and movement
organized itself into two systems of relationship: the heads of my
companions moved further and further apart from each other and
the canoe's green bottom from them, while the riverbanks
flashed backward. That moment of emergence into a cosmos
other than the one we were in a second before endowed sensual
objects with great clarity. I was a poor swimmer then, and along
with a religious effort of will I felt an astonishment that this self
here, in the middle of the Rhine, was identical with that self of
time past. I reached out for the grasses on the shore, longed for,
washed by whirlpools, and while I struggled with the current
they grew as gigantic as cathedrals.

After changing into the training suits lent us by the German
river police in the town of Waldshut, we drew up a sorry account

of our situation. The Germans had pulled our canoe out of the Rhine a few miles lower than the place we took our spill. They had also rescued two knapsacks—but not the one that held our passports and money. Was our journey over? Absolutely not. First of all we had to find our way to the nearest consulate and get new passports; and after that we would see. The pleasant and generous policemen lent us a few marks for the trip to Zurich. Well-rested, and warmed by the coffee our hosts had served us, we crossed into Switzerland on the ferry. There the compartment of a Swiss electric train, similar to the interior of a streetcar, impressed us more than the waterfall at Schaffhausen.

Our story was received somewhat skeptically in the consulate. They promised us an answer within a few days, after they had verified it by telegram. Meanwhile, however, our stomachs were growling. In the park we sat down on a bench and searched our pockets for small change, counting out how much we could buy. There was only enough for the cheapest purchase, cheese; and we divided it up with our jacknife into daily portions, keeping in mind the days ahead. We also made a valuable discovery: in the squares, very tasty water spurted out of the jaws of bronze animal heads. Pewter cups on chains invited the passerby to drink.

The night we spent at the Salvation Army ended badly. At dawn I was awakened by someone scratching me on the foot; a fat policeman stood over me asking for documents. There followed a few hours of arrest until we were freed by a telephone call from the consulate, but we had stopped believing in this tidy country. Our decision, the next day, to leave the city was proof that we did not understand civilization. Along the lake for miles stretched nothing but private villas with their private gardens and private docks; but to us a lake was still a synonym for nature. Weak from hunger, we succumbed to alternate fits of laughter and fury. To shut yourself up in your own house, fence yourself off from others and say, "This is mine," one had to be a pig. In this place we felt very strongly that ownership is pitiless, that it works against those whom it excludes. So we headed for the mountains, and every evening for the next few days we came back to the same forest clearing. Mornings we were bothered by the cold, but through the fog came the sound of cowbells, and we were afraid to light a fire lest we attract a man with a stick and hear shrieks of "That's mine!" Where we were from, no one cared whom the forest belonged to. It was for animals, hunters, and vagabonds.

The consulate finally presented us with new passports and lent us a sum of money to get to the nearest consulate in France, which was the one in Strasbourg, because we did not want to forgo Paris. So we set off again for Waldshut. There we found out, however, that it would take a long time to repair the canoe and even longer to sell it. On the other hand, if we were to pay back our debt to the policemen from the sum in our pockets, we would have nothing left for the rest of the journey. We made a getaway at the crack of dawn, bidding farewell to our canoe, which we left lying outside the police station as security. Our new plan envisaged a crossing on foot through the Black Forest to Basel.

Slopes overgrown with grass to the knees. Black masses of spruce. Climbing, climbing, and then a view of the valley, with its sharp church steeple. We were in excellent humor and our hike went off with jokes and singing. On the afternoon of the third day, after having done around sixty miles of mountain trails, we set foot in Basel.

We began our acquaintance with Western Europe, thus, from her center, for surely the shores of the upper Rhine are that. Ours was an introduction from the side of oaken beams hewn in the Middle Ages; of the Zum Wilde Mann inn, decorated on the outside with painted sculpture; of jutting eaves, of ironsmiths in leather aprons resembling gnomes in a fairy tale.

We were not the only ones who appreciated that taste. Young Germany was then on the move, already perverting its attachment to the past, changing it into a myth of blood and soil. One could have called that era the era of the *Wanderervögel*. We met them everywhere. In twos, threes, on foot or riding bicycles. They would gather in groups in front of a Deutsche Jugend Herberge and sing. One of them always directed. Our efforts to make contact failed. They were overly polite, overly quiet, but at the same time contemptuous and hostile to foreigners. Wrapping ourselves up in blankets in the dormitory, we listened to the breathing of the sleepers. The future was already there, among those beds. Today I sometimes think that Elephant's closest neighbor could have been the Gestapo officer who later tortured him during questioning. Elephant was not cut out to sit in jail as a member of an underground organization, or to bear the twisting of his limbs and beating of the face, or finally, with what scrap of his consciousness remained after he had broken his legs in a suicidal jump from a window, to comprehend with relief that his poor body was dying. No one was cut out for it. But the jovial Elephant was called to a life of gentle humor and friendly chats over wine. His mind was liberal and skeptical, resistant to the temptations of heroism. His death, and the death of others like him, tips the scale of guilt for those contemporaries of ours, the *Wanderervögel*, more heavily than the death of young enthusiasts.

I cannot help but consider those dormitories we slept in as an extract of Germany. For some reason I am convinced that if none of those sleepers was to kill Elephant (a "London agent," according to Europe's temporary rulers), then at least one of them, while sitting in the trenches on the Eastern front, must have heard Robespierre's shrill voice speaking through the Moscow radio.

Elephant, however, as we stood on the bridge near Basel, was pulling up his trousers, which had fallen below his navel. The bridge led to the French border town of Saint-Louis, and we were reading the inscription on a sign. France—our spiritual sister—welcomed us. The sign prohibited Gypsies, Poles, Romanians, and Bulgarians from entering the country. The scornful glances we exchanged took care of our Western allies. We crossed the bridge.

What was France to us? Was it what appeared as we pressed

on the door handle of a bistro in search of a glass of beer? The
door opened onto a fragment of a movie. It was like thinking you
were entering your own room, but walking into an audience with
a Cardinal. A big room. Air dense with heat and smoke. Workers
holding glasses of wine in their hands; girls sitting on their laps,
mouths open in song; and lots of eyes turned toward us in surprise. We retreated in a paroxysm of timidity, ashamed of our
lack of worldly experience.

But above all we met suffering humanity in France. The train
took us through Alsace, along the Vosges, and standing at the
window we tried to count the number of dead for every mile of
cemetery. Geometrical patterns, formed by rows of small crosses
leaving wings of shadow and light behind them, covered the
landscape as far as the line where sky meets mountains. We were
not indifferent to that view, if only because the Unknown Soldier
was then one of the most honored themes in the poetry we read.

Sunburned and ragged, our faces covered with stubble, we did
not look too unlike living and suffering humanity, and so they
treated us like their own. We found ourselves among a polyglot
mass of workers, mainly Poles, roving about in search of jobs. At
that time Poles in France had the status that was later to devolve
on North Africans—a labor force used for the heaviest jobs and
getting the least pay. Eyes winked at us significantly, elbows
poked us in the side: "On the bum, eh?" In Strasbourg we had no
trouble finding the consulate: steel-helmeted police, supplied
with stacks of guns, bivouacked in the neighboring streets. In
front of the consulate a crowd of clamoring, gesticulating men
swarmed; others sat on the sidewalks or huddled in groups.

Learning comes quickly to the young. In this birthplace of
freedom and revolution, it had not taken us long to see the seamy
side. Robespierre's nickname came from his high school days,
when he became famous for a highly enthusiastic composition
about the Jacobins; in me Kropotkin had left a deep impression.
We were sensitive to the smell of misery and brutality. Rubbing
shoulders with that tragic mass, we came to an opinion of our

own about France, and it was close (though not in every shade) to what I hold now. France's beauty evokes the greatest tenderness. Her symbolic role as the heart of Europe will never allow her to be condemned, for from her every ash a phoenix is born. Here freedom is possible as it is nowhere else, because the pressure of social convention stops at the threshold of the private hearth and no one is compelled to live like his neighbor. Yet the price of this freedom is often indifference to the fate of the silent and the humiliated: live and die as you like. What Robespierre, Elephant, and I said to each other—that France's essence had embodied itself in capitalism or capitalism had embodied itself in France until the two became one—was not stupid. But we did not take into account the weight of past centuries and we were not familiar with those other Western countries where one's neighbor gives a helping hand, takes an interest in you—and in exchange demands conformity.

The worm of our privileged position gnawed at our consciences. For we had pressed through, finally, to the consul; he received us kindly, invited us to dinner, and gave us train fare to Paris. As students, we belonged to his sphere. And of course it was tourism that interested us, not social probing. For me, the interior of the cathedral in Strasbourg, with its gloomy immensity, still surpasses all the cathedrals I was to see later on. In Colmar's narrow streets Robespierre's German came in handy because the passersby did not understand French when we asked directions. Bursting with our impressions from Alsace, we boarded the train and immediately fell asleep on the hard benches in third class.

It was a summer morning. Four or five o'clock. Gray-pink, iridescent air like the enamel inside a shell. We inhaled Paris with open nostrils, cutting across it on foot, diagonally from the north toward the Seine. The moist flowers, the vegetables, the coffee, the damp pavement, the mingling odors of night and day. Where the wide sidewalks changed into a marketplace, we took pleasure in submerging ourselves in the human stream, its color, movement, gestures, and glances. We lost count of the streets, we forgot about our own existence, our bodies were simply instruments registering impressions; the promise was infinite; it was the promise of life. On the deserted Place de la Concorde, the sight of the pearl-gray expanse between the Arc de Triomphe and the trees in the park made us want to draw deep breaths. Branches of trees emerged like huge feathers from the fog. There was not a soul in the Tuileries except for one pair on a stone bench. She was bending her head back under his kiss. He had a flower in his buttonhole. Further on, through the mist, the river already shone in the sun. We walked over the Pont des Arts toward the Boulevard Saint-Michel, without bringing to those names anything other than what we ourselves saw there; and that was enough.

Today, the most amazing thing about Paris for me is that it still exists. Man's fleetingness seen against a background of unchanging nature affords an inexhaustible subject for meditation; but if the background is created by man himself, the contrast is all the more intense. That whole sea of human eyes (vainly we mask a desire that is overwhelming and orgiastic with some inadequate word, vainly we isolate ourselves with trifles from something more profound than ourselves) floods Parisian architecture year after year: certain eyes and faces perish and die, but the flood never lets up. Those eyes, whose secret I tried then to guess, have been surrounded by wrinkles, they have lost their glow, but the city is the same, and today I can walk along a street in Paris as avid as ever for something more than just an amorous adventure. At the same time, that ever-renewed contact between old stones and successive generations awakens an image in me, I do not know why, of kings sleeping amid a tangle of stone lilies, like dried-up insects in winter.

We trod the sidewalks of the Boulevard Saint-Michel, licked the cool fountain spray from our lips in the Luxembourg Gardens, where children were floating little sailboats and prodding them with long sticks. The children are here today too: the same, bewitched into immortal elves, or others?

Our emotions in Paris cannot be presented simply as youthful rapture. An ambition to reach a heart that seems difficult to get at sometimes turns into love; it is similar with Eastern Europeans. Their snobbery seasons their experience of this storied city. They have a sense of personal achievement: "I, Stash or Jack, have finally made it!" they say to themselves, and tap their foot on the sidewalk to make sure they are not dreaming. Besides, they are burdened with a longing for a homeland other than the one assigned to them from birth. Poland weighed on us. To live there was like walking on a sheet of ice underneath which grimaced a million deformed, nightmarish faces. The lack of a uniform standard made it impossible to take a man "as he is"—the forefront of the picture was always dominated by his status: white-collar, peasant, Jew. And it was not the politics conducted during our childhood that bred this state of affairs, but whole centuries. Whether such a desire to escape from an insoluble problem is good or bad I do not judge here; I only declare that it exists and that spasmodic patriotism is sometimes a compensation for an inner betrayal. (Are Poles not similar in this to certain homosexuals who, frightened of their abnormality, impose marital fidelity on themselves?)

Our low condition—we lived in the "Palais du Peuple" on the rue Glacière—did not spoil our delight. That sonorous name designated the Salvation Army shelter. Lodgers were let into the dormitories only in the evening. Each received a sort of cabin— the beds were partitioned off from each other by a screen. On a table near the bed was a Bible. Early in the morning the whole company was driven downstairs for breakfast, which could be had for a few cents. In the evening a free supper was obtainable in return for polite singing of the psalms, and sometimes we waited patiently through the evening service. A skinny carrot-top blew the trumpet while a giant Negro pounded a drum in time with the pious crowing of bums from various countries, who fidgeted impatiently, sniffing the odors from the kitchen.

At the Colonial Exposition, the French Empire displayed its splendors: pavilions in Moroccan style, Madagascan and Indo-

Chinese huts (inside, an imported family went through the motions of their daily routine for the tourists). That whole exhibit was actually outrageous, as if it had been an extension of the Vincennes Zoological Gardens, in which it was held. After one tired of looking at black, brown, or yellow people in their cages, one went to look at the monkeys, the lions, and the giraffes. That, of course, did not bother the organizers of the exposition; perhaps they even chose the place for the very reason that the natives, the wild animals, and the palms went well together, just as they did on postage stamps. And we, too, childish and eager for the exotic, considered it more or less normal: if there are colonies, then it cannot be otherwise. Yet something rankled within us: petit bourgeois, red in the face after soaking up their wine, unemployed Polish vagrants in the dives near Saint-Paul, the smell of poverty in the "Palais du Peuple," the incredible ugliness of family gravestones in Père Lachaise cemetery, fit for the heroes of Flaubert. Was this a world for which we were not yet grown up enough, or did we have the right to oppose it with our otherness?

They acquired their colonial empire late, while we in the East knelt in admiration before their culture, the beauty of their books, the excellence of their painting. But who were these people here, who thought in the highest spiritual registers? While military expeditions mowed down the colored peoples, acquired countries and ports, these people here in Paris enjoyed freedom by refusing to identify with their own government, or even nation, although they, even the poor, simultaneously profited from all this power and wealth. All that collective wealth appeared to them as a natural gift. They were proving the rule: let not thy left hand know what thy right hand doeth. But their lofty words received wings, thanks to the very down-to-earth efforts of their generals, prefects, and merchants. Their revolt against the bourgeoisie concealed a secret respect for order, and they would have quaked had someone told them that if they carried their rebellion to its conclusion, it would mean no more little bakeries, no more package-goods stores or bistros with their cats dozing in the sun behind the windowpane. Theirs was always a secure revolt because their bitterness and their nihilism rested on the tacit understanding that thought and action were measured by different standards: thought, even the most violent, did not offend custom. Any other nation, had it permitted itself such a dose of poison, would have long ago ceased to exist; for France it was healthy. Only when carried to different soil did her slogans, books, and programs reveal their destructive force, among people who took the printed word literally.

But that silent understanding—which allowed them to revolt, not knowing and yet knowing that monuments would be erected to them and that their works would find a place in libraries and museums built with money squeezed from the toil of variously colored peoples—brought extraordinary results and, justly, they were admired by the whole world. An observer of this situation might have some doubts about the permanent stance of the initiates at the top of the social pyramid. If they glanced down and became infected with the suffering of the millions below, the responsibility would kill them, their art would die. If they wanted to know nothing, they would have been hypocrites, and their art, protected by an illusory purity, would have been hypocritical in its very form, and therefore ephemeral. But they were neither oppressed with despair nor hypocrites; they drew a line beyond which sound, color, or word should not go. They knew the secret of balance—a disturbing secret, to tell the truth—and perhaps artists and philosophers are not too praiseworthy if their knowledge of the fate of the humiliated and the disinherited must always remain "within bounds."

On our walks about the city we were conscious that this was the capital of a great power and our every sensation was colored by that awareness. When I arrived in Paris after the Second World War, it seemed small to me, as if the rush of history had pushed it aside: an Alexandrian town, drawing its reason for existence from the preservation of its treasures, preparing for its new function of a city-monument. A Soviet diplomat, assuming my

solidarity as a Slav, said to me then: "We'll teach them to work!"
His threatening tone, the triumph, the revenge in his voice, his
Russian self-inebriation ("Europe is ours") offended me, who understood more of the entangled, never straight paths of civilization than he. He felt superior to them because he knew the
depths of hells, while Paris had been barely touched by the wing
of every cyclone—a fact that made me angry, too, although in a
different way. Standing with my glass of vodka at receptions in
the Soviet Embassy, I watched how Leftist luminaries of French
literature and art minced around that diplomat, seizing upon his
every word, nodding approval—polite little boys in front of their
teacher. The magic unguent of power must have rubbed off upon
me, too, a new arrival from the East, with my broad non-Western
face, but I was ashamed of it.

A Russian could treat them only with contempt, because
France, discreet and hidden, was inaccessible to him. I, on the
other hand, penetrated her gradually, beginning with that summer in 1931. It may be that my training began with the letter I
wrote to Oscar Milosz whom up to then I knew only through correspondence. He answered, fixing a day and advising me to buy
myself a suit. In the letter a money order was enclosed. I exchanged my short pants and khaki shirt for a cheap suit from the
Samaritaine department store, and on the appointed day boarded
the train for Fontainebleau. I was nervous because it was a great
event.

In the Hotel de l'Aigle Noir, I guessed from the bowing of the
staff that I was visiting a person who was highly esteemed there.
I knocked, and for a long time I stood on the threshold, unconscious of where I was, uncertain whether I had not perhaps mistaken the number. His room was full of chattering birds and the
flapping of bright wings. Lots of cages with African birds, the
daylight coming and going on the perches, a breeze from the garden rippling the curtains.

He had thick, arched eyebrows, a high forehead, graying,
rumpled hair—good hair for plowing one's fingers through. Tall,

slightly bent, he seemed to take up more space than his body. His masterful air inspired respect and he himself showed respect to others; the servants valued most of all, perhaps, his attentiveness, the gift that renders one aware of the presence of another man. It was apparent who he was from the way he held his head, and from his eyes, which seemed to draw a circle about him so that the rest of his person remained in the background.

His eyelids, like those of a tired bird of prey, disclosed hot black lava or, rather, smoldering coals; there was an aura of bridled violence and pride about him, an aura of the desert, which suggested an image from the pages of the Bible. "*Aimer les hommes d'un vieil amour usé par la pitié, la colère et la solitude*" ["To love people with an old love worn by pity, anger, and loneliness"]—those were words from a poem of his. He knew the language of birds, and when he talked to them as we walked along the avenues of the park at Fontainebleau, they flew from all over to sit on his outstretched hand.

He did not have a foreign accent when he spoke Polish. Our conversation began with his questions about family affairs. I noticed a signet ring on his finger, and said that I did not wear a signet because it would have gone against my democratic convictions. (In Poland, that mania was characteristic of people I despised.) "That's bad. You should remember that you are a *seigneur de Labunava.*" I fell silent, not knowing whether I had run up against a confirmed stuffiness or whether in the West one could freely admit one's origins in public without exposing oneself to ridicule. Soon I understood that by emphasizing his aristocratic origins (his biographers exaggerate this, but he himself was the instigator), he was looking for a way of separating himself from the "*temps de laideur ricanante*" ["age of jeering ugliness"]. He guarded his solitude and did not recognize many of the values generally accepted in his epoch.

Kind to my ignorance, he listened to my remarks about France. He was not an observer. He loved his adopted country in every detail, in its past, in the tissue of its daily life. "Careful,

careful. As long as you must give out opinions on France, remember—we were walking along the park fence on the street side where men in blue denims were repairing the gas pipes—that in every French worker like those there lives two thousand years of civilization." Then he lapsed into one of his furies, to which I later became accustomed: *"Vous, les Slaves, vous êtes des fainéants! Fainéants!"* ["You Slavs, you are idlers! Idlers!"]. I remembered that exclamation well, long after his death, as I listened to the deep Russian voice saying: "We'll teach them to work!" Who was right? Does virtue express itself in the patient shaping of the landscape over the centuries, in the bustling about the vineyards, in the carving of oaken Louis XIII and Louis XV wardrobes, in the slow, rhythmic work of a skeptical and experienced people who lighten the strain of their tasks with pauses, a chat, a glass of wine—or is it expressed by sudden thrusts of will capable of raising a St. Petersburg out of the swamps on the Neva, and of releasing interplanetary rockets from the empty steppes? Men who understand their place in the world differently cannot be measured by a common standard.

ON OSCAR MILOSZ

IN 1924 a small book by Oscar Milosz was published in Paris under the Latin title *Ars Magna*. It consisted of five chapters or, as he called them, "metaphysical poems," the first of which was written in 1916. *Les Arcanes*, written in 1926 and published in 1927, is both a sequel to and an expanded version of the first book. It contains only one "metaphysical poem," but is appended with a voluminous commentary. I came into possession of these books as a young man of twenty, and both, I can say without exaggeration, decided my intellectual career. Or, more precisely, the questions inspired by them—and which I would put to myself unremittingly—decided my career. Both make fiercely difficult reading, exasperating in the way their author deliberately frustrates the reader's progress by mixing Cartesian discourse with poetic ambuscade. Among the French admirers of Milosz's verse few have ventured into that inhospitable region demanding unstinting dedication, which, or so it is claimed, lies so at the periphery as to be incidental to an appreciation of the poetry. Some fifty years later the "metaphysical poems" would become the subject of a doctoral dissertation assigning them a central place in the Milosz oeuvre.*

Even in those days I debated whether these works were translatable into Polish—assuming the translator could make sense of them, which was far from being so in my case. After playing around with a few sentences, I decided that the text, demanding as it was intellectually, would prove inaccessible. Besides, there was hardly a Polish reader who, because of unavoidable associations with a taboo Romantic and Modernist vocabulary, would not have bridled at such works. Yet my translator's ambition must have entrenched itself, as the project was eventually realized, albeit much later, indeed as recently as a few years ago. I have now translated both works, not into Polish but into English. Why now? No doubt because it coincided with an urge to bind together, clasp-like, the earlier intuitions with the later insights; it was a way of closing the circle. But the time it consumed! Time devoted just to a careful reading of sentences so intractable as to gain in clarity only when vetted in another language. The English version, as a consequence, is probably a shade more transparent than the French original, and this opinion is not mine alone. I worked on it, in other words, principally for myself, though not without the thought that I was acquitting myself of an obligation by acting as an intermediary between Milosz and a small coterie of American readers. Quite hypothetical readers, by the way, and this because of the deceptive similarity these works bear to other works belonging to the genres of occultism, theosophy, and Eastern esoterica. There are those who are so repulsed by this genre as to shun anything even faintly resembling it. Others, though attracted, might feel cheated on opening a Milosz work—Oscar Milosz was quite blunt in declaring himself against spiritual imports from the East. Only one group, it would appear, finds his "metaphysical poems" neither abstruse nor unread-

---

*Defended by Jean Bellemin-Noel at the Sorbonne, in 1975. I should add, however, that I find his interpretation, based on a Lacanian Freudianism, untenable.

able—the Blakeans. There is nothing to suggest that Oscar Milosz knew Blake. Yet the similarities are pronounced.

Even though today the boundary between poetry and prose has become sufficiently blurred, the terms still preserve at least a practical utility. Although styled "metaphysical poems" by their author, the works themselves elude either rubric. Rather, they form a distinct category of their own, grounded in a specific human situation embracing both the author and the reader. Before describing that situation, a few prefatory remarks about the history of our modern, "obscure" poetry. The climax of the artistic revolution in Europe coincided with the time of my childhood and adolescence, that is, with the second and third decades of our century. But my lifetime has also witnessed a corresponding disenthrallment, not because the various "isms" foundered but because they triumphed, and in so doing revealed the emptiness of their promises. Occasionally a genuine poet might profit from the tolerance forced on the man on the street by a rowdy avant-garde, but the conquest proved to be another prank staged by that mistress of irony, History, because, thanks to it, an "obscure" poetry became mainstream: a situation of "all-talk-and-no-listening," of "all-writing-and-no-reading." Milosz, though he lived in avant-garde Paris, was lukewarm to the "isms" of his time. If some avant-gardists were driven by unconscious motives to court a clientele through obfuscation, through mystery, thereby acting as the true heirs to that theory proclaiming the "priesthood of art," Milosz was a man decidedly in search of something else—a way to cloister his work in a specific language inaccessible to all but the chosen. Solitude and a wounded pride made him regard any concessions as a compromise beneath his dignity. An abhorrence for the ugliness of the age, which he judged to be criminal and vulgar, disposed him to resistance through an insurgent form. The title of his 1910 novel, *L'Amoureuse Initiation*, is telling, initiation being the way by which in the past a few attained to alchemy and the study of the Cabala, two versions of the science of mystery held by him in high regard. In bolting the door to his domain he has been quite successful. *Ars Magna* and *Les Arcanes* take the form of prophetic letters, addressed neither to the author's nor to the following generation but to the author's great-grandson, in the firm belief that he would inhabit a happier age, one more receptive to truths unknown to his forebears, with the exception of the author himself. Other formal consequences follow: since the man of the future will grasp intuitively the author's message, no further elaboration is needed, hence the author's extremely hermetic style.

The situation of the intended reader is no less worthy of consideration. If the message of these works is addressed to later generations, then their publication is strictly a protective measure; their aim is preservation in the future, not approbation in the present. Who, then, is this sufficiently enlightened reader? Almost certainly a citizen of the future, at the very least a one-eyed man among the blind, which is very gratifying to the ego and therefore insidious. By giving the author his due, the reader must count himself among the privileged, one of the few on the face of the planet to be afforded a glimpse beyond the curtain of tomorrow. But since few can imagine themselves to be so gifted, the works lose in credibility. Let us assume that the author was entirely misguided, deluding both himself and others; that he was not altogether in his right mind. Even granting this were so, the reader not only cannot breathe a sigh but risks falling victim of an even worse dilemma. If the pages before him are more mesmerizing than beautiful, then he must sense the impropriety of applying purely literary criteria. The most fitting adjective for such works would seem to be the word "sublime." That this category exists can no more be documented than the taste of bread can or even needs to be verified. It impresses itself on us whenever the intensity native to it makes any work devoid of it seem bland and jejune by comparison. If sublimity is merely the power of militant faith, of apostolic fervor, why should it imbue these works and not the confessions of countless cranks and fanatics? What makes one work sublime and not another? Unfortunately, it seems always to be accompanied by a lack of decorum. Blake's *Prophetic Books* belong to the category of the sublime, but the inscrutability of their code militated against their publication. Blake engraved them in copper, accompanying them with illustrations, thereby creating a poetic-graphic whole, and printed them in limited editions for collectors of his art. It is not even certain whether his closest collaborator, Catherine Blake, understood anything of her husband's philosophy.

The sublime nature of Milosz's "metaphysical poems" is not of this century, which suggests that sublimity is no longer within our power, or so I have always imagined. As we travel in search of his spiritual homeland, we all but pass over the Positivist half of the nineteenth century and find ourselves in the company of Goethe and a handful of poets whom he repeatedly invoked by name: Hölderlin, Lamartine, Byron, Heine, Edgar Allan Poe. These "elective affinities," in combination with numerous personal statements, allow us to retrace his persuasions back to the Middle Ages, to the Renaissance, and to the dawn of the modern era. He saw himself in a certain tradition, convinced that a hermetic science going back to the Pythagoreans had been transmitted through the ages, and that the legend of the Templars was not a fabrication. Milosz was greatly indebted to his contemporary, the French scholar René Guénon, in whose study *L'Esotérisme de Dante* he discovered a thesis postulating Dante's membership in the Order of the Templars. And it was Dante who, along with Goethe, embodied for Milosz the most sublime poetry since the New Testament. The hermetic line that persisted during the Renaissance (in the form of alchemy and a Christian Cabala) labored to sustain the unity of religion and science, a unity that was subsequently undone. It was to this second, clandestine Renaissance that Milosz paid the most tribute, because only it contained the promise of future reconciliation, not only of religion and science but of religion, art, and philosophy—the future that he addressed was hailed by him as the "new Jerusalem." The hermetic tradition was continued by three who stand at the very threshold of the modern: Paracelsus, or Theophrastus Bombastus von Hohenheim (1493–1541); the Polish alchemist Sendigovius, or Michał Sędziwoj (1556–1636); and Jakob Boehme (1575–1624). Despite the traditional date given for the breakup of religion and science, Descartes is cast by Milosz not as the father of rationalism but as an intuitionist, a "man parading in a mask," and a Rosicrucian. If Descartes was distorted by his successors, Milosz, who described himself as "a son of Descartes," was not one of them. The science and philosophy of the Age of Reason were to blame for the tragedy of modern man: spiritual vacancy, isolation of the individual, the minatory character of civilization as a whole. But the underground tradition endured, thanks to Martínez Pasqualis, Saint-Martin, and Swedenborg. If Milosz could speak of Goethe as his "spiritual master," then he would claim Swedenborg as his "celestial master," based on the triadic division of the earthly, the spiritual, and the celestial.

A topography not exactly unknown to us. With some modifications, it stands as the topography of all the Romantics, testifying to their awareness of the disinheritance and to the defense mechanisms adopted by the alienated man. The past as the refuge of a genuine homeland, a lost homeland. The present as exile. The future as both a radical renewal and a restitution of the past. The Polish Romantics, in this sense, were the quintessential Romantics: for them the three time boundaries were set off by political events, and theirs was a homeland literally lost. This literalness, at the same time, shifted the problem to the international realm and deadened—it was not the time to weep over the roses—all sensitivity to the internal predicament of the "disinherited mind." Milosz, an exile, a foreigner in the fullest sense of the word, was a Romantic by reason of his nostalgia alone; in his private mythology, the lost land of childhood grows imperceptibly to become the ideal realm of a yet to be reborn mankind. He differs from the Romantics, both Polish and Western, in his fixing on the causes and effects of the scientific-technological revolution, recalling both Blake and Goethe in this regard. If for both of these Newton symbolized the scientific method of the "lens," then all the more so did he for Milosz, who with recourse to physics practiced a meta-physics.

Even if we assent to the Brzozowskian thesis of our age as a continuation of Romanticism, of the Romantic schism, there is little to be gained by labeling as a "Romantic" a man nurtured around the turn of the century and whose literary maturity dates from around 1914. Moreover, *Ars Magna* and *Les Arcanes* were written during the most intense phase of the author's diplomatic and political career, bearing witness to his newly acquired expertise in economics and the social sciences. During the First World War, as the bearer of a Russian passport, he was assigned to the Press Office of the French Ministry of Foreign Affairs (he was fluent in Russian, English, and German); after 1918, he represented independent Lithuania, organized the Lithuanian legations in Paris and Brussels, and sat on commissions of the League of Nations. He was too sensitive to the interplay between the various sectors of human praxis to be suspected of having a purely "spiritual" vision of European history. The scientific-technological revolution had brought the working masses— "more alive, more receptive, and more anguished than ever" —into prominence; and it was the aim even of Milosz's most seemingly esoteric meditations, including the "metaphysical poems," to save the masses from the slaughters of war and the surrogate religions of ideology. Late in life he wrote: "Not the events themselves but their spiritual consequences cry out for men of inspiration. The Russian Revolution sought to manufacture its own bard. But the new social order, much less its poet, will not be summoned to life by the mechanical imposition of a materialist doctrine." Both in his critique of the present, of bourgeois and proletarian society, and in his anticipation of a new age, Milosz was simultaneously a Romantic and a subversive, a stance that for me, shaped as I was by Polish Romanticism and Brzozowski, seemed entirely natural. The reader, by force of intellectual habit, may bridle at this pursuit of a link between a hermetic vi-

sion and revolutionary flux. Yet today's scholar will readily concede a bond between the Blakean oeuvre and the Industrial Revolution, just as Blake himself conceded it.

Milosz's early poetry—and not only the very early poetry but
the work up to around 1911, or when he was already in his thirties—is usually classified, perhaps not inappropriately, as a late
example of French Symbolism. The latter, in turn, is one of the
postures assumed by the poet in Ulro, whether through the invention of a wholly imaginary universe, intended as an anti-
world, or through irony, sarcasm, blasphemy, melancholy, or
despair, all of which figure prominently in the work of Milosz
and make him read at times like the tragic Jules Laforgue, who
died prematurely. Poems of a more sanguine tone are also in evidence, proof of how poetic movements roughly contemporaneous to one another, regardless of the country, tend to converge:
around this same time, Polish poetry was moving from modernist
melancholy to the buoyant optimism of a Leopold Staff. The subsequent shift in Polish poetry corresponding to the triumph of
Cubism would yield its first experiments in the years prior to
1914. Oscar Milosz did not obey the trend. For him these formed
merely the latest heroics of those condemned to Ulro, now performed with the help of masks, costumes, and a pseudo-blasé
buffoonery. He sought not innovation, in this sense, so much as
release from Ulro, and for a long time he labored in ignorance as
to the way. In France only Claudel, thanks to his religious poetry,
could claim to be an innovator of a different kind. Milosz, meanwhile, had made his decision, renouncing his melancholy Romantic patrons in favor of a personal quest. Subsequently he
would write his "metaphysical poems," which stand as one of the
curiosities of the age, plus a handful of poems recognized as his
finest. As a poet he is as much an anachronism as Leśmian was in
Poland. Which in the course of decades ceases to have any bearing, one way or the other.

DESPITE ITS MODEST BEGINNINGS (the novel around
1800 was still not considered a respectable genre like
lyric poetry, the epic, and tragedy), the novel matured
rapidly and became a "mirror" of customs, of human psychology,
of ideas that were in circulation in society, and it even participated in philosophical and theological disputes. The question
arises: Is film developing in the same way, from frivolousness to
high seriousness, not only competing with the novel, but even
trespassing on its terrain, exploring every problem that my contemporaries are preoccupied with?

Nicola Chiaromonte insisted that this analogy is misleading. I
am trying to reconstruct those conversations around a table in the
village of Bocca di Magra near Carrara in the summer of 1963.
Lots of red wine. All of us motorboating over to the bay with its
marble cliffs, where the swimming was magnificent. And those
discussions—Nicola, his wife Miriam, Mary McCarthy, Janka,
and I. Chiaromonte is one of those heroic figures of the twentieth
century who have to be forgotten so that someday, when just

deserts are fairly distributed, their fame will be even greater. He was an intellectual with an honest, independent mind; he understood the totalitarian systems he fought against. He had fought against Fascism in Italy, his fatherland; against Franco in Spain as a pilot in Malraux's division (reading Plato); after the war, against Soviet Communism, as co-editor (with Ignazio Silone) of the journal *Tempo Presente*. I had come across his name during my first stay in America when I read, with appreciation, his essays in *Partisan Review* and *Politics*. Well, Nicola, who at that time was a respected theater critic in Rome, argued over wine that the ambitions of film directors—Fellini, Antonioni, for instance—don't match their intellectual preparation, that in their effort to equal the great writers of the nineteenth century they reveal their intellectual poverty and their susceptibility to social clichés. I remember his harsh pronouncements whenever I go to the movies in the hope of nourishing both my eyes and my mind, only to walk out into the street afterward with a bad taste in my mouth, a feeling of shame, or simple rage. Such superb technique, such expertise at taking beautiful photographs, and such trash? One might even think that the medium itself, due to the necessity of introducing action to keep the viewer from falling asleep, contains within itself the unmasking of the novel's devices, which are unpleasantly revealed in it, while the writer, working with verbal material, has many other ways of grabbing his readers' attention. One way or another, the characters and their mutual relations lose their multidimensionality. Words, should a director attempt to rely on them, vanish with the passing moment once they are uttered; they do not remain before our eyes as in a book. Perhaps responsibility for these meager results should be placed on financial and social pressures, on the character of a given civilization, or on the selection (artistically *in minus*) of the type of person who is suited to be a director, who has to be too much a man of action, a politician, a financier, for the Muses to love him.

· · ·

"But," someone will object, "film has produced masterpieces."

True enough. But it may well be that these are solely film masterpieces, limited to that medium, and untranslatable into the thoughts and sensibilities that were the strength of the novel in its prime. There have been exceptions, but nonetheless, a viewer such as I has the constant feeling of the almost limitless possibilities of film that have not as yet been realized. Perhaps the chief contribution of cinema in this century is that its formulations and devices have fertilized literature—both poetry and prose—quite wondrously, and painting, too.

I have constructed my own imaginary films without being at all eager to write screenplays. There is one film in particular that I watch on my private screen. I am not the only one who knows the first and last names of the people who appear in it.

Leon Schiller. At that time when I used to get together with him, along with Stefan Jaracz, Edmund Wierciński, and Bohdan Korzeniewski, Schiller lived on one of the top floors of the Prudential building in Warsaw and was famous for his wide-ranging reading, which was exceptional even among the well-read people of occupied Warsaw. It was simple: he needed no more than four hours' sleep and could devote the rest of the night to reading. For us who were so much younger than him, he was a looming presence, replete with his whole past as a director—and as a singer. He would sit at the piano and sing the cabaret songs of Young Poland, which I would never have heard were it not for those evening gatherings. Try as I might, I cannot recall where this took place. But I hear distinctly:

The wind is laughing outside the windowpanes.
Damn it, this life is so bad.
No, I won't drink anymore.
Tomorrow I'll start living differently.

Or from another song, warmer and more heartfelt, though only the beginning:

> *My beloved is so ugly,*
> *Her little teeth are rotten . . .*

I owe my near certainty that Young Poland's popular songs derived chiefly from Paris to my participation in those sessions with Schiller, and often with Teofil Trzciński. Schiller, after all, had lived in Paris from 1907 to 1909, then again from 1910 to 1911, when he belonged to the Society of Polish Artists on rue Denfert-Rochereau (just like Oscar Milosz).

I can't picture Schiller, a legendary figure in the history of the Polish theater, as a director and a theater critic; but I can see him taking his seat at the piano and singing. The texts and notes could probably be found, even though his collections burned up along with his apartment in Warsaw. He was a short man, with a large head, a heavy, somewhat athletic build; dark-complexioned, blue-eyed, dark-haired. He struck me as very advanced in years; he wasn't sixty yet, but he was one of those people who look older than their years.

Schiller took his secrets to the grave; I don't think they were preserved anywhere. He was so multidimensional that any attempt to tailor him to a cinematic model would inevitably trivialize him.

Henryków. Warsaw's underground theatrical life can be divided into two periods; before the shooting of Igo Sym, and after that event, when Schiller and Jaracz were arrested (1941) and sent to Auschwitz. They were gotten out with great difficulty several months later. Not long ago, at Charles de Gaulle Airport in Paris, I purchased a book called *Des Écrivains et des artistes sous l'occupation (1940–1944)* by Gilles Ragache and Jean-Robert Ragache; reading it, I came to the conclusion once again that the German occupation of France was fundamentally different from the occupation of Poland. It is possible that this can be explained by the German inferiority complex with regard to French culture and their utter contempt for the "subhumans" to the east of Germany. But the behavior of Poles and Frenchmen was also different. Had Igo Sym gotten a license to operate theaters in France, it would have been seen as nothing special; and yet in Poland he was executed as a traitor (because he had declared himself a Reichsdeutsch, since he was born in Austria) and as a demoralizer of actors (by inciting them to collaboration; i.e., to playing in a theater licensed by the occupying powers). Who shot him is still unknown; the Germans suspected Dobiesław Damięcki, who had to change his name and flee Warsaw with his wife, Irena Górska-Damięcka. After the attack on Sym, attempts at founding an official theater virtually ended; there were a few departures from this principle later on, at the very end of the occupation. Most actors worked as waiters and waitresses (for example, in the elegant Arria Café on Mazowiecka Street, "At the Actresses"). Readings of new plays, in Polish and in translation, took place in private apartments, where numerous theater productions were also mounted. The underground Theatrical Council monitored all this, issued pronouncements on what was permitted, prepared a repertoire for after the war, commissioned translations of plays, and devised plans for the organization of theaters. Leon Schiller had the deciding voice in the Council, although Edmund Wierciński and Bohdan Korzeniewski were the most active members.

People in Poland didn't immediately understand the Germans' intentions of carrying out their policy of extermination, and many people believed at first that it was an ordinary occupation by victorious forces in wartime. That explains, for instance, why people registered in the appropriate German office for permission to practice various professions, including the profession of man of letters. In our circle, Ferdynand Goetel advised people to register, and several were persuaded by him, including Jerzy

Zagórski, for instance. Jerzy Andrzejewski and I were opposed, but I have loyally to declare that at that time, in 1940, it was still possible to be deceived.

It was Jerzy Andrzejewski, I believe (I saw him very often), who told me one wintry day before Christmas 1942 that we were invited to visit the nuns in Henryków for a performance of Schiller's *Pastorałka* [Christmas Play], which he himself had edited. I had never heard of Henryków. It turned out it was somewhere on the other side of the Vistula, to the northeast; I had never been in that area. The Benedictine Sisters had a nunnery there and also an institution for female juvenile offenders, mainly prostitutes who had been rounded up on the streets of Warsaw by the blue (Polish) police.

. . .

So, the trip to Henryków. First, Janka and I went by tram from our stop on the corner of Independence Avenue and Rakowiecka Street to the city center; there we met Jerzy and took the tram to Praga across the Kierbedź Bridge. The grayness of the city under the occupation, the grayness of a wet winter; being crammed into the jam-packed tram, the first car of which was reserved for Germans. From Praga, a suburban rail line. I don't remember it at all, other than that we had already met people we knew who were traveling with the same goal in mind. I also remember nothing about Henryków, up to the moment when we were led into what I think was the chapel, with rows of low benches; the audience, about a hundred people, were seated on these benches; mainly well-known faces, actors, writers, painters, people from the university.

Stanisława Umińska. Let us go back in time. The city of Warsaw in the early twenties does not fit easily into the imagination, chiefly because the era that began before World War I developed slowly and over a long time and was still alive in the twenties, although it was already making way for the fashions and customs of the new era. Caps, lots of visored caps—the insignia of the lower classes; soft-brimmed hats—the indispensable accessory of the upper classes (no one would dare go outside with a bare head); the flat-crowned black hats of pious Jews in their long overcoats; women liberated from their corsets but still in nineteenth-century attire; on the streets, wagons pulled by horses, horse-drawn cabs, automobiles. And definitely in the air the triumph of independence regained against all odds, self-assurance stemming from the victory in the 1920 war with Russia (how many Poles had ever experienced a victorious war?), along with the poverty of the working-class districts and the unemployed, the shouts of newsboys crying out the sensational headlines, with the mutual accusations of the parties in the Sejm, the frequent dissolutions of the government. Photos of London or New York at that time may be of help, because in every decade large cities share the common spirit of the time. Warsaw's specific feature, most likely, was its transformation from a "western Russian" city with strong provincial residues into the nation's capital. Cafés, newspaper offices, theaters, many theaters, poets reciting on stage, already famous even though so young, barely past twenty, like a sign that everything was just beginning, but all those things—literature, art, fashion—are separated from today by the hiatus of war, just old stuff packed off to a museum forever.

. . .

What did it mean then to be young and a talented actress? Stanisława Umińska quickly made a name for herself. She was famous for playing Puck in Shakespeare's *Midsummer Night's Dream*. It was said to be an exceptionally well-acted Puck. For that, one needs charm, boyish beauty, a light step. *The Literary News* of June 15, 1924, features a large photograph of her with the caption: "One of the most marvelous and interesting actresses of the young generation, the splendid creator of Consuelo (*He Who Gets Slapped*), Lidia (*What Is Most Important*), has achieved a new success with her intelligent, focused realization of the role of Berta (*A Cricket in the Hearth*)."

One might conclude that the editor printed this praise because he was aware of Umińska's liaison with his collaborator on *The Literary News*, Jan Żyznowski, and knew of the couple's journey to Paris to seek medical treatment for him. I read about Żyznowski in *The Dictionary of Contemporary Polish Writers*:

b. June 15, 1889, in Warsaw, to a family of landed gentry. The son of Antoni and Michalina (*née* Jamiołowska) Żyznowski. He went to Paris a couple of years before the First World War to continue his literary and artistic studies. He was in Paris when the war broke out and was one of the first in the Polish community to join the Polish Legion of Bayonne. After his discharge in 1915 he went to Russia and worked on the Petersburg daily *The Voice of Poland*. After his return to Poland, he took part in the 1920 war. After demobilization, he became the director of the art-criticism department in the journals *Res Publica*, *The Illustrated Weekly*, and *Miss*. For a few months in 1924 he was in charge of the department of art-exhibition reviews at *The Literary News*. Terminally ill with cancer, he traveled to Paris for radiation therapy. Shot at his own request by his fiancée, the stage actress Stanisława Umińska, he died July 15, 1924, in Paris.

. . .

Paris in the year 1924 will always be a mystery for me because of the artistic explosion there. After all, only a few years had passed since the great slaughter, and people were walking along those streets who not so long before had been in the hells of Verdun or the battles on the Somme. It would seem that after such a descent into the abyss the general tone of thought, of art, of literature ought to have been gloomy. And in neighboring Germany it was, and also in England, which had lost a significant percentage of its young elite. T. S. Eliot's *Waste Land*—a satiric and catastrophic poem—was well suited to the mood over there. But France, where every little town erected a monument with the names of the fallen, in some places amounting to two-thirds of the male population, acted as a conductor for the current of euphoria that was encircling the planet and once again attracted all the enthusiasts of a revolution in art and literature. It was the time of the "expatriation" of numerous American writers and artists, too; Hemingway and Gertrude Stein were the most famous among them. The peak years of Montparnasse and its cafés—not so much the Closerie des Lilas (it peaked before 1914), as La Rotonde and La Coupole with their chairs occupying the entire width of the sidewalk, and their cosmopolitan crowds that did not, however, include tourists as they would in a later Paris (which creates a fundamental difference in atmosphere).

The two of them in that euphoric Paris: Żyznowski and Umińska. On the terrace of La Coupole, sipping Dubonnet and looking at the parade of pedestrians. Just to think that never, not for all eternity, will anyone know what they talked about and how they reached their decision. They had come to seek hope from the doctors. When there was none, what remained was the faithful love of a woman who did not recoil from a helping act, from a remedy that must have horrified her. And immediately afterward, the Paris newspapers filled with a sensational story that exactly matched the expectations of this city of modernist bohemia's daily scandals: an actress had shot her lover.

. . .

The trial, too, was sensational. The faces of the French jury, the rituals—is it possible to penetrate closed doors? The story was a moving one and must have struck people right in the heart, especially women, even though the accused was the wrong nationality. At that time, the little towns of northern France were

swarming with Poles who had come to work in the mines and
factories, often straight from the countryside, who were not necessarily considered members of the white race, but rather were
perceived as the sort of foreigners whom people frighten children
with, like Algerians later on. In the police blotters the Poles were
the chief perpetrators of theft and murder, which is where the
expression *les bandits polonais* comes from.

The verdict was an even greater sensation: Not guilty. This
meant not only that murder is sometimes not an offense but also,
perhaps, that murder to shorten (or, in this case, to avert) someone's suffering should not be punishable.

Perhaps Umińska, seeking anonymity above all, fleeing human eyes and tongues, found a haven somewhere in France; perhaps she returned immediately to Poland. But not to the theater,
in any event. She considered that chapter in her life to be over.
She entered a nunnery. One can explain this decision in various
ways, and all explanations are based on conjecture. In a Catholic
country, a nunnery was, traditionally, a shelter for unmarried
women who belonged to that category for a number of reasons:
familial, financial, personal, not necessarily because of vocation.
"Entering a nunnery" was also a synonym for escape from the
world after some personal drama. Umińska could fall back on a
certain tradition, and the nunnery gave her the anonymity of an
assumed name, which was important to her. It is also possible to
conjecture that, in choosing the discipline of the cloister, she was
meting out punishment for her deed, which she could not forgive
herself, or for forsaking Żyznowski by not having accompanied
him in death. The most difficult thing, obviously, is to come up
with hypotheses about the nature of her religious faith and her
gift of prayer. One ought not to forget that our inner life is never
static, that every month and every year introduces changes, that
therefore some of our features atrophy while others develop.

In the course of many years spent in the cloister, Umińska, as
happens to all nuns, must have been moving simultaneously in
both a vertical and a horizontal direction. The former describes

the history of the human soul in lonely contemplation, striving toward God; the latter refers to the daily affairs of a closed community of nuns, the numerous and multifaceted relationships among the sisters. Individuality is forged then in the inescapable collision of characters. It could not have been easy for Umińska, because she was very different from her new environment; she was above it on the intellectual level, perhaps, but most of all, despite her youth, by virtue of the experience that the theater, love, and her personal tragedy had given her. Adaptation was first of all a matter of humility, or of working at humbling her separateness. She may have been helped in this also by her ability to feel her way into various roles. One way or another, she became a model nun, valued by her order for her piety, tact, and kindness toward others. In 1942 she was the prioress of the cloister in Henryków.

We do not know if she had completely broken with the theatrical community during her years as a nun, or if, on the contrary, she had maintained certain friendships or at least had followed what was happening in the theater. When, however, Schiller was invited by her to Henryków after he was ransomed out of Auschwitz, her conversations with him were certainly an extraordinary moment for her. One would have to explain how it came about, at whose initiative——his, hers, or perhaps friends who sought a safe place for him, especially after several months of imprisonment in Auschwitz.

Schiller and a cloister——the two didn't fit. Although at that time in occupied Warsaw the old divisions were less clear and Schiller's past was less important than his status as the most prominent figure in Polish theater. Before the war he was known as a leftist, but I, for one, found out just how engaged Schiller had been only when I was recording my interviews with Aleksander Wat. Schiller supported the Communist *Literary Monthly* financially and it was only out of tactical considerations that he didn't join its editorial board. Many meetings of Communist sympathizers took place in his (exquisite) apartment. That Schiller was a confirmed Communist cannot be questioned, a "salon Communist," as it were; after all, his value for the Party consisted exclusively in the politicization of the theater—that was his language, he spoke his mind in it. He was the object of attacks in the rightwing press and from time to time he would lose his theaters. After the war, when he joined the Polish Workers' Party and wrote his autobiography in 1946 as a candidate for the Sejm, he spoke a great deal about those persecutions, but he did not mention the typical Polish arrangements—that is, his friendships with government dignitaries who somehow managed to protect him. There is also, of course, no mention of his attitude toward religion, even though a theoretician and practitioner of "grand theater," a director of Mickiewicz's *Forefathers' Eve,* Krasiński's *Undivine Comedy,* and Słowacki's *Silver Dream of Salomea* could not possibly *not* have thought about such matters.

In Henryków, Umińska put at his disposal her young prostitutes as raw acting material, and in this way Schiller was able to keep his director's hand in practice. His stays in the nunnery, however (he moved there permanently in 1943), were not limited to that. "At that time he became a Benedictine oblate and took the monastic name 'Ardalion,' " according to the *Biographical Dictionary of the Polish Theater* (1972). An oblate is a lay person who adheres to the rules of monastic life but does not take vows. The monastic rules included partaking regularly of the Eucharist, which means that Schiller became a practicing Catholic. Various hypotheses are possible. A revolutionary change had taken place in him in an extreme situation; that is, in Auschwitz. Stanisława Umińska converted him. Or else, despite the anticlericalism he had developed in his youth in clerical Cracow, this man of luminous erudition and intelligence was sufficiently endowed that he could exist on several levels simultaneously, reconciling his revolutionary beliefs with his secret religious experience. Perhaps my intuition misled me, but I sensed a great inner concentration in Schiller, a core that was not revealed to anyone, as happens with people who have mystical inclinations.

As far as I know, Schiller never attempted to write anything about that. Shortly before the Uprising, he returned to Warsaw from Henryków; he was deported to Germany after the Uprising. Immediately after the war ended, he organized a theater there for Poles under the aegis of the YMCA. Afterward, in People's Poland, he acted effectively and in every way as a committed revolutionary and Party member, a delegate to the Sejm, so there could be no cause to speak of any private deviation. In general, during the Stalin years, people believed that he was zealous out of a deep conviction and was becoming more fanatic than was appropriate, than even the Party wanted him to be. Nonetheless, I wasn't at all surprised when I learned from Wat that this dogmatic Communist by day prostrated himself before the crucifix at night.

. . .

Pastorałka. "She makes the entrance of a great actress," said Jerzy when the prioress entered the hall with her nuns to occupy the first rows of benches. He was expressing what we all felt: respect for her beauty (still present) and her dignity.

I did not know *Pastorałka.* In 1919, Schiller had arranged folk carols and folk songs as *An Old Polish Manger Scene*; later, in 1922, he presented it as *Pastorałka* in the Reduta Theater. I pass on this information now; I don't think that I was aware of it at the time; at most, I'd heard something or other about it. Lo and behold, it was not a Greek tragedy, not a work by Shakespeare, not a romantic drama that afforded me the most powerful theatrical experience of my life, but a folk spectacle, a Manger scene, a Nativity play, performed by poor girls from the Warsaw streets who had never been in a theater. Without a doubt, Polish carols possess a particular charm, freshness, sincerity, good humor, that simply cannot be found in such proportions in any other Christmas songs, and perhaps one ought to look at them for the essence of Polish poetry. My susceptibility to that performance can be explained by my having listened to carols from childhood, but also because only the theater has such an impact, appealing to what is most our own, most deeply rooted in the rhythms of our language. One might say, then, that the cause of my later bad relations with the theater abroad was its foreign intonations.

In a Nativity play, just as in Greece once upon a time, the plot is not at all surprising, because it is already decided, known by heart. Also, the characters are already formed and everything takes place in between: between the character and its incarnation by the actor, between the text and its enactment, in speech, in song, in dance.

The Mother of God was dressed in blue, of course; small, almost childlike, thin, blond. She appeared against a background of many centuries of tradition in which she had been depicted just that way in painting and in polychrome sculpture, although another tradition also exists of a Madonna with olive skin, black-eyed and black-haired. The director had chosen her unerringly, perhaps because of her voice. It was a tiny, mouse-like voice which, when she sang, made my throat constrict with emotion. I was partaking of a mystery which, simultaneously, revealed the essence of theater. That essence is, most likely, the human possibility of *being someone else*, which, if you think about it, means that every man is the home of many personalities that dwell within him potentially, that are never realized, because only one of them appears on the outside and proffers the mask that is accepted by others. A change in a configuration through a change of participants brings forth other hidden and heretofore suppressed personalities. The purity and holiness of the Mother of God were undoubtedly her own, this girl actress's, although at the same time she was someone else and that someone else had recently sold herself to German soldiers for a couple of zlotys. Thus, the theater is, or ought to be, a celebration of human multifacetedness and plasticity which make it possible for every man and every woman to bear within himself or herself an entire range of experiences and aptitudes, from the highest virtue to common evil, while being vaguely aware of this and therefore capable of resonating with the actors on the stage. The question arises: To what degree is it necessary for us to be aware that we are watching dual beings on the stage, that that girl, for example, is "playing" the Mother of God while being both "herself" and her? In the "lifelike" theater, we are told to forget about that duality, and probably that is why it is a low genre of theater. But here, in Henryków, an amateur spectacle was transformed into a professional act by an excellent director, so I insist that the trenchancy of that theatrical performance can also be explained by our knowledge of who those children were who had been so clearly transformed into a theater company. And, perhaps, more than one of us was thinking that, in order to play the Mother of God like that, it would be difficult not to undergo an inner transformation, so that she, the performer, was also present, along with her unimaginable future life story.

St. Joseph was dressed in a sort of brown burnoose, with the staff of a wanderer; he gently escorted Mary in their flight across Egypt. I can see that scene and hear Mary singing in her thin little voice; although I am not absolutely certain of the words, I shall write them down from memory:

Just a few steps, Joseph
Just a few steps, Joseph
After all I cannot
Run so far away.

In *Pastorałka*, tender, quiet melodies are interwoven with bursts of joyous carols and triumphal dances. At the very beginning, the arrival of the shepherds in the manger and their presentation of their gifts offers an occasion for this *vivace*. In Poland, it isn't easy to separate "folk" elements from the contributions of Church writers and musicians, not to mention seminarists and minstrels who worked for the parish. The most intense activity occurred in the seventeenth century; thus, old

Polish "folklore" and, most of all, the carols bear a strong imprint of the Baroque. The shepherds bring with them the earthy humor of the countryside, their games and buffoonery, but the seminarist who is in charge of keeping order also joins them:

Contrabasses and tenors
We split up into two choirs
Hey, hey, hey!

I remember the melodies of those merry carols and the joy of the performers, who seized the opportunity to discharge their energy in a permissible fashion—a discharge of energy that was doubtless very necessary in that severe institution. The dramatic part escapes me entirely, the dreadful adventures of Herod and Death, but to this day I am united in enthusiasm with Janka and Jerzy, who are sitting beside me, and with the entire audience, when *Pastorałka* concludes with a Dionysian dance. This is total madness, an unbridled frenzy on stage, a letting-go beyond all bounds, although the words are as plain as can be.

The rapture of the dancers, their crazy leaps and turns were like elemental movement.

Since I saw that *Pastorałka*, I have held on to the conviction that I know what true theater is, and I have applied that measure to my later evenings at the theater, usually with negative results. Obviously, one could say that specific conditions coalesced into that fervid reception (not only mine) of Schiller's spectacle: visual starvation in the drab colorlessness of the occupied city, and the absence of theatrical or cinematic entertainment; the exceptional nature of the production as a reward for the lengthy jostling on the tram and suburban rail line; and even the surprise discovery of so much acting talent among that accidental collection of girls. Perhaps an audience's receptivity is always helped by somewhat similar conditions, for, after all, the creation of a magic space, of a colorful spectacle unfolding despite the surrounding insufficiency of color, belongs to the very essence of theater. A sudden change in inner rhythm, due to the leap from one reality to another, is also necessary. *Pastorałka* in Henryków belongs to a series of somehow therapeutic performances in a Europe contaminated by the totalitarian plague; these performances took place in the occupied cities, the ghettos, the prisoner-of-war camps. I do not want to believe, however, that a true theatrical experience is possible only in times of great upheavals.

No, I would not want to transfer to the screen the film I have fashioned in my imagination. The more intensely Schiller is present, the more Umińska is a tangible presence, and even Żyznowski, of unknown appearance, the more clearly I see the girls from *Pastorałka*, who today, if they are still alive, are old women—the more powerfully can I sense the poverty of cinematic devices compared with the richness of human characters and fates. All these individuals exist simultaneously in their various phases, but it is impossible to capture that temporal dimension in linear fashion, in an unfolding plot, despite the ever more frequent use of the flashback technique. Nicola Chiaromonte was probably correct when he denied the possibility of film ever rivaling literature. Fine. But then where are those exceptional virtues of literature? No doubt they, too, are modest. But the impotence of literature when it attempts to capture and preserve reality in words is a separate topic entirely.

BROGNART: A STORY TOLD
OVER A DRINK

ONCE QUITE A WHILE AGO, in the fifties, I found myself in Marles-les-Mines, a small town in Pas-de-Calais,
a black coal-mining region. A wet winter. In the fields
the dazzling green of winter wheat, inky waste heaps and movement in the air: the turning gears of the lifts. It rained almost incessantly in Marles; walls blighted with dampness, mud between
pavement stones, skeleton trees. The first passerby I asked for directions, a miner with skin tattooed by coal dust who was returning from work carrying a lantern, answered in the language in
which I addressed him. I have a sharp eye, he was a Pole; probably half the people in Marles understood Polish. The hue of light
there is murky, foggy, and whenever the door of a café was
opened, a gust of steam burst forth (maybe I'm unfair in trans-
ferring the smoke and the steam to the light there in general).
There were bikes in front of the tiny cafés and inside, over shots
of *calvados*, everyone was talking about Brognart. And there in
Marles, the matter gripped and moved me.

I'm not the one to say how the scales of my good and evil will
come to rest, but sometimes I think that one thing might pre-

vail—those moments when I've felt like running, shouting, because nobody, no one could do it, and it was up to me. I decided
that I at least would not remain silent. I questioned residents,
went to neighboring Bruay (the two small towns are divided only
by somewhat of a ravine) and from a young schoolteacher got
Brognart's notebooks: analyses of *Le Cid*, the *Iliad*, in the spindly
handwriting of a diligent pupil. That teacher believes to this day
that I was a fraud or a spy, because I did nothing with my strong
resolution. If Hell is paved with good intentions, then here the
scales tip against me. For, after all, I had not intended to run
around the world with my tongue hanging out, taking part in the
defense of the tortured, especially not in a country like France
where there are enough writers and journalists sensitive in general to the fates of their fellow countrymen. But no Frenchman
had the slightest idea about that which befell Brognart, and no
one would have been able to identify with him; their imagination
didn't reach that far. A different training of the imagination was
needed here—mine, from the East of Europe—and I well knew
that only I was available.

I made a few attempts, and always found reasons for pushing
Brognart aside. What sort of obstacles were these? First of all,
Brognart was no longer alive. He was part of that numberless
mass, that mass of the beaten, the downtrodden, the maimed, in
the eighth century before Christ or in the twentieth after—time
doesn't matter here. Why him then, him in particular: why sympathy for him, why objection to his death? Even if I limited myself to my own lifetime, it was an inadequate reason because
millions like him had perished (and the shirt is closer to the body
than the jacket, goes a Polish saying): I would rather have chosen
someone better known to me than a Frenchman. To tell you the
truth, there was something enigmatic in my sudden emotional
response to the talk in Marles-les-Mines. I suspected that Brognart interested me so much because he was a substitute, connected by various unnamed strings to this or that person tangible
for me. But a good reason was lacking: here were cars, theaters,

flowers, trains stuffed with skiers, that human vortex which seals its losses up tightly. They didn't want to find out about things uncomplimentary to themselves, so what did one Brognart mean? To step onto the forum, to remind them, only so they could yawn and turn away from the bore or wink knowingly: another shrewd fellow, even a skillful one, increasing his political assets.

Because Brognart had already become a political matter, not of his own will—for what can a teenager, with his analyses of Corneille and Racine, know about politics? As a local issue in Pas-de-Calais, it was used in an election. Elsewhere it was invading philosophical and literary salons where to mention it other than with a smirk would have been tactless. And although I didn't care about tact, this prohibition paralyzed me in one very specific, indirect way. I was too involved with this story emotionally. Out of simple respect for the main character I preferred to remain silent, to avoid the suspicion (if only in my own eyes) that I was using Brognart as one more argument to justify myself or to defend my own virtue. Of course I saw quite clearly the outlines of the book I could have put together, even its scheme and particular chapters. But had it appeared, who would have needed it? Some would have scoffed at it, citing it as an example of the "falsified consciousness" of its author; others would have dismissed it politely or tokenly praised it. Because what to me was an abyss, the vision of an abyss, to them was only a weapon in a political game played for reasons other than some Brognart. But I admit the whole story is fantastic, absurd, atypical, so even those others would have avoided it, embarrassed.

I won't beat around the bush any longer. Brognart (first name Gilbert), the son of a foreman, was born in Marles. His father's family, and his mother's, were native peasant families that had been digging around in the soil for generations before anyone suspected that there was coal beneath it. Later their land, and they didn't diminish it by parceling, gained in value so they quit farming and took up new work in the coal mines, always keeping, however, this bit of security on the records, so that it was said in

Marles that these families were, well, you know, well off, and this house was theirs and that one, and this and that plot of land. But as is usual in France, niggardliness instead of ostentation, and groans that there wasn't enough for bread and wine. Gilbert's father left his mother when Gilbert was little, obtained a divorce, and married for the third time. Gilbert saw him rarely because the boy grew up in Marles with his mother, grandmother, and aunts, while his father lived and died in Auchel. His mother fretted over her only son maybe even more than mothers usually fret over their only sons. It was something of a desperate love, whether for reason of the divorce or for who knows what dramas in this family that was, it seems, dying out. One of her sisters, for example, was deranged—English Tommies raped her when they were stationed there during the First World War and something snapped in her head.

But it doesn't seem that Gilbert was particularly spoiled or pampered. He was a completely normal boy, diligent, matter-of-fact, serious, liked by his friends and good in sports. He showed no tendencies toward any extravagance or daydreaming beyond the needs of his immediate surroundings. He wasn't overly ambitious; after the École Primaire, he stayed on at the same school in the next grades (the École Primaire Supérieure, according to French nomenclature); afterward, the Collège Moderne. He was preparing himself for mining school, planned on receiving his engineering diploma there and then returning to Marles. He was strong in mathematics and physics. From what his teacher told me about him I've formed, I think, an accurate picture: a typical peasant from northern France, phlegmatic, slightly ironic, not exhibiting his emotions, and in addition to this a strong will, stubbornness, and independence. He never played a double game; he always said what he thought, this especially the teacher emphasized. In a group, in the classroom, or on the playing field, he was dynamic. At first he rode a bike to school in Bruay; then, when he turned sixteen, his mother bought him a motorcycle (the only trace of spoiling, though not much; a bike or motorcycle is a necessity there). A motorcycle accident gave proof of his composure: his front tire blew, but he didn't lose his head. When he received pocket money from his mother, his greatest pleasure was in buying things for others—if he saw that a friend wanted something, he bought it immediately. Reasonably sociable, he belonged to one organization, the Jeunesse Étudiante Chrétienne.

Brognart's photographs fit the teacher's report: the pleasant face of a stable teenager. Strong chin, delicately shaped lips, a prominent nose somewhat childlike in its pudginess. A direct gaze, alert, somewhat lyrical. It was exactly, I suppose, his eyes and lips that struck me because they reminded me of the eyes and lips of someone close to me in my family. In some of his pictures, it's true, Brognart wore glasses, the kind in a thin metal frame, and there the likeness began to blur.

With all his sobriety he wouldn't have been a kid if he hadn't been drawn by playing around, sniffing the world and roaming. Naturally he was crazy about traveling, about adventure. In Marles he found a companion in this, became friends with the son of a butcher, a Polish family, natives of the city of Toruń. It happened that the relatives of the Polish boy invited him to Toruń for summer vacation, and he immediately suggested to Gilbert that they go together. This was an exceptional opportunity. Up to this time Gilbert had never been outside of France, actually not beyond *le Nord*, so he asked his mother to let him go. She probably didn't want to, there is that French mistrust of strange lands, but it was difficult to refuse him—he had just passed his *bachot* exams and was going to enter mining school in the fall. This happened in 1939. Brognart had just turned eighteen, he was born the first of June, 1921. Whether Marles was familiar with international politics, I don't know—Marles isn't Paris. It is likely, however, that his mother had reservations because he didn't get his way immediately, and left for Poland only in the second half of August.

Toruń is a beautiful city, and there in the family of his friend he found a group of boys his age. Everything was new—the ar-

chitecture, the river, the kayaks—so time passed delightfully and
it was in this way that the war took Brognart by surprise in
Poland. I say the word *war* but it sounds wooden, inexact. War
can mean the Greeks in Troy or big headlines in newspapers
read over coffee where it doesn't directly apply to us and simply
marks the ups and downs of the stock exchange. Here, however,
it wasn't this at all, but a consuming fire from the heavens which
buzzed and shook from machines moving across them, and below
in the fields the red centers of fires blinked in the smoke as one
human society, straining its limits, revealed itself, showing that
which is beneath every human society. Those who haven't seen it
are lucky. Fleeing the German army and taking bombed roads,
Brognart started out on foot for the south with three of his Toruń
companions. The three soon turned back because German tanks
were everywhere and were already circling Warsaw. He, however,
knowing neither language nor country, reached Warsaw after a
few days and nights and headed for the French embassy (pangs of
conscience, probably, and the thought of his mother).

I said that the story had been developing into a book. In it
would have figured not just the experiences of Brognart but the
wanderings of his comrades as well: experiences instructive to
some and uninteresting to most. Because in Marles I questioned
the family of the butcher as well (they answered reluctantly but
I did get something out of them), and it occurred to me to ask
them about what had later happened to the other three boys.
They had returned home to the occupied city. One of them, apparently the most adventurous, didn't stay there long, instead
made his way south again, to Warsaw and beyond, into the mountains between Poland and Slovakia. In the first winter of the war,
young people stole across there on skis. He got to Hungary and
then to France, where he entered the Polish army forming there.
He was evacuated to England with his division, underwent
schooling to become a pilot, and flew in bombers over Germany:
now he was the punishing fire. He died near the end of the war
from shock suffered when landing a damaged plane.

For the second boy it went quite differently. He was mobilized and incorporated into the Wehrmacht; the Germans considered Toruń a German town and its citizens Germans. He found a chance to surrender to the Allies in Italy, and then wore a Polish uniform. After the war, when the army was transported from Italy to England, he could have remained there but didn't want to. He returned to Poland, studied, and was already passing his final exams in engineering when he was put in jail. The new powers quite diligently arrested all those who at one time were in the Polish army in the West (not necessarily in the Wehrmacht, of which they were much more tolerant).

The third boy—that friend of Brognart's from Marles—got stuck in Toruń, pined for his parents and France, and worked in a factory. The Gestapo arrested him for belonging to an underground organization, and he landed in a concentration camp, Stutthof near Gdańsk. He wasn't there long because he arrived when the German imperium was already reaching its end, but he suffered some internal damage. Later he registered at the university. All was well, he seemed healthy, when one day going up the stairs he fell and died of heart failure.

A digression, the three different fates of one generation in one country. I don't have to make things up, to add anything. But none of the three was struck by such a misfortune as Brognart's. The first of the three had his manly triumphs, his joy; the second, if they did not let him rot too quickly, certainly got out of prison in a few years; and even the third, if he suffered much, did not suffer long.

In Warsaw Brognart found there was no longer any French embassy, that it had been evacuated to the East. How he fended for himself, where he turned, what he ate, where he slept in this alien, unknown city of chaos, of contradictory rumors and panic, along whose dark streets the wind carried the papers of offices and departments which no longer existed, I don't know. He stayed there long and survived the siege (not a bad siege, either: entire streets shot into the air in fountains of brick, on the thoroughfares horse carcasses from which you carved out a steak, and so on). Afterward, in the vanquished capital, the German police picked him up in October, but, keeping him a while, they released him, probably because they did not have time to spend on such trifles as citizens of other countries, already in the bag anyway. Brognart must have reasoned, quite logically, that instead of waiting until they put him into some kind of internment camp he should get himself to a neutral country that harbored his consulates. And of the two countries that divided Poland, one was neutral; it received what it did as payment, as the interest on its neutrality. The border (by virtue of a pact between them) ran not far from Warsaw, and, in November, Brognart crossed this border avoiding the sentries as many then did.

They say that man learns everything, though not right away (his imagination is too confined by his habits). Brognart probably thought that he would find a French consulate immediately, or if not, that he would get on a train and go to Moscow the way one rides from Marles to Paris. When he was told this wasn't allowed he turned quite naturally to the authorities to help him. With the bureaucracy of his own country, the country with the oldest bureaucracy in Europe, he was familiar. He did not know, however, that compared to others this bureaucracy was quite democratic even before the French Revolution. He had never given it any thought. Now he had to find out what happens when no one lifts a finger because the individual has no so-called "natural rights." Furious, he told himself that if this was so, then he would manage without anyone's help. Here and there he gathered bits of information, from which he concluded there were French consulates in neighboring Baltic countries, then still independent. So he simply went. It is even difficult to reproach him with carelessness. The expedition from Warsaw emboldened him though it shouldn't have, it was much easier. In addition even Poles, who it would seem have a calling to know the customs of their neighbors, were naïve; they set out in whole groups, like Brognart, only to get out from under the power which had been imposed without asking anyone's opinion. Some made it, some didn't. Perhaps I would have let the whole Brognart matter in Marles-les-Mines go right by me if I had had no concrete images of my own to link me to such border crossings. But I did have them, and strong ones, and I assure you that to experience this is something, after which the years pass and life is ever wondrous, each day like a gift. Well, Brognart got caught on the Latvian border. They kept him in various prisons stuffed with louse-infested masses of humanity: with the young such as himself who wanted to get to the West to the army, with old men and women, and with all nationalities: Poles, Jews, Lithuanians, Belorussians, who were there for various improprieties but mainly for coming from the wrong social strata.

In such a situation a resourceful and stubborn youth remembers, naturally, that a shipwrecked man ought to pass on news of himself in a bottle entrusted to the sea, and should not lose faith because there is always the chance that someone will fish the bottle out. So Brognart, and here you can see his thoroughness, wrote carefully on the wall of every cell in which he found himself his first name, last, and a request to notify his family. And he didn't err in his calculations. Except that the currents carried his bottle, or not so much the bottle as those who fished it out, a long time—about six years. It was only after the war that letters came to Marles from Polish officers and soldiers of the army which had been in Italy, at one time occupants of the same prisons. Some had read his inscription, others had the Frenchman for a cell-mate.

After months in jail, Brognart was read a verdict. Let no one say that rights are not respected there. After all, the rule of law is an attribute of culture and it was invented in the same place as other clever items such as the toothbrush, the steam engine, electricity, and the parliamentary system. To make normal use of the law or elections—well, no, but the fiction even increased the desire for ritual. Brognart probably understood nothing of the ceremony, because in his mind some relation between crime and punishment was supposed to exist; that's what he learned in school, from literature, and from his environment. He didn't, moreover, even understand the language in which he was being spoken to. If they showed him on their fingers how many he got, eight, he didn't get the sense of it right away: that they meant eight years. And if he despaired then here, too, he was wrong. Whether five or eight, it was all the same since the goal was to maintain the same number of working hands in the concentration camps as the weaker prisoners died out. He was transported to one such camp near Archangelsk.

This descendant of generations of thrifty and industrious peasants was resistant. Even for people accustomed to a cold climate from childhood, to live through even four winters there was quite a feat, the average that could be expected from a healthy man. But the seasons came and went, and Brognart wouldn't give in. He continually sent his bottles to sea, believing in rescue. After the war not only did his mother know that he was somewhere in Russia but even the French embassy had received a letter from him (smuggled somehow) in which he gave exactly the what and where. Efforts began, and when his whereabouts were known—at the mouth of the River Pechora—the Russian authorities stopped denying there was such a person. Still it was a long time before they officially admitted that he existed, condemned by legal verdict with an added sentence of ten years "for spreading malicious rumors," and that a review of the trial was impossible. In other words, there in the camps of the north Brognart had not learned docility and just as earlier, in school, always said what he thought.

What his mother lived through I won't attempt to guess. When you mail letters and requests every day, go from one institution to another, go to Thorez too—falling literally at his feet, begging him to save your son—when such attempts last for years, it's possible to break down. Later, when I was in Marles, his mother lived in a psychiatric institution (put there, it's true, at her own request).

Brognart died in 1951. Not a bad accomplishment: eleven years. Families of Russian or Polish prisoners would agree here, too, that few dragged their feet in the camps for such a long time, practically an eternity. The official notice of his death was dispatched to the French embassy with the appropriate delay, about a year later, and then the sensational dailies in France related Brognart's case in the *faits divers* section. Only in Marles and in the neighboring districts did the event receive a lot of publicity. There, in *le Nord*, it was mainly the Socialists and Communists who were fighting over votes. The Socialists made an argument of Brognart and this was very uncomfortable for the Communists, because of course it mattered to them to refute all defamation. In Russia, yes, there were corrective camps for political transgressors, for fascists and Hitlerites, but who would shed tears over criminals if not an agent of American imperialism? And they had a strong point, because in France didn't *collabos* have to be punished? So everyone, even if they had doubts, kept their mouths shut. Besides, it was so far away, who could check? The countries and the people were faceless. Now unfortunately there was one concrete man, with a face, and that has a stronger impact than an abstract ten million. Brognart? What did he have to do with politics, the kid, why everyone in Marles knew him! That is why they had to find a way. The Communist press dragged out his insane aunt, combined that with the illness of his mother, and had a ready thesis. It was a case of heredity, those alleged reports which Brognart had passed on about himself were the fantasies of a madman. I think the articles were effective; in any case I know that shortly thereafter, when I returned to Paris, talk of Brognart began to die down, until it died out forever.

Now I'll confess my emotional attachment. In the photograph Brognart looked like my cousin, and the moments which I spent in the house of these relatives are important to me even to this day. That cousin, also an only child, is for me quite enigmatic. I sometimes think about what he would have been like, had he grown up. He was sensitive, lyrical, musical, and in addition possessed the very contradictory characteristics of his parents. He was a bit like the heroes in Thomas Mann's early stories. He was fifteen when the Nazis shipped him from Poland to a concentration camp in Germany, and seventeen when he died there. I can't talk about it. If they had only shot him. But no—the essence of that time was imposed on him, precisely on him.

I want to dwell for a moment on the basic difficulty that explains why it was better to keep quiet about the various Brognarts. Sure, you were allowed to lament the victims of Hitlerite camps, it lowered no one's literary prestige, and if the reader was bored it was with respect. But nothing could help my cousin or any other victims of the Nazis, and I felt no desire to speak of the past. But now masses (enough to populate a medium-sized European country) like Brognart were still going out to labor each morning, and the same sun shone upon us. It's ridiculous, I know, to take upon yourself misfortunes which are not your own. Am I my brother's keeper? Then why did the Left Bank cafés feel universal responsibility, why did they jump from "cause" to "cause" in chronic excitement: in Mississippi they're torturing Negroes, Madagascar isn't being granted independence, villages are burning in Indochina. Here they weren't ashamed of sentimentality. So other criteria must have been used, other springs were tilting the scales unevenly. Before the mythical East, "aah" with indrawn breath, as before a very great mountain. There lay progress, the direction of history, and you should not incur its disfavor but protect your name in the face of posterity. The causes they would take up were honorable, guaranteed by the future. Just like those others taken up by Lamennais or Victor Hugo or Zola, who cared about being warmly mentioned by posterity. Since there is no Heaven, let there at least be a heaven of good repute. Besides, there were always plenty of those bustling around Europe who made a profession of anti-Communism to squeeze money out of Americans; they were generally avoided by respectable intellectual company out of fear of catching leprosy.

Nothing is simple here, French rationalism is a legend, unless reducing everything to eloquence is taken for rationalism. It is, rather, a ritual, like ants feeling each other with their antennae. Although I could have been ironical, I did not treat lightly their cleverness and sensitivity to convention which sets fashions for the enlightened at the eternal supper at Madame Verdurin's, fashions which later infect Japan or America. The direction of history which they flaunted was not mere nonsense to me, though I rather suspected that it did not have in store for them what they had so safely planned. Nevertheless, my pride suffered. If not actually upon Brognart, then I was writing about related matters and ruining my good name. That is, my work was lined with steadily wounded ambition rather than with regular cowardice. I imagined how I looked in their eyes—a maniac, an émigré, in other words a reactionary—and my tone took on desperate hues. Now that all this is behind me, I only know that I would not repeat similar experiences for any price. I molded a mask for myself, a political one that distorted my features, though I have never had strong political interests and never made claims to much political acumen. I wondered instead why amazement at human foolishness was forbidden. Around me they were all swimming in a haze and driveling as if these were not serious matters of life and death that lay deeper than some form of politics. But my surprise really reached its peak a bit later when the ban was lifted, because then one single nasty man was purported to be guilty of all the crimes. Why the breakdowns, why the feigned innocence of two-year-olds? Either you see the state as an institution to which individuals delegate a part of their power and then exercise control, or you believe in a messianic state, and then, in the face of the greatness of the cause, tears shed over the destruction of some number of little human machines are truly crocodile tears. The Mexican priests who offered human sacrifices to keep the sun moving and assure a harvest would likely have been just as depressed had it been proven to them that the sacrifices were unnecessary, having no influence on the movement of the sun. As for me, I simply disliked the monopolistic state, the state-messiah—and this regardless of whether or not it was promised a splendid future—so I was surprised. No, not so much at their breakdowns and disillusionments, but more at the ease with which they immediately mended their shattered faith in the wise movement of history, without drawing any conclusions.

For me these problems were only the surface, and I blamed myself for not reaching deeper and not presenting myself as I really was. I felt guilty of deception. I had to return to myself, to learn how to outline my own hidden convictions, my own real faith, and through this to bear witness. It's a lot of work and I haven't yet learned how to do it. But since I had already begun, Brognart wasn't of much use because he would have steered me toward questions which were too blatant and which would have screened things more difficult for me and more real. Those few people who were against current political fashions and saw me as a valuable ally made dour faces because the world is divided into two blocs, and if you are in one you must beat the hell out of the other, while I was slipping away, withdrawing. What sort of politician was I? Such a mask was not made to fit my face; it was inauthentic, the bondage of circumstance. In human destiny I was looking for sources, and not for the rivers that spilled on downstream.

So I buried Brognart, which does not mean that he didn't haunt me. He haunts me to this day, ever more closely merged with my cousin, so that I can barely tell them apart. It's not really their faces, they show up faintly, it's more their inner state, my imagining of this or that moment behind wire. Peace to their poor souls.

ALPHA THE MORALIST

THE HISTORY of the last decades in Central and Eastern Europe abounds in situations in regard to which all epithets and theoretical considerations lose meaning. A man's effort to match up to these situations decides his fate. The solution each accepts differs according to those impalpable factors which constitute his individuality.

Since the fate of millions is often most apparent in those who by profession note changes in themselves and in others, i.e., the writers, a few portraits of typical Eastern European writers may serve as concrete examples of what is happening within the Imperium.

The man I call Alpha is one of the best-known prose writers east of the Elbe. He was a close friend of mine, and memories of many difficult moments that we went through together tie us to each other. I find it hard to remain unmoved when I recall him. I even ask myself if I should subject him to this analysis. But I shall do so because friendship would not prevent me from writing an article on his books in which I would say more or less what I shall say here.

Before the war, he was a tall, thin youth with horn-rimmed glasses. He printed his stories in a certain right-wing weekly that was held in low esteem by the literary circles of Warsaw, which were made up chiefly of Jews or of people who looked with distaste on the racist and totalitarian yearnings of this publication. The editor of the weekly had to some degree discovered him, and had reason to congratulate himself upon his choice, for Alpha's talent was developing rapidly. Very shortly, his first novel began to appear serially in the weekly. It was later published by one of the leading houses, and created a great stir.

His main interest was directed toward tragic moral conflicts. At the time many young writers were under the spell of Joseph Conrad's prose. Alpha was particularly susceptible to Conrad's style because he had a tendency to create solemn and hieratic characters. Night fascinated him. Small people with their powerful passions in a night whose silence and mystery embraced their fate in its gigantic folds—this was the usual formula of his novels and stories. His youthful works resembled Conrad's in their majesty and silence, and in a sense of the immensity of the inhuman, indifferent world. Alpha's position was metaphysical and tragic. He was tormented by the enigma of purity—moral purity and purity of tone in what he wrote. He distilled his sentences. He wanted each to be not merely a statement but, like a phrase in a musical composition, irreplaceable and effective in its very sound.

This need for purity, I would say for otherworldly purity, was basic to his character; yet in his relations with people he was haughty and imperious. His pursuit of purity in his work was closely linked to his personal arrogance; the former was his sublimation, his other ego, the repository of all his hopes. The more he worried about his disordered private life, the more highly he prized his redeeming activity, which is what his writing was for him, and the more he accorded to it the nature of a solemn rite. The one rank that could have sated his ambition was that of a cardinal. Slow movements, the flow of scarlet silk, the proffering of a ring to kiss—this for him was purity of gesture, self-expression through the medium of a better self. There are certain comic actors who dream all their lives of playing a serious, dignified role; in him, much the same motives were at play. Alpha, who was gifted with an exceptional sense of humor in conversation, changed completely when he began to write; then he dwelt only in the highest registers of tragedy. His ambition reached further than fame as an author of well-written books. He wanted to be a moral authority.

The novel I mentioned, which was his first big success, was widely acclaimed as a Catholic novel, and he was hailed as the most gifted Catholic writer, which in a Catholic country like Poland was no small matter. It is hard to say whether or not he really was a Catholic writer. The number of twentieth-century Catholic authors is negligible. So-called conversions of intellectuals are usually of a dubious nature, not significantly different from transitory conversions to surrealism, expressionism, or existentialism.

Alpha was the kind of Catholic so many of us were. This was a period of interest in Thomism and of references to Jacques Maritain in literary discussion. It would be wrong to maintain that for all these "intellectual Catholics" literary fashion alone was at stake; one cannot reduce the clutching gestures of a drowning man to a question of fashion. But it would be equally incorrect to consider literary debates based on a skillful juggling of Thomist terminology as symptoms of Catholicism. Be that as it may, the "intellectual Catholics" colored certain literary circles. Theirs was a special political role; they were foes of racism and totalitarianism. In this they differed from the Catholics proper, whose political mentality was not entirely free of worship of "healthy organisms" (i.e., Italy and Germany) and approval of anti-Semitic brawls. The Communists despised Jacques Maritain's influence as degenerate, but they tolerated the "intellectual Catholics" because they opposed the ideas of the extreme right. Soon after he published his novel, Alpha began to frequent the circles of the "intellectual Catholics" and the left. Sensitive to the opinion people held of him, and taking the writer's role as a moral authority very seriously, he broke with the rightist weekly and signed an open letter against anti-Semitism.

Everyone looked for something different in Catholicism. Alpha, with his tragic sense of the world, looked for forms: words and concepts, in short, textures. This tragic sense in him was not unlike Wells's Invisible Man, who when he wanted to appear among people had to paste on a false nose, bandage his face, and pull gloves over his invisible hands. Catholicism supplied Alpha's language. With concepts like sin and saintliness, damnation and grace, he could grasp the experiences of the characters he described; and, even more important, the language of Catholicism automatically introduced the elevated tone that was so necessary to him and lulled his longing for a cardinal's scarlet. The hero of his book was a priest, a sure sign of the influence of French Catholic novelists, and above all Bernanos, but also an expression of Alpha's urge to create pure and powerful characters. The action took place in a village, and here his weaknesses revealed themselves. He was so preoccupied with building up moral conflicts that he was blind to concrete details and incapable of observing living people. Having been raised in the city, he knew little of peasants and their life. The village he described was a universal one; it could just as easily have been Breton or Flemish, and for this reason it was not a real village. The characters seemed to be wearing costumes alien to them (like young nobles dressed as shepherds in pastoral literature), and their speech was uniformly alike.

The story played itself out against a barely sketched-in background, but it was powerfully welded together and the critics received it enthusiastically. It ran into several editions quickly. He received a national award for it which brought him a large sum of money. It is possible that the prize jury took into account not only the artistic merits of the book, but also certain political advantages to themselves in choosing him. In those years, the government was clearly flirting with the extreme right and the choice of Alpha seemed a wise move. The right would certainly be satisfied; whereas the liberals would have no reason to attack the decision for after all everyone was then free to believe as he pleased and to write as he believed.

Despite fame and money, in his heart Alpha never considered his novel and his collection of short stories good books. Still, the position he had won permitted him to be as haughty as he loved to be. He was recognized as the author of profound and noble prose, whereas his colleagues could hardly hope to reach a wide public otherwise than by creating a cheap sensation. Their books were either glaringly naturalistic, especially in a physiological sense, or else they were psychological tracts disguised as novels. Men of letters lived in the intellectual ghetto of their literary cafés; and the more they suffered from their isolation from the life of the masses, the stranger and less comprehensible their styles became. The bitterness Alpha felt in spite of the success of his first books was something he found difficult to define, but the moment when he realized that there was something wrong with his writing was decisive for the rest of his life.

A great doubt assailed him. If his colleagues doubted the worth of their work, suspended as it was in a void, then his perplexity took on larger proportions. He wanted to attain a purity of moral tone, but purity in order to be genuine must be earthy, deeply rooted in experience and observation of life. He perceived that he had blundered into falseness by living in the midst of ideas about people, instead of among people themselves. What he knew about man was based on his own subjective experiences within the four walls of his room. His Catholicism was no more than a cover; he toyed with it as did many twentieth-century Catholics, trying to clothe his nudity in an esteemed, Old World cloak. He was seeking some means of awakening in his reader the emotional response he wanted, and obviously the reader on finding words like "grace" or "sin," known to him since childhood, reacted strongly. But there is an element of dishonesty in such a use of words and concepts.

Alpha no longer knew whether the conflicts he created were real. Hailed as a Catholic writer, he knew that he was not; and his reaction was like that of a painter who having painted cubistically for a while is astonished to find that he is still called a Cubist after he has changed his style. Critics, deceived by appearances, reckoned his books among those that were healthy and noble as opposed to the decadent works of his fellow writers. But he realized that he was no healthier than his colleagues who at least did not attempt to hide their sorry nakedness.

The war broke out, and our city and country became a part of Hitler's Imperium. For five and a half years we lived in a dimension completely different from that which any literature or experience could have led us to know. What we beheld surpassed the most daring and the most macabre imagination. Descriptions of horrors known to us of old now made us smile at their naïveté. German rule in Europe was ruthless, but nowhere so ruthless as in the East, for the East was populated by races which, according to the doctrines of National Socialism, were either to be utterly eradicated or else used for heavy physical labor. The events we were forced to participate in resulted from the effort to put these doctrines into practice.

Still we lived; and since we were writers, we tried to write. True, from time to time one of us dropped out, shipped off to a concentration camp or shot. There was no help for this. We were like people marooned on a dissolving floe of ice; we dared not think of the moment when it would melt away. War communiqués supplied the latest data on our race with death. We had to write; it was our only defense against despair. Besides, the whole country was sown with the seeds of conspiracy and an "underground state" did exist in reality, so why shouldn't an underground literature exist as well. Except for two or three Nazi propaganda organs, no books or magazines were printed in the language of the defeated nation. Nonetheless, the cultural life of the country refused to be stifled. Underground publications were mimeographed on the run or illegally printed in a small format that was easy to circulate. Many underground lectures and authors' evenings were organized. There were even underground presentations of plays. All this raised the morale of the beaten but still fighting nation. National morale was good, too good, as events toward the end of the war proved.

In the course of these years, Alpha successfully realized his ambition to become a moral authority. His behavior was that of an exemplary writer-citizen. His judgments as to which actions were proper or improper passed in literary circles as those of an oracle, and he was often asked to decide whether someone had trespassed against the unwritten patriotic code. By unspoken accord, he became something of a leader of all the writers in our city. Underground funds went into his hands and he divided them among his needy colleagues; he befriended beginning writers; he founded and co-edited an underground literary review, typed copies of which were transmitted in rotation to "clubs" where they were read aloud in clandestine meetings. He ranked rather high among those initiated into the secrets of the underground network. His actions were characterized by real humanitarianism. Even before the war he had parted with his rightist patron, who had voiced the opinion that the country needed to institute its own totalitarianism. (The patron was shot by the Gestapo in the first year of the war.) When the German authorities set out to murder systematically the three million Jews of Poland, the anti-Semites did not feel compelled to worry overmuch; they condemned this bestiality aloud, but many of them secretly thought it was not entirely unwarranted. Alpha belonged to those inhabitants of our town who reacted violently against this mass slaughter. He fought with his pen against the indifference of others, and personally helped Jews in hiding even though such aid was punishable by death.

He was a resolute opponent of nationalism, so nightmarishly

incarnated in the Germans. This does not mean, however, that he had Communist leanings. The number of Communists in Poland had always been insignificant; and the cooperation between the Russians and the Germans after the Molotov-Ribbentrop pact created conditions particularly unfavorable to the activity of Moscow followers. The Communist Underground was weak. The hopes of the masses were turned toward the West, and the "underground state" was dependent on the Government-in-Exile in London. Alpha, with his barometer-like sensitivity to the moral opinions of his environment, felt no sympathy for a country that awakened friendly feelings in almost no one. But like the majority of his friends, he was anxious for far-reaching social reforms and for a people's government.

He and I used to meet often. It would hardly be an exaggeration to say that we spent the war years together. The sight of him was enough to raise one's spirits. He smiled in the face of all adversity; his manner was nonchalant; and to symbolize his contempt for hobnailed boots, uniforms, and shouts of "Heil Hitler," he habitually carried a black umbrella. His tall, lean figure, the ironic flash of his eyes behind his glasses, and the anointed air with which he strode through the terror-plagued streets of the city added up to a silhouette that defied the laws of war.

Once, in the first year of the war, we were returning from a visit to a mutual friend who lived in the country. As I remember, we were arguing about the choice of a train. We decided against the advice of our host, who had urged us to take a train leaving half an hour later. We arrived in Warsaw and walked along the streets feeling very satisfied with life. It was a beautiful summer morning. We did not know that this day was to be remembered as one of the blackest in the history of our city. Scarcely had I closed my door behind me when I heard shrieks in the street. Looking out the window, I saw that a general manhunt was on. This was the first manhunt for Auschwitz. Later millions of Europeans were to be killed there, but at the time this concentration camp was just starting to operate. From the first huge transport of people caught on the streets that day no one, it appears, escaped alive. Alpha and I had strolled those streets five minutes before the beginning of the hunt; perhaps his umbrella and his insouciance brought us luck.

These years were a test for every writer. The real tragedy of events pushed imaginary tragedies into the shade. Whichever of us failed to find an expression for collective despair or hope was ashamed. Only elementary feelings remained: fear, pain at the loss of dear ones, hatred of the oppressor, sympathy with the tormented. Alpha, whose talent was in search of real and not imaginary tragedy, sensed the material at hand and wrote a series of short stories which were published as a book after the war and widely translated. The theme of all these stories can be defined as loyalty. Not for nothing had Conrad been the favorite writer of his youth. This was a loyalty to something in man, something nameless, but strong and pure. Before the war, he tended to call this imperative sense of loyalty moral, in the Catholic sense. Now, fearing falseness, he affirmed merely that this imperative existed. When his dying heroes turned their eyes toward a mute heaven, they could find nothing there; they could only hope that their loyalty was not completely meaningless and that, in spite of everything, something in the universe responded to it.

The morality of his heroes was a lay morality, with a question mark, with a pause, a pause that was not quite faith. I think he was more honest in these stories than in his prewar writings. At the same time, he expressed accurately and powerfully the state of mind of the countless underground fighters dying in the battle against Nazism. Why did they throw their lives into the scale? Why did they accept torture and death? They had no point of support like the Führer for the Germans or the New Faith for the Communists. It is doubtful whether most of them believed in Christ. It could only have been loyalty, loyalty to something called fatherland or honor, but something stronger than any name. In one of his stories, a young boy, tortured by the police and knowing that he will be shot, gives the name of his friend because he is afraid to die alone. They meet before the firing squad, and the betrayed forgives his betrayer. This forgiveness cannot be justified by any utilitarian ethic; there is no reason to forgive traitors. Had this story been written by a Soviet author, the betrayed would have turned away with disdain from the man who had succumbed to base weakness. Forsaking Christianity, Alpha became a more religious writer than he had been before, if we grant that the ethic of loyalty is an extension of religious ethics and a contradiction of an ethic of collective goals.

In the second half of the war, a serious crisis in political consciousness took place in the "underground state." The underground struggle against the occupying power entailed great sacrifices; the number of persons executed or liquidated in concentration camps grew constantly. To explain the need of such sacrifice solely on the basis of loyalty left one a prey to doubt. Loyalty can be the basis of individual action, but when decisions affecting the fate of hundreds of thousands of people are to be made, loyalty is not enough. One seeks logical justification. But what kind of logical justification could there be? From the East the victorious Red Army was drawing near. The Western armies were far away. In the name of what future, in the name of what order were young people dying every day? More than one man whose task it was to sustain the morale of others posed this question to himself. No one was able to formulate an answer. Irrational dreams that something would happen to stop the advance of the Red Army and at the same time overthrow Hitler were linked with an appeal to the honor of the "country without a Quisling"; but this was not a very substantial prop for those of a more sober turn of mind. At this moment, Communist underground organizations began to be active, and were joined by some left-wing Socialists. The Communist program offered more realistic arguments than did the program of the London-directed "underground state": the country, it was fairly clear, was going to be liberated by the Red Army; with its aid one should start a people's revolution.

Gradually the intellectuals in the Underground became impatient with the irrational attitudes that were spreading in the resistance movement. This irrationality began to reach the point of hysteria. Conspiracy became an end in itself; to die or to expose others to death, something of a sport. Alpha found himself surrounded by living caricatures of the ethic of loyalty he expounded in his stories. The patriotic code of his class prohibited him from approaching the small groups whose policy followed Moscow's dictates.

Like so many of his friends, Alpha felt himself in a trap. Then, for the first time in his writing he invoked his sense of humor, using it to point up the figures he knew so well, the figures of men mad for conspiracy. His satires bared the social background of underground hysteria. There is no doubt that the "underground state" was the handiwork of the intelligentsia above all, of a stratum never known in Western Europe, not to mention the Anglo-Saxon countries. Since the intelligentsia was, in its customs and ties, the legatee of the nobility (even if some members were of peasant origin), its characteristic traits were not especially attractive to the intellectuals. The intellectuals of Poland had made several attempts to revolt against the intelligentsia of which they themselves were a part, much as the intellectuals in America had rebelled against the middle class. When a member of the intelligentsia really began to think, he perceived that he was isolated from the broad masses of the population. Finding the social order at fault, he tended to become a radical in an effort to establish a tie with the masses. Alpha's satires on the intelligentsia of the Underground convinced him that this stratum, with its many aberrations, boded ill for the future of the country if the postwar rulers were to be recruited from its ranks—which seemed inevitable in the event of the London Government-in-Exile's arrival in Poland.

Just when he was passing through this process of bitter and impotent mockery, the Uprising broke out. For two months, a kilometer-high column of smoke and flames stood over Warsaw.

Two hundred thousand people died in the street fighting. Those neighborhoods which were not leveled by bombs or by the fire of heavy artillery were burned down by SS squads. After the Uprising, the city which once numbered over a million inhabitants was a wilderness of ruins, its population deported, and its demolished streets literally cemeteries. Alpha, living in a distant suburb that bordered on fields, succeeded in escaping unharmed through the dangerous zone where people in flight were caught and sent to concentration camps.

In April of 1945, after the Germans had been expelled by the Red Army (the battles were then raging at the gates of Berlin), Alpha and I returned to Warsaw and wandered together over the mounds of rubble that had once been streets. We spent several hours in a once familiar part of the city. Now we could not recognize it. We scaled a slope of red bricks and entered upon a fantastic moon-world. There was total silence. As we worked our way downward, balancing to keep from falling, ever new scenes of waste and destruction loomed before us. In one of the gorges we stumbled upon a little plank fastened to a metal bar. The inscription, written in red paint or in blood, read: "Lieutenant Zbyszek's road of suffering." I know what Alpha's thoughts were at that time, and they were mine: we were thinking of what traces remain after the life of a man. These words rang like a cry to heaven from a shattered earth. It was a cry for justice. Who was Lieutenant Zbyszek? Who among the living would ever know what he had suffered? We imagined him crawling along this trail which some comrade, probably long since killed, had marked with the inscription. We saw him as, with an effort of his will, he mustered his fleeting strength and, aware of being mortally wounded, thought only of carrying out his duty. Why? Who measured his wisdom or madness? Was this a monad of Leibniz, fulfilling its destiny in the universe, or only the son of a postman, obeying a futile maxim of honor instilled in him by his father, who himself was living up to the virtues of a courtly tradition?

Further on, we came upon a worn footpath. It led into a deep mountain cleft. At the bottom stood a clumsy, huddled cross with a helmet on it. At the foot of the cross were freshly planted flowers. Somebody's son lay here. A mother had found her way to him and worn the path through her daily visits.

Theatrical thunder suddenly broke the silence. It was the wind rattling the metal sheets hanging from a cliff-like wall. We scrambled out of the heap of debris into a practically untouched courtyard. Rusting machines stood among the high weeds. And on the steps of the charred villa we found some account books listing profits and losses.

The Warsaw Uprising begun at the order of the Government-in-Exile in London broke out, as we know, at the moment when the Red Army was approaching the capital and the retreating German armies were fighting in the outskirts of the city. Feeling in the Underground was reaching a boiling point; the Underground Army wanted to fight. The Uprising was intended to oust the Germans and to take possession of the city so that the Red Army would be greeted by an already-functioning Polish government. Once the battle in the city began, and once it became obvious that the Red Army, standing on the other side of the river, would not move to the aid of the insurgents, it was too late for prudence. The tragedy played itself out according to all the immutable rules. This was the revolt of a fly against two giants. One giant waited beyond the river for the other to kill the fly. As a matter of fact, the fly defended itself, but its soldiers were generally armed only with pistols, grenades, and benzine bottles. For two months the giant sent his bombers over the city to drop their loads from a height of a few hundred feet; he supported his troops with tanks and the heaviest artillery. In the end, he crushed the fly only to be crushed in his turn by the second, patient giant.

There was no logical reason for Russia to have helped Warsaw. The Russians were bringing the West not only liberation from Hitler, but liberation from the existing order, which they wanted to replace with a good order, namely their own. The "underground state" and the London Government-in-Exile stood in the way of their overthrow of capitalism in Poland; whereas, behind the Red Army lines a different Polish government, appointed in Moscow, was already in office. The destruction of Warsaw represented certain indisputable advantages. The people dying in the street fights were precisely those who could create most trouble for the new rulers, the young intelligentsia, seasoned in its underground struggle with the Germans, and wholly fanatic in its patriotism. The city itself in the course of the years of occupation had been transformed into an underground fortress filled with hidden printing shops and arsenals. This traditional capital of revolts and insurrections was undoubtedly the most insubordinate city in the area that was to find itself under the Center's influence. All that could have argued for aid to Warsaw would have been pity for the one million inhabitants dying in the town. But pity is superfluous wherever sentence is pronounced by History.

Alpha, walking with me over the ruins of Warsaw, felt, as did all those who survived, one dominant emotion: anger. Many of his close friends lay in the shallow graves which abounded in the lunar landscape. The twenty-year-old poet Christopher, a thin asthmatic, physically no stronger than Marcel Proust, had died at his post sniping at SS tanks. With him the greatest hope of Polish poetry perished. His wife Barbara was wounded and died in a hospital, grasping a manuscript of her husband's verses in her hand. The poet Karol, son of the workers' quarter and author of a play about Homer, together with his inseparable comrade, the poet Marek, were blown up on a barricade the Germans dynamited. Alpha knew, also, that the person he loved most in his life had been deported to the concentration camp at Ravensbrück after the suppression of the Uprising. He waited for her long after the end of the war until he finally had to accept the idea that she was no longer alive. His anger was directed against those who had brought on the disaster, that terrible example of what happens when blind loyalty encounters the necessities of History. Just as his Catholic words had once rung false to him, so now his ethic of loyalty seemed a pretty but hollow concept.

Actually, Alpha was one of those who were responsible for what had happened. Could he not see the eyes of the young people gazing at him as he read his stories in clandestine authors' evenings? These were the young people who had died in the Uprising: Lieutenant Zbyszek, Christopher, Barbara, Karol, Marek, and thousands like them. They had known there was no hope of victory and that their death was no more than a gesture in the face of an indifferent world. They had died without even asking whether there was some scale in which their deeds would be weighed. The young philosopher Milbrand, a disciple of Heidegger, assigned to press work by his superiors, demanded to be sent to the line of battle because he believed that the greatest gift a man can have is the moment of free choice; three hours later he was dead. There were no limits to these frenzies of voluntary self-sacrifice.

Alpha did not blame the Russians. What was the use? They were the force of History. Communism was fighting Fascism; and the Poles, with their ethical code based on nothing but loyalty, had managed to thrust themselves between these two forces. Joseph Conrad, that incorrigible Polish noble! Surely the example of Warsaw had demonstrated that there was no place in the twentieth century for imperatives of fatherland or honor unless they were supported by some definite end. A moralist of today, Alpha reasoned, should turn his attention to social goals and social results. The rebels were not even an enemy in the minds of the Germans; they were an inferior race that had to be destroyed. For the Russians, they were "Polish fascists." The Warsaw Uprising was the swan song of the intelligentsia and the order it defended; like the suicidal charges of the Confederates during the American Civil War, it could not stave off defeat. With its fall, the Revolution was, in effect, accomplished; in any case, the road was open. This was not, as the press of the new government proclaimed in its effort to lull the people, a "peaceful revolution." Its price was bloody, as the ruins of the largest city in the country testified.

But one had to live and be active instead of looking back at what had passed. The country was ravaged. The new government went energetically to work reconstructing, putting mines and factories into operation, and dividing estates among the peasants. New responsibilities faced the writer. His books were eagerly awaited by a human anthill, shaken out of its torpor and stirred up by the big stick of war and of social reforms. We should not wonder, then, that Alpha, like the majority of his colleagues, declared at once his desire to serve the new Poland that had risen out of the ashes of the old.

He was accepted with open arms by the handful of Polish Communists who had spent the war years in Russia and who had returned to organize the state according to the maxims of Leninism-Stalinism. Then, that is in 1945, everyone who could be useful was welcomed joyfully without any demand that he be a Red. Both the benevolent mask under which the Party appeared and the moderation of its slogans were due to the fact that there were so uncommonly few Stalinists in the country.

Unquestionably, it is only by patient and gradually increased doses of the doctrine that one can bring a pagan population to understand and accept the New Faith. Ever since his break with the rightist weekly, Alpha had enjoyed a good opinion in those circles which were now most influential. He was not reprimanded for having kept his distance from Marxist groups during the war; authors who had maintained such contacts could be counted on the fingers of one hand. Now the writers of Poland were a little like virgins—willing, but timid. Their first public statements were cautious and painstakingly measured. Still it was not what they said that mattered. Their names were needed as proof that the government was supported by the entire cultural elite. The program of behavior toward various categories of people had been elaborated by the Polish Communists while they were still in Moscow; and it was a wise program, based on an intimate understanding of conditions in the country. The tasks that lay before them were unusually difficult. The country did not want their government. The Party, which had barely existed before the war, had to be reorganized and had to reconcile itself to the knowledge that most of its new members would be opportunists. Left-wing Socialists had to be admitted into the government. It was still necessary to carry on a complicated game with the Peasant Party, for after Yalta the Western allies demanded at least the semblance of a coalition. The most immediate job, therefore, was to bridge the gap between the small group of Communists and the country as a whole; those who could help most in building this bridge were famous writers who were known as liberals or even as conservatives. Alpha fulfilled every requirement. His article appeared on the first page of a government literary weekly; it was an article on humanism. As I recall it, he spoke in it of the ethic of respect for man that revolution brings.

It was May 1945 in the medieval city of Cracow. Alpha and I, as well as many other writers and artists, had taken refuge there after the destruction of Warsaw. The night the news of the fall of Berlin came was lit with bursts of rockets and shells, and the streets echoed with the fire of small arms as the soldiers of the victorious Red Army celebrated the prospect of a speedy return home. The next morning, on a fine spring day, Alpha and I were sitting in the office of Polish Film, working on a scenario. Tying up the loose ends of a film is a burdensome business; we were putting our feet up on tables and armchairs, we were pacing the room, smoking too many cigarettes and constantly being lured to the window through which came the warble of sparrows. Outside the window was a courtyard with young trees, and beyond the courtyard a huge building lately transformed into a prison and the headquarters of the Security Police. We saw scores of young men behind the barred windows on the ground floor. Some had thrust their faces into the sun in an effort to get a tan. Others were fishing with wire hooks for the bits of paper which had been tossed out on the sand from neighboring cells. Standing in the window, we observed them in silence.

It was easy to guess that these were soldiers of the Underground Army. Had the London Government-in-Exile returned to Poland, these soldiers of the "underground state" would have been honored and feted as heroes. Instead, they were incarcerated as a politically uncertain element—another of History's ironic jokes. These young boys who had grown used to living with a gun in their hands and surrounded by perpetual danger were now supposed to forget their taste for conspiracy as quickly as possible. Many succeeded so well in forgetting that they pretended they had never been active in the Underground. Others stayed in the woods, and any of them that were caught were thrown behind bars. Although their foe had been Hitler, they were now termed agents of the class enemy. These were the brothers of the young people who had fought and died in the Warsaw Uprising, people whose blind self-sacrifice lay on Alpha's conscience. I do not know what he was thinking as he looked at the windows of those prison cells. Perhaps even then he was sketching the plan of his first postwar novel.

As his whole biography demonstrates, his ambition was always boundless. He was never content to be just one among many; he had to be a leader so that he could justify his personal haughtiness. The novel he was writing should, he believed, raise him to first place among the writers active in the new situation. This was a time when writers were trying to change their style and subject matter, but they could not succeed without first effecting a corresponding change in their own personalities. Alpha was undergoing a moral crisis which was personal to him, but at the same time a reiteration of a conflict known to many of his countrymen. He sensed in himself a power that flowed from his individual but simultaneously universal drama. His feeling for the tragedy of life was seeking a new garment in which to appear in public.

Alpha did not betray his belief in himself. The novel he wrote was the product of a mature talent. It made a great impression on its readers. All his life he had circled around the figure of a strong and pure hero. In his prewar novel, he had used a priest; now he drew a representative of the New Faith, a fearless old Communist who after spending many years in German concentration camps emerged unbroken in spirit. Returning to his devastated homeland, this hero found himself faced with a chaos which his clear mind and strong will were to convert into a new social order. The society he was to transform showed every sign of moral decay. The older generation of the intelligentsia, personally ambitious and addicted to drink, was still daydreaming of help from the Western allies. The youth of the country, educated to principles of blind loyalty and habituated to an adventurous life in the Underground, was now completely lost. Knowing no goals of human activity other than war against the enemy in the name of honor, it continued to conspire against a new enemy, namely the Party and the government imposed by Russia. But given postwar circumstances, the Party was the only power that could guarantee peace, reconstruct the country, enable the people to earn their daily bread, and start schools and universities, ships and railroads, functioning. One did not have to be a Communist to reach this conclusion; it was obvious to everyone. To kill Party workers, to sabotage trains carrying food, to attack laborers who were trying to rebuild the factories was to prolong the period of chaos. Only madmen could commit such fruitless and illogical acts.

This was Alpha's picture of the country. One might have called it a piece of commonsense journalism had it not been for something that always distinguished him as a writer: pity, pity for the old Communist as well as for those who considered him their enemy. Because he felt compassion for both these forces, he succeeded in writing a tragic novel.

His shortcomings as a writer, so clearly evident in his prewar works, now stood him in good stead. His talent was not realistic; his people moved in a world difficult to visualize. He built up moral conflicts by stressing contrasts in his characters; but his old Communist was as rare a specimen on the Polish scene as the priest he had made his hero before the war. Communists may, in general, be depicted as active, intelligent, fanatic, cunning, but above all as men who take external acts as their domain. Alpha's hero was not a man of deeds; on the contrary, he was a silent, immovable rock whose stony exterior covered all that was most human—personal suffering and a longing for good. He was a monumental figure, an ascetic living for his ideas. He was ashamed of his personal cares, and his refusal to confess his private pain won the sympathy of the readers. In the concentration camp he had lost the wife he dearly loved; and now it was only by the greatest effort of his will that he could compel himself to live, for life had suddenly become devoid of meaning. He was a titan with a torn heart, full of love and forgiveness. In short, he emerged as a potential force capable of leading the world toward good. Just when his feelings and thoughts were purest he died, shot by a young man who saw in him only an agent of Moscow.

One can understand why Alpha, living in a country where the word "Communist" still had an abusive connotation, wanted to portray his hero as the model of a higher ethic; but that ethic can be evaluated properly only when we see it applied to concrete problems, only when its followers treat people as tools. As for the society the old Communist wanted to transform, an accurate observer would have seen in it positive signs and not merely symptoms of disintegration. The intelligentsia, that is, every variety of specialist, were setting to work just as enthusiastically as the workers and peasants in mobilizing the factories, mines, railroads, schools, and theaters. They were governed by a feeling of responsibility toward the community and by professional pride, not by a vision of socialism along Russian lines. Nevertheless, their ethic of responsibility bore important results. Their political thinking was naïve, and their manners often characteristic of a bygone era. Yet it was they, and not the Party, who reacted most energetically at first. The younger generation was lost and leaderless, but its terroristic deeds were at least as much a product of despair as of demoralization. The boys that Alpha and I had seen in the windows of the prison were not there because of any crimes they had committed, but only because of their wartime service in the "underground state." Alpha could not say all this because of the censorship, but his expressed pity for these boys permitted the reader to guess at what he left unsaid. However, his failure to present all the facets of the situation altered the motivation of his characters.

His book was entirely dominated by a feeling of anger *against the losers.* This anger was essential to the existence of Alpha and many like him. The satiric attitude toward the underground intelligentsia which marked the stories he wrote toward the end of the war now manifested itself in the chapters of the novel that mocked absurd hopes for a sudden political change. In reality, these hopes, no matter how absurd the form they took in members of the white-collar class, were far from alien to the peasants and workers. Alpha never knew the latter intimately, so he could, with much greater ease, attribute the belief in a magic removal of the Russians to a special characteristic of the intelligentsia which, unfortunately, was not distinguished for its political insight.

A novel that favorably compared the ethic of the New Faith with the vanquished code was very important to the Party. The book was so widely publicized that it quickly sold over 100,000 copies, and in 1948, Alpha was awarded a state prize. One city donated to him a beautiful villa furnished at considerable expense. A useful writer in a people's democracy cannot complain of a lack of attention.

The Party dialecticians knew perfectly well that Alpha's hero was not a model of the "new man." That he was a Communist could be divined only from the author's assurances. He appeared on the pages of the book prepared to act, but not in action. Alpha's old hero had merely traded his priest's cassock for the leather jacket of a Communist. Although Alpha had changed the language of his concepts, the residue of tragedy and metaphysics remained constant. And even though the old Communist did not pray, the readers would not have been surprised to hear his habitually sealed lips suddenly utter the lamentations of Jeremiah, so well did the words of the prophet harmonize with his personality. Alpha, then, had not altered subjectively since his prewar days; he still could not limit himself to a purely utilitarian ethic expressed in rational acts. Faust and King Lear did penance within his hero. Both heaven and earth continued to exist. Still one could not ask too much. He did not belong to the Party, but he showed some understanding. His treatment of the terrorist youth even more than his portrayal of the old Communist demonstrated that he was learning. It was too early to impose "socialist realism"; the term was not even mentioned lest it alarm the writers and artists. For the same reason, the peasants were assured that there would be no collective farms in Poland.

The day of decision did not come for Alpha until a few years after he had published his novel. He was living in his beautiful villa, signing numerous political declarations, serving on committees, and traveling throughout the country lecturing on literature in factory auditoriums, clubs, and "houses of culture." For many, these authors' trips, organized on a large scale, were a painful duty; but for him they were a pleasure, for they enabled him to become acquainted with the life and problems of the working-class youth. For the first time, he was really stepping out of his intellectual clan; and better still, he was doing so as a respected author. As one of the top-ranking writers of the people's democracies he could feel himself, if not a cardinal, then at least an eminent canon.

In line with the Center's plan, the country was being progressively transformed. The time came to shorten the reins on the writers and to demand that they declare themselves clearly for the New Faith. At writers' congresses "socialist realism" was proclaimed the sole indicated creative method. It appears that he lived through this moment with particular pain. Showing incredible dexterity the Party had imperceptibly led the writers to the point of conversion. Now they had to comply with the Party's ultimatum or else rebel abruptly and so fall to the foot of the social ladder. To split one's loyalties, to pay God in one currency and Caesar in another, was no longer possible. No one ordered the writers to enter the Party formally; yet there was no logical obstacle to joining once one accepted the New Faith. Such a step would signalize greater courage, for admission into the Party meant an increase in one's responsibilities.

As the novelist most highly regarded by Party circles, Alpha could make but one decision. As a moral authority he was expected to set an example for his colleagues. During the first years of the new order he had established strong bonds with the Revolution. He was, at last, a popular writer whose readers were recruited from the masses. His highly praised prewar novel had sold scarcely a few thousand copies; now he and every author could count on reaching a tremendous public. He was no longer isolated; he told himself he was needed not by a few snobs in a coffeehouse, but by this new workers' youth he spoke to in his travels over the country. This metamorphosis was entirely due to the victory of Russia and the Party, and logically one ought to accept not only practical results but also the philosophical principles that engendered them.

That was not easy for him. Ever more frequently he was attacked for his love of monumental tragedy. He tried to write differently, but whenever he denied something that lay in the very nature of his talent his prose became flat and colorless; he tore up his manuscripts. He asked himself whether he could renounce all effort to portray the tragic conflicts peculiar to life in a giant collective. The causes of the human distress he saw about him daily were no longer the same as in a capitalist system, but the sum total of suffering seemed to grow instead of diminish.

Alpha knew too much about Russia and the merciless methods dialecticians employed on "human material" not to be assailed by waves of doubt. He was aware that in accepting the New Faith he would cease to be a moral authority and become a pedagogue, expressing only what was recognized as useful. Henceforth, ten or fifteen dialectical experts would weigh each of his sentences, considering whether he had committed the sin of pure tragedy. But there was no returning. Telling himself that he was already a Communist in his actions, he entered the Party and at once published a long article about himself as a writer. This was a self-criticism; in Christian terminology, a confession. Other writers read his article with envy and fear. That he was first everywhere and in everything aroused their jealousy, but that he showed himself so clever—so like a Stakhanovite miner who first announces that he will set an unusually high norm—filled them with apprehension. Miners do not like any of their comrades who are too inclined to accumulate honors for having driven others to a speed-up.

His self-criticism was so skillfully written that it stands as a classic declaration of a writer renouncing the past in the name of the New Faith. It was translated into many languages, and printed even by Stalinist publications in the West. In condemning his previous books he resorted to a special stratagem: he admitted openly what he had always secretly thought of the flaws in his work. He didn't need dialectics to show him these flaws; he knew them of old, long before he approached Marxism, but now he attributed his insight to the merits of the Method. Every good writer knows he should not let himself be seduced by high-sounding words or by emotionally effective but empty concepts. Alpha affirmed that he had stumbled into these pitfalls because he wasn't a Marxist. He also let it be understood that he did not consider himself a Communist writer, but only one who was trying to master the Method, that highest of all sciences. What was remarkable about the article was the sainted, supercilious tone, always Alpha's own, in which it was written. That tone led one to suspect that in damning his faults he was compounding them and that he gloried in his new garb of humility.

The Party confided to him, as a former Catholic, the function of making speeches against the policy of the Vatican. Shortly thereafter, he was invited to Moscow, and on his return he published a book about the "Soviet man." By demonstrating dialectically that the only truly free man was the citizen of the Soviet Union, he was once again reaching for the laurels of supremacy. His colleagues had always been more or less ashamed to use this literary tactic even though they knew it was dialectically correct. As a result, he came to be actively disliked in the literary ghetto. I call this a ghetto because despite the fact that they were lecturing throughout the country and reaching an ever larger public the writers were now as securely locked up in their collective homes and clubs as they had been in their prewar coffeehouses. Alpha's fellow authors, jealous of the success his noble tone had brought him, called him the "respectable prostitute."

It is not my place to judge. I myself traveled the same road of seeming inevitability. In fleeing I trampled on many values that may determine the worth of a man. So I judge myself severely though my sins are not the same as his. Perhaps the difference in our destinies lay in a minute disparity in our reactions when we visited the ruins of Warsaw or gazed out the window at the prisoners. I felt that I could not write of these things unless I wrote the *whole* truth, not just a part. I had the same feeling about the events that took place in Nazi-occupied Warsaw, namely that every form of literature could be applied to them except fiction. We used to feel strangely ashamed, I remember, whenever Alpha read us his stories in that war-contaminated city. He exploited his subject matter too soon, his composition was too smooth. Thousands of people were dying in torture all about us; to transform their sufferings immediately into tragic theater seemed to us indecent. It is sometimes better to stammer from an excess of emotion than to speak in well-turned phrases. The inner voice that stops us when we might say too much is wise. It is not improbable that he did not know this voice.

Only a passion for truth could have saved Alpha from developing into the person he became. Then, it is true, he would not have written his novel about the old Communist and demoralized Polish youth. He had allowed himself the luxury of pity, but only once he was within a framework safe from the censors' reproaches. In his desire to win approbation he had simplified his picture to conform to the wishes of the Party. One compromise leads to a second and a third until at last, though everything one says may be perfectly logical, it no longer has anything in common with the flesh and blood of living people. This is the reverse side of the medal of dialectics. This is the price one pays for the mental comfort dialectics affords. Around Alpha there lived and continue to live many workers and peasants whose words are ineffectual, but in the end, the inner voice they hear is not different from the subjective command that shuts writers' lips and demands all or nothing. Who knows, probably some unknown peasant or some minor postal employee should be placed higher in the hierarchy of those who serve humanity than Alpha the moralist.

TIGER

MY FRIEND Tiger had prophesied in Warsaw that after the war I would do a lot of traveling. I laughed it off, but he said: "You don't have to believe me." To have seen the crown of an African king on my head would not have surprised me more than the fulfillment of his prediction. Me in America and on motor trips via the New York–Boston highway to Cape Cod's oceanside forests . . . There was a certain flavor about the letters "DP" on my Chevrolet license plates. For millions of Europeans then, they stood for that dreary and lowest of fates: "Displaced Person," but here they simply replaced the words "Diplomatic Personnel." In the little blue book that listed the names and addresses of diplomats accredited in Washington, I figured as the Second Secretary at the Embassy of People's Poland. And I was almost ready to grab every passerby and beg his pardon for my appearing as someone I was not. We always feel ourselves from the inside other than people see us—the clothes we wear are not our skin—but this revolt against the roles society imposes on us has many pitfalls.

I could fill many pages describing the Red Army's passage

through Poland or my conversations with its officers and soldiers.
I could also meditate over the cyclone that ruined families, fortunes, and whole classes, or try to explain why, after the overthrow, a non-Party poet warranted the privilege of being sent to
America. Adventures with Polish censorship or the internal affairs of a "Red" embassy in the United States would also provide
tasty morsels. But all of that, it seems to me, can be dispensed
with. I want to get to the heart of my five years as a writer and a
diplomat for a people's democracy. And the heart of it was my
philosophical star, Tiger.

He who would minimize our conflicts and decisions by ascribing them exclusively to Poland's geographical position and the
terms of the Yalta agreement, which had delivered the country
over to the administrators of the Eastern section of our planet,
would be making a mistake. The scene of our speculations and
concern was not only Poland but the world. Poland, however, had
given us a bitter knowledge incommunicable to people in the
West, whom we watched smiling inwardly. We could seek compensation for our suffering only in a malevolent wisdom that
was manifestly higher than theirs. In our dialogues, we made deliberate use of metaphors and allegories. Powerless and ruined
Greece, our beloved Greece, stood for Europe, and we often spoke
of France as Alexandria because she had become stylized in the
antiquated rituals of her grammarians and rhetoricians. As for
the United States, was it not Rome, avid for peace, bread, and
games?

It took some time before Tiger and I caught up with each
other after the war. I had been living in Washington quite a
while when I received a letter from him, postmarked Paris. Both
he and his wife had been deported from Warsaw to camps in Germany, and after the entrance of the Allies, they had worked there
as translators from German to English for the British Army.
Later they took up residence in the Latin Quarter in Paris. At
first they considered themselves refugees; but before long they
decided to declare their loyalty to the new Poland. An exchange

of letters prepared for our encounter, which I looked forward to very much.

The air in America, even summer in Washington with its 98 percent humidity, did not make me lethargic. It exhilarated me. The air in Poland is always oppressive; one breathes in elements of melancholy there that constrict the heart, and one always has the feeling that life is not completely real; hence the constant yen to drink vodka in the hope that an inaccessible normality will be restored. But even in Western Europe things had never seemed so concrete to me, so weighty, so filled with a material, temporal value. I did not need moss-covered ruins or medieval churches or Roman aqueducts; the little white houses in the green grass and the sound of power lawn mowers were enough.

Washington, D.C.—an impersonal machine, a pure abstraction—I reduced to the branches of the tree outside my window and the singing of birds the color of vermilion. But I liked New York, I liked to melt into her crowds. Most of all I got to know the American countryside, which restored me, after a prolonged interval, to my boyhood. Like all Europeans I had painted for myself a false picture of technology's reign in America, imagining that nothing was left of nature. In reality her nature was more luxuriant even than the wooded regions where I grew up, where the farmer, plowing with a wooden plow, has for centuries been wreaking effective destruction. Outside of New York City, the asphalt highways were like swords thrown into the thickets to signify that man belonged to a different order, that he was fundamentally a stranger to the snakes, turtles, chipmunks, and skunks who perished under the wheels of cars while trying to cross the unnatural band; the place where their line of march intersected the line of the driver's will somehow resembled the encounter of human destinies with the intentions of the godhead. I plunged into books on American flora and fauna, made diplomatic contacts with porcupines and beavers in the forests of Pennsylvania, but I was most drawn to the Northern states: Vermont and Maine. Maine spruce trees shrouded in white fog at sundown and sunrise were not, in my eyes, substitutes for my Lithuanian spruce. Had I used them to satisfy my nostalgia, it would have robbed them of their own individual beauty. But the waist-high grass showering me with droplets of dew, the fallen trees with their tangle of roots, the hidden presence of the moose and the bear——what a surprising kinship of emotional tradition! This America of trees and plants, fragrant with the hay reaped on forest meadows, fitted over me smoothly and I ceased to be a foreigner in her. None of us "Easterners," regardless of how long he may have lived in France or England, would ever be a Frenchman or an Englishman; but here, at barn dances where everybody, both grownups and children, danced together, one could forget. I realized then that the popular legend about America, cut off by an ocean as if by the waters of Lethe, was justified.

I wanted to forget. In my dreams, fragments would come back to me: a road between the pines above a craggy river bank, a lake with a string of ducks on it; but people above all, uninvited guests, shadows, mostly ordinary men, unintelligent, modestly ambitious, cruelly punished for wanting only to live; various peasants, Jews from ramshackle little towns, a colleague from my high school and university days——a pedant, a plodder, the owner of an idiotic collection of empty cigarette boxes, dreaming of a career as public prosecutor, tortured in some Siberian camp; another, a bald lecher with batlike ears, who told enthusiastically about a garrisoned small town: "We came to Skidel and . . . paradise, I tell you, not a town! Every house a brothel!" They shot him as he stole over the same border I had crossed in 1940; after hearing about it, I could never rid myself of the image of his short, fat fingers clawing at the moss in a death spasm.

All the same, America was difficult to get used to. My circumstances brought about an acute recurrence of my old sickness, which I may have suffered from even in high school. As far as I know, it does not figure in any psychiatric handbook. It consists of a disturbance in one's perception of time. The sick man constantly sees time as an hourglass through which states, systems, and civilizations trickle like sand; his immediate surroundings lose the force of reality; they do not last at all, they disintegrate; in other words, being is unreal, only movement is real. Those who plant flowers, till the fields, build houses are deserving of pity because they are seen as participants in a phantasmagoric spectacle, and to him they are no more real than to a demon who flies up to their windows at night and peeks through the pane. They are foredoomed because the order in which they have established themselves and which shapes their every thought and feeling is, like every order, ripe for destruction.

It may be that not only individuals but whole nations suffer from this illness, if their misfortunes have lasted a long time and they cannot tolerate the sight of others who are dully complacent. Their envy drives them to seek solace in visions of the punishment awaiting those whom Fate has unjustly spared. Perhaps the classic example of such an incurable was Alexander Herzen. In 1847 he left Czar Nicholas I's empire for Western Europe, which in the same year he judged thus: "The world we live in is dying; it ought to be buried so that our heirs may breathe more freely; but people think they must cure it and they postpone death." "The aged world has grown stooped in its aristocratic livery, especially since the year one thousand eight hundred and thirty; its face has taken on an ashen hue." "This is the *facies Hippocratica*; it tells doctors that Death has already lifted his scythe." The world around him seemed senseless because only upheavals, ruin, and apocalypse made sense. "In Paris boredom is gay; in London boredom is safe; in Rome boredom is majestic; in Madrid boredom is stuffy; in Vienna stuffiness is boring."

A hundred years after him I had, as one can see, a few things in common with those poor Russians. I could not stop my mind from coursing through the ages like a projectile, seizing general characteristics and lines of development, speeding up the processes of becoming. In other words, I was troubled by an excess of what Americans so strikingly lack. No doubt this is why Tiger claimed that I had a dialectical mind. Dialectical or catastrophic? It is not quite the same thing, but almost. In any case, from it came my power of discernment, my capacity for seeing time brutally condensed, and my pride in dominating the anthill immersed in the daily bustle; that is, in the meaningless. I walked the streets of Chicago and Los Angeles as if I were an anthropologist privileged to visit the civilizations of Incas or Aztecs. Americans accepted their society as if it had arisen from the very order of nature; so saturated with it were they that they tended to pity the rest of humanity for having strayed from the norm. If I at least understood that all was not well with me, they did not realize that the opposite disablement affected them: a loss of the sense of history and, therefore, of a sense of the tragic, which is only born of historical experience.

All their aggressiveness had been channeled into the struggle for money, and that struggle made them forget the bloody lessons of the Civil War. Later on, every one of them had so trained himself to forget, that during the Depression he regarded unemployment as shameful proof of his own personal inability. I esteemed these men; I was an admirer of their America. At least no one here could justify his laziness by sighing: "If only nations were not predestined, if it weren't for the Czar, if it weren't for the government, if it weren't for the bourgeoisie . . ." But, paradoxically, that triumph of the individual had wrought an inner sterility; they had souls of shiny plastic. Only the Negroes, obsessed like us (Oh, what a morning when the stars begin to fall!), were alive, tragic, and spontaneous.

For someone like myself, who had heard and kept at the back of his mind the prophecy "America will be destroyed by fire, England by fire and water, and Russia by a falling piece of the moon," an evening such as the one I spent in Columbus, Ohio, was unhealthy. Sunday. A deserted main street. Flickering lights on billboards and movie houses. To kill time before my train left, I went into the only little theater there. The pure vulgarity of that burlesque show, stripped of aesthetic drapery, plebeian, was fit for immigrant workers' camps of the last century; even apes would have understood the copulative movements of the girls on stage. A diversion for lonely males. But in the bar across the street the lonely were deprived even of the consolation of stammering their confessions to the bartender, for all eyes were riveted on the television screen. Was this the highest that *l'homme sensuel moyen* could reach when left to himself, undismayed by the cyclones of history? The inside of the train, which I boarded a while later, was decorated with large reproductions of French Impressionists.

And then there was that constant masquerade of "Communism and Anti-Communism." I could tell them a thing or two about Communism, but I had to put a seal over my lips. And anyway it would not have been worthwhile; the same words meant something else to them and something else to me. I spotted the Achilles' heel of their system: the selection of mostly unqualified politicians and statesmen. Worse still were those lady enthusiasts at our receptions in the Embassy, admirers of progress in the East, hens pleading for a few kernels of lying propaganda. A perverse, comic masquerade. For what really preoccupied me were studies on T. S. Eliot and W. H. Auden, anthologies of American poetry, the work of Faulkner and Henry Miller, the poetry of Robert Lowell and Karl Shapiro, periodicals such as *Partisan Review* or Dwight Macdonald's *Politics*, and exhibits of modern art. It was not American diplomats who dispensed information about intellectual America (so little known in Europe then), but a Red.

Millions of people who care about money. I cared about it little. I was not born into a class that knew how to prize it and I had walked out of too many burning cities (literally or metaphorically) without looking back: *omnia mea mecum porto*. Soft carpets, gadgets, neat little houses I associated with flaming destruction. My superiors interpreted that somewhat aristocratic detachment from earthly goods as a sign that I would not succumb to capitalistic temptations.

The Embassy was a dog collar, a waste of time, a tedious place, and just as at the Polish Radio before the war, if I showed some diligence it was rather ironical. My lunch hour brought relief. I ate quickly in the cafeteria and then browsed through the new books at Whyte's Bookshop—I have always been an addict of reading in bookstores. If I could not wiggle out of a cocktail party, I put in a ten-minute appearance and then escaped. During those years in occupied Warsaw at least I acquired the ability to do solid work. Here I returned home around seven, ate supper, took an hour's nap to separate myself from the day's nonsense—then wrote until 2 a.m. In the morning I dashed to the office at breakneck speed, cursing the red lights. I yawned all day and waited for evening.

Only that double life could have earned me the right to breathe and to walk the earth like everyone else. Because from the moment Janka and I disembarked from the British liner on the shore of the Hudson River, it all seemed like the highest outrage. The gigantic city itself was an outrage because it stood there as if nothing had happened—it had not received a single notch from a bomb—and the people in the streets of Manhattan were free from what flowed in me like molten lead. The absurd paperwork that piled up on my desk and the letter lying on top of it, from a camp near Archangelsk, was an outrage. The letter had been received in Poland by relatives of the prisoner and sent to me with the request for a package for him. I had to live with the image of camps and trainloads of prisoners heading toward them. So orange juice, milk shakes, and a new shirt were outrageous. The constant lying of my colleagues and superiors, our mutual feigning of half-wittedness and innocence, was outrageous. And so was my unexpected meeting on Fifth Avenue with a Warsaw actress who had worked as a cocktail waitress during the German occupation. When asked what happened to her husband, she replied with a shrug, "Imagine! Joe was one of the first to run up to that German tank that was loaded with dynamite in the Old Town district [giggle]. Blown to pieces! They must have picked up the head and legs on the balconies! [giggle]."

Yet I was a completely different person than I had been before the war. The pen in my hand was different, and no matter how painful the world was, I felt no urge, as I had before, to escape into a lofty art. On the contrary, my extraordinary situation, which no American could have grasped, gave me an impetus and I knew I would have been poorer for not facing up to it. I do not want to pretend that I was tranquil or composed, because mentally I thrashed about in a furious sort of inner debate. But I was convinced that as long as we live, we must lift ourselves over new thresholds of consciousness; that to aim at higher and higher thresholds is our only happiness. While living in the Government-General, I crossed one of those thresholds—when we finally begin to become the person we must be, and we are at once inebriated and a little frightened at the enormous distance yet to be traveled. During my nightly vigils, when I accomplished so much work (for that alone society should have paid me), I constantly thought of Tiger, and I was aware, through the very possibility, through my very openness to the world, of how much I owed him.

Words cannot describe the fascination with someone's personality or an intellectual friendship. Tiger did not resemble the professional philosopher who divides time into intellectual activity and "all the rest" of life, which is given over to habit and prevailing custom. He philosophized incessantly and with his whole body: he was all movement, impersonating, parodying—now with love, now with hostility, now with mockery—various attitudes and opinions. He did not argue, he danced philosophical systems by transposing them into the behavior of their adherents. For me, he incarnated a truth that Europe was discovering anew: that philosophy, despite the university departments, is not mere speculation; that it both nourishes itself on everything within us and impregnates our whole being; and that if it does not help us to judge a man, a piece of sculpture, a literary work, it is dead.

The Marxists taught much the same thing, and they had attracted me as a young man because I sensed in them something vital and bracing. At the same time their dogmatism repelled me.

I met Tiger in the way a river, hollowing out a bed for itself on a plain, meets a second river; it had been inevitable, a foregone conclusion. And it had consequences for me, of course, that were both political and artistic. Because "Tigerism" was a philosophy of action. Yet it was such a difficult one that only a few worthies, selected by the master himself, could hope to gain access to it. To practice it one had to cultivate "historical humor"; that is, one had to master a skill, like swimming or running, rather than a body of knowledge capable of being set forth in theories. Reality, according to him, was a changing, living tissue; it was woven out of countless interdependencies in such a way that even the tiniest detail germinates infinitely; and at the joints that keep its structure mobile, man is able to insert the lever of a conscious act.

Before the war, Tiger had frequented artistic circles, for the subject of style was paramount in his phenomenological analysis. It would be no exaggeration to say that he regarded the choice of one style or another as a matter of life or death. The fate of humanity, according to him, does not depend upon the foolish moves of its politicians but upon revolutions so discreet that scarcely anyone perceives them. With unequaled virulence, he cudgeled modern art almost in its entirety, because no matter how one looked at it, it derived from Romanticism, and Romanticism was Enemy Number One; it was damp, tearful, and, by necessity, always led to inner falsity. Thus Heraclitus' maxim "A dry flame is the best and wisest soul" seemed to contain the future of the earth. Tiger, with his usual flair for caricature, ridiculed Chopin: "Drowned maidens being dragged, from whose hair, ploom, ploom, ploom, water drips," and insisted that he would only listen to music "when a dozen or so little Germans"——here he blew out his cheeks and tooted on an invisible flute. These metaphors for the initiated connoted much more than a taste for Mozart. Tiger really cared about only one thing: salvation. And woe to those who think that in the twentieth century they can save themselves without taking part in the tragedy, without purifying themselves through historical suffering.

I sent the results of my nighttime jottings to him in Paris with the fullest confidence in his judgment. He did not always see the highest merit in my work, but then not just anything could satisfy a reader of Plato's *Republic* and Browning's *The Ring and the Book*, and this made every word of praise from him all the more valuable. My natural secretiveness delighted in our conspiracy; with malicious tongue-in-check, I wove my sentences perversely, hoping to win his approval. For it was we who were really changing the world, slyly, patiently, from within; we were the worm in the apple. And for precisely this reason my superiors had no cause to doubt my loyalty, or to fear that I would cross over to the émigré camp. I had come a bit too far from prewar Poland and her compulsive intellectual patterns. It is probably difficult to explain to students trained exclusively in Euclidean geometry just what non-Euclidean geometry consists of. Similarly for us (Tiger, me, our mutual friends) it was hard to convey our vision of the death of an epoch—an epoch in which inert matter, under the mask of spiritualism, tyrannized over men's minds; an epoch in which philosophy and poetry, disdained for "having nothing to do with life," were no more than accessories, flowers, an adornment of salons.

My post—as diplomat in the service of a bankrupt state—obviously did not entitle me to feel superior. Those people, however, who showed a more or less open disgust toward us (who had sold our souls to the devil) did not see the extent of the moral problem. And it could not have been otherwise, as long as they separated "serious" activities (struggle for power, drawing of borders, international treaties, and so on) from the individual's physiological existence. While they argued about Roosevelt, Truman, and Stalin, I would shrug my shoulders: "That's not what it's about." In despair they asked me what, then, was it about? Silence. I was not a politician, and despite my daily dose of press clippings I did not measure time by a political yardstick. On the other hand, I would have been threatened with moral disaster had I chosen the South Sea Islands, where I could have looked forward to nothing but "birth, copulation, and death," and where the price of turning one's back on the action was an empty heart. Like a sportsman, I kept in condition by being present in the collective work, present in the literature of my language, not as one who partakes in its lasting accomplishments (it is not up to us to decide that) but as a sharer in its moments here and now.

Many were amazed at my cunning or my insensibility to totalitarian atrocities; they saw my stance as the height of hypocrisy. But it was not, perhaps, hypocrisy. In the teaching of "Ketman" practiced by Mohammedan heretics in Persia (it is not unlike the Jesuit *reservatio mentalis*), a distinction was made between the goal toward which we fervently and passionately strive and the veils by which the prudent screen it from view. After an era of liberal loosening up, the human species, or at least the greater part of it, was once more entering a period when, unfortunately, refined methods of keeping silent were needful. I pass over the usual cynics bred in such circumstances; their subterfuges are shallow. On the long list of my shortcomings I would not include cynicism. In spite of its great cruelties, I praised my time and I did not yearn for any other. Nor did I pine for Poland's prewar social-economic order; anyone who dreamed of its resurrection was my adversary. In this sense, my service at the Embassy coincided with my conviction. However, I wished my country a considerably better fate than that of a Stalinist province. Similarly, I wished something much better for Polish literature than the half-witted police theories that had gradually come to enmesh it. I drew strength from my friendship with Tiger, from the wrath and sarcasm of that passionate pilgrim. He believed that it was our duty to carry the precious values of our European heritage across the dark era, even though one were to be surrounded for whole decades by nothing but absurdity, blood, and feces. Wear a mask, throw them off the scent—you will be forgiven if you preserve the love of the Good within you.

I have no intention of covering up our wretchedness. We were held in political pincers of a kind that previous generations, happily for them, had rarely known. Tiger, to someone who judged only his exterior without entering into more complex motives, might be pitiful, perhaps even contemptible. But let his would-be accusers not fall into the trap of their pharisaic virtue, which can be upheld only as long as they see a simple contrast between white and black. Tiger was filled with a great dread. In truth, he was a Franz Kafka abandoned in the middle of a planetary cata- clysm. To defend himself and what he loved from the intellectu- ally inferior, he had only his intelligence, and he never doubted that it would triumph, although the moment of its public unveil- ing was still far off. Thus he behaved like those insects who re- semble a piece of bark or a blade of grass.

In his letters from Paris, when he still had refugee status, he jokingly described his talks to émigré groups. Did he lie in those lectures? Not exactly. The double meaning in speeches about free- dom probably eluded his listeners. He used to complain to me that "Fascists pay too little." As I read this—or another aphorism: "A system that cannot guarantee us a few francs a month is doomed to extinction"—I never attributed it to self-interest on his part. If the émigrés, instead of raving about "pure politics," which led nowhere, had founded research institutes and publish- ing houses, and subsidized the intellectuals, they would have shown they were worth something. If the capitalistic West had known how to support people like Tiger, instead of leaving their success or failure up to chance, it would not have been what it was. Tiger and his wife, both bookworms, had modest needs. "Fascists pay too little": the humorous wink disguised an intricate reasoning. If they pay us (philosophers, poets, artists) too little, it is because they hold us in contempt, which proves they are re- actionaries destined to lose. Their defeat will be accomplished through us, as a just punishment for the iniquities of exploitation and colonialism.

Powerless Europe in 1948 had already been described in the Book of Joshua. The inhabitants of the land of Canaan trembled when the Israelites arrived on the Jordan, because they knew that the Lord had delivered Canaan over to the newcomers and that nothing could resist His will. At the sound of the Israelite trumpets, dismay filled the hearts of Jericho's defenders. Now the trumpet of Communism resounded so loudly in Paris that the more discerning were convinced that efforts to resist the verdict of historical Providence would be futile, and they decided to imitate the harlot, Rahab, who saved herself and her family by aiding the Israelite spies. Or, if one prefers, there are other chapters of biblical fulfillment from which to draw analogies. The citizens of the declining Roman Empire, eaten up by boredom and inner emptiness, wandering over a wasteland touched by drought, felt weak in the face of Christian fanatics announcing the good news of the Last Judgment. Thus when Tiger spoke of "Christians," it was understood he meant Communists. The allegory was justified insofar as the idea of inevitable progress or of a hidden force behind the scenes—implacable toward all who disobeyed the Teacher's commands—took its origins from Christianity: without Christianity, after all, there would have been no Hegel or Marx. The sacred merely underwent secularization, the immanent replaced the transcendent.

In any case, should not the wise man have drawn conclusions from the inevitable? Of what use were the courage and energy of Julian the Apostate, who endeavored to resuscitate the cult of pagan gods? He who resisted change then was certainly not a friend of humanity. The convert, on the other hand, served the Good if he built a bridge between Christianity and Plato. Was that not the position we were in? Tiger, of course, adored Hypatia, the last pagan philosopher of Alexandria, not the dirty, terrifying mob of Christians who tore her apart. And yet, he said, the future did not belong to Hypatia but to the Christians.

Tiger envied my placement in the right camp, although it was due not to my merits but to circumstances. He implored me to restrain myself, for there was no lack of heartrending shrieks in my letters to him; it is unpleasant to be surrounded, as I was every day at the Embassy, by shrewd fellows who fidgeted nervously whenever you chatted with them, so anxious were they to run to their typewriters and punch out a report on some unorthodox remark dropped by their colleague. Today, reflecting on Tiger's political maneuvers in Paris, I see many reasons for his behavior. I think about it as if I were plunging into my own life to snatch from its tangle of many threads that most essential strand of my own destiny.

It does not matter how we name the basic opposition: heaviness and lightness; life taken as it is and life shaped anew; matter and spirit; walking on all fours and soaring in flight. What was my mutiny as an adolescent and then as a young man if not a refusal of that directionless existence of "hogs"? As a child I safeguarded myself against grownups by my passion for nature, my aquariums, my ornithological books. To grow up and destroy that élan which they, in their sobriety, disdained seemed awful to me. My almost unhealthy conviction that sexuality is evil may have had its source not only in the teachings of our Father Prefect but also in those moments when, as a child, I observed that it is precisely sexuality that makes fools of adults, weighing them down, depriving them of the capacity for disinterested enthusiasm.

My hero was the brave nineteenth-century naturalist, such an ardent collector of insects that on his wedding day he forgot about his beloved waiting at the church; he was discovered in his tails, high in the branches of a tree where he was just about to lower his top hat over a rare species of beetle; at this sight the bride-to-be fell fainting into her mother's arms and the enthusiast of knowledge remained a bachelor forever.

In choosing poetry later on, I remained loyal to the pledge I made to myself: that I would never be like them and succumb to the force of inertia. Through poetry, in other words, I wanted to save my childhood. But what fiery sword protects the artist? Only his faith in an objective value. For those who live passively, values melt away; they wane in the encounter with what is considered the "real." Herein lies the secret of their impotent lives. And hence the traditional alliance between artists and revolutionaries.

Because revolutionaries, with or without success, also search for objectively grounded values. They are saved by their violent "yes" or "no," by their upsetting the somnolent routine into which spiritual heaviness imprisons us. Their deed is equivalent to the creative act of an artist; it lifts them above themselves by demanding full surrender: no one puts words on paper or paint on canvas doubting; if one doubts, one does so five minutes later.

If Tiger in Paris leaned to the side of the Communists, it was because philosophy for him was an art, an incessant effort to acquire oneness (of the same sort that the scholar in tails and top hat achieved while perched in the tree). Being in the right camp was a calculation, yes, but of a higher order. Because he who does not constantly overcome himself—i.e., does not learn and does not act—disintegrates within; but if a man is to grow, social reality must be flexible, not rigid, not established as it is in the West. And nothing other than that chaos of new forms, after all, had made me decide to stick to People's Poland. It was my shield against those who spend all their time earning, spending, and amusing themselves.

It is worth noting that Tiger, although he scoffed at Romanticism, was himself a Romantic. His hatred for the "hogs" was a hatred for an unphilosophical way of life, or to put it another way, for *l'homme sensuel moyen*. The latter had to be made into a philosophical being, even if he had to be terrorized into it. I understood, more or less, that our friendship was nourished by my old resentment toward nature, my fear of her cruelties—*nature* meaning both the one outside us and the one within us. I could disapprove of my pride and my contempt, which masked my fear, but I doubt whether any kind of psychoanalysis would have cured me of impeding my feelings, which I constantly filtered through irony, because nature builds a trap out of them and lures us into animal satiation that lets us pass our lives without leaving a trace.

L'homme sensuel moyen in Poland had every reason to yearn for distant America because to him it really was heaven, while the dictatorship of the Party was hell. It made me ashamed to think of Kijo, on whose farm I had once dug potatoes. Now I was as far above him as the old aristocrats with their jabots and swords. Had not the Romantic dividing of people into those called to the things of the spirit and those who are ordinary breadwinners been grafted onto the new social relationships, thus confirming the common origin of Romanticism and Marxism? Tiger could declare his love for people, but only "people" as an idea; in reality he feared the man in the street, who was insensitive to the subtleties of the intellect and absorbed in his biology. That boor should not be allowed to touch him; one had to intimidate the boor. In the capitalist system he becomes a bit too bold if he can jangle money in his pockets. I was less subject than Tiger to that fear, thanks no doubt to my rural-patriarchal remembrances from childhood. My tradition was more "populist" than his, and through that I was exposed to the temptations of common sense. Economics, for example, was not translatable for him, as it was for me, into images of plows, horseshoes, buckets, varieties of crops. In fact he had no notion at all about economics. Primarily, he was concerned with the need for defense against the primitive thinking of the rightist intelligentsia and against its biological penchant for nationalism. And I was with him in this because of my own hostility to the Right. Give them a parliamentary multiparty system and they would start flexing their muscles, while he, Tiger, would stand before them naked and defenseless.

At the beginning of summer in 1949, I boarded a plane for Europe. Flying over Newfoundland, where the snow was just barely melting, I thought of the countryside around Wilno. It would have been covered over with the same gray moss of coniferous forests dotted with the clear eyes of lakes. Then, in the icy twilight, the black ocean was below us with white plumes of icebergs. In the morning, the emerald color of Ireland. After America, Paris reminded me of sleepy Bruges, which I had visited before the war. Instead of canals there was the Seine, where swans could have glided and ivy could have completely enveloped the old stones. For me, there was a close connection between that tranquility and the vogue for Existentialism and Communism. They were just talking in their sleep. I munched *hors d'œuvres* while exchanging polite clichés with a crowd of "progressive" writers at various receptions, but I did not attempt to break down the wall that stood between me and them. Their warmed-over Jacobin ideas did not coincide with any reality; they were social diversions. It was not my place to enlighten them or to betray what I thought of them.

But how sweet to recover my past in the narrow streets near the Panthéon, where once I had walked to my classes and to the swimming pool. It was a Proustian experience. While my footsteps and Tiger's echoed in those streets, I was both the new and the old me; I felt the strangeness of time passing and of the city, unchanged by time, waiting for our encounter. In the familiar wink of Tiger's black eyes, I read the whole distance I had covered from my days as a student and a beginning poet here, groping about in a magma of words and feelings, as yet unprepared for the dryness and agility of an intellect such as Tiger's.

Our friendship was not an exchange between equals who give and take mutually from each other. He wanted to dominate me completely, so he hoisted himself onto a teacher's platform and from there directed a threatening finger at me. He did it jokingly, but he was quite serious. I accepted the position of an inferior, a faithful listener, although some of my silences shook his self-assurance because they told of my reservations. This tactic was in keeping with my hygienic habits: one should yield as much ground as possible to one's partner, since what cannot be defended is not worth being defended. Even so, we found ourselves more than once raising our voices against each other. But I felt at home with his historicism, so I profited from those lessons. Yet my inner castle did not fade; on the contrary, it acquired clarity, thanks to the contradiction. In America, the contradiction inclined me toward *movement*, while in Paris, through my conversations with Tiger, it drove me back toward *being*, and I tried to diagnose my case. Whoever commits himself to movement alone will destroy himself. Whoever disregards movement will also destroy himself, but in a different way. This, I said to myself, is the very core of my destiny—never to be satisfied with one or the other, only at moments to seize the unity of these opposites.

Tiger had just entered the French Communist Party. Later, after his return to Poland, this proved to be a thoroughly useless step. Not to go back would probably have been impossible for him; perhaps if he had known how to put himself across in book form, he could have found something to do abroad; but he wrote with difficulty and his language conveyed nothing of that dance, that mimicry, that brilliant acting-out of his ideas. To express himself bodily he had to have a group of friends responsive to every allusion, people, that is, who shared common historical experiences. He could find that only in Warsaw.

To prepare himself for his journey into lands he knew to be gloomy, he decided to limber up by rubbing himself with the ointment of slogans. For instance, I knew he was repelled by the saccharine, humanity-loving stanzas of Aragon and the rest of the French Communists. But now the sentimental speeches, articles, and poems did not infuriate him; they moved him, because Zeus (historical Providence) had given them his blessing. True, his emotion was more like that of a father surrounded by prattling children: "Not bad for seven-year-olds, not bad." He could manage nicely rounded sentences of praise for something, and immediately after (even though we might have been completely alone) whisper *into my ear*: "Trash!" He used to say that there was an "odor of brimstone" about Communist meetings, and the shiver that ran through him when he smelled that brimstone came from the pleasure of intellectual penetration: Evil is a test of what is *real*. Thus when the unpleasant subject of concentration camps cropped up in our conversation, there were always two stages in his response. First he would wither and contract: although he was splendidly informed about the millions of people behind barbed wire, he did not want to "weaken"; that is, to imagine the extent of their suffering. Then he would break into yells: he accused me of common sense (which is reactionary), of sympathy for fools—and here, for a second, he was sincere, for it afforded him satisfaction that fools—i.e., unphilosophical creatures who could threaten him, delicate Franz Kafka—were being oppressed. That would never happen to him, of course, because he was clever. It seemed as if cruelty, if it were abstract enough, strengthened his convictions: the more shadow a thing makes, the greater and more powerful it is. But if he kept himself pumped up with the lives of the saints—Thorez's autobiography, *Le Fils du peuple*, lay on his night table—for balance he read Arthur Koestler and Orwell's *1984*. Such a reading diet provided him with the necessary "historical humor."

What is this monster, historical necessity, that paralyzed my contemporaries with fear? I was stopped by that question. It should be remembered that, not being a so-called Westerner, I harbored some strong resentments. We can rub our hands now; those Westerners will get what they deserve. They did not prevent the build-up of Hitler's war machine, although it lay in their power. They did not come to Poland's aid, although they had sworn to. At the Nuremberg Trials, General Jodl admitted that the Germans escaped disaster in September 1939 only because the 110 French and English divisions failed to take action against the 25 German divisions left behind on the Western front, and Marshal Keitel revealed that the German General Staff had been amazed by that inaction. One could have interpreted the Allies' behavior, both then and later, in two ways: either as a series of mistakes on the part of their statesmen, or as the inevitable consequence of a mysterious paralysis. If, however, one applied the popular saying "When the Lord God desires to punish somebody he takes away his reason," one was but a step away from recognizing a general law. I did not spend as much time pondering that problem then as I did later; there are monsters that cannot be subdued in hand-to-hand combat. One must tear oneself away from their gaze and look into oneself. I was prevented from that then by my human situation. And, to tell the truth, I was more taken up with how things actually were than with establishing general laws. The fact was that we were firmly lodged inside a totalitarian system.

The reasons for my quarrel with Tiger went deep into his as well as my own past; doubtless the concrete traditions I had brought out of my childhood, when I used to wander through the forests with a gun, and my mother's peasant-Lithuanian practicality disposed me to look rather indulgently on the too slick, city-bred flights of his thought. This is just what bothered him. It may be that I was better anchored in history than he, although he was superior to me in the agility of his mind. I did not approve of the plus sign he placed next to the idea of necessity. What has to be (if we ourselves do not fool ourselves into believing it has to be) simply is, but there is no immanent divinity that guarantees the moral glory of what is irreversible. If there were, we would have to pay homage, for example, to that Mohammedan guard in a Stalinist jail who advised a Polish prisoner to sign what was asked of him, exclaiming: *"Allah dayët polozhenye!"* [Russian for "Allah provides the situation!"]. By this reasoning, Allah invested Stalin with power; therefore whoever respects Allah yields to power. But the prisoner did not believe in an immanent Reason embodied in the secret police, and he resisted. In so doing, he pushed back the boundaries of necessity.

The problem with choosing between madness (a refusal to recognize necessity) and servility (an acknowledgment of our complete powerlessness) is that one act of obedience can be the start of a downward slide. A man cannot bear the thought of being crushed by a physical compulsion; therefore he deifies the force that rules over him, investing it with superhuman traits, with omniscient reason, with a special mission; and in this way he saves a bit of his own dignity. The Russian writer Belinsky, for instance, made use of Hegel during a certain phase of his life, to deify czardom. I realized that my freedom of maneuver remained

intact only as long as I lived abroad behind the screen of diplomatic service, and yet I was threatened with sliding because we
are drawn into compromise almost without our being aware of it.
My support was none other than Tiger. Like Penelope, he ripped
what he was weaving and treated his political speeches as no
more than a comic opera set to the music of impeccable ortho-
doxy. At the same time he swore that another, a humanist revolution would follow, and it was for this, his revolution, that we
ought to work. A tender friend, he was very demanding of those
he loved: what was allowed to inferior beings was not for people
whose salvation he cared about. He put me on my guard against
those unfortunates (especially pro-government Catholics) who
were condemned in advance to become tools of the secret police.

He also advised me to stay as far away as possible from the literary milieu. Writers, with few exceptions, he did not take seriously. He thought they lacked the intellectual training for their
new status, and for that reason had to sink to the rank of common
lackeys. Of course he heartily despised "Zhdanovism," but he
found it understandable that the phenomena of decay in Western
literature and art had to provoke an equally lifeless attack. Whoever bears the taint of bad style deserves no better. For him the
artificial sweetness in the works of French Communists corre-
sponded to the decadent traits of the French literary language.
He encouraged me to write about that taint. Only one contemporary French writer found grace in his eyes—a Thomist, Étienne
Gilson—and he was an enemy, because anything that smacked of
Aristotle was a personal insult to that admirer of Plato.

Tiger forbade me to publish certain poems. For example, the
poem I wrote after a stopover in Detroit. After being taken up to
the twentieth floor by the hotel porter, I sat in my plush and overheated room, near the radio trickling music, and looked down at
the neons below me, the garages, the traffic—metal fish circulating in an aquarium—and was so powerfully struck by the universal blunting of human desires here that an image crossed my
mind of a man being sucked out from inside as one sucks out an

egg through a straw. And from that image came a poem about man torn from himself, about alienation. No political motives prompted me. Tiger, however, was of the opinion that the specialists in anti-Americanism would be too pleased by the work and would pervert my intention by reading into it a zeal to bend to Party directives.

Tiger was contradictory, someone will object. But only for those who have never found themselves inside a magic circle. Perhaps, too, my attempt to present his tricks and leaps is awkward; the word never exactly fits the serpent's undulations or the cat's soft fur. His grimaces, snorts, shouts, the whole theater, I always looked upon as but temporary disguises of the real Tiger. The real Tiger was one with the real, the deeper, me, revealed through poetry. Poetry is a constant self-negation; it imitates Heraclitean fluidity. And only poetry is optimistic in the twentieth century, through its sensual avidity, its premonitions of change, its prophecies with many meanings. Even if we leave no immortal works behind us, the discipline itself is worthy of praise. Tiger shrugged off my populist nostalgia with impatience; yet in bestowing upon me the glorious title of dialectician, he was alluding favorably to my origins; that is, to feudal vestiges unencumbered by petit bourgeois habits. This meant, more or less, that he would not have thought well of me had I eliminated the tension born of the conflict between thesis and antithesis; in other words, had I either lapsed into the comfort of moral intransigency or attached myself solely to the present by writing for the Party. But poetic discipline is impossible without piety and admiration, without faith in the infinite layers of being that are hidden within an apple, a man, or a tree; it challenges one through becoming to move closer to what *is*. Such was my inner castle, a castle of prayer, and our friendship was secured by my resistance.

All the same, ordinary human despair must be given its just due. From Paris I went to Poland, where I spent my vacation. The whole country was bursting with suppressed hatred for its rulers and their Russian employers. The Normans after the conquest of England could not have been more isolated from the population than the new privileged caste (I, by the very cut of my clothes, carried the mark of that caste), and more than once I noticed fear in the eyes of those who passed me in the street. Terror is not, as Western intellectuals imagine, monumental; it is abject, it has a furtive glance, it destroys the fabric of human society and changes the relationships of millions of individuals into channels for blackmail. In addition, Poland's economy, a captive of ideological requirements, made one's hair stand on end. It brought to mind Gulliver's observations about the land of the Balnibarbi, administered by the enlightened Academy of Projectors, where "the people [at the top] are too much taken up in their own speculations to have regard to what passed here below," and where "the people in the streets walked fast, looked wild, their eyes fixed, and were generally in rags."

No wonder, then, that Paris, after such a vacation, was not very gay, nor was that morning when my plane, because of a slight defect in the motor, stopped in New Brunswick, Canada, after a night flight over the ocean—even though the green landscape at dawn delighted me as I breathed in the fragrance of the spruce forests. I fell into a crisis that was to drag out over whole months, made more painful because there was no one with whom I could share my burden. An American could not have understood such strange modern conflicts. In official Washington there resided only one poet, though one, it must be said, of high caliber: St.-John Perse. It was he to whom I confided my misery. It seems I bored him terribly. The author of *Anabasis*, ensconced in his lofty solitude of a voluntary exile, looked upon the moral tempests and struggles of his contemporaries as one regards the ebb and flow of the sea. I attempted, nonetheless, to squeeze the opinion out of him about literature as action, about a writer's responsibility when he sees that he can get through the net of censorship only at the cost of daily concessions. I spoke badly. I stammered. In that glittering light (sun, neon, the chirping of birds—cardinals, their red like the red in the seventeenth-century paintings of La Tour) Europe lost the weight of existence, and I tried in vain to explain my turmoil.

No one will blame me, perhaps, for having sought out authorities. That was my purpose when, instead of going straight from New York to Washington one day, I turned off for Princeton. Princeton to me meant two streets. On one lived Christian Gauss, the Professor Emeritus of French Literature; he and Mrs. Gauss, old Parisians, had been contemporaries and friends of Oscar Milosz. On the other stood Albert Einstein's little house. My irony and sarcasm only somersaulted on the surface; they did not destroy my childlike enthusiasm for people and human affairs. My nature demanded that I bend my knee before something or someone—to praise. Einstein's white mane, his gray sweatshirt with the fountain pen clipped to the front of it at the neck, his soft voice, the serene gestures of his hands in front of an old wooden statuette of the Madonna, everything about him appealed to my father complex, my yearning for a protector and leader. I felt remorseful toward him because of the disgrace of what had happened during the first Congress in Defense of Peace, held in Wrocław, Poland, in 1948: fear of the Russians prevented his appeal from being read—it called for the creation of a world government to control atomic energy. I was grateful for his melancholy smile, proof that he understood, that he did not condemn people who are powerless in spite of their good will.

To tell the truth, Einstein could not have helped me. In the problem that interested me, he was moving upon uncertain ground. As an exile he had no fondness for that condition, and he reacted more on an emotional level: "You had better stick to your country." His advice did not surprise me because I had repeated the same thing to myself often enough. To justify it he fell back on his optimism: one should not be hasty; the terror and the absurdity of dogmas will not last forever; no, they certainly have to end sometime. Despite all my veneration for him, a little ironical imp in me tore him from the pedestal that people had erected to this successor of Newton, and I saw him as one of many, part of a certain generation of Europeans. He was a humanitarian; his mind had been formed in an era when nothing could have shaken the prevailing assumption that man is a reasonable creature, and that if he falls into madness it is only temporary. The criterion for that era had been the individual man, who dominated the collectivity, who was safeguarded by inviolable law and empowered to protest by the ballot. But for my generation man was already the plaything of demonic powers born not in himself but in an interhuman space created by both him and his fellow-man. So I walked out of the little house on Mercer Street and my car door banged shut, and I drove past the mileage signs numbly, a stranger to my own body. All of us yearn naïvely for a certain point on the earth where the highest wisdom accessible to humanity at a given moment dwells, and it is hard to admit that such a point does not exist, that we have to rely only upon ourselves.

Nevertheless, in the fall of 1950 I said farewell to America. That was probably the most painful decision of my life—though none other was permissible. During my four-and-a-half-year stay, I had grown attached to the country and wished it the best. Its overheated civilization may have sometimes irritated me, but at the same time I had never come across so many good people ready to help their neighbor, a trait that could be all the more valued by this newcomer from the outer shadows, where to jump at one's neighbor's throat was the rule. Yes, but even if I had consented to a separation from Tiger—Tiger, already a professor in Warsaw, I mention here only as a symbol of *all* hope, of that hope to which his undulating leaps gave assent; that whoever proposes Marxism to mankind takes in hand a scorpion whose tail is filled with the dialectical poison—even if I had wanted to cancel my share in the community the easy way, old-fashioned honor would never have permitted me to flee in such a manner. To announce that I intended to stay in America and obtain a position at some university would have been too simple and, therefore, ugly. For an average American my behavior would look insane, but I did not deceive myself either, and when I embarked in New York my teeth were chattering.

ZYGMUNT HERTZ

Z YGMUNT, a buzzing bee in search of the sweetness of
life, and the demonism of great historic events: it is difficult to reconcile the one with the other. He grew up in
Poland in the 1920s, when virtually nothing of what was to happen later seemed possible. He came from a respectable family and
I assume that those who knew him before the war could see in
him many character traits that were common to the spoiled only
sons of patrician families. A handsome man, reasonably well-to-
do, who ordered his clothing from fine tailors; an habitué of cafés
and dance halls, sociable, popular, he probably had a reputation as
a typical gilded youth, although his enlightened, well-educated
father, a social worker in Łódź and also a bit of a littérateur, had
infected him with a love of books. After completing his studies
and his military service in an artillery academy, Zygmunt became
an office worker in the Solvay firm, which sold caustic soda. He
made a decent salary, bought automobiles, traveled, lived. He met
a young woman who had recently completed her law studies and
was already making a name for herself in a law firm, and he
married her. Zosia was lovely and her beauty went hand in hand

with exceptional virtues of character, which Zygmunt probably noticed immediately. He was quick-witted and impressionable, and, I think, had a thoroughly cheerful temperament, and thus he was free of any pangs of conscience because he had so many earthly goods and so much happiness and others did not. His skepticism and, as it were, innate liberalism protected him from both the profound soul-searching and the ideologies of our century. A private man by temperament and predilection, he shied away from politics.

When the two totalitarian states concluded the Ribbentrop-Molotov pact, replete with a clause about the division of the spoils, and unleashed the Second World War, Zygmunt was thirty-one years old. The division was carried out and as a result of the official slogan—*Nikakoi Pol'shi nikogda ne budet* [There will never again be any kind of a Poland]—roughly one and a half million Polish citizens were deported into the depths of Russia. Among them were Zygmunt and his wife, who were sent to fell timber in the Mari Autonomous Republic. His life as a lumberjack was to surface repeatedly in Zygmunt's conversation. The convoy of citizens of a state that had ceased to exist, sent off to the northern forests, came upon piles of wood that had been lying there for years due to lack of transportation and by now were rotted, like the already rotted remains of the Kuban Cossacks, the people who had chopped down that wood—which did not put the newcomers in too joyous a mood.

When I met Zygmunt in 1951, he had already lived through the exodus of Anders's army, Iran, Iraq, and the Italian campaign, after which the demobilized artillery lieutenant Hertz had attached himself to the three-man cooperative in Rome that founded the publishing house which was officially called the Instytut Literacki [Literary Institute] but was popularly known by the title of its journal, *Kultura* [Culture], and which was shortly afterward transferred to Maisons-Laffitte on the outskirts of Paris. Obviously, I have no intention of writing the history of *Kultura* here, but a few observations seem to be unavoidable.

Time is the enemy of our attempts at preserving reality, for it keeps piling new layers upon already existing layers, so that it is inevitable that we keep on projecting into the past. The great terror in Poland in 1951 already escapes our imagination, but it is easier to understand its causes than the phase through which the West European, or at least Parisian, spirit was then passing. This spirit, if we are to believe its pen-wielding spokesmen, was wallowing in existential melancholy because of its lost chance, that is, because the western part of the continent had been liberated by the wrong, read "capitalist," army. The few people who stammered out that maybe this was actually for the good were condemned as American agents, socially ostracized, and also dragged into the courts. The trial of David Rousset, a former prisoner of Hitler's concentration camps and author of the book *L'Univers concentrationnaire*, was being held at that time. He had the audacity to write somewhere that there are concentration camps in Russia, too; hence the trial for libel (I don't recall on what acrobatic legal foundation it was mounted) brought against him by *L'Humanité*. Under these conditions, the émigré journal *Kultura* was absolutely isolated; in other words, the situation bore no resemblance at all to the position of the émigrés after 1831, when the European spirit welcomed them as the defenders of freedom—which frequently counted for far more than the disapprobation of governments. In our century, only at the end of the fifties or, for good measure, only in the sixties, was there a lifting of the taboo, that is, a grudging admission that émigré journals are not necessarily the hangouts of scoundrels, fascists, and agents, and that one might even invite their contributors to one's home.

So there was Zygmunt in an unavoidably heroic situation simply because, despite his inclinations, he had done some instructive traveling and now could only shrug his shoulders at the buffoonery and disgrace of the European mind strolling along boulevard Saint-Germain. Also because while other old hands like him quietly busied themselves with making money in this

West that wasn't, after all, the worst of all places, he had become a member of a cooperative that couldn't have been more obviously dedicated to impractical goals. Worse yet, he, such a private person, who so loved his own belongings and his own ways, had stumbled into a commune. This word has acquired so many meanings that perhaps it would be better to replace it with another word: *phalanstery*. This will not change the fact that *Kultura* was an insane undertaking that, for want of money, could exist only if its cooperative lived together, ate together, and worked together, giving to each according to his modest needs, no more. Zygmunt, I suspect, must have felt tempted to leave many a time. And considering his talent for getting along with people, his knowledge of languages, his energy, industriousness, he would have succeeded anywhere, in whatever he undertook to do. But he had made an emotional investment. Wonder of wonders, that commune or phalanstery or *kolkhoz*, the *Kultura* community, was to endure for decades.

The beginnings of our friendship. That first *Kultura* house, a rented *pavillon*, immensely ugly and inconvenient, on the avenue Corneille; the cold of winter in the outskirts of Paris, with scant heat from the potbellied *chaudières*, loaded with coal; and that district of chestnut-tree-lined avenues that went on for kilometers, piles of dry leaves, and also something reminiscent of the nineteenth century in Tver or Sarajevo. It was there that Zygmunt became the witness of my by no means imaginary sufferings. And though someone may remark that it is his own fault if a humiliated man suffers, since he deserves punishment for his pride, still, the pain is not any the less.

I started writing *The Captive Mind* on avenue Corneille, but the simplest questions were missing from it, for I truly had no one whom I could ask them of. If, as long as I remained on the Communist side, I benefited not only from material but also from moral privileges, on what incomprehensible magic grounds had I, escaping from there, been transformed into an individual whom everyone considered suspect? After all, over there it was sufficient not to be with them one hundred percent, to publish a "Moral [or dissident, as we would now say] Treatise" and be engaged in translating Shakespeare, to be considered a decent man. And a second, or maybe the same, question: Does an animal have the right to escape from a forest that has changed ownership? The European spirit had a ready-made opinion on this and it stood guard with a double-barreled shotgun, that European spirit incarnated in my Paris of Éluard, Aragon, Neruda, with whom I used to share a drink not so long ago. Because Zygmunt also knew about my miserable financial situation and visa complications, which caused me to be separated from my family for three years, he considered my situation to be dreadful. He watched over me tenderly, took care of me, and whenever I went to the city he made sure that I had a couple of francs for lunch and cigarettes. When I accepted his offerings, I was too preoccupied with my own troubles to value those gifts at the time, but I did not forget about them, and for years afterward there was a good deal of ordinary gratitude in my affection for him.

Zygmunt was already a fatty at that time, but vigorous, with a thickset body, healthy. A glutton, a gourmand, a tippler, and above all a talker, the personification of jovial humor and a passion for sociability. I say "passion" because he seemed to have a built-in radar that directed him unerringly to warm relations with others, to laughter, gossip, anecdotes, stories. He could not have borne isolation. And he himself radiated such warmth that in the gloomy house on the avenue Corneille he would take the chill out of whatever the stoves could not warm up. He often irritated me with his excesses: he would keep popping into the study, its air thick with the smoke from my cigarettes, for I lived and wrote there, and just sit down and begin a conversation; his desire to do so was stronger than his decision not to get in the way.

"Czesiu, don't talk, you'll say something stupid. Write." Zygmunt's advice, which I often repeated to myself later on, was very apt, and it referred to my bad habit of pronouncing extreme, offensive opinions out of spite. His advice was directed especially at my relations with *Kultura*, which at that time were not particularly harmonious. After all, we were creatures who were neither made nor molded in the same ways, and our meeting, at the intersection of different orbits, did not take place without friction, for which my provocations were chiefly responsible. Zygmunt, as his advice indicates, did not let himself be taken in, because he distinguished between my spoken and my written speech. He tolerated the former; the latter, he trusted.

I didn't treat Zygmunt as a friend at that time, as someone whom one chooses and with whom one is supposed to have an intellectual understanding. He was more like a classmate, assigned to us without our participation. I sought other partners for my talmudic hair-splitting. In my eyes Zygmunt was a preserved specimen of the prewar intelligentsia, who had been formed by *Wiadomości Literackie* [The Literary News], *Cyrulik* [The Barber], *Szpilki* [Pins], with a philosophy transmitted by Boy and Słonimski of "The Weekly Chronicles," while I was bent on breaking away from prewar Poland in both its manifestations— the liberal and the "national." And yet, as it turned out once again, intellectual friendships and loves often take a dramatic turn, while those other ones, founded on sympathies that are harder to grasp, are often more enduring. We were not standing still, after all; we were changing, Zygmunt and I, in a way that, I think, brought us closer.

Identity crises are thresholds in everyone's life on which we can smash ourselves to pieces. To know who one is, what role to adopt and in relation to which group of people, even a small group, how one is viewed by others: in all of this, one's profession plays a prominent, if not key, role. That is also why I have never advised individuals who were already immersed in certain professions to emigrate from Poland—especially not writers and actors. I myself, after all, had to change my profession and accept the fact that in the eyes of those who surrounded me I would be only a university professor. Before that came to pass, I had accumulated a good many interesting experiences. The obstacles aren't what's important here, although I was certainly hurt when a young Parisian author, who had been recommended to me as a translator, said outright that he would love to translate me, but if he did, he could publish nothing of his own because "they" control the literary journals. Some years later I was overcome with hollow laughter when I learned that a famous Parisian publishing house had given my new book (*Native Realm*) to a Party writer from Warsaw to referee—which is better, to be sure, than the French police of the nineteenth century gathering information about émigrés in the czarist embassy. But let me not exaggerate the obstacles. In 1953 I represented France in the Prix Européen in Geneva, although the French jury surely knew that my manuscript was a translation from the Polish. It was success that terrified me, because that's when I realized that in writing for foreigners I did not know and could not know who I am, and that it was necessary to end my French career. These adventures could not but lower my aspirations. I chose my language, unknown in the world at large; that is, I chose the role of a poet of Vistulania, as Zygmunt called it.

In light of these adventures of mine, I can summarize Zygmunt's great internal battles as I observed them; I came to feel more and more respect for him because of them. Those who have held in their hands the *Kultura* annuals and the books published by the Literary Institute, and those who will hold them in their hands in the future, ought to think for a moment about the kitchen pots, the preparation of breakfast, dinner, and supper by those same three or four individuals who were also responsible for editing, proofreading, and distribution, for washing up, for doing the shopping, fortunately an easy task in France, and should multiply the number of these and similar domestic tasks by the number of days, months, and years. And also think about string, about wrapping paper, about dragging, carrying, handing over the parcels at the post office. Zygmunt's identity crisis was not unrelated to his former self-indulgence; that is, to his unenthusiastic purging of his self-will. Had he had a taste for renunciation, were he an ideological fanatic, he could have entered more easily into the skin of a manager, a cook's assistant, a shipping clerk, and a porter. But his relations with ideas were always less than cordial. Absolutely polite, loyal, he opened up only to people, not to far-reaching intentions which were abstractions for him. Who should he have been, how did his acquaintances, and perhaps he himself, view him? The director of a large, smoothly functioning enterprise, several telephones on his desk, secretaries, conferences, and, at home in his villa, an infinitely generous, genial host, a patron of artists, a collector of *objets d'art*, a benefactor of orphanages and hospitals. Undoubtedly all this was within his grasp, only under the condition that he get started in good time. But in the meantime, year after year slipped away in packing, transporting the packages in a handcart to the Maisons-Laffitte station, loading them into the train, unloading them at the Gare Saint-Lazare, shopping, cooking, etc.

Only if a collective lasts long enough will it appear *ex post* as an idyll, on the strength of its very survival. As a matter of fact, its daily life is full of tensions between individuals, and since Zygmunt was sensitive to individuals, he often suffered greatly. For it is not easy to accept the modest place that somebody has to occupy in a collective, and although it is clear that somebody has to take on the jobs for the physically strongest, this demands no small amount of self-discipline. Zygmunt's struggles with himself, his search for solutions, and finally his acceptance of the identity of an almost anonymous worker——that is the substance of his mature years.

Again I must turn to the distortions introduced by time. If one were to believe the Warsaw press of the 1950s, *Kultura* was a powerful institution that was equipped by the Americans, almost the equivalent of Free Europe, with the same number of personnel (everyone judges by his own situation) as is necessary in Poland to publish a journal and books. Visitors from Poland were astonished to discover that this picture had nothing in common with reality and was one more example of the fabrication of legends in which the creators of those legends themselves eventually begin to believe. But today, when *Kultura* has passed its thirtieth anniversary, the significance if not the image ascribed to *Kultura* at that time no longer looks like an exaggeration. For *Kultura* undoubtedly has exceeded in longevity and in influence everything that the Great Emigration achieved after 1831, and has its chapter in the history of Polish writing, or, quite simply, in the history of Poland. Lo and behold, Zygmunt the bee, buzzing today above otherworldly meadows, is a historical personage. Only, when he made his choice, he did not know he would become one. The whole undertaking could have fallen to pieces and vanished without a trace, or the uncertain, unpredictable political conditions in Europe could have put an end to such experiments.

Can fat people experience deep emotions? Zygmunt was a combination of delicacy and gluttony, emotional circumspection and hooting laughter. His abdomen continued to grow larger and he came to resemble Zagłoba. Marek Hłasko addressed him as "Uncle." But Zagłoba's mouth probably wasn't shaped like his: very sensual and somehow infantile, prepared to accept a pacifier or a swig of aqua vitae, capricious and nervous. He was born a hedonist and he was governed by the pleasure principle. And he found an abundance of pleasure in this world. Thanks chiefly to him, the necessity of a communal kitchen at *Kultura* turned into delights of the table, into feasts, revelries, because there was no stinting on food at least. Guests—non-stop, from everywhere, from European countries, from Poland, from America—assuaged his passion for company, his enormous curiosity about faces, characters, biographies. The trips to Paris with the packages gave him the opportunity to meet with one person or another over a glass of wine, to talk and gossip and watch the crowd. So it was that by following his natural inclinations Zygmunt discovered his true calling and his talent. And when he discovered it, everything began to fall into a discernible pattern, the individual scattered pieces of the puzzle of predestination now fit together, and what at first had seemed resignation turned out to be the most ambitious of choices.

In brief, Zygmunt was a *philanthropos* by calling, a friend of people, and his ability to do good for people could have found no better application anywhere than in that peculiar zone "between Poland and abroad." Zygmunt lived and breathed Vistulania; he empathized, flew into a fury, rejoiced, felt ashamed because of what was going on over there, treated his involvement with it as an illness, but an incurable one, one that he had stopped struggling against. As was his wont, this constant worry over Poland always took on a concrete form: the level of earnings, prices, labor conditions, personal freedom or lack thereof; that is, the fate of real people whom he knew through their names or through a detailed, though imagined, knowledge of their daily life. An idea would suddenly pop into his head about active participation, about offering assistance. The list of people who owe their fellowships to Zygmunt, their foothold in Paris, their invitations abroad, would be enormous. He thrived on his intrigues, deliberated over his moves, whom to set in motion, whom to target through someone else—just as he tormented me for the longest time until I agreed to go see Jean Cassou, the director at that time of the Musée d'Art Moderne, with a certain young female artist, who immediately seated herself on the Parisian potentate's desk (and was victorious). How many similar intrigues there were, telephone calls, urgings, reminders! It looked as if Zygmunt had said to himself one day: "Here I am, no greater future awaits me, so let's do as much good as possible." If I have not emphasized his participation in the political formation of *Kultura*'s profile, it is because he was ruled by his sympathy, anger, pity, his wonder at the noble and revulsion at the base—that is to say, in him everything had its beginnings in an ethical reflex. And as he grew ethically, enlarging his personal field of activity, his role as inspirer, intermediary, superb public relations man in the service of independent thought grew apace, and in this way, it can be said without exaggeration, his presence transformed and humanized the house of *Kultura*.

A skeptic. He responded with disbelief to the possibility of reforming a system guarded by its neighbor's tanks. As for those
whom he helped, he had few illusions and noticed the mark of
pettiness on them, of habits acquired in the struggle of all
against all for mere pennies. He did not doubt, however, that he
would have been just like them and, who knows, would probably
have done some swinish things like many of them if he lived
there. Zygmunt was always delighted that he was living in
France, but also that he was not dependent on anyone in that
West from which he expected so little. The house of *Kultura* on
the avenue de Poissy, already an institution, already affluent,
with its large library and paintings by Polish artists, was like an
island that had emerged from the swirling seas, between one cataclysm and the next, and Zygmunt the skeptic would often express the hope that he would not live to see the next cataclysm.

I weep for Zygmunt for extremely egotistical reasons. Is there
anything one can have on this earth that is better than a few
friends holding each other by the hand, who together create a circuit and feel the current running through it? For me, after my
emigration from there to America in 1960, Paris was just such a
little circle of friends, but it was Zygmunt above all who held us
together, it was his current we felt most powerfully, and now, as
in a dream, our hands reach toward each other's but cannot connect. So my point of reference eastward from California has lost
its distinctness. One might also give a different interpretation to
the feeling of emptiness that has suddenly descended on me. For
two decades Zygmunt was my faithful correspondent. He lovingly
practiced an art that has been virtually forgotten today; his letters
were charming, brilliant, intelligent, sometimes so amusing that
they set off spasms of laughter, although his macabre Warsaw
humor was dominant. And from those letters I learned not only
what was going on among our Paris friends but also all sorts of
Warsaw gossip through which the daily life of Poland was revealed, because Zygmunt's ambition was to know everything—

and if throughout such a long period of exile I somehow did not feel that I had ever left Poland, it was thanks to him most of all.

Very likely, we were linked by being mired in Vistulania, he through his passion to know, I through language, in ways that were as complicated in him as in me, *odi et amo*. I never noticed any snobbery in his eager socializing with artists and writers; he was, if I may say so, a natural kibitzer and guardian of the arts, which stemmed from his curiosity about this particular species of animal. He knew this species and good-naturedly observed the parade of hunchbacks as, with more or less grace, they toted their variously shaped humps around, usually tormented with grief that they were who they were and not somebody else. Zygmunt had an aphorism for this: every woman of easy virtue dreams about being a nun, every nun about being a woman of easy virtue; a tragic actor wants to make people laugh and a comedian wants to play Hamlet. If I complained, he would remind me of this as consolation. In any event, in his opinion I was good-looking for a hunchback, which is to say, he saw certain manifestations of normalcy in me. As a matter of fact, our friendship was consolidated outside literature, as it were. His grumbling about "philosophizing"—in which he included my essays—didn't bother me in the slightest. I have written various things out of inner necessity, but not without an awareness of the merely relative significance of intellectual edifices, so that Zygmunt's voice, the voice of the average reader, no doubt alerted me to something there.

"Czesiu, write for people!" But what did Zygmunt mean by writing "for people"? He thought *The Issa Valley* was my best book. Many of his letters exhorted me: "When are you going to write about the Dukhobors?" Once, when I came to Maisons-Laffitte from America, as we sat around the table I talked about a Dukhobor ceremony that I had seen with my own eyes in the woods of British Columbia, and Zygmunt's love of comically unbelievable sights found this almost too satisfying. Instead of accommodating myself to Zygmunt's request, I again wrote some "philosophizing," *The Land of Ulro*, only to hear again, "Why don't you write for people?" This was already the summer of 1979, after Zygmunt's operation, when he was growing weaker by the day. I didn't cite my poetry (perhaps too difficult?) in my defense, but asked him: "What about my translation of the Psalms? Isn't that for people?" He thought for a moment. "Yes," he said, "that is for people."

What good are our triumphs and defeats if there is no one for them to warm or chill? Zygmunt was upset when things went badly for his friends and rejoiced when they went well. One of his last letters is exultant because Czapski's paintings had finally "caught on" in the market, and in his old age he had begun to sell a lot of pictures. And now I can't help thinking that Zygmunt, who witnessed my triumphs and my miseries, was the first person I wanted to please with a report of some piece of good luck, as if I owed him this for worrying about me when I was down. Living as we do in a fluid, hurried civilization, in which titles, names, fames change with great rapidity, we learn to value personal ties, and when someone like Zygmunt passes away, it is immediately apparent that nothing counts if we have no one in whose presence we can weep or boast.

Zygmunt was never ill, and having made it to seventy in good health, he considered that an achievement in itself. I have to mention here a fairly recent dinner party at Jeleński's, at which Zygmunt, in contrast to the rest of the company who were drinking wine, drained a bottle of vodka all by himself. I took him to the Gare Saint-Lazare by taxi and he started up the steps, unsteady but in control. The next day I asked him why he'd done that. "To test. If I can." At the same time, however, he was stoically pondering the briefness of time and grieving, but not for himself. He was also thinking about what would happen to his collection of abominations for, incorrigible scoffer and perverse tease that he was, he had amassed a large collection of decorations for distinguished service, from various epochs, like the czarist medal *"Za usmirenie polskogo miatezha"* ["For pacification of the Polish rebellion"]. What Polish museum would be pleased by such a bequest?

He was balancing his accounts, then, when there was still no hint of illness. So I was not surprised by his letter from the hospital after he learned that he had a tumor and was awaiting surgery. I have no intention of exploiting his correspondence; it is private. I will only permit myself to quote from this particular hospital letter, dated July 22, 1979:

Affairs in our fatherland are *non existing.** For the time being, calm. Very little is happening. From the perspective of the operation somehow in the course of a few days everything has assumed the size of dwarfs. Mentally, I feel terrific. I have lived for 71 years, up till 1939 in luxury considering conditions in Poland—before I was 31 years old I had managed to own 3 automobiles, then that *drôle de guerre*, what can I say, you know those times that have continued to this day.

True: from 1939, the kolkhoz. At my uncle's in Stanisławów, in the Mari Autonomous Soviet Socialist Republic, in the army, then *Kultura* for the last 32 years. I have met hundreds of interesting people, whom I would never have known even had I been not a bureaucrat but the director of Solvay. I have never done anything truly swinish to anyone. I have been quite useful, I have rendered crucial service to a couple of people, there is a small group of people whom I can count on. So what's the problem? I will not go down in the history of literature as you will. So what? I have no qualifications. You will go down, but so what?

I'm holding up as well as before and I hope that I will remain in good shape until the end. I'm even amazed, because it turns out that I have "character"; that's blatant nonsense, I don't. Most likely in painful situations like this some kind of

*"*Non existing*" in English in the original.

whalebones materialize to keep a man stiff, or else the whale-bones disappear and a man is turned into jelly. I am fortunate that the former eventuality came into play.

Not everything had lost importance for him: "the most essential thing" was his thoughts about his wife. Opposed to all melancholy, he comforted himself immediately: "But then, why should I kick the bucket? After all, it's not inevitable."

And just think, in his hospital bed, as always, he was planning his jolly prankster's tricks: "Should worse come to worst, a bit of mischief. I shall request, not I, but it's already been arranged for here in Paris, that Paweł Hertz will place an obituary notice in *Życie Warszawy* [Warsaw Life] and order a Mass at St. Martin's. I won't learn who 'was sick,' 'was out of town,' 'had business obligations.' It will be a riot."

There is something terribly upsetting in writing about dead friends: one subject used to associate with another subject, and although his understanding of the secret of the other's personality was incomplete, and frequently replaced by an "objectifying" glance, still, it was an exchange, every judgment remained open to correction. But then all of a sudden: an object. And the embarrassing incompleteness of a description of an individual human being from the outside, the usurpation of divine vision, or, quite simply, a totalitarian intervention as this unique being is subsumed under "the universal," "the typical." That's where the falsity of literature lies, literature that supposedly depicts man "from the center" but actually constructs him so that a whole will be pieced together, subject to the law of form. There is nothing to hide. I have Zygmunt's portrait in front of me instead of Zygmunt, and I am piecing together details that are supposed to represent him, leaving room for only an insignificant number of contradictory details. A rare thing: to live one's life as a good and honorable man. Because I understand that this is a rarity, the demands of construction guide my pen. But the most important thing for me is what remains of Zygmunt's subjectivity, of his appetite, the greed with which he would toss back a glass of whiskey, his jokes, intrigues, pranks: all the motion, the incompleteness, the change through which, imperceptibly for him and for others, his destiny was being fulfilled—for who among us ever expected that from a distance Zygmunt would begin to look like a statue?

PITY

IN THE NINTH DECADE of my life, the feeling which rises
in me is pity, useless. A multitude, an immense number of
faces, shapes, fates of particular beings, and a sort of merg-
ing with them from inside, but at the same time my awareness
that I will not find anymore the means to offer a home in my poems to these guests of mine, for it is too late. I think also that,
could I start anew, every poem of mine would have been a biography or a portrait of a particular person, or, in fact, a lament
over his or her destiny.

PART TWO

ON THE SIDE

OF MAN

DEAR JERZY,
  Doubt is a noble thing. I believe that if there were
a recurrence of the biblical experience of Sodom, it
would be necessary to seek the righteous among those who pro-
fess doubt rather than among believers. And yet, as you know,
doubt is traditionally bathed in a glow and accorded dignity
solely because it serves the seekers of truth as a weapon. Indeed,
the most fervent people are doubters. Allow me, then, to take
both sides, and do not think that when I speak as one who knows
with a certainty, I do not also doubt; do not think, either, that
when I doubt I am not also sensing right beside me, close enough
to touch them, definite, indisputable things. Just as human sight
is capable of taking in only one side of an apple, human speech
cannot encompass any phenomenon in its total roundness. The
other side always remains in shadow. You summon me to assist in
the struggle against armies of the most varied moral laws, armies
equipped with swastikas, hammers and sickles, portable shrines,
banners. Each of them insists that only its system of values is
salutary, appropriate, useful. Each of them rushes around the

world, exhorting people to join its ranks. Looking at this variety
of mutually contradictory laws, you ask what is it that could convince you that your own intuition will not lead you astray; you
ask about criteria, about guidelines. You ask, won't this stage be
subject to constant change in response to particular social conditions, to a person's origins and upbringing, and if that is the case,
can that constantly shifting line, that function of the most diverse
factors, be the standard by which the currents and ideas creating
contemporary history should be measured?

Yes, this is a vague, uncertain foundation, so vague and uncertain that it is easy to doubt its existence. All it takes is to raise one
human generation in a new, changed way, instilling in it a different good and a different evil, and what a dozen years ago would
have elicited universal indignation will elicit universal praise.
The elasticity of human nature appears to have no limits; indeed,
our own age is an age of monstrous experiences which prove this
alleged truth clearly and persuasively. But still I must console
you. Attempting to appeal to that nebulous element, the kernel of
common sense in man, is nothing new, by any means; it is not like
the discovery of a new continent. On the contrary, it is as old as
the world, or, at any rate, as old as culture that can be traced back
to ancient Greece. This element has been known by a great variety of names throughout history. Depending on the epoch, and
on intellectual and linguistic development, it has been called reason, *daimonion*, common sense, the categorical imperative, the
moral instinct. And although different faiths and different laws
prevailed, enforced by the might of the sword, more than one
Socrates drank poison in the name of that vague, wondrously indefinable voice, more than one humanist was burned at the stake.
Only yesterday, Aldous Huxley, whose *Jesting Pilate* is such depressing, unpleasant reading (since it reveals the weakness of the
West), that skeptical Huxley took a trip around the world in
search of verities, and in this summary of the results of his journey he states that although almost all his convictions were demolished as a consequence of his contact with the immense

variety of human beliefs, passions, and customs, still, he was able to preserve one conviction. That one conviction was his belief in the similarity of human nature, irrespective of race, religion, and language, his belief in the identical moral sense and similar definition of good and evil, be it in Europe or China or the Polynesian islands. Could it be that people like Huxley were the last, unworthy heirs of the European tradition? Could it be that their judgment was the last of the old world's delusions, a weak and deformed reflection of the final wave of humanism? And that in that case one ought to look at the extermination of people in camps, in prisons, with new eyes—look at it as a battle between red ants and black ants, without recognizing either the one or the other as in the right but rather granting that both species are right? Or perhaps we should instead admit that some human right, some fulfillment of moral law belongs to one side and that their persecutors do not share that right. But if we take that position, we return to the vague kernel of ethical intuition; verily, this is not something that has long since been put to rest, that should have been consigned by now to oblivion.

At this point in my argument, I am overcome with shame. I bow my head in sorrow over my own tendencies, which prod me toward a greater zealousness than I desire. It is enough for me to loosen the reins a bit, and I begin to pontificate in the manner of a prophet or preacher. . . . Knowing how easily I lapse into exaltation, I fear that I will soon mention the devil who summons people to Mass by ringing his tail. I have very few qualifications to be a bard. So let us quickly extinguish exaltation with renewed doubt; let us return to bitter, scathing questions.

Over the last few years, observing the spectacle in which we all are also actors, I have been astonished—no less, I am sure, than you—by the plasticity of human nature. That man can endure relatively easily the loss of his property, of his family, his beloved profession, is not what I find most astonishing. That he grows accustomed to hunger, to cold, to being beaten about the face and kicked also fits within the boundaries of the understand-

able. But beyond that stretches a dark expanse of wonders, as yet
unsuspected perspectives. Let us take the question of one's relationship to death. In so-called normal times (and perhaps ours actually are normal) death is surrounded by a ritual of magic
gestures, incantations, and rites. The smell of death makes the
neck hair of animals stand on end, but humankind drowns out
the terror with the beating of tom-toms, the sound of organs,
and the singing of mournful songs. Until recently, in Belorussia
women mourners still keened over fresh graves. These rites give
death the character of a singular event, the appearance of a phenomenon that disturbs the natural order; they make of death an
event that is utterly specific, seemingly unrepeatable. As far as I
can recall from my reading of the scholarly literature on this
matter, the idea that death is inevitable is alien to primitive
tribes—they ascribe death, if it is not the result of being eaten by
wild beasts or being killed during warfare, to the influence of evil
spells. Perhaps this, too, testifies to a ceremonious attitude toward
death (if I may call it that). It is a different matter when, as today, new ideas are being born—for example, the idea of the mass
extermination of people, akin to the extermination of bedbugs or
flies. There is no longer any place for ceremoniousness. After a
while these striking changes penetrate the psyche of the masses,
who daily confront this phenomenon. A person lived, spoke,
thought, felt. Then, the next day he's gone. ("*Jego voobshche
nigde net*"—"In general, he's nowhere," as a certain Bolshevik
told me when I asked him about the fate of Bruno Jasieński.)
Death makes no more of an impression than the drowning of an
ant makes on its comrades parading beside it on the tabletop. A
certain insectivity of life and death, as I'd like to call it, is created.
I suspect that we are beginning to look at man partly as a living
piece of meat with tufts of hair on his head and his sexual organs, partly as an amusing toy that speaks, moves—but all one
has to do is raise one's hand and squeeze the trigger and an ordinary object is lying in the same place, as inert as wood and stone.
Who knows, perhaps this is the path to absolute indifference, in-

cluding indifference to one's own death. It may happen that with good training and appropriate schooling people will die easily, from a lack of desire; they will treat dying as almost an everyday activity, between two shots of vodka and a cigarette that they won't get to smoke.

In any event, this will certainly lead to indifference to the death of others and to a change in the classification of murder as an ugly deed. Causing someone's death is dissociated from the reek of demonism, pangs of conscience, and similar accessories of Shakespearean drama. Young men in perfectly clean uniforms can then shoot people while gnawing on a ham sandwich. Yet another novelty is connected with this: criminal law, paralleling the ethical feeling of civilized societies, has linked punishment to the fact of guilt. Because X is guilty, X must die, or must be placed behind bars. Today, the issue of guilt is fading into the background, and how pernicious or dispensable a given individual may be in relation to society has emerged in the foreground. X dies, even though he did nothing bad; he dies because his hair color, the shape of his nose, or his parents' background is considered a sufficient sign of his perniciousness. And it is difficult to cry out that this is happening outside the law, that these discoveries of a destructive war are the same as collective responsibility. On the contrary, the development of criminal law is clearly moving in this direction; the German and Russian criminal codes are symptomatic (see their definition of crime).

Down the road lie unequal rights and unequal obligations. For some one hundred years the democracies of the West have held to the conviction that all people are equal under the sun and should be judged according to the same principles—which in practice came down to a glaring inequality, depending on the amount of property people owned. The Middle Ages knew a strict caste system, which was gradually tempered by modern mores. The murder of a knight was not the same then as the murder of a merchant or a peasant, although genuine religiosity placed certain limitations on that disparity. In Sparta, as Taine reports, youths who trained for battle in camps would come out onto the roads at night in order to kill a couple of late-returning helots from time to time, for the experience and to prove that they had mastered the soldier's trade.

Today, the same differentiation is surfacing again, the same inequality of obligations and privileges. The claim that the democratic concept of equality is a definite model and ideal, and that what we see around us is a distortion and perversion, is therefore, at the very least, a doubtful proposition. To choose among the ebb and flow of the most varied aspirations of human mores, to take one period (and a rather short one, at that) as a model, and to condemn others—is that not a gross error, yet another error of untroubled evolutionism and faith in Progress?

Take the problem of freedom of thought. True, there have been periods when freedom of thought was placed very high, making it one of the hallmarks of man. But those years (from the start of the Renaissance, shall we say, until the end of the nineteenth century) are not particularly binding on us. Excellent educational results (and despite everything, we must include among them results that the Soviet Union can boast of) were achieved by the total elimination of independent thinking, and it turned out that people can get along quite well without freedom of thought. The question can also arise whether with the development of such technological means of communication as radio, film, and the daily press, freedom of thought is possible at all. Does this not mean constant infection with whatever ideas are in circulation, and even that when the masses are given ostensible freedom they may succumb to total unification?

Evidently, human plasticity is great and the search for constants, for an "eternal man," might turn out to be a risky undertaking. It does not seem to me, however, that this plasticity is limitless. It gives one pause that even the most incompatible moral-political systems appeal to the same elements in man and, independently of the various forms assumed by whatever ethical currents are in circulation, they make use of a similar ethical judgment. The call to heroism and sacrifice, whether in the name of the German people or the Socialist fatherland of the working people, incorporates a scheme that is in no way different from the praise of patriotism and masculine courage in Plato's time. The propaganda of the various fascisms rolls out images of a "new order," in which, in contradistinction to the former democratic lack of order, people will be able to live happily, without fear of unemployment, wars, and economic pressure, that product of "Judaeo-plutocracy." The working people will be surrounded by care, mothers will have better conditions than in societies based on respect for money, and participation in the universal well-being and harmony will be shared among the people according to their deserts.

The falsehood of such assurances does not alter the fact that they appeal to the sense of rightness, to the thirst for justice in man. Propaganda devotes a great deal of effort to creating in soldiers faith in a "just cause," and the execution and torture of "worse" peoples has been given an equally broad justification.

These are not merely enemies—for enemies the chivalric code, so highly valued in Germany, demands a certain respect. These are enemies of the human race, subhumans, and as such they are released from the prescriptions of ethics. Photographs of Poles, Jews, or Soviet commissars, appropriately retouched, are supposed to convince the viewer of the fundamental difference of these creatures, to inculcate faith in their inferiority. The principles of honor and ethics remain in place, but, as we know, they always apply only to relations among people. Certain groups of people are bracketed out, and from then on it is permissible to condemn them without breaking these noble commandments in any way. The presentation of the Germans as a people who have been wronged and hemmed in until now—oh, those hastily unearthed strata of *ressentiment*—is no different than the depiction of the proletariat as an oppressed class, which at long last is meting out justice. I dare say, too, that the moral sense as a motor force is very much alive both in Fascism and in Communism, and that when we observe the monstrous things they do in practice, we should ascribe them not so much to the disappearance of all ethical brakes as to a change in motivation. This means that within those various armies that carry around the swastika, the hammer and sickle, portable shrines, and banners, there is one and the same ethical scheme, and that only its being filled with various contents is what gives these varying results. One can compare this to an algebraic model: depending on the values assigned to the symbols in an equation, various combinations are possible. National Socialism praises fraternity, collegiality, righteousness, nobility in relations between people, only "people" here means Germans, and, more exactly, good Germans who follow their Führer's commands. The French newspapers, which have lately been trumpeting the ideology of "national revolution" with a significant dose of cynicism, have been competing with each other in elaborating images of the nobility and beauty of the "new order." Lies like that are extremely comforting. The person who lies demonstrates that he recognizes a fictitious image as more alluring than reality. Indeed, propaganda is perhaps nothing but an appeal to man's instinctual sense of what ought to be—a perverse appeal, to be sure, which falsifies innate proportions. And although from time to time in the speeches of Fascist men of state an open confession of crime can be heard that makes the blood run cold in our veins, the majority of their statements are lies, sentimental appeals to God to bestow His blessings, and the rending of garments over the other side's lack of morality. This demonstrates that Machiavelli's prescription is immortal and that a ruler would be acting badly if he appealed exclusively to man's basest urges. On the contrary, while doing evil, he must robe himself in the toga of a benefactor of humanity, a savior, one who exacts vengeance for injuries—a precept that today's pupils of Machiavelli are following quite faithfully on the whole. Yes, yes, this is all as old as the earth, this is all known and undoubtedly only the absence of a necessary distance places in our mouths a sentence about man's total plasticity, the total novelty of what is being played out in front of our eyes.

Since we agree that even in the seemingly most predatory armies and programs an elementary ethical sense is surrounded with a certain degree of deference, we confront another problem. That same ethical scheme, that same sympathy for the good and disinclination toward evil lead to such varied deeds and are filled with such varied contents! The hierarchy of ethical values is easily overturned and its ranks reassembled. A German, a model son, husband, loving father of a family, will torment a subhuman, a Jew or a Soviet soldier, because he is obsessed with his vision of duty and justice, which commands him to cleanse Europe of similar vermin. The fact that a characteristic dose of sadism is added to the mix still does not undermine my example. A purely bestial sadism, naked and plain, occurs much more rarely than motivated sadism, equipped with all the arguments needed to make it into a noble and positive inclination. Jews and Bolsheviks are responsible for the war, they are harmful, they murdered Germans, they are subhumans, they are filthy, they belong to the lowest race, which is incapable of culture—rationalizations like these come to the aid of sadism, the beast that slumbers in every man, when it feels like going on a rampage with impunity—with impunity, which is to say, on the margins of the ethically ordered rest of his life, leaving him clean hands that can stroke a child's head or light the candles on the tree on Christmas Eve. What contents, then, should we use to flesh out a structure for an ethical norm, what should it be aimed at if it is not to lead us into depravity? Does a single true content exist while others are a counterfeit and a fraud? Contrary to all those powerful slogans of historicism, which denies that there are immutable, constant elements, I believe that one such element does exist. Every serious Christian will have no trouble agreeing with me, since the one, eternally binding truth of the Gospels does not permit any deviations or sophistry. I said in my previous letter that I am searching for a reliable foundation apart from any faith and that I see that foundation in the ethical instinct—or whatever one might like to call it; that is the sole example in a vortex of dubious things. And now here I am, all confused. How can it be, one might ask, if that same ethical drive without which it is impossible, in general, to build civilization, at one time justifies slavery, then again lauds the burning of sorcerers at the stake or the slaughter of tens of thousands of Albigensians, and on another occasion is perfectly comfortable accepting the extermination of non-German peoples—can one accept that as a higher instance, as a model for deeds and ideas?! It is, perhaps, only an innate drive to assign value, but *how* to make those distinctions remains an open question, and once again we are deprived of any fixed point.

Here we touch upon the fundamental argument that has been going on for centuries in the bosom of Western civilization between the pessimistic and optimistic conceptions of man. Christianity has not looked with confidence upon man's innate capacity to distinguish between good and evil. The virtue of the Stoics, which existed without divine assistance, sinned in Christianity's view by an excess of pride. Human beings' innate inclinations, if not illuminated by the light of grace, could lead, in the opinion of the Church, solely to sin, blindness, and error. In addition, the Western Church looked with a certain amount of disbelief upon the earning of that grace in isolation, upon the settling of accounts between God and a human soul within the privacy conferred by four walls. *Ecclesia* was to be the intermediary, the dispenser of grace by means of the sacraments created for that purpose. And although human reason was not actually surrounded with contempt, reason had always to follow the path of God's law; reason—to use the language of the Church doctors—had to be illuminated by the sun of supernatural knowledge. This lack of confidence in man's possession of common sense, this reliance not on the average person's intuition but on the opinion of *Ecclesiae militantis*, expresses a pessimistic view of human nature as marred by original sin and incapable of distinguishing between good and evil without resorting to extraordinary means. The Renaissance and Reformation were acts of faith in autonomous morality, in the grain of truth within each person; they applauded natural reason. The bonds of the Church organization and the assistance of the sacraments were unnecessary since each human being possesses a voice which dictates unerringly what he should do and what he should not do. Grace and damnation became a mystery of the human heart, for which no priest can offer relief nor any encyclical simplify the path. That was the germ of faith in man as the judge of his own actions; that is how man grows to colossal proportions: master of his own destiny, answering for it only and exclusively to God. And then along comes that optimist Rousseau, reared in the Protestant spirit, and he proclaims man's natural goodness, paints in the most exuberant colors all the innate drives of the human animal, accusing civilization of perverting them. Next comes the optimist and Protestant Nietzsche, summoning man to total liberation from the chains of "slave morality," inciting to a transformation of civilization in the spirit of power and health, but not truth, and pronouncing the slogan "Let truth die, let life triumph!" (And so it did, poor, mad philologist.) Nietzsche is seconded by the Protestant and optimist Gide, his ardent admirer. And then these new men come along, these ultra-moderns, these worshippers of the magnificent beast in man, whom we know so well. I have a book by a young Nazi poet, presented to me by the author in 1935. I pick it up and read the dedication: *"Au dessus de la loi le Créateur a posé la vie"* ["The Creator placed life above law"]. Yes, we know it; that's the way it is. Life is superior to law, life fashions and creates laws for its own purposes, life breaks laws when it needs to, and life is man—magnificent, not answerable to any court of law, free, deriving from himself the rules governing his conduct.

Slow down, slow down. I am too incensed. More than one Catholic writer speaks of Protestantism like this; we need only mention Maritain. This is the way Naphta would have phrased it had his quarrel with Settembrini, inscribed in the pages of

Mann's *Magic Mountain*, flared up again today. Faith in man has had some fine representatives, however, who, wary of Rousseau's and Nietzsche's perverse excesses, were measured in their claims and drew entirely different conclusions from their optimistic conception of man. I need only mention Anglo-Saxon literature as an example. Nevertheless, I must admit that whoever wishes to seek moral authority in man and to base himself on it, whoever believes in man's right to an autonomous resolution of ethical problems, is taking the path of Humanism and the Reformation and not the path of the Catholic Church. The path that leads from Luther to Rosenberg, as you correctly say, is by no means crooked, while Rosenberg is separated from Catholicism by an abyss.

No, I harbor no illusions. All noble humanitarians, debating to the present day the rights of man and of the citizen, are descended from the same spiritual family that the Church has condemned on many occasions, thus giving proof of the Church's wisdom. And just as the germ of monarchism and totalitarianism persists within democracy, so a germ of slavery persists in their appeals to complete freedom of conscience and thought. Man became free, but being free, he created certain historical ideas and bent his neck under the yoke which he himself had created. Soon the idea of self-sufficient humanity took hold. It was contaminated by the corrosive acids of the work of philosophers whose goal it was to prove that "man" is an abstraction, that "Man" with a capital *M* does not exist, that there are only tribes, classes, various civilizations, various laws, and various customs, that history is filled with the struggle of human groups, and that each of them brings along different ethics, different customs, and a different worldview. Like Marx, they yearned to prove that "being defines consciousness" or, as my Nazi poet says, that "the Creator placed life above law." On the heels of this came the necessity to replace the idea of one's fellow man with a narrower idea, the idea of the proletariat or the Aryan, and instead of "do no harm to your fellow man" they began saying "do no harm to your countryman" or "do no harm to a worker." And now, my dear friend, I shall share with you my greatest doubt. Without religious and metaphysical underpinning, the word *man* is too ambiguous a term, is it not? From the moment it is deprived of traits such as an immortal soul and redemption through Christ, does it not disintegrate into a vast number of possibilities, of which some are better, others worse, some deserving of protection and cultivation, and others of absolute extinction? Finally, is it really possible to invent a single ethics, since the *daimonion*, left to its own resources, turns out to be something like Pythia? His pronouncements can be interpreted any which way, however one wishes——Mr. Goebbels is well aware of this. I am not comforted in the least by the opinions of writers like Huxley. Rolling down a steep slope toward valleys inhabited by the wolves of totalitarianism, along with all of Europe, they seem to be unaware of this, and they mistake a brief period of as yet incompletely disrupted equilibrium between freedom and slavery for a permanent state. I am not comforted by allusions to European tradition; Europe's cart has driven more than once along this rutted path, but she has forgotten the dark moments of the past. . . .

And so, what remains is to give up the attempt to discover an ethical authority in man, to shrug one's shoulders in response to the hopelessness of human justifications, and if one is to fight, then to do so only as a member of a threatened nation, only as enemy against enemy! There is something within me that rebels, something that demands that I assess justice and pass judgment on them both, the persecutor and the persecuted, according to a standard different from that of patriotic exaltation.

Allow me to end my letter with this doubt. May it balance out my frequent impulsiveness.

SPEAKING OF A MAMMAL

1

TEN YEARS AGO, the news of Hiroshima found me in
Cracow, and if I did not give it then the attention it deserved, it was because I was busy with something else.
Anxious to preserve in a concrete form the vision of things newly
seen, I was working on a scenario for a film. Its main figure was
to be a city which before the war numbered more than a million
inhabitants, but which, by the use of ordinary bombs and dynamite, was changed into a desert of burnt-out streets, twisted iron
and crumbling barricades: this city was Warsaw. The idea of the
film came to me from the story of a man who, after having lost
his ties with civilization, had to face the world alone——Daniel Defoe's Robinson Crusoe. Once the Nazis had deported all the population which survived the battles of the Polish uprising of 1944,
only isolated men, leading the lives of hunted animals, hid in the
ruins of Warsaw. For every one of those men, the previous history of mankind had ceased to exist. They each had to solve anew
the exceedingly difficult problem of finding water and crusts of

bread in abandoned cellars; they were afraid to light a fire lest they betray their presence; and they trembled at the echo of a human voice.

My intention was to portray a Robinson Crusoe of our times. The earlier Crusoe's misfortune was to find himself on a scrap of land not yet touched by the power of mind capable of transforming matter. The misfortune of my Crusoe came about as a result of the use of the power of mind over matter for suicidal aims.

A few years later the film was produced by the State-owned Polish Film Company. Before shooting, however, the scenario provoked so many serious political objections that the producers had to make constant revisions every few months—without my participation. For Robinson Crusoe is, as we know, an asocial individual. His faithful Friday does not suffice to create a society. So the producers introduced two Fridays, and then again two, until the number reached a dozen, all imbued with a fine ideological zeal. They even included a heroic Soviet parachutist (yet unknown at that period in Warsaw). Thus, a film whose original purpose was to show the terrible landscape of a dead city and to warn men of their folly was transformed into a piece of paltry propaganda. Not only was it a deformation of truth; it was completely counter to truth.

I have recounted this adventure in order to draw from it a number of conclusions. That summer of 1945, when the blast over Hiroshima revealed the omnipotence of Faust, who started his career around 1505 by delving in magic, I was walking along the medieval streets of Cracow trying to push my political passions to the side. I had all the reason in the world to hate the Nazis, but to show that hatred in the film would have diminished the force of evil of which they were only an instrument. Rather, I preferred simply to mark their presence as a lurking danger. Without any sympathy for Stalin and Beria, I passed over their part in the destruction of Warsaw also. The important thing was the ruins, and the man who lived in them, an average man, a worker in his forties who never studied magic or social doctrines, whose problem was to survive in a city which our civilization had created and then transformed into a desert.

The conflict between that concept and the wishes of the Polish film directors was serious and in a sense symbolic. That the directors represented the Communist Party, and that they tried to use the film to the immediate advantage of the Party, was only one facet of the problem. In trying to avoid "deviation" they committed an absurdity: their attitude serves to point up the incommensurability between Faust's technical progress and his knowledge about himself. "What is man?" I wanted to ask. "Let us not stop at such a vague notion!" they exclaimed. "What we want to know is whether he is a friend or an enemy. How can we tell if in your film he appears alone?" "He is a victim," I replied.

2

For many centuries, no one questioned the existence of "human nature." It was protected by the authority of the religions which erected a barrier between man and the rest of creation; a justified barrier, since no animal has a consciousness of time, nor does it know that it has to die. In order that a mentality such as that of the Polish film directors could arise (for me they are an example of politics in the pure state), it was first necessary that there be a steady development of scientific research and that this development be linked to the movement of historical transformations. At first, the earth ceased to be the center of the universe; then the evolution of organisms became universally accepted; and as the human fetus was shown to repeat at certain stages in its development aspects of the life cycles of other species—to possess in fact some of the features of fish and frog—it was denied that human beings could pretend to be different from other living matter.

The promulgators of the nineteenth century's social doctrines were, however, torn between conflicting motives: between their quest to subject all phenomena to scientific law and their insistence on engineered social change. On the one hand, they leaned heavily upon biology where it helped them to abolish *ius naturale* and to supplant the concept of the immutability of moral rules with that of continuous change. But at the same time, they revolted against those biological tenets which held that man was subject to the same primitive struggle for life which characterizes the lower species. If what is called "instinct" were always man's guiding inspiration, he would merely be a part of nature, and the hope of constructing an ideal society would prove illusory. Hence the fierce anti-naturalism of the Marxists, finding expression in their revulsion at a literature which portrayed the most elementary forces of sex and of violence. They are even more hostile to the idea of a special divine privilege, thanks to which man would carry within himself a set of inextricable aspirations and limitations. Seeking a specific difference between man and other vertebrates, Marxists found it in the fact that no animal has a history as the sum of transmittable experiences. To try to speak of man outside his historical context is to speak of a leaf without a tree. It is clear therefore why they interpret Defoe's Robinson Crusoe as only a tale about a young English merchant of the seventeenth century who treats his island as a capitalistic enterprise and so carries Society within himself—and why my Robinson Crusoe caused them lively anxiety.

The Marxist dilemma only symbolizes the confusion that has arisen over our concept of man: deprived by scientific critique of its root in metaphysics, humanitarianism has become either shallow or ineffective. The mechanistic notion of the universe which was the basis of science simply did not square with the notion of individual choice which is the basis of moral philosophy. Since my early youth—and I have lived in a time not particularly favorable for Europe—I have heard bitter words directed at humanitarians who clasp their hands piously in sorrow over cruelty yet are incapable of proposing means to combat it. I am familiar with a great number of literary works whose subject is the defeat of defenseless goodness; the heart bursting with eagerness to help fellow creatures regardless of their race, religion, or political affiliations is scorned by authors whose sarcasm hides their betrayed love. And it must be conceded that the position of humanitarianism is very weak. If the Vatican refers to the dignity of man, it does so in accordance with logic, for it backs it with metaphysical essence; while the tenderhearted intellectuals are the inheritors of a scientific view of life, and the concern they show for the intelligent animal among whose total achievements can be found such items as slavery, concentration camps, and gas chambers does not seem sufficiently motivated. As they have been unable to found any value through science, they have taken recourse in half-measures: they either do not confess that they are metaphysicians, or they are imperfect, half-hearted Marxists who deserve a condescending smile from the true Marxists for not taking the only step which could lead them, in any case apparently, out of the impasse: namely, to "engage" themselves in history and politics. Yet if the "humanitarians" did submerge themselves in history, they would be forced to renounce a *general* sympathy for all, and simply wish life to friends and death to enemies.

It is enough to establish the weakness of their basic premise; we must avoid proposing remedies which would be easy but ineffective. An element of pathos has been introduced by the fact that the eminent Western scientists who foresaw the danger from the use of atomic energy belong to that humanitarian type. With concern for all the inhabitants of our planet, they advance the opinion that an atomic war would bring extinction to all mankind, and this reflects their groping for a common denominator which would enable us to grasp the substance of man and thus re-create a feeling of planetary community. But their efforts often have to start from zero because of a too-complete insertion of the human species into the chain of evolution forged in the nineteenth century. The British biologist Haldane exclaimed at an international congress, "I am proud that I am a mammal!"

The greatness and the defeat of the humanitarians are

reflected in the figure of Albert Einstein. Many things were changed by his death; his former adversaries today pretend to have been his admirers. In Warsaw, when the reconstructed city is decked out for the numerous congresses and festivals, huge portraits of Newton and Einstein are hung on the fronts of the houses in the neighborhood of Copernicus' monument. It was not so during Einstein's lifetime. The Theory of Relativity, however much it was discussed in small specialist circles, was considered bourgeois and hence was not mentioned in public. His warnings about the catastrophic possibilities of atomic power were received with the prescribed shrugs of the shoulder.

"The World Movement for the Defense of Peace" came into being through the initiative of a few Polish Communists, and the first Congress for the Defense of Peace took place in Poland, in 1948, in Wrocław. On that occasion Einstein sent a message which raised panic among the organizers. He had displayed the extraordinary lack of tact to speak in it in the defense of all mankind, leaving no possibility for a division into bad men and good men, i.e., for demonology, which was after all what really mattered. He proposed as the only successful means of salvation the creation of a world government capable of controlling atomic energy. The message itself was not read. In order not to lose an important propaganda effect, however, a falsification was committed: a short letter which Einstein had enclosed with his message was presented as the message. These facts can be easily verified; the *New York Times* published the two texts, together with a short commentary by Einstein.

The same reasons that led the successor to Newton to be considered in the East as a harmless crank exposed him in America to the reproach of naïveté. His sense of responsibility as the father of the Bomb forced him to condemn a lack of foresight in the United States similar to that of the participants at the Wrocław Congress. In so doing, he brought upon himself the suspicion of softness and almost of sympathy with the Reds. To his eternal glory it should be said that he tried until the very end to awaken world public opinion—in this twentieth century lacking a unifying principle. The last appeal—that of Bertrand Russell—which he signed does not deny the existence of a "titanic struggle between Communism and anti-Communism," but asks us to consider ourselves above all as "members of a biological species which has had a remarkable history, and whose disappearance none of us can desire."

One wonders whether this minimum definition "biological species" can serve as a bridge connecting believers in mutually hostile philosophies. The nudity of that definition, after the thousands of years of creative thought which produced works of art, subtle constructions of dogma and meditations upon the qualities of the soul, is depressing. In any case, it shows the seriousness of the present moment. No prisoner of a concentration camp of our era would dream of asking pity for himself in the name of biological kinship with those who condemned him; he knows that he was discarded by them as historically harmful, and it is that harmfulness which defines him in the first place, and not his membership in the tribe of *Homo sapiens.* Cosmic perspective has been completely lost, and the best image of the earth would be of a ship on which the passengers murder each other, indifferent to the sea surrounding them. For politicians brought up on Leninist-Stalinist strategy, the acquisition of the new perspective called for in the last appeal signed by Einstein will be very difficult. Training inclines them to see in every call to hold fast to the helm either a ruse or a sign of resignation from the use of one's arms, an indication of a lack of faith in one's own forces. Yet they cannot fail to see something revolutionary in the enforced moral discipline: the humanitarians clearly and for the first time since the nineteenth century are realists as well. In the West, if people are moved by that appeal, it is by the very nudity of the term used. The scientists who wished to reach out to all mankind eventually concluded that it was hopeless to continue to refer to fraternity, to the special vocation of man, to human rights—and by this withdrawal, they relegated those words to a dying phraseology. We are confronted, thus, by a crucial manifesto which concedes that we do not possess any universally accepted language to express "the quality of being man."

3

If I permitted myself to start this article with a picture of Warsaw destroyed, it was not without the intention of showing how different the mental climate in Europe was from that in America at the moment when the newspapers brought the announcement of the greatest discovery ever made. The "acceleration of history" in the few decades preceding that discovery was sensed by the Americans only as continuous technical progress, and the act of liberating atomic energy appeared to their eyes as something nearly divine, as well as demoniac and tragic; it was a sudden shock. In Europe, this "acceleration of history" demonstrated its force in the span of one generation: the First World War broke out; seemingly indestructible powers—the Russian Czarist Empire and the Habsburg monarchy—fell; the Revolution of 1917 flared up; Nazism and Fascism culminated in the Second World War and Russia marched far beyond its 1914 borders, taking into its orbit little countries which had previously separated themselves from it, as well as nearly all the former Habsburg domain. To one witnessing these events, the rise and decline of State organisms, the appearance and disappearance of chiefs, the millions of graves and the ashes of other millions scattered over the fields, all combined to make up a film running at a crazy tempo. Human affairs had exploded like the mushroom of the atomic blast. As for technical advancement, it turned to the witness its ominous face—nights of bombardment, electrified barbed wire around borders, factories producing soap made from human fat, trailer trucks transformed into portable gas chambers in which were being exterminated the "mammals" that filled Haldane with such pride, while a driver-executioner quietly smoked his pipe. Hiroshima did not introduce anything startling into that picture. On the contrary, it was received as something that was inevitable.

These violent events were accompanied by phenomena in the field of thought which can be compared to a chain reaction. We can assign to the nineteenth century the role of a scholar's study room in which concepts were elaborated that to the contemporaries of the period seemed but theoretical; although in the succeeding century these same concepts managed to move heaven and earth. To complete the analogy with the development of physics, all the doctrines that people have accepted as worthy of being enriched with their very blood were born in the same Germany that is the source of the Bomb. Hegel, Feuerbach, Marx, and Nietzsche were Germans, and it is rightly being said that the common feature of their teachings is their portrayal of the stupefaction of man when he recognizes that beyond him there is nobody in the Universe, and that he does not owe his attributes to any deity. In the past, Faust made his pact with the Devil. In the nineteenth century he rejected that help as an infringement upon his independence. For Hegel, God dissolved into the Movement, identified Himself with the Movement. For Feuerbach, and after him Marx, He became a humiliating product of the "alienation." In the "God is dead" of Nietzsche, there is as much of triumph as there is of pain. Yet not until the twentieth century were conditions created in which the awareness of the new situation could spread, and what had been Promethean upheavals would be looked upon as commonplace. European literature, concealing philosophy under a symbol and a parable, faithfully notes this awakening.

"How to create Value?"—this is the question continuously repeated in that literature. If all Value has its source only in man, and he himself genuflects before what he has made an object of worship, he must be tortured by doubt as to his choice of idol, because he evidently could have chosen something else. Some of the writers worshipped before the altar of Art as the most au-

tonomous and self-sufficient activity. This did not satisfy those
more passionate, those who were moralists by temperament. We
can see for how long a period of time these problems continued to
absorb the attention of writers when we look at a few dates. Let
us remember that Kafka's *Trial* was written as early as 1914—and
that Kafka (who died in 1924) achieved fame in Europe in the
thirties. The moralists wandered through the "arid plain" of T. S.
Eliot waiting for a new revelation; since it was not forthcoming,
they proclaimed catastrophe. Very early, around 1913, some of
them discovered a general panacea for all ailments: action, and
from that time on, action (political) has been the main problem
of European literature. This penchant can be explained by ascribing demiurgical qualities to the Act of Faust, not only as far as
the shaping of matter is concerned: action creates Value, thus
man becomes a god.

The first movement to proclaim this openly was futurism; its
creator, Marinetti, later supported Mussolini. Yet it would not be
correct—although it is often done—to link the cult of action for
action's sake to the extreme Right or Fascist movements alone.
The most eminent Communist writers in Europe used first to
reach the outermost limits of nihilism, and then, if they did not
commit suicide, ended by finding a haven of faith in the Revolution, using it, as we might suppose, as a drug without which life
and creation would have been impossible for them. This was the
path followed by Mayakovsky, son of a family of public officials,
who started out by embracing futurism; by Bertholt Brecht, a ni-
hilist ironist in his first phase; by the sophisticated French poets
Aragon and Éluard; and by many others.

One of the most interesting cases of polarization is Malraux,
an author typical of the period we are dealing with, who placed
his faith in the autonomous grandeur of man, at first in revolution, then in the history of art. Here we should come to a halt—
although it is difficult to resist a glance into the future, and to
hold back comment on some of the new barrels for the old wine.
It is the word "engagement," introduced after the Second World

War, that now holds our attention, as well as the renaissance in France of German philosophy, particularly that of Hegel via Sartre.

If one wished to assemble an anthology of writing in the various European languages for the period of 1930 to 1939 in which the approaching annihilation was predicted with despair, fear, or sometimes even joy, he would find himself with a collection almost the size of an entire library. There is nothing strange in the fact that for a great number of Europeans experiencing the oppressive atmosphere of those years and the sufferings of war, there existed a connection between anticipation and accomplishment. Nazism liquidated what illusions remained about the innate goodness of man, and discouraged people from relying upon their irrational impulses. Alone in the universe—and unable to rely upon his own instincts—where was a prisoner, or a relative of a prisoner or of a man shot to death, to look for rescue? The successes of Communism among the intellectuals were due mainly to their desire to have Value guaranteed, if not by God, at least by history. With resistance, but at the same time with relief, they subjected themselves to a discipline which liberated them from themselves.

While in America atomic energy quickly became a main topic of conversations, articles, and books, and served to arouse the collective anxieties, nothing similar could be observed on the European continent. There apocalypse was routine. The great majority of the inhabitants of the countries which found themselves within the Russian orbit avidly awaited the dropping of bombs on the heads of their new masters, or even on their own. In Poland, unknown hands covered the walls of factories during the night with pleas to Truman to come to a decision. In the Western part of the continent, the possibility of a quick mass death was received as not the worst eventuality—and people returned to their everyday occupations. This culminating achievement of scientific technique was reached at the moment of Europe's political, economic, and spiritual defeat, when, having exported its anti-transcendentalist philosophy to Russia and its technique to America, it passively watched how its own rays, projected onto the crystals of foreign civilizations, were reflected back upon itself. Flightiness, or apathy, or rather the great weariness of people who have lost much, who do not make plans because their future does not depend on them, not only made it impossible for them to accept as a real possibility that the Promethean effort of Faust could well mean the end of the long career of the species; it also closed their eyes to the vistas opened up by the rational use of nuclear energy for the prosperity of the species.

In the nineteenth century, continental Europe produced a writer of genius in the field of science fiction: Jules Verne, whose writings were a testimonial to Europe's faith in continuous progress. Today, however, if the European public reads about heroes of the distant future, it finds them in translations from America. This does not mean that Europeans are insensitive to those visions; the dimension of time remains, after the disappearance of the dimension of eternity, the only sphere of hope. Perhaps with the beginning of interplanetary voyages, hope will find new nourishment in the dimension of space, as in the era of the explorations of the earth in the sixteenth, seventeenth, and eighteenth centuries. As to the public in the Popular Democracies, its vision of the future comes from different sources; it must live not in the sad present, but in expectation of the perfect future happiness of grandchildren and great-grandchildren—a much more enticing happiness than that offered by American science fiction. The only flaw one can find in this vision is that such perfection can only be attained after the "final battle" for the earth has been fought. Speaking to his son, a poet of a Popular Democracy tells the boy that he will see during his own lifetime "an immense rainbow erected across the sky"; and he compares history to a patient weaver who intertwines his threads in such a way that they eventually will form the most beautiful pattern attainable.

4

As a consequence of the foregoing circumstances, Einstein's warning, which urges humanity to acquire a completely new perspective, will not strike a responsive chord among those Western European intellectuals who are keeping themselves busy discussing the adventures of dialectics. Reading their books, it is impossible to resist feeling that they are trying to relive a philosophical pageant staged a hundred years ago in Germany— while in America and Russia the sequel is being actively performed. These intellectuals would prefer to suffer the greatest humiliations rather than concede that they are conservatives untouched by the potentialities of the Atomic Era. But the complexity and diversity of Europe are such that their work, together with the instinctive unwillingness of the masses to face the too-difficult dilemma, nevertheless accomplish a useful function through the interplay of these two elements with less conspicuous tendencies of thought. This useful function might be described as that of a brake on the desperate impulses of the modern mind to fall far back, beyond the evil which resulted from reaching for forbidden fruit from the tree of knowledge.

The "tragic sense" awakened by the shock of the first blast turned a few Americans to a kind of religion which is a negation of human achievements. What is more natural, after all, in the final hour of accounting, than to condemn Faust's first pact with the Prince of Shame who offered him eternal youth? The long story of the presumption of Reason is said to have begun with the Renaissance; at the outermost limits, punishment was waiting. Is it not then only fair to recognize the error and to concede with humility that the disappearance of the very substance of man shows us the overly high price we paid for the progress of science?

The Europeans who, thanks to their experiences, domesticated, so to speak, the "tragic sense" view such repentance with suspicion, finding in it a temptation to simplify what should not be simplified. Too-easy solutions can have a very harmful effect when we have to accomplish a task which requires patience. The centuries which separate us from the Middle Ages are not like a blackboard which can be easily sponged off, leaving no trace of what had previously been written on it; we can no longer accept as our own the view of life of Dante, while at the same time launching artificial satellites into the ionosphere. That static image of the world is inaccessible to us; it was not known at that time that man is a historical being and is submitted to society to such an extent that the very air he breathes is conditioned by it. The importance of Marxism, always in the foreground of European quarrels, is that it forbids us to forget that fact; but man cannot be reduced to just a part in history; history is unable to produce a moral judgment unless we ascribe magic qualities to it. Marx saw that history is subjected to determinism, that it is of the realm of matter. It is extraordinary therefore that in looking for *justice*, he ascribed to matter a capacity for producing justice. After all, why does history subjected to necessity automatically produce a happy Communist society? What god watches over it? We can understand that matter through evolution produced man. Why should it care that he be happy and live in a happy society? No one yet can understand why matter should have been "a machine for the manufacture of Good," as Simone Weil says. This is the main contradiction at the base of today's major philosophical controversy, and it cannot be bypassed.

Now, it would not be fair to leave the picture as I have painted it. Life in Europe, through all the great disasters which have fallen upon it in succession, would be impossible if it were not for the existence of some subterranean rivers that only once in a while reveal their presence. Access to them is difficult, and the initiated do not like to show others the paths leading to them; these are rivers of jealously guarded hope. In the Western part of the continent, as in the Popular Democracies, those who quench their thirst at these waters recognize each other instantly with the first words spoken. Occasionally one of these rivers comes to the surface, and we give it the name of a person. One such person is Simone Weil. Her very style distinguishes her writings from the sentimental works of the demagogues. We immediately recognize that her attention is concentrated on the central problem of recovering the notion of human nature. Yet her approach is wary, as is the way of all those who have no illusions about the possibility of returning to a point left behind long ago, and who appreciate the new instruments placed at our disposal. It is no accident that she is constantly concerned with the philosophical bases of Marxism, which she considers "the highest spiritual expression of bourgeois society." From a criticism of an internal contradiction in Marxism between its scientific element and its prophetic element, she comes to a criticism of all attitudes which attempt to overcome the contradiction inherent in man by masking it, and create in this manner an artificial unity.

"The essential contradiction in human life," she says, "is that man, having as his very being a striving toward the Good, at the same time is submitted in all his being, in his thought as well as in his body, to a blind force, to a necessity that is absolutely indifferent to the Good. This is the way things are; and this is why no human thinking can escape from the contradiction."

We can deal with the contradiction in two ways: "The illegitimate way is to put together incompatible thoughts as if they were compatible with each other. (For instance, matter as a machine for the manufacture of Good.) The legitimate way, in the first instance, when two incompatible thoughts come to mind, is to exhaust all the resources of one's intelligence to try to eliminate at least one of the two. If that is impossible, if both impose themselves, we must then recognize the contradiction as a fact. Then, we must use it as if it were a tool with two prongs, like a pair of pliers, to enable us to enter, with its help, into direct contact with the transcendent domain of the truth inaccessible to human faculties."

It is worth mentioning that Weil finds the equivalent of that procedure in mathematics. Her thinking, like that of others moving in the same direction, does not counsel resignation; on the contrary, it seeks to recognize limitations and to profit from that "limit situation." Her writings hold an additional interest for me because there are many similarly inclined minds in the Popular Democracies. Since all youth there is given Marxist schooling, the intellectual movement is intense. Young people are put in touch with one of the most complicated of philosophies; they come out of it either with little more than a certain number of easily assimilated slogans, or else with a desire to pull down the wall of these slogans—and then they see for the first time the vicious circle of historically determined ethics. The frequent cases of conversion of young Marxists to Catholicism are but one of the symptoms. It happens more frequently than not, that dialectical materialism is being secretly considered as merely an efficient work theory, unable to provide answers to more basic questions.

I would not like to conclude this article by making too-far-reaching prognostications. Granting that Faust needs two poles, that of creation and that of destruction, it is difficult to believe that he would not someday be able to recover the equilibrium at present lost between them. This may take much time. Yet we would be unjust if, living in a period when destruction prevails, we were to accuse him of being only a criminal. Let us rather assume that he is now again entering the stage of research on man to which he is compelled by discoveries in physics. He has left this field fallow in the past, and he concedes it. Neither Hegel, nor Marx, nor Nietzsche provided him with the tools; or rather, they provided him with tools ill-adapted for the immense territory waiting for the plow. But Faust does make valiant attempts, again and again, with what is at his disposal. A certain European fatalism, which advises men to plant the apple trees today, even if the end of the world were to come tomorrow, can be of help to him; it counsels him to do, at all costs, what must be done—even though it is quite possible that death will overtake him in the act.

FACING TOO LARGE
AN EXPANSE

To BE FORCED into a confrontation with nature. For example, to find oneself in the mountain forests somewhere along the Feather River, unprotected among the boulders, the five-foot-thick trunks of pines, the maze of dry, parched earth. We are usually protected, to some degree, by the praise and condemnation we portion out, by the part we take in exchanging boasts and deceptions, by clinging to one another—the scientist concentrates on other scientists, the printer on other printers, the artist on other artists, the politician on other politicians. All this makes for a cocoon of constantly renewed dependencies, which infuses time with value—progress, regression, evolution, revolution, a revolution in the preparation of dyes, topless bathing suits. The deeper we immerse ourselves in that cocoon woven of speech, pictures moving on screens, paper spat out of rotary presses, the safer we are. But the consistency of that cocoon varies and is different from one country to the next. I do not wish to play games with chains of causes and effects, and so will simply acknowledge that this continent possesses something like a spirit which malevolently undoes any attempts to subdue it.

The enormity of the violated but always victorious expanse, the undulant skin of the earth diminishes our errors and merits. In the presence of the pines by the Feather River, or on rocky promontories spattered by the ocean's white explosions where the wind bears the barking of sea lions, or on the slopes of Mt. Tamalpais, where the border of ocean and land, shattered into promontories, looks like the first day of creation, I stand stripped and destitute. I have not achieved anything, I have taken no part in evolution or revolution, I can boast of nothing, for here the entire collective game of putting oneself above or beneath others falls apart. Strangeness, indifference, eternal stone, stone-like eternity, and compared to it, I am a split second of tissue, nerve, pumping heart, and, worst of all, I am subject to the same incomprehensible law ruling what is here before me, which I see only as self-contained and opposed to all meaning.

I do not number myself among those who seek unusual landscapes, nor do I take photographs of nature's panoramas. To itself neither beautiful nor ugly, nature no doubt is only a screen where people's inner hells and heavens are projected. But the majestic expanse of the Pacific seacoast has imperceptibly worked its way into my dreams, remaking me, stripping me down, and perhaps thereby liberating me. For a long time I cunningly forbade myself to encounter that chaos which dispenses with valuation; I tried not to overstep the limits of what is human and thus inclines one to predictions either hopeful or gloomy; I imposed discipline on myself—I devised work, commitments, always aware that I was only being evasive, postponing the moment when I must clash with what awaits me close at hand.

We spread papers on a table beneath a tree and try to write or add columns of figures; the uneasy leaves, stirred by the wind, the birds in flight, the drone of insects—that incommensurability between open space and the operations of the mind—immediately drive us to a place with four walls where our activities seem to acquire importance and dignity. Cocoons, caves, rooms, doors, enclosures, lairs, those underground galleries where Cro-

Magnon man ventured, though endangered by cave-dwelling hyenas, so that in the farthest, deepest corner, he could draw magical beasts by torchlight: only there did his work become enormous, only from there could it govern the fate of the live animals on the surface of the earth.

Now I seek shelter in these pages, but my humanistic zeal has been weakened by the mountains and the ocean, by those many moments when I have gazed upon boundless immensities with a feeling akin to nausea, the wind ravaging my little homestead of hopes and intentions.

RELIGION AND SPACE

. . . a blasphemous identification of space with infinity
Since all our ideas have their origin in our idea of place, a
psychology not based on an analysis of our conceptions of the physical
universe must be subjective and erroneous.

OSCAR MILOSZ, *Les Arcanes*

IT IS WORTH STUDYING philosophical systems in order to
dismiss them; not they, but the imagination, concerns me.
My imagination is not like that of someone who lived when
Thomas Aquinas's worldview was reflected in Dante's symbols,
though its fundamental need—to reduce everything to spatial relations—is the same. Space, however, has undergone certain dis-
turbances. To begin where I am: the Earth, instead of being a
stable, solid foundation, slips out from beneath my feet, and were
I, by some miraculous dispensation, suspended above it, liberated
from gravity, other regions, other landscapes would move past beneath me. Moreover, they already do so in my imagination, for,
though I know it to be absurd, I choose to be an incorporeal on-
looker, outside the system, in front of a screen on which the

planet revolves. In so doing, I lose the possibility of dividing things into "above" and "below." Drawing a vertical line above me, I will not reach the boundary where the world ends and heaven's spheres begin to circle the throne of God. Neither will any plumb line allow me to bore deeply enough through the geological strata to come upon the caverns of Hell. A seething infinity surrounds me on every side and eludes the powers of my mind.

There has been considerable reflection on the origins of the phenomenon known as individualism, on Byronic despair—the revolt of the individual who considers himself the center of all things, and their sole judge. No doubt, it was the contents of the imagination itself which forced this to happen, as soon as hierarchical space began to somersault. Anyone who looks into himself can reproduce the course of the crisis. The imagination will not tolerate dispersal and chaos, without maintaining one Place to which all others are related, and, when confronted with an infinity of relationships, always relative only to each other, it seizes upon its sole support, the ego. So why not think of myself as an ideal, incorporeal observer suspended above the turning Earth?

Unfortunately, it was difficult to preserve the ego's lofty privileges. The "I" saw the Earth as one of a multitude of bits and pieces in space and saw itself on that Earth as one of a multitude of organisms subject to the law of transformation; that is, it became something outside its own self. A monstrous doubleness, a monstrous contradiction, enough to justify the complaints of tender souls. What is worse, time, always strongly spatial, has increased its spatiality; it has stretched infinitely back out behind us, infinitely forward into the future toward which our faces are turned. When Dante was alive, neither nature nor (secular) history, stabilized and recurrent, gave occasion for any such anxieties. Today I cannot deny that in the background of all my thinking there is the image of the "chain of development"—of gaseous nebulae condensing into liquids and solid bodies, a molecule of life-begetting acid, species, civilizations succeeding each other in turn, segment added to segment, on a scale which reduces me to a particle. I do not like this and I would prefer that chain to be another human fiction, because the resultant compulsion to renounce my faith in my five senses corrupts me, Adam.

Perhaps only our Romantic ancestors experienced the crisis in their imagination acutely; later there was a gradual effort to forget it, for some sort of futility, the futility of too far-reaching inquiries, seemed to result from it; better to return to human affairs, life among people. But after all, here, by San Francisco Bay, people gather at least once a week and praise God in Episcopalian, Baptist, Congregationalist, and Catholic churches, and in synagogues, and for all America, religion is what religion must certainly be in a land of human aloneness—I, Nature, and God. And it would truly be frivolous to try to evade questions which belong to everyone, though most people are ashamed to ask themselves those questions. They have experienced the collapse of hierarchical space, and when they fold their hands and lift up their eyes, "up" no longer exists. Let no one say that religion can manage without such primitive directions to orient people. Not the theologians' dogma, but human images of the universe, have determined the vigor of religions. The Descent of God and the Ascension are two of the spatial poles without which religion becomes pure spirituality devoid of any toehold in reality, a situation not to man's measure. One of the Soviet astronauts said in an interview that he had flown very high but had not seen God anywhere. It is not clear whether one should smile at this or not, for those who kneel and raise up their eyes differ from the astronaut only in that they would wish to shift the spheres of heaven further away—a billion light-years away, to where the universe ends—but they are unable to carry out that operation; their faith is a struggle between an instant of intuition and an hour of indifference or weariness.

What could be more fascinating than to look into their minds at that struggle between the desire to believe and the inability to, as when you have almost caught a butterfly but end up with a

handful of air. I do not understand why we have allowed ourselves to be cowed by fashion and have relinquished important
fundamental inquiries so that only churchmen, intimidated and
constrained by their defenses, will at times admit to their religious troubles.

I am not afraid to say that a devout and God-fearing man is
superior as a human specimen to a restless mocker who is glad to
style himself an "intellectual,". proud of his cleverness in using
ideas which he claims as his own though he acquired them in a
pawnshop in exchange for simplicity of heart. Besides, it seems to
me that we are born either pious or impious, and I would be glad
were I able to number myself among the former. Piety has no
need of definition—either it is there or it is not. It persists independently of the division of people into believers and atheists, an
illusory division today, since faith is undermined by disbelief in
faith, and disbelief by disbelief in itself. The sacred exists and is
stronger than all our rebellions— the bread on the table, the
rough tree trunk which *is*, the depths of "being" I can intuit in
the letter opener lying in front of me, entirely steeped and established in its "being." My piety would shame me if it meant that I
possessed something others did not. Mine, however, is a piety
without a home; it survives the obsessive, annihilating image of
universal disjointedness and, fortunately, allows me no safe superiority.

Religion and space: but now the old is meeting with the new.
The old; that is, space conceived by the imagination as an infinitely extended, all-embracing body in which the chunks of
manifold worlds are stuck like raisins in a cake. The new means
space-creating movement, for, since space is relative and not absolute, why would we ascribe to it the features of a cake or an elephant and be amazed by its grandeur? And here Movement, the
destroyer of hierarchy, reveals talents which its enemies, who defend the hierarchy at any cost, never suspected. In his romantic
frock coat, standing on a mountaintop, the solitary admirer of his
own ego succumbed to panic when faced with his own insignifi-

cance beneath the stars. But would that reaction be appropriate now when "the greater" and "the lesser" are losing meaning, subverted by relativity? Movement causes dematerialization and infamous matter, burden of burdens to the faithful, thins into light and whirls into the original "*Fiat lux*" as in the works of those medieval philosophers who interpreted the creation of the world as the transmutation (*transmutatio*) of non-physical, divine light into light which today we would call physical. But the more time became spatialized in the imagination, the faster it produced its contradiction, "meta-time." In spite of the theologians' warnings, eternity always assumed the guise of infinite extension; only the relativity of multiple equivalent times has revealed a new dimension which does not possess extension or the other features we had ascribed to space. Only then could we imagine all events and actions from all times persisting simultaneously, an enormous conglomeration (another clumsy spatial metaphor) of film frames.

In the opinion of certain Protestant writers, the "death of God" touched the root of all America's religions, leaving them vital only in the realm of morals and customs. The ravenous insect eating out the heart of religious faith is certainly more than a textbook model of the universe, and it is not enough to part company with Newton to find the universal reference point. Nevertheless, when here at night in these hills, near the brightly illuminated atomic laboratory where experiments beyond my understanding are conducted, I analyze my imagination, I realize that it is no longer entirely of the nineteenth century and that, in any case, I have been freed from an image of space as a solid body and container.

CARMEL

CONTINENT'S END

At the equinox when the earth was veiled in a late rain,
    wreathed with wet poppies, waiting spring,
The ocean swelled for a far storm and beat its boundary,
    the ground-swell shook the beds of granite.

I gazing at the boundaries of granite and spray, the
    established sea-marks, felt behind me
Mountain and plain, the immense breadth of the continent,
    before me the mass and doubled stretch of water.

I said: You yoke the Aleutian seal-rocks with the lava and
    coral sowings that flower the south,
Over your flood the life that sought the sunrise faces ours
    that has followed the evening star.

The long migrations meet across you and it is nothing to
    you, you have forgotten us, mother.

You were much younger when we crawled out of the
  womb and lay in the sun's eye on the tideline.

It was long and long ago; we have grown proud since then
  and you have grown bitter; life retains
Your mobile soft unquiet strength; and envies hardness,
  the insolent quietness of stone.

The tides are in our veins, we still mirror the stars, life is
  your child, but there is in me
Older and harder than life and more impartial, the eye that
  watched before there was an ocean.

That watched you fill your beds out of the condensation of
  thin vapor and watched you change them,
That saw you soft and violent wear your boundaries
  down, eat rock, shift places with the continents.

Mother, though my song's measure is like your surf-beat's
  ancient rhythm I never learned it of you.
Before there was any water there were tides of fire, both
  our tones flow from the older fountain.

ROBINSON JEFFERS

Not far from the steep coast of Big Sur, legendary as a hermitage for hippie Buddhists, is the small town of Carmel with its mission, the tomb of Father Junípero Serra, and another monument as well—a little-remembered stone house by the water, built by the poet Robinson Jeffers when today's elegant tourist and vacation spot was only a fishing settlement. In that house Jeffers wrote works dedicated to the contention that nature, perfectly beautiful, perfectly cruel, and perfectly innocent, should be held in religious veneration, whereas the human species was a sick excrescence, a contamination of the universal order, and deserved only annihilation. One may suppose, however, that both his withdrawal into seclusion (made possible by income received from relatives in banking) and the direction his thoughts took were not without their connection to World War I. The scorn shown mankind by the creator of *inhumanism* stemmed from an excess of compassion, and many of his poems attest to his having read the newspapers with a sense of tragedy, wishing neither side victory. In his mature years it was his fate to follow from his solitude the massacres of the thirties and forties, and what issued then from his pen was laced with fury and sarcasm. To favor one side over another, when he thought them both equally criminal monsters tearing each other to pieces, was, in his eyes, a naïve submission to propaganda.

I began to visit Carmel little more than two years after his death. The cypress groves he planted to outlive his name had been cut down because, in expanding, the little town had absorbed that valuable property. Of the former wilderness there remained only the crash of the waves spraying against the rocks, but the hill where his house stands is separated from the sea by an asphalt road hissing with tires. The gulls danced in the wind as they always do, but a helicopter was flying above them, its rotor blades clacking. The too-fertile humanity which Jeffers predicted would suffocate on its own stinking excreta was now swarming in the deserts, on islands, and in the polar zones, and there was not much reason to believe that one could break free of its grasp.

We spent a long time walking around Jeffers's low granite house. Two large dogs were lying on the grass by the fence, a face appeared for a moment at the window. The tower standing a bit off to one side struck me most. It was there, I thought, that Jeffers would often go to meditate and write, listening to the ocean breathe, trying in his own words to be true to that single, age-old rhythm. Not to digress, I later learned that he had built the tower for his wife, Oona, and so he must have only rarely worked there. The rough-hewn stones he fitted and joined made the building formless, and that worked well. Why didn't he maintain the

stone's inherent modesty all the way through? But no, he stylized
a bay window, an early medieval arch; denying history, taking
refuge from it by communing with the body of a material God,
in spite of everything he may still have seen himself as one of his
own barbarian ancestors on the cliffs of Scotland and Ireland.
That permanent oddity half covered in ivy, that romantic monument raises various suspicions, even as far as Jeffers's poetry itself
is concerned.

Who knows, he may have been just an aesthete. He needed to
see himself as a being elevated above everything alive, contemplating vain passions and vain hopes, thereby rising above time as
well. He seems to have been impressed at some point by tales of
knights in their aeries, pirates in their lookouts by the sea. Even
during my first visit to Carmel, I asked myself if I was like him,
and, perhaps flattering myself, answered no. I was sufficiently
like him to re-create his thoughts from within and to feel what
had given rise to them. But I did not like my own regal soarings
above the Earth. That had been forced upon me and deserved to
be called by its name, exile.

I also would have been unable to oppose eternal beauty to human chaos. The ocean, to him the fullest incarnation of harmony,
was, I admit, horrifying for me. I even reproached Jeffers for his
descriptive passages, too much those of the amateur painter who
sets up his easel on a wild promontory. For me, the ocean was primarily an abyss where the nightmares located in the depths of
hell by the medieval imagination came ceaselessly true, with
endless variations. My kinship with the billions of monsters devouring each other was threatening because it reminded me who
I was and their unconsciousness did not absolve me from sin.

Did Jeffers consider consciousness only an unforgivable flaw?
For him the nebulae, the sun, the rocks, the sea, sharks, crabs,
were parts of an organism without beginning or end which eternally renews itself and which he called God. For he was a religious writer, though not in the sense that his father, a Calvinist
pastor, would have approved. Jeffers studied biology as a young

man, and once having accepted the mathematical system of cause and effect, he dethroned the Jehovah who makes incomprehensible demands of his subjects, who appears in a burning bush and makes a covenant with one tribe. Personal relations with a deity who graciously promises people that by remaining obedient to his commands they will escape the fate of all the rest of creation were, to his mind, only proof of what lengths human insolence and arrogance could reach. But Jeffers was even less able to reconcile himself to the scandalous figure of Jesus, which caused his stern and pious father to weigh all the more painfully on him; in rising from the dead, Jesus had broken a link in an infinite chain, thus making it known that the chosen would be wrested from the power of cause and effect, a power identified with hell. This was close to the claims of the modern revolutionaries who proclaimed universal happiness, but always for tomorrow, and Jeffers could not bear them. His God was pure movement pursuing no direction. Universes arose and died out in Him, while He, indifferent to good and evil, maintained his round of eternal return, requiring nothing but praise for His continued existence.

This is very impressive even if Jeffers's attraction to piety and veneration was not unique among the anti-Christians of his time. He composed hymns of complete acceptance, and it is unclear whether he was more a Stoic or the heir of his Calvinist father, who trembled before *Deus terribilis*. Perhaps those were not hymns but psalms of penance. And it is because of his ardent bitterness that I acknowledge his superiority to his fellow citizens who sat down at the table, folded their hands in prayer, and said: "God is dead. Hurray! Let's eat!"

I have focused on his particular obsession. Whenever he wrote about people (usually dismal tales of fate, causing unbridled instincts to crush all the protagonists), they are reduced in size, tiny insects crawling along the piled furrows of the planet. He achieved that perspective by contrast with the background. Or, perhaps more important, his characters diminished as the action progressed, until finally the main hero, having committed mur-

der, flees to the mountains, where his love, his hate, and the body
with the knife in it now appeared ridiculous, inessential, pin-
points lost in infinity. What did that mean? Dimensions are a
function of their distance from the eye. Like everyone else, Jeffers longed for a hierarchically ordered space divided into bottom, middle, and top, but an impersonal and immanent God
could not serve as a keystone to a pyramid. Jeffers granted himself the superior position at the summit, he was a vulture, an eagle, the witness and judge of mortal men deserving of pity.

We used to walk the beach at Carmel fairly often, gathering
pieces of wood, shells, and stones, smooth and pleasing to the
touch. The cries of running children and the barking of their
dogs vanished in the double roar of wind and surf. In the hollows
shielded by the dunes, vacationers built fires, grilled frankfurters
on sticks, took snapshots. Nearly all of them were unaware that
Jeffers's house was nearby. Jeffers, if one overlooks a handful of
admirers, has been almost completely forgotten. But, after all,
whatever his faults, he was truly a great poet. Even in his own
lifetime he did not have many readers, and before condemning
his misanthropy, one must recall that he was neglected by people
who placed great value on meat, alcohol, comfortable houses, and
luxurious cars, and only tolerated words as if they were harmless
hobbies. There was something paradoxical in my fascination with
him; I was surprised that I, a newcomer from lands where everyone is burdened with history, where History is written with a capital *H*, was conducting a dialogue with his spirit though, had we
met, we would not have been able to understand one another.

But I did conduct that dialogue. He was courageous, and so he
broke through the spiderweb of invisible censorship as best he
could, and compared with him, others were like dying flies utterly tangled in that web. They had lost the ability to be simple;
they were afraid that if they called bread bread and wine wine
they would be suspected of a lack of refinement, and the more
caught they became in the perversions of their cultivation, the
less sure they were of it. He bet everything, drew his own conclu-

sions in voluntary isolation, making no attempt to please anyone, holding his own. Just as he appears, distinct, in photographs—the thin, proud face of a sailor, the narrow lips—Jeffers's work resembles nothing else produced in this century; it was not done for the cultural stock markets of the great capitals, and seemed intentionally to repel them by the violence of his tone, which is forgivable but only if the violence includes no preaching. His work is distorted, turn-of-the-century, tainted like that tower of his, but after all, he had to pay something too, like everyone else here. In contrast to the products of the jeweler's chisel to which we have become inadvertently accustomed, his work is striking in its simplicity, its roughness, but at the same time there was something sickly in his simplicity. The tasks he set himself no doubt exceeded his strength, and not his alone. In a time when no one knows what to believe in and what not to believe in, he studied himself and drew a distinct line expounding his image of God, the universe, and the human species, for which he foretold a quick finish. He understood the whole of his work as a new *De rerum natura,* and how could such ambition proceed without reversals?

I fumed at his naïveté and his errors; I saw him as an example of all the faults peculiar to prisoners, exiles, and hermits. But here in Carmel, where he had his body burned and his ashes strewn to the wind, his spirit, perhaps reincarnated in the gulls or pelicans flying over the beach in majestic formation, challenged me to wrestle and, through its courage, gave me courage.

TO ROBINSON JEFFERS

*I*F YOU HAVE NOT READ *the Slavic poets*
so much the better. There's nothing there
for a Scotch-Irish wanderer to seek. They lived in a childhood
prolonged from age to age. For them, the sun
was a farmer's ruddy face, the moon peeped through a cloud
and the Milky Way gladdened them like a birch-lined road.
They longed for the Kingdom which is always near,
always right at hand. Then, under apple trees
angels in homespun linen will come parting the boughs
and at the white kolkhoz tablecloth
cordiality and affection will feast (falling to the ground at times).

And you are from surf-rattled skerries. From the heaths
where burying a warrior they broke his bones
so he could not haunt the living. From the sea night
which your forefathers pulled over themselves, without a word.
Above your head no face, neither the sun's nor the moon's,
only the throbbing of galaxies, the immutable
violence of new beginnings, of new destruction.

All your life listening to the ocean. Black dinosaurs
wade where a purple zone of phosphorescent weeds
rises and falls on the waves as in a dream. And Agamemnon
sails the boiling deep to the steps of the palace
to have his blood gush onto marble. Till mankind passes
and the pure and stony earth is pounded by the ocean.

Thin-lipped, blue-eyed, without grace or hope,
before God the Terrible, body of the world.
Prayers are not heard. Basalt and granite.
Above them, a bird of prey. The only beauty.

What have I to do with you? From footpaths in the orchards,
from an untaught choir and shimmers of a monstrance,
from flower beds of rue, hills by the rivers, books
in which a zealous Lithuanian announced brotherhood, I come.
Oh, consolations of mortals, futile creeds.

And yet you did not know what I know. The earth teaches
More than does the nakedness of elements. No one with impunity
gives to himself the eyes of a god. So brave, in a void,
you offered sacrifices to demons: there were Wotan and Thor,
the screech of Erinyes in the air, the terror of dogs
when Hekate with her retinue of the dead draws near.

Better to carve suns and moons on the joints of crosses
as was done in my district. To birches and firs
give feminine names. To implore protection
against the mute and treacherous might
than to proclaim, as you did, an inhuman thing.

ESSAY IN WHICH THE AUTHOR
CONFESSES THAT HE IS ON
THE SIDE OF MAN, FOR LACK
OF ANYTHING BETTER

I HAVE often been asked why I, a poet, with a clear-cut vocation, engage in inanities; that is, write about things which
can be grasped only in an improvised fashion, resisting precision. I, too, reproach myself for this and am consoled by the fact
that, thus far, I have not written panegyrics in honor of any
contemporary statesman—although more than once I have ex-
pended time on projects perhaps no less useless. But what I am
doing now is not without function, at least for me. I am examining what is hidden behind my tendency to slip into social themes.

The world, existence, may be conceived as a tragedy, but, unfortunately, that view is no longer our specialty. Tragedy is grave,
hieratic, while today we are assailed at every moment by monstrous humor, grotesque crime, macabre virtue. The dismal antics
in which we all, willingly or not, have taken part (for these antics
were History with a capital *H*) seemed to enjoin us to sprinkle
our heads with ashes and weep like Job—but our Job shook with
laughter for his own fate and, at the same time, for the fate of
others. Every television switched on, every newspaper taken in
hand evokes pity and terror, but a derisive pity, a derisive terror. I

am no exception: while sympathizing with the victims of terror, I cannot control the sarcastic spasms wrenching my face when, for example, I learn that the police of a certain totalitarian state have made a series of arrests disguised as doctors and hospital attendants, having also painted their police cars with red crosses to look like ambulances. Those arrested were beaten unconscious, then carried off on stretchers by the "attendants." As has already been observed many times, reality's nightmarish incongruence has outstripped the boldest fantasies of the satirists. The entire style of my century is an attempt to keep pace with this depressing and ridiculous abomination, and can be felt in drawings, paintings, theater, poetry, the style of the absurd, and in our fierce and bitter jeering at ourselves and the human condition.

This style unites everything: the solitude of man in the universe, his imagination disinherited from a space related to God; images of what is taking place on the surface of the entire planet, which are constantly bombarding us; the neo-Manichaean hatred for matter; Promethean defiance in the name of human suffering is sent into a void, since there is no addressee. This medley of ingredients makes for an ambivalent style, and nearly every work can be interpreted with equal validity either as metaphysical despair or as a curse hurled at man's cruelty to man, at evil society.

I do not like the style of the absurd and do not wish to pay it homage by using it, even if I am assured that it derives from protest. Black gallows humor is too much an admission of complete impotence; mockery has long been the only revenge for the humiliated, the oppressed, slaves. Although today's sensibility is so blunted that, without the stimulation of tricks from the Grand Guignol, our voice is heard by practically no one, contempt for fashion has, on the whole, kept me from making concessions. Possibly my need for order is exceptionally great, or perhaps I am classical in my tastes, or perhaps mine are the ways of a polite, naïve boy who received a Catholic upbringing. I think, however, that in my need for order, my reluctance to grimace hellishly in response to the absurd, I am quite average, except that I am less ashamed of my heart's demands than other people.

I do not like the style of the absurd, but neither do I like the natural order, which means submission to blind necessity, to the force of gravity, all that which is opposed to meaning and thus offends my mind. As a creature of flesh, I am part of that order, but it is without my consent. And with absolute sobriety I maintain that although today our imagination cannot deal with a division of existence into the three zones of Heaven, Earth, and Hell, such a division is inevitable. Man is inwardly contradictory because he resides in between. For me, the talk of some Catholics—wishing to buy their way into the good graces of the unbelievers—about the goodness of the world, is no more than a fairy tale. On the contrary, I do agree with Simone Weil when she says that the Devil does not bear the title Prince of This World in vain. Certainly, the causes and effects that govern matter with mathematical necessity do not entitle us to hurl abuse at God or at any X designating the very basis of existence. If we can leave our humanity aside for a moment and put our human sense of values out of mind, we must admit that the world is neither good nor evil, that such categories do not apply to the life of a butterfly or a crab. It is, however, another matter when we are dealing with our own demands, demands peculiar to us amid everything alive. Then indifferent determinism assumes diabolical features and we have the right to suppose that God has leased the universe to the devil, who, in the book of Job, is one of Jehovah's sons. "The war we wage with the world, the flesh, and the Devil" is not a contrivance of Spanish mystics but occurs within us and as well between us and the indifferent necessity surrounding us. I am twofold: to the degree that I am the kin of the butterfly and the crab, I am the servant of the Spirit of the Earth, who is not good. If there were no man, there would be no Devil, for the natural order would not have been contradicted by anyone. Since it is contradicted, its ruler, Satan, the Spirit of the Earth, the demiurge of nature, battles with what is divine in man for the human soul. And only the covenant with God allows man to disengage himself, or rather to attempt to disengage himself, from the net of immutable laws binding creation.

I am, thus, frankly pessimistic in appraising life, for it is chiefly composed of pain and the fear of death, and it seems to me that a man who has succeeded in living a day without physical suffering should consider himself perfectly happy. The Prince of This World is also the Prince of Lies and the Prince of Darkness. The old Iranian myths about the struggle of Darkness with Light, Ahriman against Ormazd, suit me perfectly. What, then, is the light? The divine in man turning against the natural in him—in other words, intelligence dissenting from "meaninglessness," searching for meaning, grafted onto darkness like a noble shoot onto a wild tree, growing greater and stronger only in and through man.

Consciousness, intelligence, light, grace, the love of the good—such subtle distinctions are not my concern; for me it is enough that we have some faculty that makes us alien, intruders in the world, solitary creatures unable to communicate with crabs, birds, animals. According to an old legend common in the first centuries of Christianity and later forgotten, Satan revolted because God ordered him, the firstborn, to pay homage to man, who had been created in God's likeness and image. From then on, all Satan's activities have had a single aim—to rival the younger brother so unjustly exalted. Or, to offer a somewhat different reading, enmity was established between us and nature.

We are unable to live nakedly. We must constantly wrap ourselves in a cocoon of mental constructs, our changing styles of philosophy, poetry, art. We invest meaning in that which is opposed to meaning; that ceaseless labor, that spinning is the most purely human of our activities. For the threads spun by our ancestors do not perish, they are preserved; we alone among living creatures have a history, we move in a gigantic labyrinth where the present and the past are interwoven. That labyrinth protects and consoles us, for it is anti-nature. Death is a humiliation because it tears us away from words, the sounds of music, configurations of line and color, away from all the manifestations of our anti-natural freedom, and puts us under the sway of necessity, relegates us to the kingdom of inertia, senseless birth, and senseless decay.

Yes, but the absurdity that afflicts us today is, first and foremost, the work of man. Civilization does not satisfy our desire for order, for clear, transparent structure, for justice, and finally, for what we instinctively apprehend as the fitness of things. The savagery of the struggle for existence is not averted in civilization. Opaque, automatic, subordinate to the most primitive determinants, and subordinating us so much that it levels and grinds us down, civilization does not approach but rather recedes from the models of a republic at long last fit for man, as postulated by philosophers for more than two millennia. That happens because the duality residing in each of us is in fact sharpened by civilization. The Devil brilliantly exploits technology in order to penetrate to the interior of our fortress and manipulate our mechanisms; that is, the determinism and inertia of what is not human drags what is divine in man down as well.

For many of my contemporaries, the Devil is the inventive, coldly logical mind, as well as the creator of the technological civilization by which we are increasingly elevated and oppressed. For that reason, many people side with the instincts and intuition of natural, individual man against the artificial and the collective. It is also true that in the popular imagination the self-confident know-it-all with his books, reducing everything to the mechanisms of cause and effect—dry, devoid of faith, indifferent to good and evil—has often been synonymous with the evil spirit. This image is maintained by the comics, film, and television, where the villain, a criminal in a white lab coat, is made omnipotent by his laboratory. For me, however, the responsibility for our misfortunes is not borne by intellect but by intellect unenlightened, insufficiently rational, cutting itself off from those gifts of ours—grace or attachment to value, by whatever name—from which it should be inseparable. I am no friend of the rationalists, either those of the eighteenth century or their successors. But if today's opponents of impersonal, repressive, inhuman knowledge are quick to cite William Blake, I am with them only because I find in Blake something different than they do. The intellect that oppressed Blake renounced impulse in favor of the fixed laws of matter, and renounced ascending movement in favor of inertia. Newton's physics horrified Blake because he saw them as a declaration of subjection, our subjection to what is; since things are as they are, there is no choice in the matter.

In modern times the great metaphysical operation has been the attempt to invest history with meaning. That is, we, as foreigners, intruders, face a world that knows neither good nor evil; our divinity is weak, imprisoned in flesh, subject to time and death; so let our labyrinth but increase, let our law, born of the challenge we hurl at the world in the name of what should be, be established. Our existence, like that of crabs and butterflies, does not lend itself to deliberations on its own purpose, all our *what fors* and *whys* fall away; meaning can only be made from what resists meaning if, from one generation to the next, there is an increase in the purely human need for justice and order, which also permits us to postulate the moment when humanity will be fulfilled. Curious dislocations and substitutions have occurred in the course of that attempt. God changed into a malevolent, cruel demiurge, the tyrant Zeus, the tyrant Jehovah, because he was the god of nature, which contradicts and dissatisfies us; many people have opposed that god with a divine hero, a leader of men, namely, the rebel Prometheus, Lucifer (who often had the face of Christ), as did the Romantic poets. Later, anyone who wished to see history in motion and directed toward a goal was required to express himself in the language of atheism. However, the change did not relieve this process of any of the traditional violence that occurs whenever ultimate concerns are at stake.

This much should be said lest I be suspected of possessing the instincts of an activist, which are, in fact, rather weak in me. The social and the political are forced onto us, since we have no defense against time and destruction outside of them. The labyrinth spun by the generations is so truly splendid, so interesting, that just to wander through it affords one much joy, and I do not blame people for never poking their noses from books or museums. And there is also the making of art, which is continually infusing human freedom with new life. But, upon closer examination, one sees that that entire humanistic space withers and dies if it's not stimulated by a reaching out from stagnant to new forms; while, by virtue of laws, which I shall not mention here, the new always allies itself with the social and the political, though sometimes in a highly roundabout way.

Our age has been justly called the age of new religious wars. That would make no sense if the Communist revolutions were not rooted in metaphysics; that is, had not been attempts to invest history with meaning through action. The liberation of man from subjection to the market is nothing but his liberation from the power of nature, because the market is an extension of the struggle for existence and nature's cruelty, in human society. The slogans used by the two camps, the adherents of the market and the revolutionaries, thus take on an aspect that is quite the reverse of what they seem at first sight. The enemies of revolution loved to appear as the defenders of a religion threatened by atheists, while those atheists hated them as the priests of an inferior god, Zeus, Jehovah, otherwise known as the Devil, who tramples the divine impulses in man. This is the meaning of History which Marxism opposed to Nature. Marxism is thus in harmony with the neo-Manichaean ferocity of modern man. Were it not, it would not exercise the near-magical attraction it has for the most active minds and would not be a central concern for philosophers.

Only when a metaphysical core is recognized in what seems to be merely social and political can the dimensions of the catastrophe that has befallen us be assessed. Hopeful thought moved into action and returned to thought, but now bereft of hope. The collapse of faith in the meaning of history as a result of the revolution which was both victorious and a failure concerns, to be sure, only Europe and North America, but we must have the nerve to admit that we neither can nor very much desire to share the hopes of Asians, Africans, and Latin Americans, for we assume tacitly, and perhaps quite wrongly, that there will be a repetition of a pattern with which we are already familiar.

It is easy to miss the essence of revolutionary intention, for it is usually obscured by sentimental and moralistic slogans. It is also easy to argue that what happened had to have happened. Marxism wanted to act against the Devil but let him in through a loophole in doctrine. That is, because of its scientific ambitions, Marxism glorified necessity, which supposedly was to be the midwife of men's freedom. In this manner, terror acquired the sanction of a *Weltgeist* invested with all the trappings of an evil demiurge. This was none too friendly a blessing for any better tomorrow. And thus, in the countries ruled by Marxists, the Prince of Lies put on a performance that made all his previous exploits pale by comparison. However, it should not be forgotten that, in retrospect, we are always inclined to ascribe to events more developmental logic than they in fact possessed.

What is the trap we are caught in today? My childhood was marked by two sets of events whose significance I see as more than social or political. One was the revolution in Russia, with all its various consequences. The other was the omen of Americanization, the films of Buster Keaton and Mary Pickford, the Ford motorcar. Now there is no doubt that Americanization has carried off complete victory: Americanization means the product of forces not only lower than man and not only outstripping him, submerging him, but, what is more important, sensed by man as both lower than and outstripping his will. Who knows, perhaps this is a punishment for man's claims on the forbidden. The more God abandoned space, the stronger became the dream of building the Kingdom of God here and now with our own hands, which, however, condemned man to a life of getting and spending. Fine, why should it be any other way? The only question is whether our twofold nature can endure a static reality, and whether we, if forbidden to reach out beyond that reality and beyond our nature, will not go mad, or, to use the language of psychiatrists, succumb to an excess of "problems." It may well be that we are healthy only when trying to leap from our own skins, in the hope of succeeding from time to time.

Something important, at least to me, emerges from what I have said. There seems to be much truth in what I have read in histories of religion about the circle symbolizing Greek thought. A circle has neither beginning nor end, on its circumference "was" flows into "is" and returns to "was." The exact opposite holds for Jewish thought, which is well depicted by the sign of the arrow. The flight of that arrow: the Covenant with God, the journey of the chosen people through the ages, the promise of a Messiah. This was inherited by Christianity, and it is the source of secular messianic dreams as well. Even the prosaic bourgeois concept of progress in the second half of the nineteenth century occasioned expectations that seem comical to us today, as can be seen in Bolesław Prus's novel *The Doll*, where the invention of a metal lighter than air was to assure universal peace and universal happiness. For me these are very personal matters. The education I received set me forever under the sign of the arrow, an education not confined to school. Yet in America, where I live, in this phase of civilization, every man must somehow cope with his situation—that of a fly trapped in amber. He is surrounded by that which has lost its ability to maintain direction and has begun to take on a circular form. Interplanetary voyages hold little promise of our entering another human dimension, and probably only the legend of flying saucers provides any outlet for our yearning for something completely other, through contact with little green men arriving here from some distant planet. The mind either behaves perversely, delighting in visions of destruction, catastrophe, apocalypse (in this respect, American intellectuals are reminiscent of their European colleagues of the twenties and thirties), or consoles itself with an eternally recurrent cosmic harmony in disharmony. Perhaps the circle is not an exact representation of Greek thought on time-space, but some kinship between Greece and India, and the present interest in Oriental wisdom may be a result of the restraints imposed upon our images of ascending movement.

In any case, America, by virtue of its entire development, whose driving force was automatic, unplanned movement, has always suffered from a certain weakness in historical imagination—yesterday and tomorrow are like today, a little worse, a little better, which is perhaps why in American films both ancient Romans and astronauts from the year 3000 look and act like boys from Kentucky. The imagination had a naturalistic orientation— man, eternally the same, eternally in the power of the same drives and needs, faced a nature also eternally the same. Commercial advertising fell into this pattern easily and contributed to its reinforcement. Advertising appeals to the physiological sides of what is "eternally human": sex; the ingestion of food (appetizing dishes which make your mouth water); excretion (pills regulating the stomach, toilet paper delightful to the touch); ugly odors (mouthwashes, deodorants).

I am ill-disposed to the philosophical propositions that current literature, art, and advertising offer me. Every man and woman I pass on the street feels trapped by the boundaries of their skin, but, in fact, they are delicate receiving instruments whose spirituality and corporality vibrate in one specific manner because they have been set at one specific pitch. Each of them bears within himself a multitude of souls and, I maintain, of bodies as well, but only one soul and one body are at their disposal, the others remaining unliberated. By changing civilizations, time continually liberates new souls and bodies in man, and thus time is not a serpent devouring its own tail, though ordinary men and women do not know this. Once, a very long time ago, walking down the street in a Polish village, I grew thoughtful at the sight of ducks splashing about in a miserable puddle. I was struck because nearby there was a lovely stream flowing through an alder wood. "Why don't they go over to the stream?" I asked an old peasant sitting on a bench in front of his hut. He answered: "Bah, if only they knew!"

THE IMPORTANCE
OF SIMONE WEIL

FRANCE offered a rare gift to the contemporary world in the person of Simone Weil. The appearance of such a writer in the twentieth century was against all the rules of probability, yet improbable things do happen.

The life of Simone Weil was short. Born in 1909 in Paris, she died in England in 1943 at the age of thirty-four. None of her books appeared during her own lifetime. Since the end of the war her scattered articles and her manuscripts—diaries, essays —have been published and translated into many languages. Her work has found admirers all over the world, yet because of its austerity it attracts only a limited number of readers in every country. I hope my presentation will be useful to those who have never heard of her.

Perhaps we live in an age that is atheological only in appearance. Millions were killed during the First World War, millions killed or tortured to death in Russia during and after the revolution; and countless victims of Nazism and the Second World War. All this had to have a strong impact upon European thinking. And it seems to me that European thinking has been circling around one problem so old that many people are ashamed to name it. It happens sometimes that old enigmas of mankind are kept dormant or veiled for several generations, then recover their vitality and are formulated in a new language. And the problem is: Who can justify the suffering of the innocent? Albert Camus, in *The Plague*, took up the subject already treated in the Book of Job. Should we return our ticket like Ivan Karamazov because the tear of a child is enough to tip the scale? Should we rebel? Against whom? Can God exist if He is responsible, if He allows what our values condemn as a monstrosity? Camus said no. We are alone in the universe; our human fate is to hurl an eternal defiance at blind inhuman forces, without the comfort of having an ally somewhere, without any metaphysical foundation.

But perhaps if not God, there is a goddess who walks through battlefields and concentration camps, penetrates prisons, gathers every drop of blood, every curse? She knows that those who complain simply do not understand. Everything is counted, everything is an unavoidable part of the pangs of birth and will be recompensed. Man will become a God for man. On the road toward that accomplishment he has to pass through Calvary. The goddess's name is pronounced with trembling in our age: she is History.

Leszek Kołakowski, a Marxist professor of philosophy in Warsaw,* states bluntly that all the structures of modern philosophy, including Marxist philosophy, have been elaborated in the Middle Ages by theologians and that an attentive observer can distinguish old quarrels under new formulations. He points out that History, for instance, is being discussed by Marxists in the terms of theodicy—justification of God.

Irony would be out of place here. The question of Providence, or of lack of Providence, can also be presented in another way. Is there any immanent force located in *le devenir*, in what is in the state of becoming, a force that pulls mankind up toward perfec-

*At the time of this writing.

tion? Is there any *cooperation* between man and a universe that is subject to constant change? So worded, the question is related to the quite recent discovery of the historical dimension, unknown to the rather immobile societies of the past. Curiously enough, Christian theologians are helpless when confronted with those issues. They are ashamed of the providentialist philosophy propagated by Bossuet and other preachers, according to whom God, a super-king, helped good rulers and punished the bad. If it were true, and certainly it is not, the enigma of every individual's commitment would still remain unsolved. At least one French theologian, Father Gaston Féssard, affirms that this is the basic intellectual weakness of modern Christians. As soon as they touch historical problems, they succumb to habits of philosophy alien to them; they become, consciously or unconsciously, Hegelians or Marxists. Their weakness reflects a gap in Thomist doctrine. In Saint Thomas Aquinas, affirms Father Féssard, there are no traces of pronouncements on the historical dimension. He was interested only in the *order of reason* and in the *order of nature*. "If the historical," says Father Féssard, "plays a capital role in Hegel, in Marx, and in many philosophers of existence, in the opinion of good judges it is, or rather it seems to be, completely absent from the Thomist doctrine." So a Christian dialectician has to invent his very conceptual tools.

Here I end my introduction. It leads toward some vital points in Simone Weil's thought.

Simone Weil was born into a family of intellectuals of Jewish origin. Her father's family was from Alsace; her mother's family had migrated to France from Russia. She grew up among people who respected learning above all, and all her life she preserved a lively interest in modern physics and mathematics. She mastered foreign languages early: besides Latin and Greek as taught in French schools (and her excellent knowledge of Greek proved decisive for her future evolution), German and English. She was not brought up in any religious denomination, and throughout her youth was not concerned with religious problems.

After having completed her university studies at the École Normale Supérieure (where one of her colleagues was Simone de Beauvoir, then a Catholic), Simone Weil started her brief career as a teacher of Greek and of philosophy. A brilliant professor, she was often in trouble with the authorities because of her eccentricity. She was politely ironic toward her bourgeois surroundings and sided with people looked at by the French middle class with horror: the militants of the labor unions and the unemployed workers. Those were the years of the economic crisis. She refused herself the right to earn money if others were starving and kept only a small part of her salary, giving the rest away to union funds and workers' periodicals. Politically she was on the left, but she never had anything to do with the French Communist Party. She was closest to a small group, "La Révolution Prolétarienne," which followed the traditions of French syndicalism. Her numerous political articles on the chances of the workers' struggle in France, on economic policy, on the causes of Nazism in Germany, as well as her studies on the mechanism of society and on the history of Europe, have been recently collected in a few volumes. Only some of them had been published in her lifetime, in little-known magazines.

The desire to share the fate of the oppressed led her to a momentous decision. In spite of bad health, she worked for a year (1934–35) as a simple worker in Paris metallurgical factories; she thus acquired a firsthand knowledge of manual labor. Her essays on that subject (a volume entitled *La Condition ouvrière*) are a terrible indictment of brutality, callousness, physical and spiritual misery. As she confesses, that year in the factories destroyed her youth and forever left the indelible stigma of a slave upon her ("like those stigmas branded on the foreheads of slaves by the ancient Romans").

When the Spanish civil war broke out, Simone Weil left for Barcelona (in 1936), where she enlisted as a soldier in the "Colonna Durutti," an anarchist brigade. I stress anarchist—she chose it because the ideal of the anarchists was utopian. But ow-ing to an accident and resulting illness, her stay in Spain was very short.

In 1938 Simone Weil, to use her words, was "captured by Christ." Nobody has the right to present her biography as a pious story of conversion. We know the pattern: the more violent the turn, the more complete the negation, the better for educational purposes. In her case, one should not use the term "conversion." She says she had never believed before that such a thing, a personal contact with God, was possible. But she says also that through all her conscious life her attitude had been Christian. I quote: "One can be obedient to God only if one receives orders. How did it happen that I received orders in my early youth when I professed atheism?" I quote again: "Religion, in so far as it is a source of consolation, is a hindrance to true faith: in this sense atheism is a purification. I have to be atheistic with the part of myself which is not for God. Among those men in whom the supernatural part has not been awakened, the atheists are right and the believers wrong."

The unique place of Simone Weil in the modern world is due to the perfect continuity of her thought. Unlike those who have to reject their past when they become Christians, she developed her ideas from before 1938 even further, introducing more order into them, thanks to the new light. Those ideas concerned society, history, Marxism, science.

Simone Weil was convinced that the Roman Catholic Church is the only legitimate guardian of the truth revealed by God incarnate. She strongly believed in the presence, real and not symbolic, of Christ in the Eucharist. She considered belonging to the Church a great happiness. Yet she refused herself that happiness. In her decision not to be baptized and to remain faithful to Christ but outside of His Church, we should distinguish two motives. First, her feeling of personal vocation, of obedience to God who wanted her to stay "at the gate" all her life together with all the neo-pagans. Second, her opposition to the punitive power of the Church directed against the heretics.

After the defeat of France she lived in Marseilles for a while, and in 1942 took a boat to Casablanca and from there to New York in the hope of joining the Committee of Free Frenchmen in London. Her intention was to serve the cause of France with arms in hand if possible. She arrived in London after a few months spent in New York. In 1943 she died in the sanitarium at Ashford, apparently from malnutrition, as she limited her food to the level of rations allotted by the Germans to the French population.

Such was the life of Simone Weil. A life of deliberate *foolishness*. In one of her last letters to her family, commenting upon the role of fools in Shakespeare's plays, she says: "In this world only human beings reduced to the lowest degree of humiliation, much lower than mendicancy, not only without any social position but considered by everybody as deprived of elementary human dignity, of reason—only such beings have the possibility of telling the truth. All others lie." And on herself: "Ravings about my intelligence have for their aim the avoidance of the question: Does she tell the truth or not? My position of 'intelligent one' is like being labeled 'foolish,' as are fools. How much more I would prefer their label!"

Tactless in her writings and completely indifferent to fashions, she was able to go straight to the heart of the matter which preoccupies so many people today. I quote: "A man whose whole family died under torture, and who had himself been tortured for a long time in a concentration camp. Or a sixteenth-century Indian, the sole survivor after the total extermination of his people. Such men if they had previously believed in the mercy of God would either believe it no more, or else they would conceive of it quite differently than before." Conceive of it how? The solution proposed by Simone Weil is not to the taste of those who worship the goddess of History; it may be heretical from the Thomist point of view as well.

A few words should be said about Simone Weil's road to Christianity. She was imbued with Greek philosophy. Her beloved mas-

ter was Plato, read and reread in the original. One can notice a
paradox of similarity between our times and the times of decadent Rome, when for many people Plato—that "Greek Moses,"
as he was sometimes called—served as a guide to the promised
land of Christendom. Such was the love of Simone Weil for
Greece that she looked at all Greek philosophy as eminently
Christian—with one exception: Aristotle, in her words "a bad
tree which bore bad fruit." She rejected practically all Judaic tradition. She was never acquainted with Judaism and did not want
to be, as she was unable to pardon the ancient Hebrews their cruelties, for instance the ruthless extermination of all the inhabitants of Canaan. A strange leftist, she categorically opposed any
notion of progress in morality, that widely spread view according
to which crimes committed three thousand years ago can be justified to a certain extent because men at that time were "less developed." And she was making early Christianity responsible for
introducing, through the idea of "divine pedagogy," a "poison,"
namely, the notion of historical progress in morality. She says:
"The great mistake of the Marxists and of the whole of the nineteenth century was to think that by walking straight ahead one
would rise into the air." In her opinion, crimes of the remote past
had to be judged as severely as those committed today. That is
why she had a true horror of ancient Rome, a totalitarian state
not much better than the Hitlerian. She felt early Christians were
right when they gave Rome the name of the Apocalyptic Beast.
Rome completely destroyed the old civilizations of Europe, probably superior to the civilization of the Romans, who were nothing
but barbarians, so skillful in slandering their victims that they
falsified for centuries our image of pre-Roman Europe. Rome
also contaminated Christianity in its early formative stage. The
principle *anathema sit* is of Roman origin. The only true Christian civilization was emerging in the eleventh and twelfth
centuries in the countries of the Langue d'Oc, between the Mediterranean and the Loire. After it was destroyed by the Frenchmen who invaded that territory from the north and massacred

the heretics—the Albigensians—there has not been any Christian civilization anywhere.

Violent in her judgments and uncompromising, Simone Weil was, at least by temperament, an Albigensian, a Cathar; this is the key to her thought. She drew extreme conclusions from the Platonic current in Christianity. Here we touch perhaps upon hidden ties between her and Albert Camus. The first work by Camus was his university dissertation on Saint Augustine. Camus, in my opinion, was also a Cathar, a pure one, and if he rejected God it was out of love for God because he was not able to justify Him. The last novel written by Camus, *The Fall*, is nothing else but a treatise on Grace—absent grace—though it is also a satire: the talkative hero, Jean-Baptiste Clamence, who reverses the words of Jesus and instead of "Judge not and ye shall not be judged" gives the advice "Judge, and ye shall not be judged," could be, I have reasons to suspect, Jean-Paul Sartre.

The Albigensians were rooted in the old Manichaean tradition and, through it, akin to some sects of the Eastern Church of Bulgaria and of Russia. In their eyes God, the monarch worshipped by the believers, could not be justified as He was a false God, a cruel Jehovah, an inferior demiurge, identical with the Prince of Darkness. Following the Manichaean tradition, Simone Weil used to say that when we pronounce the words of the Lord's Prayer "Thy kingdom come," we pray for the end of the world as only then the power of the Prince of Darkness will be abolished. Yet she immediately added that "Thy will be done on earth" means our agreement to the existence of the world. All her philosophy is placed between these two poles.

There is a contradiction between our longing for the good, and the cold universe absolutely indifferent to any values, subject to the iron necessity of causes and effects. That contradiction has been solved by the rationalists and progressives of various kinds who placed the good in this world, in matter, and usually in the future. The philosophy of Hegel and of his followers crowned those attempts by inventing the idea of the good in movement, walking toward fuller and fuller accomplishment in history. Simone Weil, a staunch determinist (in this respect she was not unlike Spinoza), combated such solutions as illegitimate. Her efforts were directed toward making the contradiction as acute as possible. Whoever tries to escape an inevitable contradiction by patching it up, is, she affirms, a coward. That is why she had been accused of having been too rigid and of having lacked a dialectical touch. Yet one can ask whether she was not more dialectical than many who practice the dialectical art by changing it into an art of compromises and who buy the unity of the opposites too cheaply.

Certainly her vision is not comforting. In the center we find the idea of the willful abdication of God, of the withdrawal of God from the universe. I quote: "God committed all phenomena without exception to the mechanism of the world." "The distance between the necessary and the good is the selfsame distance as that between the creature and the Creator." "Necessity is God's veil." "We must let the rational in the Cartesian sense, that is to say mechanical rule or necessity in its humanly demonstrable form, reside wherever we are able to imagine it, so that we might bring to light that which lies outside its range." "The absence of God is the most marvelous testimony of perfect love, and that is why pure necessity, necessity which is manifestly different from the good, is so beautiful." She allows neither the Providence of the traditional Christian preachers, nor the historical Providence of the progressive preachers. Does it mean that we are completely in the power of *la pesanteur*, gravity, that the cry of our heart is never answered? No. There is one exception from the universal determinism and that is Grace. "Contradiction" says Simone Weil, "is a lever of transcendence." "Impossibility is the door of the supernatural. We can only knock at it. Someone else opens it." God absent, God hidden, *Deus absconditus*, acts in the world through persuasion, through grace which pulls us out of *la pesanteur*, gravity, if we do not reject his gift. Those who believe that the contradiction between necessity and the good can be solved on any level other than that of mystery delude themselves. "We have to be in a desert. For He whom we must love is absent." "To love God through and across the destruction of Troy and Carthage, and without consolation. Love is not consolation, it is light."

For Simone Weil society is as subject to the rule of necessity as all the phenomena of the world. Yet if Nature is nothing but necessity and therefore innocent, below the level of good and evil, society is a domain where beings endowed with consciousness suffer under the heel of an ally and tenant of necessity, the Prince of Darkness. She says: "The Devil is collective (this is the God of Durkheim)." Her stand in politics is summed up in a metaphor she used often, taken from Plato. Plato compares society to a Great Beast. Every citizen has a relationship with that Beast, with the result that asked what is the good, everyone gives an answer in accordance with his function: for one the good consists in combing the hair of the Beast, for another in scratching its skin, for the third in cleaning its nails. In that way men lose the possibility of knowing the true good. In this Simone Weil saw the source of all absurdities and injustices. Man in the clutches of social determinism is no more than an unconscious worshipper of the Great Beast. She was against idealistic moral philosophy as it is a reflection of imperceptible pressures exerted upon individuals by a given social body. According to her, Protestantism also leads inevitably to conventional ethics reflecting national or class interests. As for Karl Marx, he was a seeker of pure truth; he wanted to liberate man from the visible and invisible pressures of group ethics by denouncing them and by showing how they operate. Because of that initial intention of Marx, Marxism is much more precious for the Christians than any idealistic philosophy. Yet Marx, in his desire for truth and justice, while trying to avoid one error, fell into another which, argues Simone Weil, always happens if one rejects transcendence, the only foundation of the good accessible to man. Marx opposed class-dominated ethics with the new ethics of professional revolutionaries, also group ethics, and thus paved the way for a new form of domination by the Great Beast. This short aphorism sums up her views: "The whole of Marxism, in so far as it is true, is contained in that page of Plato on the Great Beast; and its refutation is there, too."

But Simone Weil did not turn her back on history and was a partisan of personal commitment. She denied that there is any "Marxist doctrine" and denounced dialectical materialism as a philosophical misunderstanding. In her view dialectical materialism simply does not exist, as the dialectical element and the materialist element, put together, burst the term asunder. By such a criticism she revealed the unpleasant secret known only to the inner circles of the Communist parties. On the contrary, class struggle, filling thousands of years of history, was for her the most palpable reality. Meditations on social determinism led her to certain conclusions as to the main problem of technical civilization. That problem looks as follows. Primitive man was oppressed by the hostile forces of Nature. Gradually he won his freedom in constant struggle against it, he harnessed the powers of water, of fire, of electricity and put them to his use. Yet he could not accomplish that without introducing a division of labor and an organization of production. Very primitive societies are egalitarian; they live in the state of "primitive communism." Members of such communities are not oppressed by other members, fear is located outside as the community is menaced by wild animals, natural cataclysms, and sometimes other human groups. As soon as the efforts of man in his struggle with his surroundings become more productive, the community differentiates into those who order and those who obey. Oppression of man by man grows proportionally to the increase of his realm of action; it seems to be its necessary price. Facing Nature, the member of a technical civilization holds the position of a god, but he is a slave of society. The ultimate sanction of any domination of man by man is the punishment of death——either by the sword, by the gun, or from starvation. Collective humanity emancipated itself. "But this collective humanity has itself taken on with respect to the individual the oppressive function formerly exercised by Nature."

Today Simone Weil could have backed her social analyses with many new examples; it is often being said that underdeveloped countries can industrialize themselves only at the price of accepting totalitarian systems. China, for instance, would have provided her with much material for reflection.

The basic social and political issue of the twentieth century is: "Can this emancipation, won by society, be transferred to the individual?" Simone Weil was pessimistic. The end of the struggle between those who obey and those who give orders is not in sight, she argued. The dominating groups do not relinquish their privileges unless forced to. Yet in spite of the upheavals of the masses, the very organization of production soon engenders new masters and the struggle continues under new banners and new names. Heraclitus was right: struggle is the mother of gods and men.

This does not mean we can dismiss history, seeing it as eternal recurrence, and shrug at its spectacle. Willing or not, we are committed. We should throw our act into the balance by siding with the oppressed and by diminishing as much as possible the oppressive power of those who give orders. Without expecting too much: *hubris*, lack of measure, is punished by Fate, inherent in the laws of iron necessity.

The importance of Simone Weil should be, I feel, assessed in the perspective of our common shortcomings. We do not like to think to the bitter end. We escape consequences in advance. Through the rigor exemplified by her life and her writing (classical, dry, concise), she is able to provoke a salutary shame. Why does she fascinate so many intellectuals today? Such is my hypothesis: If this is a theological age, it has a marked bias for Manichaeism. Modern literature testifies to a sort of rage directed against the world which no longer seems the work of a wise clockmaker. The humor of that literature (and think of Beckett, Ionesco, Genet), if it is humor at all, is a sneer, a *ricane-*

ment, thrown in the face of the universe. Professor Michael Polanyi has recently advanced the thesis that the most characteristic feature of the last decades has been not a moral laxity but a moral frenzy exploding in the literature of the absurd as well as in revolutionary movements. Political assassination has been practiced in the name of man's victory over the brutal order of Nature. Yet the belief in the magic blessings of History is being undermined by the very outcome of that belief: industrialization. It is more and more obvious (in the countries of Eastern Europe as well) that refrigerators and television sets, or even rockets sent to the moon, do not change man into God. Old conflicts between human groups have been abolished but are replaced by new ones, perhaps more acute.

I translated the selected works of Simone Weil into Polish in 1958 not because I pretended to be a "Weilian." I wrote frankly in the preface that I consider myself a Caliban, too fleshy, too heavy, to take on the feathers of an Ariel. Simone Weil was an Ariel. My aim was utilitarian, in accordance, I am sure, with her wishes as to the disposition of her works. A few years ago I spent many afternoons in her family's apartment overlooking the Luxembourg Gardens—at her table covered with ink stains from her pen—talking to her mother, a wonderful woman in her eighties. Albert Camus took refuge in that apartment the day he received the Nobel Prize and was hunted by photographers and journalists. My aim, as I say, was utilitarian. I resented the division of Poland into two camps: the clerical and the anticlerical, nationalistic Catholic and Marxist—I exclude of course the *aparatchiki*, bureaucrats just catching every wind from Moscow. I suspect unorthodox Marxists (I use that word for lack of a better one) and nonnationalistic Catholics have very much in common, at least common interests. Simone Weil attacked the type of religion that is only a social or national conformism. She also attacked the shallowness of the so-called progressives. Perhaps my intention, when preparing a Polish selection of her works, was malicious. But if a theological fight is going on—as it is in Poland, especially in high schools and universities—then every weapon is good to make adversaries goggle-eyed and to show that the choice between Christianity as represented by a national religion and the official Marxist ideology is not the only choice left to us today.

In the present world torn asunder by a much more serious religious crisis than appearances would permit us to guess, Catholic writers are often rejected by people who are aware of their own misery as seekers and who have a reflex of defense when they meet proud possessors of the truth. The works of Simone Weil are read by Catholics and Protestants, atheists and agnostics. She has instilled a new leaven into the life of believers and unbelievers by proving that one should not be deluded by existing divergences of opinion and that many a Christian is a pagan, many a pagan a Christian in his heart. Perhaps she lived exactly for that. Her intelligence, the precision of her style were nothing but a very high degree of attention given to the sufferings of mankind. And, as she says, "Absolutely unmixed attention is prayer."

THERE WAS ONCE A YOUNG WOMAN by the name of
Sorana Gurian. She emigrated to Paris in the 1950s from
her native Romania after adventures about which, she
felt, the less said the better. In Paris her life of poverty as a
refugee did not particularly disturb her. In fact, of the group of
students, young writers, and artists among whom she lived she
was the first to make her way; a good publisher, Julliard, accepted
her first and second novels. Then, all of a sudden (how could it
have happened if not all of a sudden?), she discovered that she
had breast cancer. An operation followed, then another. Although
cases of recovery are rare, they do occur; after the second operation, her doctors were optimistic. Whether Sorana had complete
confidence in them I do not know. In any case, one battle was
won. Being a writer she had to write about what concerned her
most, and she wrote a book about her illness—a battle report on
her fight against despair. That book, *Le Récit d'un combat,* was
published by Julliard in 1956. Her respite, however, lasted only a
year or two.

I met Sorana shortly before her death; through mutual friends she had expressed a wish to meet me. When I visited her in her small student hotel on the Left Bank, she was spending most of the day in bed with a fever. We talked about many things, including writers. She showed me the books on her night table; they were books by Shestov in French translation. She spoke of them with that reticent ardor we reserve for what is most precious to us. "Read Shestov, Miłosz, read Shestov."

The name of Sorana Gurian will not be preserved in the chronicles of humanity. If I tell about her, it is because I cannot imagine a more proper introduction to a few reflections on Shestov.

Lev Shestov (pen name of Lev Isaakovich Schwarzmann) was born in Kiev in 1866. Thus by the turn of the century he was already a mature man, the author of a doctoral dissertation in law, which failed to bring him the degree because it was considered too influenced by revolutionary Marxism, and of a book of literary criticism (on Shakespeare and his critic Brandes). His book *Dobro v uchenii grafa Tolstogo i Nitsshe—filosofiia i propoved'* [*The Good in the Teaching of Count Tolstoy and Nietzsche: Philosophy and Preaching*] was published in 1900. In the same year he formed a lifelong friendship with Nikolai Berdyaev, one that was warm in spite of basic disagreements that often ended in their shouting angrily at one another. His friendship with Berdyaev and Sergei Bulgakov places Shestov in the ranks of those Russian thinkers who, about 1900, came to discover a metaphysical enigma behind the social problems which had preoccupied them in their early youth. Shestov's philosophy took shape in several books of essays and notes written before 1917. His collected works (1911) can be found in the larger American libraries. The fate of his writings in Russia after the revolution, and whether their meaning has been lost for new generations, is hard to assess. In any case Shestov expressed himself most fully, it seems to me, in his books published abroad after he left Russia in 1919 and settled in Paris, where he lived till his death in 1938. These are *Vlast' klyuchei: Potestas Clavium* [*The Power of the Keys*], 1923, and *Na vesakh Iova* [*In Job's Balances*], 1929; those volumes which first appeared in translation, *Kierkegaard et la philosophie existentielle*, 1938 (Russian edition, 1939), and *Athènes et Jérusalem: Un essai de philosophie religieuse*, 1938 (Russian edition, 1951); lastly, those posthumously published in book form, *Tol'ko veroi: Sola fide* [*By Faith Alone*], 1966, and *Umozrenie i otkrovenie: Religioznaia filosofiia Vladimira Solovyova i drugie stat'i* [*Speculation and Revelation: The Religious Philosophy of Vladimir Solovyov and Other Essays*], 1964.

Shestov has been translated into many languages. Yet in his lifetime he never attained the fame surrounding the name of his friend Berdyaev. He remained a writer for the few, and if by disciples we mean those who "sit at the feet of the master," he had only one, the French poet Benjamine Fondane, a Romanian Jew later killed by the Nazis. But Shestov was an active force in European letters, and his influence reached deeper than one might surmise from the number of copies of his works sold. Though the quarrel about existentialism that raged in Paris after 1945 seems to us today somewhat stale, it had serious consequences. In *The Myth of Sisyphus*—a youthful and not very good book, but most typical of that period—Albert Camus considers Kierkegaard, Shestov, Heidegger, Jaspers, and Husserl to be the philosophers most important to the new "man of the absurd." For the moment it is enough to say that though Shestov has often been compared with Kierkegaard he discovered the Danish author only late in his life, and that his close personal friendship with Husserl consisted of philosophical opposition—which did not prevent him from calling Husserl his second master after Dostoevsky.

I am not going to pretend that I have "read through" Shestov. If one is asked whether one has read Pascal, the answer should always be in the negative, no matter how many times one has looked at his pages. In the case of Shestov, however, there are obstacles other than density. His oeuvre is, as Camus defined it, of "admirable monotony." Shestov hammers at one theme again

and again, and after a while we learn that it will emerge
inevitably in every essay; we also know that when the theme
emerges, his voice will change in tone and sustain with its usual
sarcasm the inevitable conclusion. His voice when he enters an
argument is that of a priest angry at the sight of holy vessels being desecrated. Convinced that he will not be applauded because
his message seems bizarre to his contemporaries, he does nothing
to diminish our resistance, which is provoked most of all by what
Lévy-Brühl, in a polemic with him, called "hogging the covers."
Shestov was often reproached for finding in Shakespeare, in Dostoevsky, and in Nietzsche much that is not there at all, and for too
freely interpreting the opinions of his antagonists (numerous, for
these included practically all the philosophers of the past three
thousand years). He dismissed the reproach with a laugh: he was
not such a genius, he would say, that he could create so many ge-
niuses anew. Yet the reproach is not without validity.

He knew he was not understood; probably he did not want
to be overly clear. But the difficulty in assimilating him is not
caused by any deviousness on his part or by any levels of ironic
meaning or aphoristic conciseness. He always develops a logical
argument in well-balanced sentences which, especially in their
original Russian, captivate the reader with their scornful vigor.
Shestov is probably one of the most readable philosophic essayists of the century. The trouble lies in his opposition to those
who separate the propositions of a given man from his personal
tragedy—to those who, for instance, refuse to speak of Kierkegaard's sexual impotence or of Nietzsche's incurable disease. My
guess is that Shestov, too, had his own drama, that of lacking the
talent to become a poet, to approach the mystery of existence
more directly than through mere concepts. And although he does
not mix genres, or write "poetic prose," one feels that at a given
moment he falls silent and leaves much unsaid because the border of the communicable has been crossed. That is why in self-
defense he sometimes quotes Pascal: "*Qu'on ne nous reproche donc*

plus le manque de clarté, puisque nous en faisons profession"—
"Then let people not blame us any more for our lack of clarity,
since we practice this deliberately."

To associate Shestov with a transitory phase of existentialism
would be to diminish his stature. Few writers of any time could
match his daring, even insolence, in raising the naughty child's
questions which have always had the power to throw philosophers into a panic. For that reason such questions have been
wrapped in highly professional technical terms and, once placed
in a syntactic cocoon, neutralized. The social function of language is, after all, both to protect and to reveal. Perhaps Shestov
exemplifies the advantages of Russia's "cultural time lag": no
centuries of scholastic theology and philosophy in the past, no
university philosophy to speak of—but on the other hand a lot of
people philosophizing, and passionately at that, on their own.
Shestov was a well-educated man, but he lacked the polite indoc-
trination one received at Western European universities; he simply did not care whether what he was saying about Plato or
Spinoza was against the rules of the game—that is, indecent. It
was precisely because of this freedom that his thought was a gift
to people who found themselves in desperate situations and knew
that syntactic cocoons were of no use any more. Sorana Gurian
after all was an agnostic, largely beyond the pale of religious tradition, and not a philosopher in the technical sense of the word.
Whom could she read? Thomas Aquinas? Hegel? Treatises in
mathematical logic? Or, better still, should she have tried solving
crossword puzzles?

What does a creature that calls itself "I" want for itself? It
wants to be. Quite a demand! Early in life it begins to discover,
however, that its demand is perhaps excessive. Objects behave in
their own impassive manner and show a lack of concern for the
central importance of "I." A wall is hard and hurts you if you
bump against it; fire burns your fingers; if you drop a glass on the
floor, it breaks into pieces. This is the preamble to a long education the gist of which is a respect for the durability of "the out-

side" as contrasted with the frailty of the "I." Moreover, what is "inside" gradually loses its unique character. Its urges, desires, passions appear to be no different from those of other members of the species. Without exaggeration we may say that the "I" also loses its body: in a mirror it sees a being that is born, grows up, is subject to the destructive action of time, and must die. If a doctor tells you that you are dying of a certain disease, then you are just another case; that is, chance is a statistical regularity. It is just your bad luck that you are among such-and-such a number of cases occurring every year.

The "I" has to recognize that it is confronted with a world that follows its own laws, a world whose name is Necessity. This, according to Shestov, is precisely what lies at the foundations of traditional philosophy—first Greek, then every philosophy faithful to the Greeks. Only the necessary, the general, and the always valid will merit investigation and reflection. The contingent, the particular, and the momentary are spoilers of unity—a teaching that dates back to Anaximander. Later Greek thinkers exalted the all-embracing Oneness and represented individual existence as a crack in the perfectly smooth surface of the One, a flaw for which the individual had to pay with his death. From a Shestovian perspective, Greek science and morality both follow the same path. The sum of the angles in a triangle equals two right angles; the general, eternal truth reigns high above breeding and dying mortals just as eternal good does not change whether or not there is a living man to aspire to it.

The "I" is invaded by Necessity from the inside as well, but always feels it as an alien force. Nevertheless the "I" must accept the inevitable order of the world. The wisdom of centuries consists precisely in advising acquiescence and resignation. In simple language, "Grin and bear it"; in more sophisticated language, *"Fata volentem ducunt, nolentem trahunt"*—"The Fates lead the willing man; they drag the unwilling." Stoicism, whose very essence is to curb the shameful pretense of transitory individual existence in the name of universal order (or, if you prefer, Nature), was the final word of Graeco-Roman civilization. But, says Shestov, Stoicism has survived under many disguises and is still with us.

Shestov simply refuses to play this game of chess, however, and overturns the table with a kick. For why should the "I" accept "wisdom," which obviously violates its most intense desire? Why respect "the immutable laws"? Whence comes the certainty that what is presumably impossible is really impossible? And is a philosophy preoccupied with *ho anthropos*, with man in general, of any use to *tis anthropos*, a certain man who lives only once in space and time? Isn't there something horrible in Spinoza's advice to philosophers? "*Non ridere, non lugere, neque detestari, sed intelligere*"—"Not to laugh, not to weep, not to hate, but to understand"? On the contrary, says Shestov, a man should shout, scream, laugh, jeer, protest. In the Bible, Job wailed and screamed to the indignation of his wise friends.

Shestov (and he was not the first, for Rozanov had already made the same suggestion) believed that Dostoevsky's most significant work was *Notes from Underground*, and considered the major novels that followed as commentaries and attempts to solve the riddle set forth in the *Notes*. He expressed this opinion in an essay written in 1921 for the hundredth anniversary of Dostoevsky's birth. Shestov believed that the true critique of pure reason was not Kant's achievement but Dostoevsky's, and in the *Notes* specifically. He admired Dostoevsky's philosophical genius without reservation—and accepted as true the disparaging rumors about his personal life, rumors spread mostly by Strakhov. It also suited his purpose to see such characters as the Underground Man, Svidrigailov, Ippolit in *The Idiot*, Stavrogin, and Ivan Karamazov as Dostoevsky's true spokesmen, and even to a large extent autobiographical portraits; and to dismiss Father Zosima and Alyosha as *lubok* (cheap block prints). To Shestov peace of mind was suspect, for the earth we live on does not predispose us to it. He loved only those who, like Pascal, "*cherchent en gémissant*"— who "seek while moaning." This approach to Dostoevsky should appeal to those critics who believe the *Notes* reveal much that this conservative publicist and orthodox Christian tried to stifle in himself. There is, however, one basic difference between Shestov and those who think of Dostoevsky as a humanist, often mentioning the vision of earthly paradise (modeled on Claude Lorrain's painting *Acis and Galatea* in the Dresden gallery) in his later writings. The vision, they believe, is proof that a young Fourierist was still alive in the conservative author of *The Diary of a Writer*. Shestov does not agree with this "humanistic" interpretation.

The narrator of Dostoevsky's *Dream of a Ridiculous Man* visits in his sleep, in a state of anamnesis perhaps, a humanity living in the Golden Age before the loss of innocence and happiness. Now for Shestov the story of the Garden of Eden, because of its unfathomable depth and complexity, spoke for the superhuman origin of the whole Scripture. Explanations of the Fall advanced by both theologians and the popular imagination seemed childish to him when compared with chapters 2 and 3 of Genesis. Dostoevsky's intuition enabled him, Shestov felt, to guess at a *metaphysical state* of man before the Fall, not just to visualize a happy Rousseauistic society: "their knowledge was higher and deeper than the knowledge we derive from our science; for our science seeks to explain what life is and strives to understand it in order to *teach others how to live* [the italics are mine], while they knew how to live without science. I understood that, but I couldn't understand their knowledge. They pointed out the trees to me, and I could not understand the intense love with which they looked on them; it was as though they were talking with beings like themselves. And, you know, I don't think I am exaggerating in saying that they talked with them!" (David Magarshack's translation). Shestov doesn't hesitate to speak of man before he tasted from the tree of knowledge of good and evil as possessing omniscience and absolute freedom. What, then, was the Fall? A choice of an inferior faculty with its passion for a *distinguo* and for general ideas, with pairs of opposites: good, evil; true, untrue; possible, impossible. Man renounced faith in order to gain knowledge. Shestov names his enemy: Reason. He even says the fruits of the forbidden tree could just as well be called synthetic judgments a priori. And if Dostoevsky's *Notes from Underground* occupies a central place for Shestov, it is because the hero screams "No!" to "two and two make four" and wants "something else."

According to Shestov, Hellenistic civilization could accept neither the God of the Old Testament nor Christ of the New Testament. It had to adapt the scandalous particularity of a personal God to its general ideas, shaped as they were through speculation. "The good is God," "Love is God"—to such equations the Hellenized citizens of the Roman Empire could give assent. But the equations are nonsensical, says Shestov, for here the abstract is put before the living. He reminds us with relish that Saint Augustine hated the Stoics as much as Dostoevsky hated the liberals; both the Stoics and the liberals recommended a morality of self-sufficing Reason.

The gnosis, when it absorbed Christian elements, was nothing more than an attempt to trim the Scriptures of their "capriciousness," of their antigenerality equated with untruth. The heresy of Marcion in the beginning of the second century, inspired by the gnosis, altogether rejects the Jehovah of the Old Testament as an evil demiurge because his *incomprehensible* behavior seems offensive to an enlightened mind. But similar Hellenization of the Scriptures continued throughout the Middle Ages. Where the Scholastics affirmed that God created the universe by making use of some preexisting laws of Nature (two and two make four, the principle of contradiction, and so on, as eternal principles) they in fact put Necessity (universal laws) above the God of Genesis. They paved the way for the modern attitude that calls religion before the tribunal of Reason. The modern mind, Shestov affirms, is completely under the spell of formulas found in their most perfect form in two representative thinkers: Spinoza and Hegel. The latter said: "In philosophy religion receives its justification. Thinking is the absolute judge before whom the content of religion must justify and explain itself." And the reader who does not share Shestov's belief in the Garden of Eden should be aware of the basic issue; by voicing his disbelief he takes the side of knowledge against faith.

Shestov opposed Jerusalem to Athens in a most radical, uncompromising manner. Those names stood for faith versus reason, revelation versus speculation, the particular versus the general, a cry *de profundis* versus the ethics of, as Ivan Karamazov said, "accursed good and evil." Shestov liked to quote Tertullian: "*Crucifixus est Dei filius; non pudet, quia pudendum est. Et mortuus est Dei filius; prorsus credibile est, quia ineptum est. Et sepultus resurrexit; certum est quia impossibile est*"—"The Son of God was crucified; this does not bring shame, because it is shameful. And the Son of God died; again this is believable because it is absurd. And having been buried, He rose from the dead; this is certain because it is impossible." Contemporaries of Tertullian, perhaps no less than their remote descendants of the twentieth century, disliked everything in the New Testament which was in their eyes "*pudendum*," "*ineptum*," "*impossibile*." Shestov's men were Pascal because he had faith in the God of Abraham, Isaac, and Jacob, and not in the God of philosophers; Martin Luther because he relied on "faith alone" and because he used to say that blasphemy is sometimes dearer to God than praise; Nietzsche because he saw through the speculative nature of ethics devised to supplant the killed God; and, finally, Kierkegaard.

Shestov's articles attacking Edmund Husserl in *La Revue philosophique* had an unexpected effect: a meeting of the two men, at the philosophical congress in Amsterdam in 1928, which developed into a friendship. They respected each other, always stressing that they stood at opposite poles in their concept of philosophy. It was Husserl who literally forced Shestov to read a thinker with whom he himself disagreed—Kierkegaard. Shestov thus found out that he was less a maverick than he had thought. It must have been quite a surprise for him to learn that Kierkegaard saw the source of philosophy not in amazement, as did the ancients, but in despair, and that he, too, opposed Job to Plato and Hegel. Those were Shestov's own most cherished thoughts. A remark by Kierkegaard testifying to his stake in the Absurd, "Human cowardice cannot bear what insanity and death have to tell us," could have been made by Shestov as well. From Kierkegaard he took the name applicable *ex post* to his own meditation, "existential philosophy" as distinguished from speculative philosophy.

No wonder Camus in *The Myth of Sisyphus*, when invoking the protagonists of paradox and the Absurd, mentioned Kierkegaard and Shestov first of all. The similarities, however, between the Parisian existentialism of the 1940s and 1950s on the one hand, and Kierkegaard and Shestov on the other, are superficial. Camus, it is true, was perhaps no less fascinated than was Shestov with Dostoevsky's *Notes from Underground*, even to the extent that his last book, *The Fall*, is essentially the *Notes* rewritten. Yet Shestov, convinced as he was that the Underground Man deserved salvation because of his longing after "something else," would not leave him a victim of his desperate, crazy, solitary ego. Certainly he was skeptical of the alternatives proposed by Dostoevsky—the peasant pilgrim Makar Dolgoruky, Father Zosima, Alyosha. Nevertheless, he was a man of the Scriptures. He would probably have gladly accepted the epithet Plato often hurled at his opponents in a dispute—*Misologos*, a hater of reason—but only to stress the absurd of the human condition, which is masked by Reason. There was a way out: "The good is not God. We must seek that which is higher than the good. We must seek God." Which means that the despair that seizes us when we are faced with the Absurd leads us beyond good and evil to an act of faith. There is nothing impossible for God and for those who truly believe in Him. An absurd affirmation, for who ever saw a mountain moved by prayer? But do we have a choice? The fruits of the tree of knowledge bring only death. It should be noted that Shestov was not a preacher; he tried only to present a dilemma in all its acuteness. Most definitely he was neither a moralist nor a theologian.

For Camus, despair was not a point of departure but a permanent state of existence not excluding happiness. He wanted us to believe that even Sisyphus could be happy. He was drawn thus by the French moralistic tradition toward some sort of accommodation with a world deprived of meaning. Perhaps it sounds strange, but his atheist existentialism is less radical than Shestov's precisely because of that moralistic (Greek, after all) bent. To Camus Shestov's God seemed capricious, wicked, immoral, and as such was rejected. "His [God's] proof is in His inhumanity." For the humanist this was unacceptable. In *The Myth of Sisyphus* Camus defines the difference between his Parisian contemporaries' position and that of Shestov: "For Shestov reason is useless, but there is something beyond reason. For the absurd mind, reason is useless and there is nothing beyond reason." Camus preserved that complete bereavement till the end. In *The Fall*, his last book, the narrator and hero settles down in a bar near the port of Amsterdam in an underground private hell where there is no aspiration and no promise.

Either/or. Shestov's categorical opposition between faith and reason reminds one of the theory of two parallel truths, elaborated in the thirteenth century; but, in fact, he rejects the truth of reason completely;* the world of the "laws of Nature" is, as he says, a nightmare from which we should waken. His criticism is directed primarily against those who eschew the fundamental "either/or" and who, even though they pronounce themselves for faith, imperceptibly move to the side of their adversary. Thus the case of all devisers of theodicy: since the world created by God is not a very happy place, something should be done to lift from God the responsibility for evil—and thence the attempts at a

---

*In the Eastern Church this radical antirationalism goes back to Saint Maximus the Confessor (580–662).

"justification of God" accomplished by means of human reason. This aspect of Shestov's struggle is well represented by his essays on Vladimir Solovyov and Nikolai Berdyaev in his posthumous volume *Umozrenie i otkrovenie*. Let us concede that his severe, unornamented style makes Solovyov sound by contrast verbose if not woolly, and Berdyaev, frequently rhetorical. But Shestov also argues well. Without detracting from Solovyov's imposing stature, Shestov accuses him of nothing less than an unintentional falsity. He "placed on his banner a philosophy of Revelation, but practiced, like Hegel, a dialectical philosophy." "The idea of a 'philosophy of Revelation' seduced Solovyov as if it were itself the Revelation and, without his noticing it, took the place of the Revelation, just as for Hegel the rational took the place of the real." What happened to Solovyov had happened before; when a mind introduces rational order into the Revelation which defies order ("For the wisdom of this world is foolishness with God," I Corinthians 3:19) it ends by taking refuge in an ethical system, in a moral ideal, to be realized of course in some future kingdom of God on earth. Solovyov, contends Shestov, came gradually to conclusions quite similar to the moralistic and antimetaphysical teachings of Tolstoy—then woke up and took fright. Solovyov's last book, *Three Conversations* (1900), is a complete reversal. It is directed at Tolstoy, but perhaps the author really settles accounts with himself. After all, its focus is the story of the Antichrist who comes disguised as a lover of mankind. Such a change in Solovyov's orientation was to Shestov's liking. The pivotal points in his interpretation of the Scriptures were the Fall and the renewal of man by his partaking from the tree of life as promised in the Apocalypse. The last event was to occur, however, in a metaphysical rather than purely historical dimension. We cannot be more specific, because we simply do not know what Shestov meant in his references to the Revelation of Saint John; we have to respect his silence. In any case, Solovyov was guilty in Shestov's opinion of an inadmissable attachment to ethics at the expense of the sacred and of bowing before the tribunal of reason, as had Spinoza and the German idealistic philosophy.

The essay on Berdyaev is most revealing. The exaltation of human freedom gave to Berdyaev's writings their tone of unbridled optimism; mankind called to collaborate with God would attain "Godmanhood" ("Bogochelovechestvo"); in this respect he may be counted among many of Teilhard de Chardin's predecessors. But for Berdyaev, the belief that free action can transform the face of the earth had its roots in the eschatological and apocalyptic orientation of the Russian nineteenth-century mind, continuing the line of Slavic messianism. When in the last pages of *The Russian Idea* Berdyaev praises the Polish messianic philosopher August Cieszkowski and his voluminous work *Our Father*, he confirms this estimation. It is precisely this lofty notion of human freedom and man's unlimited possibilities in the pursuit of good that Shestov attacks. He suspects that for his friend freedom is an expedient means of explaining away the horror of existence. Evil in the world results from man's freedom, man could only have been created free, thus Berdyaev does not go beyond the Christian doctrine. Yes, but his teachers are German mystics—Meister Eckhart, Jakob Boehme, Angelus Silesius—who affirm that a sort of dialectical movement *preceded* the creation of the universe. The ideas of these mystics were to inspire the whole of German idealistic philosophy which Shestov belabors now in the person of its precursors. According to the German mystics man's freedom—meaning the possibility of evil, which has existed since before the beginning of time—is due to the dark force of the preexisting Naught that limits the power of God. Indeed, above God the mystics put *Deitas*, an eternal law. But this is the gnosis! exclaims Shestov. In striving to equate the good with God, Berdyaev made God depend on man in His struggle against a dark preexisting nothingness to such an extent that man, absolutely necessary to God, began to play the central role. Why should "Godmanhood" succeed where God fails? Why not transform "Godmanhood" into "Mangodhood"? And that, Shestov feels, is what Berdyaev does in fact. His philosophy of freedom, presumably an existential philosophy, deals with the illusory, exaggerated freedom of the Pelagians and is not existential; the latter is a philosophy *de profundis* recognizable by its refusal to explain away suffering and death, no matter which "dynamic process" is supposed to achieve the victory of the good. When Ivan Karamazov says that the tear of a child outweighs all the possible harmony of the universe, he cannot and should not be answered with historical dynamism.

Perhaps Shestov in his polemic with Berdyaev "pulls the blanket to his side" a little. Yet if we compare his essay on Berdyaev with his essay on Husserl (his last, written in 1938 to honor the memory of his friend who had just died) we must conclude that, contrary to appearances, Shestov probably had more in common with Husserl than with Berdyaev, even though in the Great "either/or" Husserl opted for science. Husserl thus intended Reason to be an instrument for discovering absolute and eternal truths untouched by relativism, truths valid for gods, angels, and men, on earth and in the universe. By "more in common" I mean the sternness proper to both men. Shestov admired Husserl precisely because he was a man ready to accept a verdict of reason even if it provided him with no comfort at all. If he himself chose the Scriptures, it was not because they brought him comfort but because he believed them to contain the truth.

Future studies of Shestov, it seems to me, should not devote more than a very limited space to the French intellectual scene, even though Shestov lived in Paris for nearly two decades. There is one exception, however. The oeuvre of Simone Weil throws some of his propositions into relief, and conversely Shestov enables us to see her basic premises better. Not that they knew each other. Perhaps Shestov used to pass her in the Latin Quarter when she was a student at the École Normale Supérieure. Her colleague there was Simone de Beauvoir, and the fate of these two women provides us with an awe-inspiring lesson. Simone de

Beauvoir was responsive to the intellectual and literary fashions of the day and became a famous but not first-rate writer, one of those who make a lot of splash in a lifetime but are soon forgotten. Simone Weil—antimodern, aloof, quixotic, a searcher for the ultimate truth—died in London in 1943 at the age of thirty-four completely unknown, but her notes and maxims published posthumously secured her a permanent place in the history of religious ideas. My mention here of Simone de Beauvoir is not totally arbitrary. Immediately after World War II she, with Sartre and Camus, was promoting the "existentialist movement." Yet the very problems that concerned Shestov remained outside her sphere of interest. To apply any epithet to Weil's philosophy would be futile; that she, as it seems, read some Shestov is not material either. What matters is a similarity of temperament in the two thinkers, expressing itself in their classicism and nakedness of style, and in general in the same attitude toward time. Shestov wrangled not only with Spinoza as if he were his contemporary, but also with Plato, and saw the last three thousand years practically as one short moment. Simone Weil's notebooks are full of quotations in the original Greek, of mathematical equations, and of references to Hinduism, Zen, and Taoism—which did not hinder her in her passionate twentieth-century commitments. But there is something else that authorizes us to speak of Shestov and Simone Weil in one breath. It is the central theme of their thought, the phenomenon of suffering and death. These are her words [from *Cahiers*, vol. 3]: "A Discourse of Ivan in the Karamazovs. Even if that immense factory brings the most extraordinary marvels and costs only a single tear of a single child, I refuse. I adhere completely to that feeling. No matter which motive people might offer me, nothing could compensate for the tear of a child and nothing will make me accept that tear. Nothing, absolutely nothing conceivable by intelligence. One thing only, intelligible only to supernatural love: God willed it thus. And for that reason I would also accept a world of pure evil, the consequences of which would be as bad as one tear of a child." Shestov could have written these lines, but they would have had a different meaning to him.

Although Simone Weil was Jewish, she was raised in an areligious family and was unacquainted with Judaism. In Kiev Shestov absorbed Jewish religious literature, including legends and folklore, at an early age. Simone Weil's sacred book was Homer's *Iliad*; her thought was inspired by Plato, later by the New Testament. She was as thoroughly Hellenized as it was possible for pupils of the French *lycées* in the early decades of our century to be. And, had Shestov lived to read her work, he would have quoted her as an example confirming his thesis about the irreconcilable feud between Athens and Jerusalem. With the exception of the Book of Job, Simone Weil did not venerate the Old Testament and spoke harshly of the God of the Old Testament and of the Jews, reproaching them for cruelty and superstition. She was totally on the side of Athens; besides, she believed Greek and Hindu metaphysics to be identical in essential points. Her God was Greek. She even hinted at the possibility of Dionysus having been an incarnation of God, before Christ. And the gnostic penchants typical of early Hellenized Christians can be easily detected in her work. For instance, in her historical essays the indignation with which she describes the French crusade against the Albigensians and the conquest of the land speaking Oc, meaning Occitan (now the south of France), is due not only to her sympathy for the massacred and the oppressed but in large part to her identification with Albigensian Christianity related through Manichaeism to the gnosis of Marcion.

Future investigation—and I do not doubt that there will be one—should be centered in the first place on Shestov's and Weil's concept of Necessity as well as on different treatments of the relationship between Oneness and the particular. For Shestov, universal Necessity was a scandal. He felt that its horror was best described by Dostoevsky in *The Idiot* where there is talk of Holbein's painting of the *Deposition from the Cross*: "Looking at that picture, you get the impression of Nature as some enormous, implacable, and dumb beast, or, to put it more correctly, much more correctly, though it might seem strange, as some huge engine of the latest design which has senselessly seized, cut to pieces, and swallowed up—impassively and unfeelingly—a great and priceless Being, a Being worth the whole of Nature and all its laws, worth the entire earth, which was perhaps created solely for the coming of that Being! The picture seems to give expression to the idea of a cold, insolent, and senselessly eternal power to which everything is subordinated." Shestov wanted man to oppose that beast with an unflinching "No."

Simone Weil's attitude, on the other hand, was similar to the wonder a mathematician feels when confronted with the complexities of numbers. A few quotations [from *La Pesanteur et la grâce*] will suffice to show this: "Necessity is a veil of God"; "God entrusted all phenomena without exception to the mechanism of the world"; "In God not only is there an analogy of all human virtues, but also an analogy of obedience. In this world He gives necessity free play"; "The distance between necessity and the good is the very distance between the Creation and the Creator"; "The distance between necessity and the good. To contemplate it without end. A great discovery made by the Greeks. Undoubtedly the fall of Troy taught them this"; "God can be present in Creation only in the form of absence"; "God is not omnipotent because He is the Creator. Creation is an abdication. But He is omnipotent in the sense that His abdication is voluntary; He knows its effects and wants them."

For Simone Weil the "terrifying beauty" of the world was mysteriously linked to mathematical Necessity. Yet she would not disagree with Shestov when he denounced "the beast," since she believed that the determinism of Nature is the domain of the Prince of this World acting on God's authority. But as a philosopher (also a college professor of philosophy) whose intellectual antecedents were essentially Greek, she would not turn against Reason. Applying ideas of reduction, she conceded as much as possible to the immutable structure of the world. The power of

God to act through Grace is, by His own will, infinitely small but sufficient to save man. It is the mustard seed of the Gospel (or the silence of Christ in the "Legend of the Grand Inquisitor"). It makes it possible for us to accept an existence which, when looked at rationally and soberly, is unbearable. Shestov fumed against Greek wisdom which led to Stoical resignation. He even reproached Nietzsche, whom he esteemed, with *amor fati*, a final blessing given to fate. Simone Weil interpreted "Thy Kingdom come" as a prayer asking for the end of evil, for the end of the world, and "Thy will be done" as an assent to the existence of a world bound by the laws of Necessity. Moreover, that heroic assent was in her view the very core of Christianity: "Just as a child hides from his mother, laughing, behind an armchair, so God plays at separating Himself from Himself through the act of Creation. We are God's joke"; "To believe that reality is love, seeing it for what it is. To love what is impossible to bear. To embrace iron, to press one's body against the cold of hard metal. That is not a variety of masochism. Masochists are excited by fake cruelty. For they do not know what cruelty is. One must embrace, not cruelty, but blind indifference and blind brutality. Only in such a manner does love become impersonal" [*La Connaissance surnaturelle*].

Why should love become impersonal? Here again Shestov would not agree. In the Jansenist "*Le moi est haïssable*"—"The I is hateful"—of Pascal, with whom he otherwise agreed, he suspected a glimmer of the old Greek nostalgia for the immutable, eternal, general Oneness in which the particular disappears. Why should we hate "I"? Was it not the "I" of Job that complained and wailed? Was not the God who would demand such an impossible detachment from us a God of philosophers rather than a God of prophets? Simone Weil's response to these questions points to her latent Platonism and to the Platonic myth of the world as a prison of souls longing after their native land, the empyrean of pure ideas. Many of her maxims amount to a confession of guilt, the basic guilt of existing, and to a desire for self-annihilation. "My existence diminishes God's glory. God gave it to me so that I may wish to lose it" [*La Connaissance surnaturelle*]. She was aware that a self-imposed renunciation of the "I" was nearly impossible, and yet she rated the very aspiration to achieve renunciation as a high spiritual attainment. She referred more than once to two lines in Racine's *Phèdre* (again we are in a Jansenist climate):

Et la mort à mes yeux ravissant la clarté
Rend au jour qu'ils souillaient toute sa pureté.
[And death, ravishing the light from my eyes,
Gives all purity back to the day they defiled.]

This is, however, an essay on Shestov, not on Simone Weil. Their judgments often converge, yet in general these two move in realms that bear only a tangential relationship to each other. Not only was she passionately interested in social problems (she worked as a laborer in the Renault factory and participated in the Spanish civil war) but her religious, even mystical, experience was drawing her to Roman Catholicism and to a discussion of religion as an institution. For very personal reasons she decided not to receive the sacrament of baptism. Nevertheless, Catholic theology and the history of the Roman Catholic Church occupy a prominent position in her writings. Shestov was dominated by a violent scorn for speculative philosophy because he believed that although it pretends to bring solace, in truth its consolations are illusory. Paradoxically he waged his war. as an antirationalist using rational argument as his weapon. We know nothing about his confessional options and not much about the intensity of his personal faith.

What could Sorana Gurian, a young woman dying of cancer, get from her reading of Shestov? Not the promise of a miraculous cure. He did not maintain that you can knock down the wall of Necessity by beating your head against it. To the sober-minded who criticized the Absurd of Kierkegaard and his faith in the impossible, he used to reply that Kierkegaard knew perfectly well the weight of reality: Regina Olsen would not be restored to him. Yet there is a great difference between our looking at ourselves as ciphers on a statistical sheet and our grasping our destiny as something that is personal and unique. Simone Weil, though she advocated the voluntary renunciation of the "I," also considered the destruction of the "I" by an external force as a sign of utter misfortune: prisoners and prostitutes are compelled by *others* to visualize themselves as *objects*, statistical ciphers, interchangeable units. Shestov did not fight science. Yet in his rebellion against philosophy we may sense an implied rejection of the terror exerted by a whole purely quantitative, scientific *Weltanschauung*. Such a scientific code of self-perception, imposed by education and the mass media, eats up our individual substance from the inside, so to speak.

To Sorana the God of the Scriptures defended by the stern priest Shestov would probably not have meant an afterlife and a palm tree in Heaven. He must have appeared to her as He did to the Russian author, as pure anti-Necessity. The question was not the existence of Heaven and Hell, not even the "existence" of God Himself. Above any notions, but revealed by His voice in the Scriptures, He is able to create anything, even a personal heaven and earth for Sorana Gurian. Or for each one of us.

DOSTOEVSKY

I TAUGHT A CLASS on Dostoevsky and have been asked many times why I have not written a book about him. I have always answered that an entire library in various languages has been written about him and that I am not a literary scholar; at most, I am a distant cousin to one. To tell the truth, however, there is another reason why.

It would have to be a book based on mistrust, and one cannot do without trust. That great writer had an influence like none of his contemporaries, with the exception of Nietzsche, on the thinking of Europe and America. Neither Balzac, nor Dickens, nor Flaubert, nor Stendhal is as universally known now. He used a form of the novel such as no one had ever succeeded in using before (or after) him, although George Sand attempted it—to present a diagnosis of an immense phenomenon which he himself had experienced from the inside and had thoroughly comprehended: the erosion of religious belief. His diagnosis turned out to be correct. He foresaw the results of this erosion in the minds of the Russian intelligentsia. The Russian Revolution found its prediction in *The Possessed*, as Lunacharsky openly admitted, and in "The Legend of the Grand Inquisitor."

Undoubtedly a prophet. But also a dangerous teacher. Bakhtin, in his book on Dostoevsky's poetics, proposed the hypothesis that the polyphonic novel was that Russian writer's invention. Polyphony makes Dostoevsky such a modern writer: he hears voices, many voices, in the air, quarreling with each other, proclaiming contradictory ideas—are we not all in the present phase of civilization exposed to this raucous chaos of voices?

His polyphony has limits, however. Behind it is concealed the fervent man of faith, the Russian millennialist and messianist. It is difficult to think of anything less polyphonic than the scene with the Poles in *The Brothers Karamazov*, a crass satire which does not fit the seriousness of this work. The treatment of the character Ivan Karamazov produces a far stronger emotional effect than polyphony would allow.

Dostoevsky the ideologue has been distinguished from Dostoevsky the writer in order to protect his greatness, which is marred by unfortunate pronouncements, and Bakhtin's hypothesis has proved a great help in this effort. In point of fact, however, one can say that had there been no Russian messianist and his passionate concern for Russia, there would have been no international writer. It was not only his concern for Russia that gave him strength, but also his fears about Russia's future that forced him to write in order to issue a warning.

Was he a Christian? That is not clear. Perhaps he thought that he would become one, because he saw no salvation for Russia outside of Christianity? But the conclusion of *The Brothers Karamazov* allows us to doubt whether the destructive forces, which he observed, had found an effective counterweight in his mind. The pure youth Alyosha, at the head of his twelve schoolboys, like a Boy Scout troop, as a projection of Christian Russia capable of saving her from Revolution? That's just a bit too sweet and kitschy.

He fled from kitsch; he sought strong flavors. The sinners,

rebels, deviants, madmen of world literature first inhabited his novels. It seems that descending into the depths of sin and shame is a condition in his works for salvation, but he also creates the damned, like Svidrigailov and Stavrogin. Although he is all his characters, one in particular was given the type of understanding that is closest to his own: Ivan Karamazov. That is why Lev Shestov suspects, justifiably so, in my opinion, that Ivan expresses Dostoevsky's ultimate inability to believe, despite his positive characters, the Elder Zosima and Alyosha. What is it that Ivan declares? He returns the Creator's "ticket" because of a single tear of a child and then relates the legend of the Grand Inquisitor, which he himself has composed, and whose meaning leads us to the conclusion that if it is impossible to make people happy under the sign of Christ, then one must try to bring them happiness by collaborating with the Devil. Berdyaev wrote that Ivan is characterized by "false oversensitivity" and no doubt the same could be said of Dostoevsky.

He wrote in a letter to Mrs. Fonvizin that if he were ordered to choose between the truth and Christ, he would choose Christ. Those who would choose the truth are probably more honorable, even if the truth appears on the surface to deny Christ (as Simone Weil argued). At least they are not relying on their fantasy and not constructing idols in their own image.

There is something that would incline me to make a softer judgment: it is the fact that Lev Shestov found the inspiration for his tragic philosophy in Dostoevsky. Shestov is very important for me. It was thanks to my reading of him that Joseph Brodsky and I were able to understand each other intellectually.

A PHILOSOPHER

THAT PHILOSOPHER was an atheist; i.e., he would not seek in the existence of the universe any signs indicating its first cause. The hypotheses of science managed without it, and he, though he had some doubts as to its methods, relied on them to learn about the nature of things. To be fair, we should add that even though he esteemed science, he did not belong to those dreamers who expect that reason would allow human beings to build a perfect society one day.

The only preoccupation worthy of a philosopher was, in his view, meditating on the meaning of religion. When reproached with contradicting himself, he would answer that man is a self-contradictory being, and thus he, in his pronouncements on the importance of religion, was in harmony with his humanity.

All splendor and all the dignity of man was contained, according to him, in religion. The very fact that so miserable a creature, so irrevocably mortal, was able to create good and evil, up and down, heavens and abysses, seemed to him incomprehensible and deserving of constant astonishment. Nowhere in the whole immense universe—not to be encompassed by imagination—was there even a shred of good, of pity, of compassion, and the questions prompted by the needs of the human heart found no response. The faithful of the chief religions of mankind did not, felt the philosopher, pay enough attention to the absolute loneliness of human consciousness under the starry sky. Even less inclined to reflect on this were followers of various shamanisms, who humanized Nature and blurred the borderline between the human and the animal kingdom.

The philosopher had a hard time coping with the idea of beauty ruled by the goddess Venus; i.e., by the force of Nature itself. He wrote a book to prove that beauty exists only where shapes and colors called to life by the goddess Venus encounter the sight and the hearing of man, two senses endowed with a magical power of transformation.

Not all religions were ranked the same by him. He assigned the highest place to those in which the opposition between man and the natural order of things was the most marked, in which, therefore, man by liberating himself from that order achieved salvation. In this respect, the first among them was Christianity; the next, Buddhism; for they both sanctified a trait exclusively human, compassion, against the stony face of the world. What could be more human than the God of Christianity, taking the shape of a man, and aware that the stony world would sentence Him to death? Because the Son reigned for eternity and in His name everything was created, it meant that the human shape and the human heart reside in the very bosom of God and suffer as they look at a world that was intended as good but was tainted by death because of the Fall.

The philosopher's respect turned first of all to the Roman, Catholic, and Apostolic Church, whose two millennia could suffice as an argument. In his century he witnessed furious attacks directed by the gates of Hell against that rock. Being a humanist, he should have rejoiced at the weakening of prohibitions that in-

terfered with natural human desires; he, however, bowed his
head before the Pope, who dared, openly and loudly, against the
whole world, to proclaim "the sign of dissent."

Aware that civilization is threatened by decay if one truth
does not provide it with a unifying bond, the philosopher in his
public statements always sided with warnings flowing from the
Vatican. He did not hide the fact that, though he was refused the
grace of faith, he would like to be counted among the workers in
the Lord's vineyard.

SALIGIA

Superbia
Avaritia
Luxuria
Invidia
Gula
Ira
Acedia

IN THE MIDDLE AGES the first letters of the seven cardinal sins formed the word *saligia*, which was thought to be doubly useful since it made it easy to memorize the names of the seven sins, or, rather, failings (*vitia capitalia*), and it emphasized their unity. That much I knew, but not long ago I was tempted to look into a few encyclopedias to check out what they had to say about *saligia*. In none of them did I find even a mention of this word. What is more, Catholic encyclopedias and dictionaries of theological terms are silent about it. Priests no longer evince much interest in sins, as if they would like to ask the world's pardon for considering this one of their primary tasks for so many centuries. They mumble even when speaking of the concept of sin, and so they are not inclined to mention the old classifications in the compendia and catechisms that they edit.

In search of a certain book that is devoted to the history of the cardinal sins, I made my way to Theology Hill. For Berkeley, in addition to its university, which is splendid in every respect, also has several graduate divinity schools, for various denominations, which are located in close proximity to each other, with a lovely view of San Francisco Bay. They collaborate in an ecumenical spirit and share their rich library collections. The best known of these schools is the interdenominational Pacific School of Religion. The late Earl Morse Wilbur was a member of its faculty; he learned Polish in order to write his two-volume *History of Unitarianism*, not without a reason, for at least half his work is filled with the travels and disputes of the Polish Arians.

I found the book about the cardinal sins, but it was in storage, where rarely requested books are kept, which leads me to the conclusion that this topic is not particularly popular with either future pastors or their teachers. In fact, the list of cardinal sins compiled by the eremites of Egypt in the fourth century was always a bit of a historical relic, since the names of the sins would stay the same but their meanings kept changing. I learned from this work that the word *saligia* was popularized by Henry of Ostia in the thirteenth century, but that for a long time it was rivaled by another version: *siiaagl* (*superbia, invidia, ira, acedia, avaritia, gula, luxuria*), signifying a different ordering of the same failings. However, *saligia* triumphed, if only for mnemonic reasons, and was adopted by the Jesuits during the Counter-Reformation.

As a child, I did not receive much moral benefit from my catechism lessons. Perhaps children in general are not prepared to understand such convoluted knowledge, and besides, too many strange associations based on the Polish names for the cardinal sins would enter my mind during those lessons.

1. *Pycha* (pride) instead of *superbia. Pych* (punt), *puch* (fluff),

pyza (a moon face or a round plate)? *Pyszałkowaty-pyzaty* (conceited and chubby)? Self-inflation beyond one's means? That's someone else, some gentleman, a *pyza-pycha w kryzie* (moon-faced, preening person wearing a ruff), definitely not I—in other words, this cannot apply to me. *Pycha* is classified instantly, just by its sound, whereas *superbia*, as Lucifer's attribute, has nuances of gravity, too, like English *pride*, French *orgueil*, German *Stolz*, Church Slavic *gordost'*.

2. *Łakomstwo* (covetousness) for *avaritia*. I saw in this a transgression that consisted of licking out jam jars or indulging my unrestrained craving for dessert, which may not be much of a problem today, but during my childhood desserts rarely appeared on our table. And who would have explained to me then that just such a yen for sweets was the mainspring of our civilization's grim history, that it provided the impetus for usury and the establishment of factories, for the conquest of America, the oppression of the peasant in Poland, the brilliant idea perfected by the pious citizens of Amsterdam that they could use their ships to traffic in slaves? Certainly, the mighty of this world have always wanted dessert. However, if they were at least gluttons, that is, individuals in pursuit of sensual pleasures, that wouldn't have been so bad. *Avaritia*, however, is rather an ascetic passion, as the French *avarice* and the German *Geiz* indicate. Should Molière's *L'Avare* be translated as *The Glutton*? English *covetousness* is closer to greediness than miserliness, but it is also a stern appetite directed exclusively at money. Both meanings, miserliness and greediness, are expressed by Church Slavic *srebrolub'e*, a literal translation of the Greek *filarguria*.

3. *Nieczystość* (impurity) instead of *luxuria*. This probably had something to do with not washing oneself? With the added implication of "shameful parts"? But the Latin word meant exuberance, fertility, abundance, primarily of vegetation, then immoderate exuberance, for example in how one expressed oneself; also excess, overweening pride, and dissolution. French *luxure* preserved some of these connotations, although it means

the same as Polish *rozwiązłość* (dissoluteness); *rozwiązłość*, not *nieczystość*, would have been a better Polish equivalent. By abandoning Latin here and making use of the Old German *Lust*, English has strayed too far from the original meaning, although the adjective *lusty* leans in the direction of exuberant, strong, and at one time was used in the sense of playful, merry. English *lust* suggests the kinds of changes that related concepts have been subjected to as a result of language and customs, especially if we compare it to the Church Slavic name for this sin: *blud* (which simply means "fornication"), taken directly from Greek *porneia*, bypassing the Latin. *Nieczystość*, by contrast, appears to be simply a translation of the German *Unkeuschheit*.

4. *Zazdrość* (envy) instead of *invidia*. The meaning of this word was completely unclear to me. Now, I know that its source is the Latin *in-videre*; *za-źrzeć*, in other words, exactly the same thing as *za-widzieć* (*zavist'* in Church Slavic). Other languages place more or less emphasis on will, yearning, although I find it difficult to say if French *envie*, English *envy*, German *Neid* adequately convey the sense of the Latin term that includes both hatred and slander.

5. *Obżarstwo* (gluttony) and *pijaństwo* (drunkenness) instead of *gula*. Originally, it meant throat in Latin; later, voraciousness and greediness, too. Gluttony and drunkenness suggested an image of laden tables, of potbellied men grunting and bellowing; obviously a grownup's sin. Only now do I wonder why Polish used two words to translate *gula*. In none of the languages I know does drunkenness figure among the cardinal sins. Church Slavic *chrevougod'e*, or belly-pleasing, was constructed on the model of the Greek *gastrimargia*; the closest thing in Polish would have been *popuszczanie sobie pasa* (loosening one's belt) in relation to both food and drink. Something unexpected happened to this failing in the course of history, perhaps because there was a time in the past when more people could indulge themselves with *gula* than in the course of the following centuries. All sorts of undernourished people could lick their chops at the thought of

stuffing their bellies just for once, and an entire poetry arose about smoked goose, kielbasa, smoked ham, kegs of beer. It was supposed to be a sin, but what else was the reward for self-restraint during Lent if not gluttony and drunkenness? And is there really a negative connotation to the French word *gourmandise*? On the contrary, if someone is a *gourmand* that's very good, it means he has a ruddy complexion, ties his napkin under his chin, and is knowledgeable about cuisine and wines; he's not a pauper. He's not quite a *gourmet*, or a connoisseur of food, but he's close to it. German *unmässig* doesn't benefit from such privileges, and the English *glutton* is also different, an insatiable gullet prone to *gluttony* or omnivorousness.

6. *Gniew* (rage) instead of *ira*. "An explosion of rage"—it wasn't hard to picture what that is. It is a short-lived physical state that is expressed in violent deeds (King Bolesław the Brave breaking into the church and in a fit of rage murdering the bishop). *Ira* doesn't present any great difficulty in translation either. *Anger, colère, Zorn,* Church Slavic *gnev*.

7. *Lenistwo* (laziness) instead of *acedia*. Polish is not responsible for the comical misunderstanding. The word is not Latin but was borrowed via the Latin directly from the Greek *akedia*, and should have been translated as *obojętność* (indifference). But for the fourth-century eremites *akedia* was the main danger, a temptation by the Devil that was most severe at noon, when all nature rests in silence, motionless under the high sun. That is when a monk would be visited by sadness and boredom. He would try to resist it with prayer, but he would be tormented by a feeling that all his exertions and his mortifications were meaningless. If he allowed himself to be defeated, he would abandon his cave and just run over to the neighboring cave in order not to be by himself. If he often succcumbed to such attacks, he had to return to the city, to be among people. *Akedia* was therefore a dangerous impediment for people dedicated to an intense spiritual life. Monastic instructions also devoted a good deal of attention to it later on, in the Middle Ages. It was frequently linked with *tristi-*

tia or *lupe*, that is, sadness; it is easiest to express it with the words *nothing matters*. The transformation of *akedia* into the (physical?) failing of somnolence and indolence took place only gradually. Neither the French *paresse*, the English *sloth*, nor the German *Trägheit* conveys the original meaning. Only Church Slavic *unyn'e* conveys it perfectly. Obviously, I didn't have the foggiest notion of what "laziness" was except for one of its variants, that is, my understandable repugnance for "iron necessity," that is, doing my homework.

The disinclination of clergymen today to classify sins is understandable, since the whole great edifice of distinctions, concepts, and syllogisms was erected quite late, achieving its ultimate form in Jesuit casuistry. Of course, the prestige of scientific research that sets itself the task of dissecting stuffed bears in order to see how they are constructed undoubtedly also had an influence. This stuffed bear, or man, is not studied by psychologists as a tangle of good and evil, or of values, but as the territory of certain "phenomena." At the same time, man's poor sins, in comparison with the luxuriant flora and fauna discovered inside him, have become abstractions similar to émigré governments and exiled monarchs.

Nonetheless. *Sed contra*, as Thomas Aquinas used to say. In each of us various interesting chains of causes and effects can be tracked down, but let someone else concern himself with this. When we are alone with ourselves, it is our goodness and our evil that perturb us and not those intriguing questions: Where do we come from and why are we here? And what if I should try to ascertain what the cardinal sins, so vague and foggy in my childhood, mean to me today? This would be no ordinary assignment, because it would imply that a new content is being interpreted in terms of the old *saligia*; that is, by discovering its imposing forms within oneself, one restores it to its sorrowful dignity.

Let us be candid. The seven cardinal sins were considered at most a spur to the actions that condemn one to eternal damnation, but not a single one of these seven nor *saligia* as a whole had of necessity to lead to utter damnation. For the *vitia capitalia* were the more or less universal manifestations of spoiled human nature, and this nature is not so spoiled as to leave no room for hope. Thus, in *The Divine Comedy*, when Dante and his guide, Virgil, emerge at the other end of the earth after their sojourn in Hell at the center of earth and begin their ascent to Mount Purgatory, they come upon seven terraces, each of which is inhabited by souls who are doing penance for one of the seven cardinal sins. The order of these terraces follows the model of *siiaagl*, not *saligia*, and I find Dante's reasoning convincing. Several tercets from Canto 17 are of particular importance here and are well worth citing in translation. When they reach the fourth terrace Virgil says:

> *"My son, there's no Creator and no creature*
> *who ever was without love—natural*
> *or mental; and you know that," he began.*
> *"The natural is always without error,*
> *but mental love may choose an evil object* [per malo obietto]
> *or err through too much or too little vigor.*
> *As long as it's directed toward the First Good*
> *and tends toward secondary goods with measure,*
> *it cannot be the cause of evil pleasure;*
> *but when it twists toward evil, or attends*
> *to good with more or less care than it should,*
> *those whom He made have worked against their Maker.*
> *From this you see that—of necessity—*
> *love is the seed in you of every virtue*
> *and of all acts deserving punishment."*

[TRANSLATED BY ALLEN MANDELBAUM]

"Love that moves the sun and the stars" is, then, the core of all things and of each living being. In the order of nature (*amore naturale*) it does not submit to moral judgments. A stone released from the hand falls because that is what the law of gravity wants;

an animal hunts another animal because that is what he is ordered to do by what has come to be called instinct. But love in the
spiritual order, which is what distinguishes man and also angels
(*amore d'animo*), can be mistaken. Its calling is to aspire to the
first good, that is, to the source of great good, that is, to God
(*primo ben diretto*). It is mistaken if it recognizes as its good
something that conflicts with this chief end, and also if it itself is
too strong or too weak. The seven terraces of Purgatory are an illustration of such errors. The three lowest signify depraved love;
that is, love that aspired to a mistaken goal. The souls whom
Dante and Virgil meet there are suffering because during their
lifetimes the magnetic needle of their love (or Will) had turned
toward themselves: *superbia, invidia, ira.* The fourth is the terrace
of *acedia*, or insufficient, somnolent love, that love that was incapable of putting to proper use the time given to mortal man. The
three highest terraces, the ones closest to the Earthly Paradise,
which is located on the highest plateau of Mount Purgatory, are
designated as the place of penance for souls whose love was excessive, because *avaritia, gula,* and *luxuria* derive from excess.
This is rather enigmatic, because the greedy, the gluttonous, and
the dissolute come out much better with their failings than do
others. Their powerful will to life appears to be centrifugal, not
centripetal; that is, it is directed toward the external world, toward its annexation. It is oblivious, somehow, of the annexer
himself: for the greedy man or the miser, money symbolically
summarizes all the delights of earth; roast meats rivet the attention of the glutton because he does not, after all, think about his
own taste—taste resides in the roast; a beautiful girl charms the
ladykiller with a promise of something mysterious, unrecognized.
If this is so, if the centrifugal will to life is the pursuit of existence as enchantment, by transgressing a certain measure it can
find satiety only in *primo ben diretto*, that is, in God; but in that
case, since there is so much of it, it would lead to saintliness. But
saintliness is not easy, which is why these three higher terraces
exist. Which is to say, since love directed outward, so to speak, to-

ward things apprehended by the senses, is not an error, at worst its excessive greediness would incline one to offer this advice: Either be saintly or you will have to have less of this love of yours. Dostoevsky follows Dante faithfully in *The Brothers Karamazov*; the *avaritia, gula,* and *luxuria* of both the elder Karamazov and Dmitri pale in comparison with a truly severe defect: Ivan's *superbia*, with which Smerdyakov's *acedia* is in league.*

SUPERBIA

If you are one of the thousand, shall we say, active poets of your time, you think about what will become of your works in a hundred or two hundred years. Either all your names will be listed only in footnotes to the intellectual history of the period, or one of you will rise above the fashions and collective customs, while the rest, although they had appeared to be individuals, will form a chorus obedient to its conductor, who will silence any voices that are too independent—independent, that is, of the epoch's style. That one poet is you, for you alone are right. But what does poetry have in common with being right? A whole lot. The arrangement of words implies choice, choice implies deliberation, and behind your words lurks a silent judgment about the many human matters that you have dealt with. If in your judgment (conscious, semiconscious, or unconscious) you are right, you will break through the cocoon of generally accepted opinions in your epoch; the others, however, will become trapped in them. For not all reasons are equal and error enjoys the same privileges as truth for only a short time. Could it be, then, that absolute criteria exist for the creations of the imagination and language? Without a doubt. But how can that be? After all, one person likes

*Sergei Gessen was the first to apply *saligia* to Dostoevsky His 1928 work, "Tragediia dobra v 'Brat'iakh Karamazovykh,' " is reprinted in the collection *O Dostoevskom. Stat'i* (Providence: Brown University Press, 1966), pp 199–229.

one thing, another likes something else, *de gustibus non est disputandum.* And yet everything that can be numbered among the works of the human spirit submits to a strict hierarchy. Our opinions about contemporary works are unstable and tentative, because only time lays bare the true hierarchy under the veils and piles of gilded rubbish. Nonetheless, at the moment when you hold your pen and compose poetry, you are extraordinarily confident of your rightness—and also of the erroneous assumptions of all your rivals. But isn't there a fraternity of poets who are also very different but who respect each other? There are such fraternities. The triumph of your mastery, however, is contained in the act of writing itself, and you know very well that you trust only the voice of your own daimonion.

It cannot be ruled out that this is the way things have worked up till now because "eternal glory" has gotten into the habit of crowning only a few greats. Considering that it is the *activity* (writing, painting, sculpture, etc.) that assumes prominence today and not the results, it is possible that the many millions of creative artists who are fleetingly famous will replace the few who are chosen. I was raised according to traditional beliefs, however, and therefore I am inclined to consider the sin of *superbia* an occupational disease. If we limited its meaning to overweening pride, we would ignore the rich ambiguity of its consequences, for pride and self-assurance are indispensable for the poet who wishes to achieve something and not retreat from his path.

I have held various opinions about poetry and literature in various phases of my life, so I might be making the mistake of reading into the past the views that I hold today. In the profession of "writer" I now see a certain embarrassing buffoonery. When we read the diaries of various masters of the pen published nowadays, we are overcome with pity: they really considered themselves "great." How many of them worshipped dry rot, their own renown, which was supported by a couple of coffeehouses and a handful of press clippings? That's how it is now, but my not very friendly attitude toward my profession was formed a long time ago, I think, in my early youth. Already at that time poetry, not to speak of literature in general, was *too little*. Let us assume that you are, potentially, better than your rivals (which I did not doubt). So what? Among the blind a one-eyed man is king, and are you really going to take pride in that title? There is no question that I wanted to be a superb poet. But that did not seem to me to be sufficient. Had I aspired to the composition of a certain number of excellent poems, that would simply have been evidence of only mild *superbia*; however, I had enough *superbia* in me for it to carry me beyond any mere authorship.

I did not ascribe to myself any extraordinary abilities or talents except for one which I would be unable to define even now. It was a particular type of intelligence capable of perceiving associations between things that others did not perceive as connected. It was also a type of imagination that was particularly sensitive to customs and institutions. One way or another, I always heard this warning inside me: *This cannot last.* And if there was a certain unreality to everything that surrounded me, could works written in the midst of this unreality be real? Especially since this did not apply to Poland alone but also, although for somewhat different reasons, to all of Europe. Somewhere, Ortega y Gasset compares the artist who is born in an unfavorable era to a woodcutter with strong muscles and a sharp ax who finds himself in the desert. I wasn't familiar with this analogy at that time, in my youth; had I known it, my auto-irony would have been expressed in the following words: "You've picked a fine time, with that strength of yours, since there isn't any wood."

It was necessary to strive for that dimension where the fates of both reality as a whole and poetry were being decided. However, it wasn't reachable by words in those days. Furthermore, no one understood my poems or, perhaps more important, I believed that no one understood them, because I felt totally isolated, the more so as we drew closer to 1939. Today, I understand this as follows: Polish society has a very strong sense of the sacral, and this explains the specific fortunes of Poles in a century of advanced desacralization. What we are talking about here, however, is such an extreme appropriation of the sacral by one goddess—Polishness—that nothing else was good enough for her. The dimension that my eyes dimly perceived in the thirties did not belong to the general Polish dimension, so my place was among the "outsiders," because they were Jews or because they were Communists or Communist sympathizers. No matter where I turned, however, there was nowhere where I felt at home. A taste for "ultimate things" gave direction to my entire life, although due to various geographical-psychological peculiarities the Polish-Catholic tonality has not been dominant in this religion of mine.

Was my imagination right, then, to warn me that this could not last? Here I should draw a distinction. Grasping the "black" sides of reality, my imagination facilitated my pessimistic diagnosis, but I should try to downplay the opinion, flattering though it is, that this was my prophetic poetic gift at work. Who knows if my rejection of life in general, punishing it for being *unreasonable*, was not even more important here? This unreason, in both individual, biological life and collective life alike, has various degrees of intensity, ranging from those that can be named (e.g., economic absurdities, unsuccessful political institutions, and so forth) to completely elusive ones, though they were always inconsistent with my need for total harmony. Thus, whether the overthrow of the existing order occurred or not, its downfall would always have seemed justified to me in advance.

My *superbia* demanded punishment, and at last it has incurred punishment. For now, in my mature years, when I open my mouth and listen to myself with the ears of those to whom I speak, what do I hear? Incomprehensible babbling, which should be counted as punishment. After repeated explosions of rage (after all, I wasn't asking for much) I had to accept this immuring of myself in loneliness as equitable and pedagogically beneficial to me. Someone who writes in Polish should not harbor illusions. If the Polish custom of respect for literature as the national shrine did not go hand in hand with utter disdain for matters of the spirit, the earth would be too beautiful a place for our sojourn here.

To be polite: I am barely lifting the curtain here, conscious of the many complications that I have overlooked, for I am obedient to the discipline of language. I am limiting myself to the twofold consequences—negative and positive—of *superbia*. Does it not frequently act as a substitute for morality? As when it forbids us certain actions because they are beneath our conception of ourselves as worthy only of the highest acts? And could someone who relies on willfulness alone really get by without *superbia*? Sooner or later loneliness drives us into crises that cannot be resolved other than by some rebirth, the shedding of the snakeskin, so that what has tormented us till now no longer concerns us. True, I prefer to believe that my *superbia* has played the role of midwife at these births but that, independent of it, more noble characters have also been at work.

INVIDIA

He has what I ought to have; I, not he, deserve it—there's a model of envy. Not that I would like to be him; quite the contrary: he is inferior to me and has been unjustly rewarded, and undoubtedly, because of his inferiority, he is unable to even appreciate it (I, as the superior one, would be able to). Envy, the daughter of pride, is so widespread a failing among literati and authors that it's funny. For instance, every piece of news about a distinction accorded to others evokes in them more or less well-concealed pangs of jealousy. It is true that it is difficult to determine the extent and intensity of envy within oneself, because it is adept at disguising itself. Coming from a provincial European backwater and emigrating three times, first to Warsaw, then to Paris, then to America (always with a marshal's baton in my knapsack?), I must have been cultivating plenty of envy within myself. Let's be fair; this was moderated, however, by an exceptional talent for idolizing, so that while sternly judging some (the many), I knelt humbly before the chosen, absolutely convinced of my own utter inferiority (though they were rarely "writers").

Let us abandon the field of art and literature, however. My century should have been called the age of *invidia* and I shall explain why immediately. Social mobility, when great masses of people suddenly, within a brief span of time, change their occupation, dress, and customs, is conducive to imitation. Strong caste divisions used to make imitation difficult (for example, a bourgeois who pretended to be a member of the landed gentry was laughed at). Imitation means close observation of another and the desire to have as much as he has (money, clothes, freedom, etc.). And here is where a personality that spreads terror appears—it exists in every person as the "I-for-others" that torments the "I-for-myself." One can imagine a state in which a person is relatively indifferent to the behavior of others, if only because their station is too high (for example, wearing folk costumes because only city people wear manufactured clothes), or because, at ease with his uniqueness, he calmly tells himself: "That's not for me." However, in the twentieth century we have been forced to be ashamed of our particularity. "I-for-myself" is, after all, always a shame and a sin, although different people will cope with it more or less successfully. When a person is constantly having it drummed into his head that others are enjoying life as they should, he does not stop to think about the illusory character of this image that depicts people from the outside, that is, in such a way that every man is "I-for-others." He looks around and starts to be envious: that person over there, he's a miserable creature, and yet look at how much he's received, how many gifts have been showered upon him—he's not below the norm, I am. This "normality" or "I-for-others" is, after all, the secret of the diffusion of the "new ethics," namely, the characteristic feature of the "permissive society." Each of us has a "calling" that comprises his diversion from the norm, an appeal directed at this and not that individual. The object of envy is not others in the guise of

Charles, Peter, or Ignatius, but in the guise of "normality" as seen from the outside, which we allegedly have too little of. "Reification," imitation, and *invidia* are closely interconnected.

But does the desire to become "the same as everyone else" really indicate that one is envious? So it seems. I don't have what he has, it's owed me, because if I should have it, then I would have a lot more (being myself, my individuality, of course). "Normality" will be an addition to my individuality, while, in my opinion, the essence of this other person is being dissipated in it.

If we divide envy according to its target—a small group based, for example, on profession, or "people in general," the latter would be more dangerous. It is easy to err when we don't want to accept our own destiny, which has been given to us alone, when we are unable to make our peace with the thought that some types of lifestyles are beyond our abilities and would even be painful for us. When we make the effort to conform, various miseries of the "man in the crowd" reveal themselves to us.

IRA

Bah, if only it were old-fashioned anger that visits us. It is bad to turn purple in the face from fury; even worse to knock someone flat with a blow to the head and kill him in a fit of rage. Even if someone doesn't carry a hatchet around with him, he may well know the belated regrets of a hothead when it's already too late to make amends. But in addition to this age-old anger, a new, modern anger appeared on the scene when we began to feel responsible for evil as members of society and participants in history. Your guts churn, you grit your teeth, clench your fists—but hold your tongue, you are a cipher and can change nothing. And you ask yourself: "Am I crazy or are they crazy? Maybe it's me, because they go right on living and feel neither indignation nor terror in the face of their own co-responsibility." If we are born with an inclination to anger, and in this lovely century, to boot, what should we do, how are we to cope? Obviously, each person receives an upbringing; just living among others shapes him. He notices that yelling and banging his head against the wall hardly help; if he is a poet, he becomes convinced that making a lot of noise is not very useful. So his anger goes underground and emerges only in disguise, transformed into irony, sarcasm, or icy calm, from which it is often hard to deduce that fury lies concealed behind it.

I spent my entire conscious life in just such maneuvers with my own anger, never, even to this day, understanding how it could be reconciled with my (truly) asocial nature. How, in fact, are we to understand the coexistence within us of contradictory impulses and habits? All the same, my guts kept churning before 1939 and during the war and after. How is it possible, someone will ask quite justifiably, to compare what is incomparable, historical periods and systems marked by a lesser intensity of evil with those in which evil approached its own paroxysm? Unfortunately, the truth is that every human society is multilayered and multilocational. What offends our moral sense does not occur simultaneously in all strata and in all places. Even where the majority of the population is dying of hunger there are beautiful neighborhoods inhabited by the sated, who listen to good music and are interested in—shall we say?—mathematical logic. One should not imagine that those who have been swallowed by a dragon won't experience moments of perfect contentment. For example, one of my memories of felicity is the day in the summer of 1941 when, after a visit to the peasant writer Józef Morton in Chrobrze near Pinczów (we got there by way of a quaint narrow-gauge track that wound through the grass-covered hills), Jerzy Andrzejewski and I got off the train at a tiny station on the outskirts of Cracow from which we had to walk to the city proper. We stopped at a roadside tavern where, in the garden, a wandering Gypsy band was playing, and then, not quite steady on our feet, we slowly entered the outlying streets, where everything, compared to Warsaw, seemed to be part of another country and another era. The

hubbub of voices and the colorfulness of the crowd in the artists'
café on Łobzowska Street reminded me of Montparnasse at the
height of its glory. The waitress who came over to our table was
Jewish, the wife of our colleague, a Warsaw poet. So happiness
had not ceased to exist—although ten days later a huge roundup
demonstrated how illusory are such oases.

It's not only the multiplicity of strata and locations in human
society that acts as a universal law. The intentionality of our attention is another law, so that the mind transforms and shuffles
all sorts of "givens." Where one person sees an injustice that cries
out to heaven for vengeance, another sees nothing; where one
person evinces no desire for rebellion, another uses guns and
places bombs. My thinking about anger is strongly marked by
years spent in America; the two zones of time and space, the European and the American, complement each other. American ter-
rorists are not too different from a certain female poet who was
quite popular in the Warsaw cafés at the end of the 1930s. Poland
at that time offered many causes for anger, but this poet (from a
family of intellectuals) was so loaded with hatred that according
to her the system was at fault for everything—for what really
ought to have been dismantled and what could not be dismantled
in Poland, as well as for everything that is immune to disman-
tling in every collective life. It was she who wrote the rash line:
"We have exchanged the Russian occupation for a Polish occupation" (as if independent Poland after 1918 was no better than
czarist Russia), but she was to suffer too much on account of her
rashness for it to be worth reproaching her for this today. Her
odious poem deserves to be mentioned, however, because in it
our own, familiar, twentieth-century anger turns simultaneously
against institutions and against, one suspects, the very existence
of anything at all. The young Americans from well-to-do white
families, no less disturbed by the fate of blacks in the ghetto than
the Russian nihilists were by the fate of the peasants, demonstrate a boundless capacity for pumping themselves up with revolutionary rhetoric, but it would be wrong to treat this lightly. The

blatant analogies with Dostoevsky's *The Possessed* are probably based on a deeper level than societal relations—most importantly, perhaps, through the figure of Kirillov, the man who condemns himself to death because, as he says, there is no God but there *ought* to be. Is anger, the mighty demon of our epoch, a Promethean outburst in the name of love of people, or is it a declaration of a grudge against a world that is too unjust for life to be worth living? Both the one and the other, I should think, although their proportions here are unclear.

It is easy to understand the anger of the oppressed, the anger of slaves, particularly if you yourself have lived for several years inside the skin of a subhuman. In my century, however, the anger of the privileged who are ashamed of their privilege was even louder. I am fairly well acquainted with this anger. Though very poor as a young man, I still knew that the couple of zlotys in my pocket was practically a fortune for the majority of people in Poland; furthermore, toward the end of the thirties I earned a lot and was able to act the role of the elegant snob. And then in America I could have served as a (doubtful) argument for the defenders of classic capitalism when they assert that "the best man wins" in it, for my work was rather appreciated. I admit that I hobnobbed with people like myself in my Berkeley and my California, people who had succeeded. "We *should* bite the hand that feeds us," one of them said to me. Perhaps. But if so, always bearing in mind the fact that well-fed, rosy-cheeked people have often gotten entangled in duplicity when they pretended that they were suffering.

ACEDIA

No one can call this failing simply laziness any longer; whatever it may once have been, nowadays it has returned to its original meaning: terror in the face of emptiness, apathy, depression. It's not isolated hermits, however, who are experiencing its sting, but the masses in their millions. A perfect reactionary would say that for their own good they should have been kept in poverty and illiteracy, so that the whip of elemental necessity would have left them only brief moments for resting but not thinking, so that they could have been protected from the influence of half-baked intellectuals exploiting the printed word. It turned out otherwise, and although the model changes depending on the country and the system, the general outlines remain the same; that is, the average man has appeared who knows how to write, read, use a motorcycle or a car. Who is also unprepared for spiritual effort and subject to the power of the quasi-intellectuals, who stuff his head with counterfeit values.

Let us not yearn for the good old days; they were not good. Certainly, the sacral daily life of the medieval city was not a figment of the imagination, for it did leave a trace in architecture and in art; but at best it can furnish a clue to the distant future, when after the present transitional phase, an ascending movement will be possible—similar, but of, so to speak, a second degree.

For the present, we are in an era when minds are being defiled, which may be the unavoidable price we pay when many human beings are granted access—not just, as in the past, the narrow stratum of the privileged. Access to what? Not to "culture"—at best, culture is reminiscent of a tightly locked iron chest for which no one has remembered to supply the key. If we may anticipate access, it will be to the "independent battles" of the human persona. Steeped in tribal customs, the individual did not need this at one time, but today, everyone is beginning to be a hermit in the Egyptian desert and is subject to the law of selection—either ascending or descending into one kind of *skotstvo* or another, to use the Russian term which, although its literal meaning is "brutishness," we are inclined, despite the linguists, to link with Greek *skotos* or "darkness."

The chaos of values makes precise distinctions impossible at present, so tributes are rendered to illusory greatnesses that are famous because they represent fashionable tendencies in a color-ful and forceful manner. This age is, in addition, an age of mon-sters—humanity has rarely seen their like—but also, as if for the sake of balance, it has produced not a few figures of gigantic pro-portions, to whom it is no shame to humbly pay tribute. The mental distance between them and the mechanized man in the crowd is probably greater than that between a medieval theolo-gian and, for example, a member of the coopers' guild. To be pre-cise: this is not a judgment based on the level of education, for many who are Nobel laureates in one field of science do not dif-fer intellectually, apart from their specialty, from their least-educated fellow men. Jacques Maritain used to say that the tone of this era has been set by people with weak heads and sensitive hearts, or people with powerful heads and hard hearts, whereas few people unite a sensitive heart with a powerful head. There is no better example of this than the marketplace in America that governs both the language of words and the language of images. Stupid nobility and ignoble commercial cleverness have become so interconnected that when judging journals, films, books, and television programs in terms of their educational influence, one must simply speak of a mass crime against what is called, inaccu-rately but not inappropriately, "human dignity."

Unfortunately, someone who will not slack off, because he knows that *acedia* (or *unyn'e*) is lying in wait for him, will soon notice that the distance between him and his contemporaries in-creases with every year, if not every month. One of the charac-teristics of intellectual work is that the same activities begin to demand less and less time; that is, one develops a capacity for ab-breviations, for shortcuts. As a consequence, one loses one's taste for the words and images supplied by the market, whence the not inconsiderable problem of the new aristocracy of refined intel-lects who, however, as I have already suggested elsewhere, move in a different sphere than half a century ago—then, it was "avant-garde" literature and art that promised more than it was able to fulfill.

Zealous and diligent by temperament, I have worked hard enough, it would seem, that I ought not reproach myself with *unyn'e*. However, I have not done what I could have and the cause was both a flawed education and states of depression that would render impossible a fruitful resistance to the delusions of my time. Obviously, this does not mean that it would have been better had I decided to put on armor early in life, so that nothing from the twentieth century could infect me, as did one of my acquaintances from my youth, who even at that time was preoccupied exclusively with Plato. That would have been an erroneous and sterile choice. Here, *nota bene*, it would be appropriate to cite the storminess of history, which is not exactly favorable to better judgment. But only a slothful person will presume to cast responsibility onto something that lies outside him.

There is nothing new about grappling with the nothingness that encircles us; man has been faced with these trials for a millennium. However, never before, it seems, not since the times of Caesar's Rome and Hellenistic civilization, has man been so defenseless. These are the consequences of the scientific revolution broken down into small pieces and acting upon the popular imagination in this form. It is possible that the vast majority of people will submit to such nihilizing pressures and will at best search for consolation in the miraculous elixirs sold by Hindu, Buddhist, or Satanic preachers.

AVARITIA

It would seem that from time immemorial there has been nothing more universal and more classic. But although greed for money has always driven people to conquest, to oppression, although it has wiped out many species of animals and threatened the entire planet with the chemical poisoning of the water and air, *avaritia* in the present does not assume only those forms that Dante was familiar with. In those days, this failing always characterized a given, specific individual; today, it is spilling over onto mechanisms that are independent of a specific individual, and this also applies to the other cardinal sins, which seem to elude naming because they are cut off from man. For example, is it a result of greed that an oil company pollutes the ocean with its tankers? If we answer in the affirmative, then we see greed where there is no individual, and therefore neither guilt nor contrition. The directors? But they are acting not as people but as a function of the collective body, which has no other aim than the amassing of profits. They are punished for decisions taken in the name of any goal other than profit. They can, it is true, resign their positions and take up something else; this will not, however, change the actions of the corporate body, which yields only to external force.

The situation of the directors of such a corporation is probably emblematic of what confronts the various, and considerably lower, rungs on the social ladder. This or that Jones or Du Pont quietly dreams of virtue; he would eat grass, drink spring water, wear a sack tied with a piece of string; but while his yearning for the Franciscan ideal may be completely sincere, he has been "captured," alas, and there is no turning back.

The new, impersonal varieties of greed could, if necessary, be considered one of the reasons why it has ceased to be a literary theme. *Avaritia* as the sinister passion of the heroes of novels has its own history, which more or less parallels the history of the "realistic" novel. Defoe, Dickens, Balzac, Zola have successors in the West at the beginning of our century, too, primarily among American writers. In Russia, *srebrolub'e* begins its literary career with Pushkin's *Covetous Knight* and occupies a not inconsiderable position in Dostoevsky's biography (he wanted to win a million at roulette) and in practically all his works. The revolution in novelistic technique that we have witnessed took place at a time when the greedy collective, which is very difficult to describe, was already active alongside the greedy individual. But also the very flight from the realia of life somehow caused the novel to stop

speaking about money. And when the human jungle stuns us
with its wild growth today, literature, occupied with passive experiences and the individual's impressions, steers away from the
vulgar questions: Who makes his living at what? Who is paid for
what? It is characteristic that the anger of American intellectuals, who, with rare exceptions, are independent of the publishing market because they live off the universities, overlooks the
crux of the matter, that is, the market, and even, on the contrary, strikes out at all limitations on the market's freedom,
even though in practice that freedom serves the tradesmen-
demoralizers. No doubt a powerful taboo is at work here, one of
the most mysterious social thermostats, by force of which revolutionary anger at everything that *avaritia* is responsible for becomes transformed into merchandise, that is, assists that same
avaritia.

More than other failings, it in particular, but also its absence,
refers us to the vague laws of personal predestination. Success
and failure, measured in money, do not appear to have an unam-
biguous link with greed or miserliness, although perhaps the
middle groups, those who are called neither to wealth nor to
poverty, are the most free of *avaritia.* In this middle group the
following principle generally holds true: you will have exactly as
much money as you need, but under the condition that you are
not particularly anxious about it.

GULA

It is painful to think about all one's great-great-grandfathers suc-
cumbing to gluttony and drunkenness; in general, it is painful to
think about the genes that one is carrying around inside oneself.
The awareness that one has Slavic genes is depressing enough to
make the "taste for pickled cucumbers and boisterousness" seem
as burdensome as irreversible Karma; the consequences of this
tendency to feasting cannot be evaded, even if subsequently they

are gracefully assigned to various geopolitical causes. A simple calculation of the time spent on feasting and thereby lost to thinking over the course of centuries can explain a lot here. Idyllic feasting may testify to an inability to tolerate the world as it is, to a yearning for a gentler world; at the same time, it is one of the chief motivations of self-contempt, for revulsion at drunks in the street seems to merge with revulsion at one's own behavior in the recent past. Low self-esteem, which, to be sure, is rooted not only in this but also in a collective incapacity (so that only individuals are energetic), leads, in turn, to paranoid reflexes; self-revulsion is extended to "them," to whomever, who are guilty of everything. That is why one should also notice more than just the loud talk, stupid bragging, and jabbering in a certain type of feasting. Drunkenness itself is less important than what is revealed by drunkenness. And what is revealed is more or less the same among all peoples, with the addition of a given society's particular characteristics. It's the latter that can be the cause of low self-esteem.

I have tried to avoid the traps set by *gula* with varying degrees of success. I admit that this may be taking my practical sense too far, but I have discovered that one can "profit from one's enemy"; that is, one can ponder those things that surface whenever we carry things too far. And what comes to the fore are reflexes, whims, resentments, and egotisms too unflattering for us to enjoy being aware of them.

LUXURIA

When talk turns to dissoluteness or licentiousness, everyone pricks up his ears; I should, therefore, discourage such expectations ahead of time. For want of other attractions, above all, the attractions of the writer's art itself, the literati compete with each other nowadays in "sincerity," and it would no doubt be possible to introduce a new distinction between high style and low style

based on this principle. A self-respecting author will not sink to
such methods, from which it follows that *belles lettres* are not
worth reading because only a very few writers in that genre stay
within the bounds of high style.

Dreams of man as happy and liberated have long stood in opposition to all prohibitions and to the hypocrisy that prefers to
forget about the libido's hold over us. But eliminating hypocrisy
solves very little. D. H. Lawrence says that Adam and Eve's first
sexual act after the Original Sin was no different, physiologically,
from what they had done many times before. The difference lay
in the fact that now each of them *saw*, that is to say, was conscious
of his own body and his partner's body as Other; moreover, each
was conscious of the fact that the partner was another consciousness. That is why they experienced shame for the first time,
were conscious of their nakedness, and hid before the sight of
God. "Who told you that you are naked?" God asked Adam.
D. H. Lawrence sought a restoration; he wanted man to be innocent, as he was *before* he tasted the fruit of the Tree of the
Knowledge of Good and Evil. This is not the place to consider to
what extent we can succeed at that. That conjunction in the Book
of Genesis: a man and a woman, the apple (or consciousness),
shame, teaches us that in any event our words will not succeed in
inhabiting the Garden of Eden and that the field of literature, or
the works of the mind, can be, at best, an area on the border and,
therefore, something that exists merely *in proximity* to love and
death in their innocently physiological aspect.

There are a number of puzzling aspects to the "sexual liberation" of the second half of our century. Its vehemence can perhaps be explained as a reaction to the entire nineteenth century,
not to the period that directly preceded it, since the years of my
youth, for example, were not particularly puritanical. Let us
agree that revolutions in mores do not occur rapidly; sometimes it
takes decades until the so-called masses embrace a universal standard. However, even if we concede this, "liberation" is striking
in its frenzy, as if it were a "feast in the time of the plague,"

whether because the death that threatens the individual has grown more threatening or because the plague is going to destroy the species. This frenzy has its seat not so much in the glands as in the mind, which is filled with shifting images that constantly bombard it from outside, and that are in turn obedient to the dynamics of their own form; in other words, the dose of vividness has to be increased continually. Such a frenzy cannot stop itself and it may well be that it will destroy itself, resulting in an ominous boredom. But it is also possible that it presages a new revolution, which would be a rather paradoxical result of these yearnings for innocence and normality. Science-fiction writers have already written about such visually-olfactorily-tactilely provoked surrogate discharges.

Beatrice is a powerful symbol in *The Divine Comedy*; that is, she is both a real person and a real idea of platonic love in precisely the same degree, or she is neither the one nor the other, because she appears instead of them, so that they cannot be separated. She also leads Dante to the summit—literally, because she leads him to the mountain of Earthly Paradise and even higher—assuming the leadership where Virgil ends his role; that is, where the natural sorcery of art ends.

The present antagonism toward all asceticism and even the particular fury with which it is mocked are sufficient cause for revealing a certain secret. The Divine Arts of Imagination, as Blake called them, are obedient to Eros' summons but at the same time are ill disposed to or, should we say, envious of the procreative urge. This conflict is an entirely serious one, for the arts demand of those who are faithful to them a constant striving without fulfillment, and whether or not the faithful desire it, the arts impose upon them their own monastic rule. There exist a sufficient number of testimonies to that effect; furthermore, the lives of artists and of people who have had mystical experiences can be cited together here, since the issue is the same. The coloring and expressiveness of all "visions," whether in dreams or waking, depend on a number of conditions; one of them is a high threshold of erotic energy. "Unfulfilled" love, from the Provençal ladies of whom the troubadours sang, and their Florentine sister, Beatrice, to the Romantic biographies, bears witness that the entire dualistic, Platonic tradition, which was revived by the Albigensians, responds to some truth in our nature. Or perhaps not to ours, that is, not to man's in general? Of the two types of totalism, the "permissive" will be more enduring than the "prohibitive," because in the former the arts of the imagination will wither of their own accord.

IF ONLY THIS COULD BE SAID

> *To deny, to believe, and to*
> *doubt absolutely—this is for man*
> *what running is for a horse.*
>
> PASCAL

IF ONLY this could be said: "I am a Christian, and my Christianity is such and such." Surely there are people who are capable of making such a statement, but not everyone has that gift. The power of dispossession, of disinheritance, is so great that language itself draws a boundary line. "In that dark world, where gods have lost their way" (Theodore Roethke), only the path of negation, the *via negativa*, seems to be accessible. It is worthwhile to ponder the difficulty of labeling oneself a Christian. This difficulty is marked by somewhat different characteristics in each branch of Christianity; to speak of "Christianity in general" would be to forget about many centuries of history and that we each belong to a particular, more or less preserved, tradition. In my case, the difficulty lies in calling myself a Catholic.

The obstacles I encounter derive from shame. We always

experience shame in relation to someone; that is why, instead of dilating on religious concepts, I am obliged to make an effort to picture the faces of people before whom I am ashamed. A milieu which is hostile to religion, which thinks of religion as a relic of a past era, would probably arouse my violent opposition and a manifestation of my own religiosity. I am not dealing with such a milieu, however. Actually, I ought to explain the word *milieu*. What I mean by this is a certain number of people, scattered among various cities and countries, but present in my imagination. When I speak about my time or my era, I refer to events that touch me directly, as well as to what I know from books, films, television, the press; but more reliable knowledge is connected to people, to those whose way of life and thinking is familiar to me, to some extent, thanks to our personal relationships. I call this group "my contemporaries" under the assumption that they can be considered to be representative of a much more inclusive group, although it would be inappropriate to base any far-reaching generalizations on them.

My contemporaries treat religious faith with respect and a lively interest, but almost always faith is something held by others that they have rejected for themselves. During the first three quarters of the twentieth century such radical changes took place in the way people lead their lives that customs which were still universal in 1900 have acquired the characteristic of exceptions, and my contemporaries experience these changes both as progress and as a loss about which nothing can be done. Once upon a time, the fundamental events of human existence were consecrated by rituals marking a person's entrance into life, fertility, and death. The birth of a child was followed immediately by his acceptance into the community of the faithful, which meant, among Christians, baptism. Then the child submitted to rites of initiation (First Communion, confirmation studies, the sacrament of confirmation). In the countries where I have spent most of my life, in France and America, the existence of these rites, even of baptism, is becoming more and more problematic. They require a decision by the parents, so they are not perceived as self-evident. One of my contemporaries, Albert Camus, once asked me what I think: Is it not a little indecent that he, an atheist, should be sending his children to First Communion? But a decision in favor of the religious education of children does not offer much help, since the language in which the catechist speaks is countered by the impression the surrounding scientific-technological civilization makes upon the imagination.

The existence of marriage rites, rich in symbolism and providing a sense of the succession of generations, is becoming even more problematic. (The central place of this rite in Polish theater—in Wyspiański's *Wedding*, Gombrowicz's *Marriage*, Mrożek's *Tango*—should give us something to think about.) Increasingly, the institution of marriage is being replaced by simply living together, which has followed upon the sundering of the link between sex and fertility. This is not just a revolution in the area of moral norms; it reaches much deeper, into the very definition of man. If the drive which is innate in man as a physiological being conflicts with the optimum condition that we call a human way of life (sufficient food, good living conditions, women's rights), and therefore has to be cheated with the help of science, then the rest of our firmly held convictions about what is natural behavior and what is unnatural fall by the wayside. This distinction between the natural and the unnatural was based on the harmony of Nature, which enfolded and supported man. Now we are forced to recognize that anti-naturalness defines man's very nature. And yet, isn't a belief in salutary cyclicity inherent in every ritual? Doesn't the ancient notion that infertility, whether of a woman's womb or of a sowed field, is a disaster provide negative confirmation of this fact? And isn't every kind of ritual dealt a blow when a species has to oppose the cycles of nature?

My contemporaries generally adhere to the rituals accompanying death, because they have to. Faced with the fact that someone has died, a particular sense of helplessness overwhelms family and friends; something has to be done, but no one knows what. This is a moment when the living gather together and form a community which unites, for the occasion, into a farewell circle. It is possible that the more activity that takes place around the deceased, the easier it is to endure the loss, or that lengthy prayers ease sorrow by virtue of something having been done. Burying someone who was movement and energy is too repulsive and at odds with our humanity for us to accept it without a pre-scribed form: the more conventional it is, the better, for as long as the deceased takes part in our tradition-sanctioned gestures and words, he remains with us; this dance, as it were, includes him in our rhythm and language—in defiance of that great Other about which the only thing we are able to say is that for us it has no properties. That is why over the course of millennia mourning rituals became richly differentiated into liturgy, the lamentations of professional mourners, the funeral feast. Of course, scientific-technological civilization cannot cope with death, because it has always thought only about the living. Death makes a mockery of it: new refrigerators and flights to other planets—what does the one who is lying here care about them? In the face of death the circle of those saying goodbye senses its own buffoonishness, just like the participants in a "demonic vaudeville," to borrow Kirillov's phrase from Dostoevsky's *The Possessed*. Whatever may be the beliefs of those gathered there, they accept a religious fu-neral with a sense of relief. It frees them from the necessity of an almost impossible improvisation at a time when, at best, one can come up with a moment of silence and the playing of a Mozart recording.

I feel obliged to speak the truth to my contemporaries and I feel ashamed if they take me to be someone whom I am not. In their opinion, a person who "had faith" is fortunate. They as-sume that as a result of certain inner experiences he was able to find an answer, while they know only questions. So how can I make a profession of faith in the presence of my fellow human beings? After all, I am one of them, seeking, as they do, the laws of inheritance, and I am just as confused. I have no idea at all how to relate to the rituals of initiation. What form should the catechization of children take? How and when should they be prepared to participate in the Eucharist? I even suspect that in a world that is alien to it, religion is too difficult for a young mind, and that in the best of circumstances it will take on the form of an alternate system in that mind, a system of "as if," having no connection with reality. One can imagine a state (let this be science fiction for the moment) in which most of the population is educated from childhood in a mundane, materialistic philosophy, only the highest elite has religion, and the citizens of that country are not allowed to concern themselves with religious problems until they are at least forty years old. Furthermore (let us enlarge upon this), this proscription was introduced not to preserve privilege but, sorrowfully, when it was noticed that despite everyone's desire, the simplest religious ideas were as difficult to comprehend as the highest mathematics and that they had been transformed into a kind of gnosis.

A Catholic ought to know what to think about today's sexual morality and about marriage, shouldn't he? Yet I have no opinion about these matters, and it is not because I am indifferent to them. On the contrary, I believe they are crucial. In this regard, it is important to remember that ideas from the late eighteenth and early nineteenth centuries have triumphed: "free love" was a slogan uniting atheists and anarchists like William Godwin, apocalyptic prophets like William Blake, and utopian socialists. The particular dialectic tension of the Industrial Revolution in its early stages, of repressive morality and the revolt against it, made their appearance. But that revolt would lead to change only thanks to science, which was developing in a context of repressive morality. Taken together, all of this bears scant resemblance to the eighteenth-century libertinism practiced by dissolute aristocrats and their ladies. It is probably not one of those revolutions of moral tolerance which occur repeatedly in history and which alternated with periods of severity. As a representative of a transitional generation, I cannot assume the role of Cato, since sexual freedom was already accepted by my generation, even if not too openly. At the same time, however, the Catholic upbringing I received imposed a severely repressive morality. This is one reason why I tend to distrust my own judgments. I can say nothing good about repression, which crippled me in some ways and poisoned me with pangs of conscience, so that I am not fit to be a teacher of conservative ethical rules. But at the same time, I ask myself this question: These inhibitions and self-imposed prohibitions, without which monogamous ties are impossible—do they not have a fundamental significance for culture, as a school of discipline? Perhaps the proponents of "free love" would be quite distraught if they could see that today their sermons seem downright puritanical. I also have nothing to say about the rupture of the link between sex and fertility, other than that it has already happened. The subtle comments of theologians seem dubious to me, and I cannot discern a difference in the methods used since their causal effect is the same: the cunning of the human mind deployed against Nature. Which does not mean that I react to the Pope's exhortations like those progressive Catholics who hear in them only the voice of obscurantism. It is, as I have said, a deeper problem than it seems, and that the Church is privately tearing its hair out over this testifies to a sense of responsibility for our entire species at a time when it is undergoing a great mutation.

But what of death? I would say that it has made an especially spectacular appearance in my century and that it is the real heroine of the literature and art which is contemporary with my lifetime. Death has always accompanied us, and word, line, color, sound drew their *raison d'être* from opposition to it; it did not, however, always behave with the same majesty. The *danse macabre* that appears in late medieval painting signified the desire to domesticate death or to become familiar with it through its ubiquitous presence, a friendly partnership, as it were. Death was familiar, well known, took part in feasts, had the right to citizenship in the *cité*. Scientific-technological civilization has no place for death, which is such an embarrassment that it spoils all our calculations, but it turns out that this is not for the best. For death intrudes itself into our thoughts the less we wish to think about it. And so literature and art start referring to it incessantly, transforming themselves into an areligious meditation on death and conducting "pre-casket somatism," to borrow a phrase from contemporary Polish poetry.

Here, perhaps, is where I part ways with many people with whom I would like to be in solidarity but cannot be. To put it very simply and bluntly, I must ask if I believe that the four Gospels tell the truth. My answer to this is: "Yes." So I believe in an absurdity, that Jesus rose from the dead? Just answer without any of those evasions and artful tricks employed by theologians: "Yes or no?" I answer: "Yes," and by that response I nullify death's omnipotence. If I am mistaken in my faith, I offer it as a challenge to the Spirit of the Earth. He is a powerful enemy; his field is the world as mathematical necessity, and in the face of earthly powers how weak an act of faith in the incarnate God seems to be.

I must add immediately that when thinking about my own death or participating with my contemporaries in a funeral ceremony, I am no different from them and my imagination is rendered powerless just as theirs is: it comes up against a blank wall. It is simply impossible for me to form a spatial conception of Heaven and Hell, and the images suggested by the world of art or the poetry of Dante and Milton are of little help. But the imagination can function only spatially; without space the imagination is like a child who wants to build a palace and has no blocks. So what remains is the covenant, the Word, in which man trusts. Who, however, will inherit life? Those who are predestined to do so. I know that I ought not play the role of a judge, yet I do, prompted by the human need to evaluate. So I divide people; that's right, I divide people—as artists used to when painting the Last Judgment—into those who go to the right and those who go to the left, into the saved and the damned. There are many among both the living and the dead whom I call bright spirits, whom I respect and admire, and so I have no doubt that they belong among the saved. But what about the others, those who are like me? Is it true that we ourselves were guilty of all those falls and internal conflicts that tear us apart, of the evil that stifles the weak impulses of our good will? Where does the responsibility for our illnesses lie—for us, patients in hospitals and psychiatric clinics, whatever our illnesses may be, whether physical or spiritual? My criteria are inadequate; I understand nothing.

My contemporaries, or, at least, those whom I value most highly, strive not to lie to themselves. This obligates me. Alas, two traps lie in wait: hypocrisy and exaltation. A man who derives from his own scrupulous fulfillment of religious prescripts a sense of superiority over others, because they are not as scrupulous, is called a Pharisee. The Church as an institution imposes rules concerning participation in its rites; attendance at Mass and confession are not a matter of the heart's needs but a self-imposed discipline accepted by the faithful. In our new conditions, however, a new temptation is born: the more I resemble my contemporaries who are leaving the Church, the more my decision to comply with these rules takes on the appearance of arbitrariness. I respond with a shrug of my shoulders—"Well, what of it?"—to all the reservations I come up with, and although I don't want to, I grab myself by the scruff of the neck. Alas, I take pride in being able to do that: a Pharisee. As a matter of fact, I don't really believe in these acts; for me, confession is a purely symbolic test of strength. What will win out—revulsion at the completely senseless activity of confessing imaginary sins or obedience to the prescriptions of our mother *Ecclesia*? In this regard, my attitude comes close to Lutheran conclusions: Man cannot know his own true evil; all he can do is trust in divine mercy, knowing that the sins he confesses to will almost certainly be nothing but a mask and a disguise. In other words, I am with all those people who have proclaimed their distrust of Nature (it's contaminated) and relied solely on the boundless freedom of the divine act, or Grace. That is why, among all the figures of the twentieth century, my writers were Lev Shestov and Simone Weil. In naming them together, I do not wish to obscure the essential differences between them which arose, first and foremost, from the fact that Shestov struggled against Greek philosophy, whereas Weil was fundamentally a Platonist. Nevertheless, even though she often quarreled with Pascal, she was closest to his thinking, and as for Shestov, he, too, praised Pascal and also Luther. That I was drawn to Shestov and Weil was also a function of their style. It is no accident that their language—Russian in Shestov's case, French in Weil's—is clear, severe, spare, superbly balanced, so that among modern philosophers they are the best writers. In my opinion, this proves that in a period when the sacral is available to us only through negation and repudiation of what is anti-sacral, the self-restraint and intellectual rigor of those two places them on the outermost boundary of the very best style, beyond which verbosity begins.

At one time I was prepared to call these tendencies of mine Protestant. With great relief, since nothing links me intellectually with Anglo-Saxon Protestants, I became convinced that it was only a few old Christian currents which had been labeled heretical after the schism and the Tridentine Council, since the warring sides needed to underline and even to invent their differences. The breathtaking casuistic distinctions developed by Catholics attempting to capture the riddle of free will and grace in Aristotelian-Thomist language do not seem convincing to me, and even Jacques Maritain's attempt to resolve this problem toward the end of his long life smells too much of casuistry. It's the same with predestination. It was part of the teachings of the Church long before Martin Luther appeared (those who are predestined to do so will inherit life), and we have been informed erroneously that this is a distinguishing feature of Protestantism.

Hypocrisy and exaltation: struggling with my two souls, I cannot break free of them. One: passionate, fanatical, unyielding in its attachment to discipline and duty, to the enemy of the world;

Manichaean, identifying sex with the work of the Devil. The other: reckless, pagan, sensual, ignoble, perfidious. And how could the ascetic in me, with the clenched jaws, think well of that other me? He could only aim for false sublimations, for deceptive Platonisms, convincing himself that *amore sacro* is his calling, and smothering the thought that I am entirely on the side of *amore profano*, even if I clasp my hands and primly purse my lips like a well-behaved young miss. Those two souls have also led me down some strange byways where it was necessary to establish my own relationship to the community, ranging from a thoroughly patriotic devotion akin to that of the nineteenth-century Philomaths all the way to fits of rage and egotistical indifference, which, of course, forced my disciplined half to adopt various disguises and enact various comedies in relation to myself. Alas, I cannot avoid mentioning those internal altercations; they demonstrate that Saint Francis's cheerfulness is not for me. Although, I must say, one of my old English friends once told me that there is a lot of *gaiety* in me, which is probably true, and means that there is such a thing as a despairing cheerfulness.

Nowadays, we tend to exaggerate the difficulty of having faith; in the past, when religion was a matter of custom, very few people would have been able to say what and how they believed. There existed an intermediary stratum of half-conscious convictions, as it were, supported by trust in the priestly caste. The division of social functions also occurred in the field of religion. "Ordinary" mortals turned to the priests, setting the terms of an unwritten contract: We will till the soil, go to war, engage in trade, and you will mutter prayers for us, sprinkle holy water, perform pious singing, and preserve in your tomes knowledge about what we must believe in. An important component of the aura that surrounded me in my childhood was the presence of clergy, who were distinguished from those around them by their clothing, and in daily life and in church by their gestures and language. The soutane, the chasuble, the priest's ascending the steps before the altar, his intonations in Latin, in the name of and in lieu of the faithful, created a sense of security, the feeling that there is something in reserve, something to fall back on as a last resort; that they, the priestly caste, do this "for us." Men have a strong need for authority, and I believe this need was unusually strong in me; when the clergy took off their priestly robes after Vatican II, I felt that something was lacking. Ritual and theater are ruled by similar laws: we know that the actor dressed up as a king is not a king, or so it would seem, but to a certain extent we believe that he is. The Latin, the shimmering chasubles, the priest's position with his face toward the altar and his back to the faithful, made him an actor in a sacral theater. After Vatican II the clergy shed not only their robes and Latin but also, at least here, where I write this, the language of centuries-old formulas which they had used in their sermons. When, however, they began speaking in the language of newspapers, their lack of intellectual preparation was revealed, along with the weakness of timid, often unprepossessing people who showed deference to "the world," which we, the laity, had already had enough of.

The child who dwells inside us trusts that there are wise men somewhere who know the truth. That is the source of the beauty and passion of intellectual pursuits—in philosophical and theological books, in lecture halls. Various "initiations into mystery" were also said to satisfy that need, be it through the alchemist's workshop or acceptance into a lodge (let us recall Mozart's *Magic Flute*). As we move from youthful enthusiasms to the bitterness of maturity, it becomes ever more difficult to anticipate that we will discover the center of true wisdom, and then one day, suddenly, we realize that others expect to hear dazzling truths from us (literal or figurative) graybeards.

Among Catholics that process was until recently eased by the consciousness that the clergy acted in a dual function: as actors of the sacred theater and as the "knowledgeable caste," the bearers of dogmas dispensed, as if from a treasure house, by the center, the Vatican. By democratizing and anarchizing, up to and including the realm of what, it would seem, were the unassailable truths of faith, *aggiornamento* also struck a blow at the "know-ing" function of the clergy. An entirely new and unusual situa-tion arose in which, at least in those places where I was able to observe this, the flock at best tolerates its shepherds, who have very little idea of what to do. Because man is *Homo ritualis*, a search takes place for collectively created Form, but it is obvious that any liturgy (reaching deep into one or another interpretation of dogma) which is elaborated communally, experimentally, can-not help but take shape as a relative, interhuman Form.

Perhaps this is how it should be, and these are the incom-prehensible paths of the Holy Spirit, the beginning of man's maturity and of a universal priesthood instead of a priesthood of one caste? I do not want this to sound like an admission that the Protestant isolation of individuals is correct, on the basis of which each individual may treat religion as a completely per-sonal matter; this is delusive and leads to unconscious social de-pendencies. It would be useless for man to try to touch fire with his bare hands; the same is true of the mysterious, sacral dimen-sion of being, which man approaches only through *metaxu*, as Si-mone Weil calls it, through intermediaries such as fatherland, customs, language. It is true that although I would characterize my religion as childishly magical, formed on its deepest level by the *metaxu* which surrounded me in my childhood, it was the adhesions of Polishness in Catholicism that later distanced me from the Church. I cannot say how I would react to this today, be-cause I have lived for a long time outside the Polish-speaking re-ligious community. With rare exceptions, for me Catholics are French, Italian, and Irish, and the language of the liturgy is En-glish. In other words, what happened inside me, of necessity, was a division into two spheres, or rather a change in only one of them, since I myself stuck with the Polish language and with everything that this language carries with it. The pain and fits of anger that "national religion" (i.e., parochialism) provoked in me, and the right-wing political ideology among those who took part in the rituals, remain in my memory, but perhaps they no longer interfere with my looking at these matters from the broader perspective of time. Catholicism, divorced by now from borscht with dumplings and nationalistic programs, seems to me to be the indispensable background for everything that will be truly creative in Polish culture, although I feel that the present moment is preparatory and portends an era of fundamental re-thinking.

Though circumstances disconnected me from the community of those praying in Polish, this does not mean that the "communal" side of Catholicism vanished for me. Quite the contrary; the coming together of a certain number of people to participate in something that exceeds them and unites them is, for me, one of the greatest of marvels, of significant experiences. Even though the majority of those who attend church are elderly (this was true two and three generations ago, too, which means that old age is a vocation, an order which everyone enters in turn), these old people, after all, were young however many years ago and not overly zealous in their practice at that time. It is precisely the frailty, the human infirmity, the ultimate human aloneness seeking to be rescued in the vestibule of the church, in other words, the subject of godless jokes about religion being for old ladies and grandfathers—it is precisely this that affords us transitory moments of heartbreaking empathy and establishes communion between "Eve's exiles." Sorrow and wonder intermingle in it, and often it is particularly joyous, as when, for example, fifteen thousand people gather in the underground basilica in Lourdes and together create a thrilling new mass ritual. Not inside the four walls of one's room or in lecture halls or libraries, but through communal participation the veil is parted and for a brief moment the space of Imagination, with a capital *I*, is visible. Such moments allow us to recognize that our imagination is paltry, limited, and that the deliberations of theologians and philosophers are cut to its measure and therefore are completely inadequate for the religion of the Bible. Then complete, true imagination opens like a grand promise and the human privilege of recovery, just as William Blake prophesied.

Ought I to try to explain "why I believe"? I don't think so. It should suffice if I attempt to convey the coloring or tone. If I believed that man can do good with his own powers, I would have no interest in Christianity. But he cannot, because he is enslaved to his own predatory, domineering instincts, which we may call *proprium*, or self-love, or the Specter. The proposition that even if some good is attainable by man, he does not deserve it, can be proved by experience. Domineering impulses cannot be rooted out, and they often accompany the feeling that one has been chosen to be a passive instrument of the good, that one is gifted with a mission; thus, a mixture of pride and humility, as in Mickiewicz, but also in so many other bards and prophets, which also makes it the motivator of action. This complete human poverty, since even what is most elevated must be supported and nourished by the aggression of the perverse "I" is, for me, an argument against any and all assumptions of a reliance on the natural order.

Evil grows and bears fruit, which is understandable, because it has logic and probability on its side and also, of course, strength. The resistance of tiny kernels of good, to which no one grants the power of causing far-reaching consequences, is entirely mysterious, however. Such seeming nothingness not only lasts but contains within itself enormous energy which is revealed gradually. One can draw momentous conclusions from this: despite their complete entanglement in earthly causality, human beings have a role in something that could be called superterrestrial causality, and thanks to it they are, potentially, miracle workers. The more harshly we judge human life as a hopeless undertaking and the more we rid ourselves of illusions, the closer we are to the truth, which is cruel. Yet it would be incomplete if we were to overlook the true "good news," the news of victory. It may be difficult for young people to attain it. Only the passing of years demonstrates that our own good impulses and those of our contemporaries, even if only short-lived, do not pass without a trace. This, in turn, inclines us to reflect on the hierarchical structure of being. If even creatures so convoluted and imperfect can accomplish something, how much more might creatures greater than they in the strength of their faith and love accomplish? And what about those who are even higher than they are? Divine humanity, the Incarnation, presents itself as the highest rung on this hierarchical ladder. To move mountains with a word is not for us, but this does not mean that it is impossible. Were not Matthew, Mark, Luke, and John miracle workers by virtue of their having written the Gospels?

WHY RELIGION?

INSTEAD of leaving to theologians their worries, I have constantly meditated on religion. Why? Simply because *someone*
had to do this. To write on literature or art was considered
an honorable occupation, whereas anytime notions taken from
the language of religion appeared, the one who brought them up
was immediately treated as lacking in tact, as if a silent pact had
been broken.

Yet I lived at a time when a huge change in the contents of
the human imagination was occurring. In my lifetime Heaven
and Hell disappeared, the belief in life after death was considerably weakened, the borderline between man and animals,
once so clear, ceased to be obvious under the impact of the
theory of evolution, the notion of absolute truth lost its supreme position, history directed by Providence started to look
like a field of battle between blind forces. After two thousand years in which a huge edifice of creeds and dogmas has
been erected, from Origen and Saint Augustine to Thomas
Aquinas and Cardinal Newman, when every work of the

human mind and of human hands was created within a system of reference, the age of homelessness has dawned. How could I not think of this? And is it not surprising that my preoccupation was a rare case?

PART THREE

AGAINST

INCOMPREHENSIBLE

POETRY

REMEMBRANCE
OF A CERTAIN LOVE

WHEN I WAS A BOY, I was quite curious about things that ran, flew, and crept, things that grew, things that could be watched and touched, and I had no interest in words. I devoured books, but I saw them as information about actual events and adventures, and if I came across some "self-sufficient" words (though I would not have been able to call them that then), descriptions of feelings or landscapes, I thought them stupid and skipped the page. Every so often, a volume of poetry would end up in my hands and would at once repel me with its falseness. The same falseness permeated the bows, smiles, and empty chitchat exchanged by adults, which was ridiculous because they thought no one would ever notice that it was all only make-believe.

Still, in another way, I was an admirer of words, though not of those formed into phrases and sentences. A naturalist, I collected May bugs asphyxiated by formalin fumes and impaled on pins, plant specimens in herbariums, bird eggs gathered in thickets at the cost of scrapes on my face and bare feet; I was certain of the special importance of my activity and I would have rejected as insulting any suggestion that I was not alone among my peers in experiencing such passion. I was a Romeo, and my Juliet was both the boundless profusion of forms and colors and the one particular insect or bird holding me spellbound for whole days or weeks. But I was falling so totally in love, let us be properly suspicious, through an intermediary. What really fascinated me were the color illustrations in nature books and atlases, not the Juliet of nature, but her portrait rendered by draftsmen or photographers. I suffered no less sincerely for that, a suffering caused by the excess which could not be possessed; I was an unrequited romantic lover, until I found the way to dispel that invasion of desires, to make the desired object mine—by naming it. I made columns in thick notebooks and filled them with my pedantic categories— family, species, genus—until the names, the noun signifying the species and the adjective the genus, became one with what they signified, so that *Emberiza citrinella* did not live in thickets but in an ideal space outside of time. There was a furious Aristotelianism in that will to catalogue; I was repeating the procedures of ordering the world around me, as if childhood, boyhood, and youth did in fact correspond to the phases through which humanity passes. Moreover, my passion had distinctly male features, it expressed the male hunger for demarcations, definitions, and concepts more powerful than reality, a hunger which armed some with swords, cast others into dungeons, and led the faithful on to holy wars.

That love had a sad end, as do many loves. Suddenly our eyes seem cleansed by a potion that has undone the spell; the unique person we elevated above all others begins to be seen objectively, subordinate to the rules which operate on all creatures with two arms and two legs. Suspicion, critical reflection—what had been a sheaf of colors, an undifferentiated vibration of light instantly turns into a set of characteristics and falls under the sway of statistics. And so, even my real birds became illustrations from an anatomical atlas covered by an illusion of lovely feathers, and the fragrance of flowers ceased to be extravagant gifts, becoming part of an impersonally calculated plan, examples of a universal law. My childhood, too, ended then. I threw my notebooks away; I demolished the paper castle where beauties had resided behind a lattice of words.

The practical consequence of my passions was an extensive vocabulary for the plants, animals, and birds of my native, northern land. My emigration from Europe, however, occurred when my attachment to names had long since forsaken me, and recognizing the kinship of American species with these other, European ones only made me think of my own life—its migration away from obdurate divisions and definitions to a harmony with the fluid and the undefined. But the truth is that I am always annoyed by that sort of musical motif played with new variations. I had known only one sort of pine, a pine tree was a pine tree, but here suddenly there was the sugar pine, the ponderosa pine, the Monterey pine, and so on—seventeen species, all told. Five species of spruce, six of fir—the largest, a rival in size to the sequoias, was not entirely a fir and, thus, its Latin name was neither *Picea* nor *Abies*, but *Pseudotsuga*. Several species each of cedar, larch, juniper. The oak, which I had believed to be simply an oak, always and everywhere eternal and indivisible in its oakness, had in America multiplied into something like sixteen species, ranging from those whose oakness was beyond question to others where it was so hazy that it was hard to tell right off whether they were laurels or oaks. Similar but dissimilar, the same but not identical, all this only leads to nonsensical thoughts, but why not acknowledge them? For example, what force is at work here, what origin—a universal law, the essence of tree? And does it contain the principle, the essence of pine, oak? Oh, classifications! Do they exist only in the mind or, in spite of everything, outside the mind as well? Jays screech outside the window (if only they were *sójki*), but they are either California jays or Steller's jays, black on top, blue-breasted with a black crest—only the cries, the thievishness, the audacity are the same as that of their kinsmen thousands of miles away in my native land. What is jayness? The brevity of their life cycle and their repetition of it through the millennia, unaware that there exists something like "being a jay" or "being a Steller's jay," contains, I think, something amazing.

A SEMI-PRIVATE LETTER
ABOUT POETRY

EVERY AUTHOR should be sensitive to criticism, should ponder it for a long time and draw conclusions from it. This statement is not as obvious as it might seem. There have been periods in the history of literature when a dismissive attitude toward criticism was part of the writer's toolbox and progress was made despite it. Critics are sometimes more susceptible to stylish and purely transitory slogans than the authors they discuss, and flogging their "isms," they construct a ponderous machine which is slow to move forward. Finally, young writers, if they are too responsive to criticism, lose more than they gain, because their vision, strongly felt but imperfectly conceived, draws down upon them thunderbolts, which they may easily attribute to the vision itself, rather than to its flawed execution.

Despite all these permutations, at this particular moment there are, in my opinion, special conditions which demand that critics and authors assume equal responsibility for establishing the voice of Polish literature. There's no helping it; a heavy block of iron cannot be lifted singlehandedly. Therefore, we must observe with some alarm the absence of literary criticism in Poland

and the gray space that book and theater reviews occupy in the weekly papers. And this is occurring at a time when, as I have said, the conditions are right for authors and critics to take each other seriously.

I was moved to write this letter by the serious and flattering review of my book of poems *Ocalenie* [Rescue], published in the May [1946] issue of *Twórczość* [Creative Writing], and written by Kazimierz Wyka, one of Poland's few literary critics. This issue reached me in New York after a two-month delay, which explains my belated response. The issues it raises are of continuing and immediate concern, however.

IS JOURNALISTIC POETRY POSSIBLE?

I pose this question while recalling the unpleasant shudders that poetic journalism elicits in people of good taste. I also know that this question has often been answered with a yes, citing Whitman and Heine, and often with a no, citing good poets who destroyed their talent by harnessing it to the service of problems pronounced upon *expressis verbis*. Every question, however, acquires a slightly different sound amid new experiences and circumstances, and new people repeat old—but only apparently old—words.

I used to be an opponent of any journalistic concerns in poetry, and I was not unique in that regard. The frequent attempts at vociferous, unmediated protest (and there were plenty of reasons for that) left a feeling of bitterness, shame, and betrayal with regard to the rules of good craftsmanship. How did it happen, then, that poems filled with invective and employing the stylistic methods of pamphlet writing, of persiflage, and even of a philosophical treatise wound up in *Ocalenie*? And how did it come to pass that despite what Wyka has to say, I do not consider them merely "rhymed documentation of reality" or a departure from my true path?

Two explanations are possible: either the author, having written those poems, grew attached to them thanks to the particular events surrounding their creation (which often happens) and is evaluating them subjectively, or the sensitive, wise critic possesses a range of sensibility which does not register certain combinations and instead of music hears rasping sounds, whistles, and inarticulate noise. Both explanations are possible, and either person may be right, but the question of two different evaluations, two different types of argumentation in relation to one and the same work, still remains—as, for example, in judging the cycle "Voices of Poor People."

Let us start right in. The main problem with contemporary poetry is what someone has called *peu de réalité*, a detachment from reality caused by remaining inside the chalk circle of rigidly defined ways of reacting to the world. This should not be confused with "living in an ivory tower," "art for art's sake," or the like because the problem is in fact a technical one. The poet, heir to the heritage of recent European poetry, finds himself, like the contemporary painter, obligated to employ laconicisms, abbreviations, and concern for new discoveries in presenting the proportions of observed material. To put it metaphorically: if the description of a blade of grass has become problematic, is there room left for a panorama including people, animals, the rising and setting of the sun? This condition, however, feels like an unbearable constriction of the terrain of poetry, and efforts at escaping from the chalk circle are a fundamental feature of the period in which we are now living.

It's the same in painting, with all due respect for the differences between these two branches of art. Picasso's exhibition in London, which allowed us to become acquainted with the work he did during the war, can serve as an example. We can admire this wartime Picasso who remains distant from classicism, who still operates with the most blatant deformation, or we can criticize him in the name of social and aesthetic puritanism, which does not permit placing a platter of herring on a woman's head instead of a hat. Still, we must take into consideration the intensity of the passion that speaks to us from those canvases. Irony, disgust, mockery, rage are too clearly present; their intention of screaming out a cry of protest through form and color is too evident for us not to notice. This is an effort to expand the possibilities of the painter's tongue, to sing a new Sophoclean tragedy in the language of Hottentots.

Last winter I spent a great deal of time in Feliks Topolski's London studio. Looking at his albums of drawings, "Great Britain in War" and "Russia in War," and also at his canvases in which masses of people of all races cluster together, propelled by the rhythm of the events that visited five continents, I thought that painting's road back to emotions and human passions is profoundly justified and that artists again have before them the prospect of hope, which had apparently vanished.

Let us not deceive ourselves. This is a period of temptations. Plenty of fluent, patriotic, ideological poems whose words ring out, whisper, and stupefy are bound to appear. No doubt there are already painters who, citing murky conversations about realism, are prepared to remind us, to represent, to immortalize. Let us leave those whitewashed graves of theirs to their proper fate. A true resolution of this issue will take place among people who understand that more than poetry's enrichment with assonance separates us from Romanticism and that one can no longer paint as if Cézanne had never existed.

Some revolutions, despite their use of slogans aimed against the past, are truer to the past than might be imagined, considering the way they swear that they are beginning anew. The so-called poetic avant-garde has created out of the poet a creature with a head covered with mathematical lumps, with exceptionally large lenses for its eyes, and suffering from atrophy of the heart and liver. Such poetry depends on noting down intellectual impressions, visual ones above all; intellect fulfills the role of an engineer of impressions so that the object of its interests is more the poetic work itself than the wide world. The godparents of this method are the theoreticians of pure poetry who, like Edgar Allan Poe, argued that poetry should not venture into the realm of passion or the field of virtue. Perhaps in a stormier era such poetry has a better chance of surviving, since a certain degree of insensitivity helps one keep one's calm and balance. It is free to legitimize itself against its attackers by citing the positive pedagogical influence it exerts in shaping the sense of rational construction. However, the aggrieved heart and liver, along with the aggrieved mind, which reluctantly agrees to perform only mathematical functions, demand their rights, and that safe "alcove for rent" becomes cramped.

When, after many years of disrupted contact with French poetry, the first books (by Éluard and Aragon) fell into my hands, I felt both satisfaction and embarrassment. I was satisfied because they fulfilled my prediction about the expanding range of topics. My embarrassment was the embarrassment of a Pole: Damn it, we could have written just like that during the war. But it never entered our mind.* We were ashamed: they were throwing themselves into patriotic themes with a degree of enthusiasm that we could not match. In situations like these we quote our great poets: Mickiewicz, Słowacki, Krasiński, Norwid. We have a tradition of suffering. But they are not terrified by the shade of Victor Hugo, and like neophytes, they are rapacious.

I think that Aragon's poetry is overrated in Poland. The thrashings he receives in France, precisely for what makes us uncomfortable, are often well deserved. Despite this, his experiments with applying the ballad style to France's struggles and hopes is as interesting (*toute proportion gardée*) as Picasso's furious drive to depict the world as monstrous or the transformations of Éluard, whom one would hardly have predicted would become a poet of underground France.

The process is taking a different turn in the Anglo-Saxon

*When this essay was reprinted in 1958, Milosz added: "This dig at those patriotic Communist orators is decidedly too delicate."

countries. But if we consider just the works of T. S. Eliot and
W. H. Auden, we will find in their poems microdramas, satires,
philosophical treatises, and comedies in the style of Aristophanes.
Right now, a book by the fine young American poet Karl Shapiro,
his *Essay on Rime*, is lying before me. It is a treatise on poetry, in
verse. I don't want to underestimate this drilling of new tunnels
by poetry, its turning back to before the nineteenth century in
search of forms of expression which are by now so entrenched
and stable that they compel the contemporary artist to utter
freshness and sensitivity.

What is this disdained journalistic writing? The journalistic
writer is a person who fights with his pen against something or
someone. We know at least several thousand good literary works
which were written against someone, and perhaps that, in fact, is
the reason why they are good and have endured. Even Dante derived great pleasure from placing his enemies in Hell. A journalistic element is present in virtually every literary work to a
greater or lesser degree, and only the writer who has developed to
perfection the disappearance of heart and liver in himself can get
rid of it completely.

Perhaps, then, in condemning journalistic elements in literature we have in mind particular variants, those which are closest
to us, cultivated over the course of, shall we say, the last hundred
years? We feel that the new artistic means, which arose in the
laboratories of the adherents of pure art, are in conflict with the
flood of words flowing freely in the works of the Romantics.

Poetic language has become as pictorial as the language of
primitive peoples, and how to introduce concepts into it without
depriving it of its conciseness is a real puzzle. It is easy for me to
agree with the condemnation of journalistic writing in the name
of such reasoning. But why should we not admit that we are
using the word "journalism" in too narrow a sense? There are
significant differences between the journalistic *Dismissal of the
Greek Envoys* by the late-sixteenth-century poet Jan Kochanowski and a Romantic tirade. No one is telling us to hew to the

latter as a model. Rather, we should deplore the fact that in Poland whenever someone wants to speak about the so-called great themes, he falls into the Romantic manner, which is supposed to be a matter of faithfulness to tradition, but to a tradition broken off well over a century ago.

I think that the key to the future should be found in considerations of artistic irony, persiflage, the dramatic forms of poetry. If I am going to be met with the rebuke that I am calling for mockery and a light tone, then there's really no reason to continue writing. Artistic irony, as I understand it, rests first of all on the author's ability to inhabit the skin of various people and, when he writes in the first person, to speak as if not he were speaking but a persona created by him. The essential meaning of a work is thus encapsulated in the author's relation to the persona. This relationship may vary from cautious approbation to heartfelt negation and on to venomous negation—thousands of variations are possible; what is attacked directly eludes us and can often be caught in this way. This is an old recipe from fine masters, but it seems to have been almost entirely forgotten. The pure Romantic manner dismisses it: the speaker and the author are one and the same. Byron felt obligated to announce what he thought of his heroes, inserting entire digressions of personal lyrical flights, not distancing himself from himself for even a moment. Only when the Romantics aspired to drama did they have to make allowances for the rules, without which drama is impossible.

I have my own view of Mickiewicz's *Ballads and Romances* and his *Crimean Sonnets*. I think I have a right to. Every Pole has his private accounting with Mickiewicz, just as an Englishman has his private accounting with the Bible. I do not consider the *Ballads and Romances* to be as Romantic a work as, say, the verse of Lamartine. If I read *Ballads and Romances* as they are read in school, I would have to come to the conclusion that the author of "A City Winter" is at the very least infantile, and I would not be able to explain their position in his work as a whole. I love them for all the shades of the distance Mickiewicz kept from the songs

and fables of the Nowogródek region, a distance filled with tender affirmation; I love them for his incarnations in the figures of
hunters and maidens, for his skill at erasing the many difficulties
he faced, and for his use of simple language. It is a work of artistic irony (not irony in the colloquial sense), and when one looks at
it in this way, it is easier to understand how he came to write *Pan
Tadeusz*. Sometimes I recite "Tukaj" to myself and think about
what it is that produces the exquisite beauty of Tukaj's speech before his death. Is it not that it is persiflage?

The *Crimean Sonnets* are, in my opinion, less a collection of
lyrical effusions and more a song sung by a solo bass voice, where
the performer is not at all identical with the total Mickiewicz, if I
may put it that way. Like Kochanowski's *Laments*, they are *ex-
temporale* on the theme of death, with a conscious selection of
patterns which exist in literature, so that in the *Sonnets* the
speaker is deliberately posed to resemble a portrait by Wańkowicz. Only this gives them their transparency and their unity of
themes, makes them, in a word, classical poems, despite the
attacks launched by pseudo-classicists.

As long as the poetic *métier* is reduced, as it is today, to assembling words and overlooks the subtleties of the author's relationship to what he supposedly is saying "from the depths of his
soul," it will be difficult to believe in the possibility of escaping
from the chalk circle, and those who do not like a journalistic
tone will be absolutely right. Poetry is divided into pure lyric and
pure satire, and obviously it cannot be tempted to touch upon human matters which are not amenable to either lyric or satiric
treatment (and it appears that there are quite a few of those). So
I prefer Krasicki's *Myszeis* [The Mouseiad], in which the phrase
"Sacred love of our beloved fatherland" appears on the occasion
of a war among mice.

Mixing together lyric and satire—a dose of lyric and a dose of
satire (Romantic irony)—will not resolve anything either. If Polish critics and poets treated their obligations seriously, they would
convene a major conference dedicated to the classical education of

youth, because only a good classical program could lend truth to Norwid's pronouncement that "Neither a shield nor a sword, but a masterpiece, is the people's weapon." One should not trust today's pedagogical positivists. From the point of view of literature, they are Romantic arsonists. In their hearts they are convinced that civilization dates from the nineteenth century and the rest is utter nonsense.

Given the present state of readers' interests and similar pressures on poets themselves, it would be presumptuous to aim at taking a very large step beyond the chalk circle. Despite this, we must make the attempt, opening ourselves up to rather peculiar interpretations. Today's reader, even a good reader of poetry, is sensitive to the so-called formal values and likes to catch the author by his words, giving his psychoanalytic inclinations free rein. A grasp of the work's entirety, the concept employed by the poet, escapes his notice. If the poet clearly signals by shaking his head and winking, then his poem will ultimately be placed among satirical or comic verse. Approval or satire. Nothing else.

"Objectivization" is a fashionable word nowadays. Are we free to use it without having thoroughly discussed the entire complexity of the author's attitude toward the lines of verse he has written? If it has a Romantic, and not a classical, form, there is no complexity. If there is no complexity, there is no objectivization——that is how I would put it. When Józef Weyssenhoff's novel *The Life and Ideas of Zygmunt Podfilipski* was published in 1898, the critics did not know what to think about the book: was it in praise of Podfilipski or was it a satire on Podfilipski? It may be that Weyssenhoff was simply a good writer (though I doubt that) and maintained a distance from his character. Let us also recall the arguments over whether the heroes of Mickiewicz's *Pan Tadeusz* are swine or models of civic virtue.

It does not discredit me that, having fine predecessors, I attempted to introduce into poetry on my own modest scale some old, but today revolutionary, principles, and that I met with misunderstanding. I wrote "The World: A Naïve Poem," "Voices of Poor

People," and a host of other poems in a similar style, after which I was operated upon with the psycho-socio-analytical method ("the poet, whether he means to or not, says that . . . After all, it is clearly stated"). Here I could introduce numerous examples from a couple of reviews. I will limit myself to one. The poem "Waltz" is very simple: a lady who is dancing the waltz in the year 1910 has, or could have had, a vision of the years of the Second World War. Two epochs: the first, during which what will destroy the existing order is still developing, and the second, during which the destruction is completed. The tragedy of ignorance of the future. When, toward the end of the poem, I say to her,

> *Forget it. Nothing exists but this bright ballroom*
> *And the waltz, the flowers, the lights, and the echoes*

that is my compassionate irony placing a blindfold over her eyes. I feel very sorry for her, because I know how it will end.

In his review, Kazimierz Wyka argues that what I say to her reveals "a quest for autonomy in the name of beauty." That's interesting. Is it because I tell her to keep on dancing the waltz? Undoubtedly, dancing the waltz has more beauty in it than a vision of concentration camps. But if she weren't dancing the waltz in her delightful ignorance, there would be no dramatic conflict, there would be no poem. Was I really obligated to add a commentary with more or less the following content: "Ah, you pathetic creature, just wait, you'll get yours!"? I would never add such a commentary, because it would express at most only a fraction of my feelings toward this person.

Perhaps this is not really a journalistic verse. The real difficulty begins when I happen to sketch certain types or individuals and to speak in their name, as in my cycle "Voices of Poor People." I suspect that when "The Poor Poet" or Adrian Zieliński begin to be treated as my own disguises (not even roles), these poems will appear too simple, even primitive, and that is how I explain why Wyka calls them "journalism," "an eloquent document." I, however, consider them to be among the most complex poems I have ever written, complex, at least, for a period when poets rarely create situations and characters.

Wyka's review has given me so much grist for my mill that I would feel uncomfortable if I did not write frankly about a phenomenon that struck me: namely, the boundary line demarcated by the critics beyond which the forbidden kingdom of journalistic writing begins. I think that this boundary is no more real than the lines demarcating latitudes and longitudes.

THE ARCADIAN MYTH

The arcadian or cytherean myth is a very old one. There is no need to seek it only among ancient Greek poets or the writers and painters of the Rococo period. Whatever name we give to it, it has reappeared for hundreds of generations. It is a dream about the happy life of the human race. Sometimes that happiness is projected back in time to a legendary golden age, as among the ancients. Sometimes, as among Christians, it is postponed until the fulfillment of time and the coming of the Savior, or until the moment of death. Maciej Kazimierz Sarbiewski, our seventeenth-century Latin poet, displays a longing for his "heavenly fatherland," which he penetrates during his lifetime by rising up to the clouds on a winged horse. (No one has written on "The Obsession with Flight in Sarbiewski," about his viewing the earth from above.) In Shakespeare, the golden age is situated in a forest on a midsummer's night, in the woods of Arden. For pseudo-shepherdesses reading *Paul and Virginia*, the land of happiness was America's wilderness. Socialism put off happiness until the future, anticipating its creation by new societies.

Faith in an arcadian myth is by no means a crime. If there were no poets to repeat continuously that humankind ought to live in such a way that it is possible to write, *"Nec supplex turba timebat / iudicis ora sui, sed erant sine vindice tuti"* ["The mass of defendants was not afraid of a judge, for all were secure even without a protector"], we would turn into a species of reptiles.

Kazimierz Wyka sees the sin of aestheticism in poets' attraction to the arcadian myth. I do not think he is right. True, one can cite eras when that aspiration was transposed into a fondness for idylls, into creating a closed, imaginary state of magical spells. His condemnation would appear directed at such aspirations. But even the happiness of primitive peoples in Rousseau contained the dynamism of contrast; it struck a blow at the spoiled society of the eighteenth century. Perhaps, then, it is the "private entertainment" of the great patrons of pure poetry that riles him? Here, too, to take the case of Rimbaud, for instance, it turns out that his personal gamble in the name of happiness was actually a contest for the happiness of the human race. A true arcadian myth, if it is rich enough, goes beyond one's personal state of bliss and is incapable of imagining happiness otherwise than as a universal condition—of the nation or of all people on earth. That is why one has to be careful with the arcadian myth, because it can transform itself into a promethean myth.

I am grateful to Wyka for drawing my attention to the dangers posed by the arcadian element in my poetry. His proof was too weak, however, to convince me. Take the ending of my poem "In Warsaw":

Was I born to become
a ritual mourner?
I want to sing of festivities,
The greenwood into which Shakespeare
Often took me. Leave
To poets a moment of happiness,
Otherwise, your world will perish.

The critic sees in this "the quest for nonconformity in the name of aesthetic contemplation, in the name of the beauty of reality." I ask him:

1. Does not every inhabitant of Warsaw experience a feeling of protest against the ruins? Isn't the sight of the destroyed capital something that disturbs the inner peace of every inhabitant of Warsaw?

2. Is it not monstrous that virtually every generation of Polish poets must fulfill the function of ritual mourners, and would not a calm acceptance of this situation be the same as sanctioning all our national manias, which always yield the same results?

3. Is the thought of conditions in Poland which would allow poets to be singers of happiness abnormal and immoral?

4. Does the critic not detect the artistic irony in this contradiction: the poet does not want to become a ritual mourner, but he is a ritual mourner?

The poem "Morning" is programmatic according to Wyka. Let us agree, willingly or not, that it is. What does it contain? In the first place, a description of morning in a Polish village during the German occupation. Second, the assertion that song breaks off when people's despair weighs it down. Third, a yearning to keep the song. Fourth, a vision of a happy Poland, which is symbolized by art, by mass art: theater and music. Fifth, a condemnation of complaining. I do not know where there is any dream of happy islands here. Or perhaps this is it:

In vain do you remember Italian vineyards
The green of England and the oceans' gleams.

Exactly, in vain. If people had been well off during the German occupation, they would not have complained. If they had not complained, they would not have had to be of two minds, to suppress their complaints while comforting themselves with a vision of the more beautiful world of the future. Then such verses would certainly not have come into being.

People in Poland dreamed during the war: about journeys, about a beautiful future Warsaw, about the taste of freedom, about food and drink. These were very human dreams, and if I gave them expression, creating images of cities where it was permitted to debate openly about the Republic (poets of arcadian myths love ancient Greece) or about a marble Warsaw of the future filled with song, sculpture, food, and drink, this only demonstrates that I lived in harmony with the population, that I was no different from anyone else.

Sometimes the world loses its face. It becomes too base. The task of the poet is to restore its face, because otherwise man is lost in doubt and despair. It is an indication that the world need not always be like this; it can be different.

NEC SUPPLEX TURBA TIMEBAT IUDICIS ORA SUI

Do arcadian elements lead to nonconformity? We need to make some distinctions. There are two types of nonconforming. One is nonconformity to the life of society, a severing of the individual from his ties with the collective, abandonment of the obligations that a particular person owes his society. Given the present trend toward a lively interest in public life after the experiences of the war, there is little probability that this is a threat for writers. Personally, I am appalled by the passion with which I read newspapers (apparently these political passions begin at a certain age).

The other sort of nonconformity, the refusal to share the moral approbation of evil, is every poet's privilege. I know Europe, every month I am getting to know America better, and I see no reason why I should have to accommodate myself and cry out that everything is for the best in the best of all possible worlds. I have too much heart and liver for this. When I wrote in the introduction to *Rescue* that I accepted the salvational goal of poetry, that was exactly what I had in mind, and I still believe that poetry can either save or destroy nations.

In conclusion, I appeal to Kazimierz Wyka. He wrote that I am a loner of an artist. That is true, but it is bad, because it seems to me that I perceive my own road better than my literary abilities allow. In sorrow I assert that at the present moment Polish literature is entering upon a renaissance of Romanticism. Critics on the left, professing to be Humanists, do what they can to urge writers in this direction. They are not Humanists, however, but Romantics masquerading as Humanists, wolves in sheep's clothing, and they are all fixated on the notion that every one of them is Erasmus of Rotterdam.

Kazimierz Wyka! If you and several other people of good faith and sound mind do not put a stop to this, it will be too late. It is no time to be shuffling around inside the chalk circle. The circle is already cracking.

Will it be a bright butterfly soaring over the earth,
Or a moth, dirty tribe of the night?

It seems it will be a Romantic moth. For Poles, whatever is Romantic is pretty, great, patriotic, national, universal—by its very nature. Just one more moment and they will become entangled in a web of lies, like the émigrés, in a slightly different, leftist-nationalist mode, which, in the final analysis, makes no difference. Kazimierz Wyka, this is the last possible moment.

RUINS AND POETRY

N OW I INTEND to speak on the experience of poetry in a strictly defined time and place. The time is 1939–1945, the place, Poland. This, I feel, will provide many of the problems already touched upon with distinct exemplification. I should remind you in advance that before World War II Polish poets did not differ much in their interests and problems from their colleagues in France or Holland. The specific features of Polish literature notwithstanding, Poland belonged to the same cultural circuit as other European countries. Thus one can say that what occurred in Poland was an encounter of a European poet with the hell of the twentieth century, not Hell's first circle, but a much deeper one. This situation is something of a laboratory, in other words: it allows us to examine what happens to modern poetry in certain historical conditions.

A hierarchy of needs is built into the very fabric of reality and is revealed when a misfortune touches a human collective, whether that be war, the rule of terror, or natural catastrophe. Then to satisfy hunger is more important than finding food that suits one's taste; the simplest act of human kindness toward a fellow being acquires more importance than any refinement of the mind. The fate of a city, of a country, becomes the center of everyone's attention, and there is a sudden drop in the number of suicides committed because of disappointed love or psychological problems. A great simplification of everything occurs, and an individual asks himself why he took to heart matters that now seem to have no weight. And, evidently, people's attitude toward the language also changes. It recovers its simplest function and is again an instrument serving a purpose; no one doubts that the language must name reality, which exists objectively, massive, tangible, and terrifying in its concreteness.

In the war years, poetry was the main genre of underground literature, since a poem can be contained on a single page. Poetry was circulated in manuscript or in clandestine publications, transmitted orally or sung. An anthology entitled *Poetry of Fighting Poland* published a few years ago (Warsaw: PIW, 1972) has 1,912 pages of poems and songs, written mostly under the German occupation. The vast majority has documentary value and, at the time, fulfilled an important function; today we would not grant them high artistic rank. Only a few show any familiarity with poetic craft. All of them, however, are characterized by that law discovered by Michał Borwicz in his book on the literature of prisons and concentration camps: they belong stylistically to the prewar period, but at the same time they try to express "the new," which cannot be grasped by any of the available notions and means of expression. This poetry is often too talkative and blatant in its calls to battle while simultaneously, on a deeper level, it behaves like a mute who tries in vain to squeeze some articulate sound out of his throat; he is desperate to speak but does not succeed in communicating anything of substance. It is only later, after the war, under the pressure of a strongly felt need to find an expression for an exceptionally trying collective experience, that Polish poetry begins to move away from the stylistic modes common to the prewar poetry of many countries.

To define in a word what had happened, one can say: disinte-

gration. People always live within a certain order and are unable
to visualize a time when that order might cease to exist. The sudden crumbling of all current notions and criteria is a rare oc-
currence and is characteristic only of the most stormy periods
in history. Perhaps the generations of Frenchmen who lived
through the revolution and the Napoleonic wars felt something
similar, and perhaps, too, Americans from the South felt they
were witness to the ruins of their entire way of life after the civil
war. In general, though, the nineteenth century did not experience the rapid and violent changes of the next century, whose
only possible analogy may be the time of the Peloponnesian war,
as we know it from Thucydides. Nevertheless, the disintegration
of which I speak had already taken place in the nineteenth century, though it was under the surface and so observed by only a
few. The pact concluded between Hitler and Stalin on August 23,
1939, brought all of Europe's poisons to the surface; it opened up
a Pandora's box. This was a fulfillment of things that were already prepared and only waiting to reveal themselves. It is necessary to keep in mind this peculiar logic of events in order to
understand how poetry reacted. Perhaps, in proclaiming the end
of European culture, Dostoevsky was, to a considerable extent,
motivated by his Russian anti-Western obsession. But it was precisely in that manner that poets in Poland perceived Europe sink-
ing in consecutive stages into inhumanity—as the end of all
European culture and its disgrace.

The main reproach made to culture, a reproach at first too difficult to be formulated, then finally formulated, was that it maintained a network of meanings and symbols as a façade to hide the
genocide under way. By the same token, religion, philosophy, and
art became suspect as accomplices in deceiving man with lofty
ideas, in order to veil the truth of existence. Only the biological
seemed true, and everything was reduced to a struggle within the
species, and to the survival of the fittest. Yes, but that reduction
had already been made. A whole system of values had been
destroyed, with its neat division into good and evil, beauty and

ugliness, including as well the very notion of truth. Therefore
Nietzsche was not entirely mistaken in announcing "European
nihilism." Yet the façade was maintained, and it provoked angry
reproaches: "You spoke of the dignity of man, a being created in
the image and likeness of God, of good and beauty, and look
what happened; you should be ashamed of your lies." Mistrust
and mockery were directed against the whole heritage of European culture. This is why many years after the war a play by
Stanisław Wyspiański, *Akropolis*, written in 1904, was staged by
Jerzy Grotowski in such a peculiar fashion. The play is composed
of scenes from Homer and the Bible and thus sums up the main
components of Western culture. In Grotowski's version, those
scenes are played by prisoners in Auschwitz wearing striped uniforms, and the dialogue is accompanied by tortures. Only the tortures are real, and the sublime language of the verses recited by
the actors is sarcastically colored by the very law of contrast.

Putting culture on trial so summarily must provoke serious
doubt, for it simplifies the human condition and in that manner
departs from truth, as happened in the past with various kinds of
Weltschmerz and *mal du siècle*. By living through disintegration
in its most tangible varieties, Polish poetry, strange as this may
sound, joined once more with Western poetry contaminated by
"European nihilism," only to give it a more radical expression.
This is true of the poetry of Tadeusz Różewicz, who made his
debut after the war. Characteristically, while putting culture
on trial, he often makes use of shorthand and symbols borrowed from that culture, as for instance in his poem "Nothing in
Prospero's Cloak," a travesty of *The Tempest*. The civilizing
power of the wise Prospero who, on his island, introduces Caliban
to the world of human speech and good manners proves to be a
sham.

Caliban the slave
taught human speech
waits

his mug in dung
his feet in paradise
he sniffs at man
waits

nothing arrives
nothing in Prospero's magic cloak
nothing from streets and lips
from pulpits and towers
nothing from loudspeakers
speaks to nothing
about nothing

Poems of this kind seem to fulfill a surrogate function, that is, they direct a global accusation at human speech, history, and even the very fabric of life in society, instead of pointing out the concrete reasons for the anger and disgust. That probably happens because, as was the case in Poland during the war, reality eludes the means of language and is the source of deep traumas, including the natural trauma of a country betrayed by its allies.

The reality of the war years is a great subject, but a great subject is not enough and it even makes inadequacies in workmanship all the more visible. There is another element which shows art in an ambiguous light. Noble intentions should be rewarded, and a literary work so conceived should acquire a durable existence, but most often the reverse is true: some detachment, some coldness, is necessary to elaborate a form. People thrown into the middle of events that tear cries of pain from their mouths have difficulty in finding the distance necessary to transform this material artistically. Probably in no language other than Polish are there so many terrifying poems, documents of the Holocaust; with few exceptions, these are poems that survived and whose authors did not. Today a reader hesitates between two contradictory assessments. Next to the atrocious facts, the very idea of literature seems indecent, and one doubts whether certain zones of reality can ever be the subject of poems or novels. The tortures of the damned in Dante's *Inferno* were, after all, invented by the author, and their fictitious character is made apparent by form. They do not appear raw, as do the tortures in documentary poems. On the other hand, because they use rhyme and stanzas, documentary poems belong to literature and one may ask, out of respect for those who perished, whether a more perfect poetry would not be a more appropriate monument than poetry on the level of facts.

After the war the annihilation of the Polish Jews appears in the poems of several writers, some of which found their place in anthologies. But, applying severe criteria, one can say that the subject is beyond the authors' capabilities and rises up before them like a wall. The poems are considered good primarily because they move us with their noble intentions. The difficulty of finding a formula for the experience of elemental cruelty is exemplified by the case of Anna Świrszczyńska. She made her debut before the war with a volume of prose poems, quite lovely and refined, which testified to her interest in the history of art and medieval poetry. And no wonder, for she was the daughter of a painter, grew up in a painter's studio, and at the university studied Polish literature. Neither she nor any of her readers could have guessed what purpose would be served one day by her predilection for illuminated manuscripts and miniatures.

During the war, Świrszczyńska lived in Warsaw. In August and September of 1944 she took part in the Warsaw Uprising. For sixty-three days she witnessed and participated in a battle waged by a city of one million people against tanks, planes, and heavy artillery. The city was destroyed gradually, street by street, and those who survived were deported. Many years later Świrszczyńska tried to reconstruct that tragedy in her poems: the building of barricades, the basement hospitals, the bombed houses caving in burying people in shelters, the lack of ammunition, food, and bandages, and her own adventures as a military nurse. Yet those attempts of hers did not succeed: they were too wordy, too pathetic, and she destroyed her manuscripts. (Also, for a long time the Uprising was a forbidden topic, in view of Russia's role in crushing it.) No less than thirty years after the event did she hit upon a style that satisfied her. Curiously enough, that was the style of miniature, which she had discovered in her youth, but this time not applied to paintings. Her book *Building the Barricade* consists of very short poems, without meter or rhyme, each one a microreport on a single incident or situation. This is a most humble art of mimesis: reality, as it is remembered, is paramount and dictates the means of expression. There is a clear attempt to condense, so that only the essential words remain. There are no comparisons or metaphors. Nevertheless, the book is characterized by a high degree of artistic organization, and, for example, the title poem can be analyzed in terms of the rhetorical figures with Greek names that have been used in poetry for centuries—anaphora, epiphora, epizeuxis:

BUILDING THE BARRICADE

We were afraid as we built the barricade
  under fire.
The tavern-keeper, the jeweler's mistress, the barber,
  all of us cowards.
The servant-girl fell to the ground
as she lugged a paving stone, we were terribly afraid
all of us cowards—
the janitor, the market-woman, the pensioner.

The pharmacist fell to the ground
as he dragged the door of a toilet,
we were even more afraid, the smuggler-woman,
the dressmaker, the streetcar driver,
  all of us cowards.

A kid from reform school fell
as he dragged a sandbag,

you see, we were really
afraid.

Though no one forced us,
we did build the barricade
under fire.

Świrszczyńska often uses the form of a miniature monologue or dialogue to squeeze in as much information as possible. The small poem "A Woman Said to Her Neighbor" contains a whole way of life, the life in the basements of the incessantly bombed and shelled city. Those basements were connected by passages bored through the walls to form an underground city of catacombs. The notions and habits accepted in normal conditions were reevaluated there. Money meant less than food, which was usually obtained by expeditions to the firing line; considerable value was attached to cigarettes, used as a medium of exchange; human relations also departed from what we are used to considering the norm and were stripped of all appearances, reduced to their basest shape. It is possible that in this poem we are moved by the analogy with peacetime conditions, for men and women are often drawn together not from mutual attraction but from their fear of loneliness:

A woman said to her neighbor:
"Since my husband was killed I can't sleep,
when there's shooting I dive under the blanket,
I tremble all night long under the blanket.
I'll go crazy if I have to be alone today,
I have some cigarettes my husband left, please
do drop in tonight."

Enterprises like Świrszczyńska's, a diary of events reconstructed many years later, are rare in postwar Polish poetry. Another poet, Miron Białoszewski, succeeded in doing the same thing in prose, in *A Memoir of the Warsaw Uprising*. Previously, his poems had given no indication that their author had the experiences he related in his memoir. Yet, when the book appeared, it shed light on a peculiar quality of his verse. *A Memoir* is a faithful, antiheroic, and nonpathetic description of disintegration: bombed houses, whole streets, human bodies disintegrate, as do objects of everyday use and human perceptions of the world. A witness of that disintegration could not help but write as Białoszewski the poet did afterward. For a long time he was not published, and no wonder, for it is difficult to find any poetry more distant from the official optimism. His poetry is mistrustful of culture, no less than that of Różewicz, but above all it is mistrustful of language, for language is the fabric from which the garments of all philosophies and ideologies are cut.

One can say that Białoszewski performs a Cartesian operation, in the sense that he effects a reduction and attempts to draw a circle, even a small one, around something in which he can believe. He appears to have divided reality into two layers: a higher layer, embracing all that creates culture, namely churches, schools, universities, philosophical doctrines, systems of government, and a second, lower layer, life at its most down-to-earth. People go to a store, they use a dish, a spoon, and a fork, sit down on a chair, open and close the door, in spite of what happens up there, "above." They communicate in a language indifferent to correct grammar and syntax, in an idiom of half words, sentences interrupted in the middle, grunts, silences, and peculiar intonations. Białoszewski wants to stay within that lower everyday world and its language. He is like a Roman who, witnessing the fall of Rome, seeks help in what is most durable because it is the most elementary and trivial and, for that reason, is able to grow on the ruins of states and empires. The poetry of the last few decades, not only in Poland but everywhere, has renounced meter and rhyme, and has begun reducing words to their components; in this respect, Białoszewski differs only by the radical nature of his

attempts. But there is something else in him, an aural mimesis—
in the common speech of Warsaw's streets he hears "rustles,
snatches, flows," and he jots them down in a nearly inarticulate
mumble. In such diction he writes of insignificant daily incidents
in his life and that of his acquaintances, mixing verse and prose,
though the borderline between them already is so blurred that
differentiation becomes meaningless. Taken together, these poems make a chronicle of the streets of the city in which he was
born and which he saw destroyed and rebuilt. What is for me
most interesting is the democratic quality in Białoszewski. Like
the other poets I just discussed, he paradoxically breaks the pattern of bohemia, so that the chasm between the poet and the
"human family" ceases to exist. This does not mean that he appeals to everybody, for, in a sense, Białoszewski is a continuator of
the avant-garde and an anti-poet. His example indicates that the
reintegration of the poet does not mean conformity with the
taste of the majority. But Białoszewski himself is not alienated—
he speaks as one of the crowd, gives himself no airs, stands at no
distance, and maintains cordial relations with the people who appear in his prose-poetry.

A diction that juggles peculiarities of flexion and a great
number of suffixes cannot be rendered in a foreign language and,
as a rule, Białoszewski is untranslatable, especially since his penchant for fragmentary, stenographic notation has increased with
time. One poem from his earlier phase, however, does give an
idea of his search for something stable, even if it is as unpreten-
tious as shopping in a store:

A BALLAD OF GOING DOWN TO THE STORE

First I went down to the store
by means of the stairs,
just imagine it,
by means of the stairs.

Then people known to people unknown
passed me by and I passed them by.
Regret
that you did not see
how people walk,
regret!

I entered a complete store:
lamps of glass were glowing.
I saw somebody—he sat down—
and what did I hear? What did I hear?
rustling of bags and human talk.

And indeed,
indeed
I returned.

The experience of disintegration during the war years probably marked Polish poetry so firmly because the order established
after the war was artificial, imposed from above and in conflict
with those organic bonds that survived, such as the family and
the parish church. One striking feature of Polish poetry in recent
decades has been its search for equilibrium amid chaos and the
complete fluidity of all values, something of sufficiently general
importance to deserve attention here. Białoszewski's program
could be called minimalist.

Taking refuge in the world of objects provided a somewhat
similar solution. Human affairs are uncertain and unspeakably
painful, but objects represent a stable reality, do not alter with reflexes of fear, love, or hate, and always "behave" logically. Zbigniew Herbert, a quiet, reserved poet with an inclination to
calligraphic conciseness, has chosen to explore the world of objects. His example confirms what I have said about Polish poetry's
rejoining Western poetry because of the disintegration that confronts them both, even if that disintegration is different in qual-

ity and intensity. Herbert is sometimes reminiscent of Henri Michaux, but his "mythopoems," as they have been called (poems on objects), are closest to those of Francis Ponge. One notable difference between the two is Herbert's personal approach to an object and Ponge's withdrawal to the role of impersonal observer. In Herbert's work a space filled with human struggles and suffering gives objects their background, and thus a chair or a table is precious simply because it is free of human attributes and, for that reason, is deserving of envy. Objects in his poetry seem to follow this reasoning: European culture entered a phase where the neat criteria of good and evil, of truth and falsity, disappeared; at the same time, man became a plaything of powerful collective movements expert in reversing values, so that from one day to the next black would become white, a crime a praiseworthy deed, and an obvious lie an obligatory dogma. Moreover, language was appropriated by the people in power who monopolized the mass media and were able to change the meaning of words to suit themselves. The individual is exposed to a double attack. On the one hand, he must think of himself as the product of determinants which are social, economic, and psychological. On the other hand, his loss of autonomy is confirmed by the totalitarian nature of political power. Such circumstances make every pronouncement on human affairs uncertain. In one of Herbert's poems the narrator hears the voice of conscience but is unable to decipher what the voice is trying to say. In another, "The Elegy of Fortinbras," Hamlet loses out because of his "crystal notions," synonymous with being unprepared for life, while practical Fortinbras pronounces an encomium to opportunism. As opposed to the human domain with its shaky foundations, Herbert tells us, objects have the virtue of simply existing—they can be seen, touched, described.

A similar motivation seems to mark the poems of Francis Ponge, except that his turning to objects signifies a desire to go beyond psychology; in Herbert the object is an element of his encounter with History. History is present in an object as an absence: it reminds us of itself by a minus sign, by the object's in-difference to it.

THE PEBBLE

The pebble
is a perfect creature
equal to itself
mindful of its limits

filled exactly
with a pebbly meaning

with a secret which does not remind one of anything
does not frighten anything away does not arouse desire

its ardour and coldness
are just and full of dignity

I feel a heavy remorse
when I hold it in my hand

and its noble body
is permeated by false warmth

Pebbles cannot be tamed
to the end they will look at us
with a calm and very clear eye

Mankind, unfortunately, is not "equal to itself." Herbert has read twentieth-century philosophy and knows the definition of man as "he who is what he is not and who is not what he is." It is precisely this that in Sartre makes man foreign to Nature, which is established in itself, equal to itself, and bears another name, "être-en-soi." It is "mindful of its limits," while man is characterized by a limitless striving to transcend all limits. The poem is therefore polemical: it indicates that poetry is not bound to avoid philosophy. So "The Pebble" cannot be numbered among the works of pure poetry.

A pebble is free of feelings, that cause of suffering. It has no memory of past experience, good or bad, and no fear or desire. Human ardor and human coldness can be viewed in a positive or negative light, but in a pebble they are just and full of dignity. Man, transient and short-lived, feels remorse when confronted with a pebble. He is aware that he himself is a false warmth. The last three lines contain a political allusion, though a reader may not notice it at first. Pebbles cannot be tamed, but people can, if the rulers are sufficiently crafty and apply the stick-and-carrot method successfully. Tamed people are full of anxiety because of their hidden remorse; they do not look us straight in the face. Pebbles will look at us "with a calm and very clear eye" to the end. To the end of what? we may ask. Probably to the end of the world. The poem ends on an eschatological note.

A final example of the unexpected turns and transfers by which poetry meets the challenge of History is provided by my late friend Aleksander Wat. Wat has left a monumental work—a memoir, *My Century*. This book tells of a life rich enough for ten, and of the peculiar dependence of one destiny upon the various philosophies of our century. In his youth, around 1919, Wat was a futurist. Next, in 1927, he published a volume of perverse parable-like tales, *Lucifer Unemployed*, a blatant example of "European nihilism." In 1929 he became editor-in-chief of the major Communist periodical in Poland between the wars, the *Literary Monthly*. After Poland was partitioned by Hitler and Stalin in 1939, Wat found himself in the Soviet zone, where he was imprisoned, accused of being a Trotskyite, a Zionist, and an agent of the Vatican. After many years in various prisons and in exile in Soviet Asia, he returned in 1946 to Poland, soon to be accused of departing from the doctrine of socialist realism. And, it should be added, that spiritually he was shaped in equal measure, as he stressed in his memoirs, by Judaism, Catholicism, and atheism.

Wat therefore typifies the numerous adventures of the European mind in its Polish variety, that is, a mind not located in some abstract space where what is elementary—hunger, fear, despair, desire—does not penetrate. Wat experienced the philosophies of the twentieth century bodily, in their most tangible forms. He spent time, as he says himself, "in fourteen prisons, many hospitals, and innumerable inns," always taking on roles imposed by the people in power: the role of a prisoner, a patient, an exile. After his period of youthful futurism he virtually abandoned poetry for a long time. He fulfilled himself as a poet in his old age. His late poems are sort of haphazard notes by a man who is locked inside "the four walls of his pain," physical pain. Moreover, Wat is inclined to see his suffering as a punishment, for he was guilty of a grave sin. That sin, widespread in this century, was defined by Nadezhda Mandelstam in her memoirs when she said that, though much can be forgiven a poet, he must not become a seducer, not use his gifts to make his reader into a believer in some inhuman ideology. Wat passed a severe judgment on his nihilistic operations in the twenties and on his subsequent work as editor of the Communist periodical that had such great influence in Poland.

Capricious, highly subjective notes—such, at least in appearance, are Wat's late poems. He speaks of himself, and yet some unexpected transmutation turns that chronicle of his own afflictions into a chronicle of this century's agonies. Wat's example seems to verify my assumption that once reality surpasses any means of naming it, it can be attacked only in a roundabout way, as it is reflected in somebody's subjectivity. Herbert's poem "The Pebble" applies a specific *via negativa* when he speaks of man's fate and praises inanimate nature which contradicts that fate. Wat's *Mediterranean Poems*, written when he was approaching seventy, are the memories of a castaway, a sick veteran of beliefs and doctrines, who finds himself in the stony landscape of the

Alpine foothills and is engaged in a major reassessment. I think it was the German philosopher Adorno who said that, after the Holocaust, poetry is impossible. In Wat's private poetic jottings there is no mention of the Holocaust or of what he, along with more than a million others, lived through during their deportation to Russia. His cry, the cry of Job, tells only of the conclusions drawn by a survivor. As in Herbert, inanimate nature becomes an object of envy.

Disgusted with everything alive I withdrew into the stone
world: here I thought, liberated, I would observe from above,
but
                                without pride, those things
entangled in chaos. With the eyes of a stone, myself
                 a stone among stones, and like them sensitive,
pulsating to the turning of the sun. Retreating into
                     the depth of myself, stone,
motionless, silent; growing cold; present through a waning
                     of presence—in the cold
attractions of the moon. Like sand diminishing in
               an hourglass, evenly,
Ceaselessly, uniformly, grain by grain. Thus I shall be
  submitted
only to the rhythms of day and night. But—
no dance in them, no whirling, no frenzy: only
                   monastic rule and silence.
They do not become, they are. Nothing else. Nothing
                else, I thought, loathing
all which becomes.

What can poetry be in the twentieth century? It seems to me that there is a search for the line beyond which only a zone of silence exists, and that on the borderline we encounter Polish poetry. In it a peculiar fusion of the individual and the historical took place, which means that events burdening a whole community are perceived by a poet as touching him in a most personal manner. Then poetry is no longer alienated. As the etymology of the term suggests, poetry is no longer a foreigner in society. If we must choose the poetry of such an unfortunate country as Poland to learn that the great schism in poetry is curable, then that knowledge brings no comfort. Nevertheless, the example of that poetry gives us perspective on some rituals of the poets when they are separated from "the great human family." Clearly, any neat division of poetry into the "alienated" and "nonalienated" will encounter serious difficulties. I pretend to no precision here.

Mallarmé's sonnet "Le Tombeau d'Edgar Poe," which I have already quoted, is a symbolist manifesto and as such provides some valuable hints. Edgar Allan Poe is called an angel who wanted "*donner un sens plus pur aux mots de la tribu,*" to give a purer meaning to the words of the tribe. Curiously enough, it was precisely Poe's use of English and his form of versification that contributed to his marginal place in the history of American poetry. But a myth needs a conflict between an angel and the hydra of the crowd, and here both Poe's life and the distance between France and America were of help. From Romanticism, of course, comes the idealization of the lonely, misunderstood individual charged with a mission in society, and thus French Symbolism emerges as a specific mutation of the Romantic heritage. Whereas in Romanticism a poet had to prophesy, to lead, to move hearts, here we have the idea of purity and defensiveness, opposed to vulgarity and dirt. On the one side, an angel and "*un sens plus pur*"; on the other, "*le flot sans honneur de quelque noir mélange,*" a wave without honor, of some black mixture. But the ending of Mallarmé's sonnet is probably crucial: Poe's granite tomb is to remain forever a landmark, not to be crossed by "*noirs vols du Blasphème,*" black flights of Blasphemy.

A landmark that will last forever. Here we can see how Mallarmé's sonnet differs from Romanticism. The relationship between the poet and the crowd is defined as stable, not imposed by circumstances that would be changed by historical movement. Society appears as given, like trees and rocks, endowed with the firm, settled existence typical of nineteenth-century bourgeois France. It is precisely that aspect of poetry in isolation as depicted in this sonnet which strikes us as incompatible with what we have learned in the twentieth century. Social structures are not stable, they display great flexibility, and the place of the artist has not been determined once and for all. To be fair to Mallarmé, let us recall that he appears to say exactly the same thing as Horace, who called himself "*Musarum sacerdos*" (a priest of the Muses) and declared: "*Odi profanum vulgus et arceo*" (I hate the profane crowd and keep it at a distance). But the similarity is illusory, for we are confronted with two different historical contexts.

Polish poets found out that the hydra so ominously present for the Symbolists is in reality quite weak, in other words, that the established order, which provides the framework for the quarrel between the poet and the crowd, can cease to exist from one day to the next. In that light, Mallarmé's sonnet is a typical work of the nineteenth century, when civilization seemed to be something guaranteed. And, of course, Polish poets may reproach their Western colleagues who generally repeat the thought patterns proper to the isolated poet. That would be a reproach for lacking a sense of hierarchy when appraising phenomena or, more simply put, for lacking realism. In colloquial speech, the word "unrealistic" indicates an erroneous presentation of facts and implies a confusion of the important and the unimportant, a disturbance of the hierarchy. All reality is hierarchical simply because human needs and the dangers threatening people are arranged on a scale. No easy agreement can be reached as to what should occupy first place. It is not always bread; often it is the word. And death is not always the greatest menace; often slavery is. Nevertheless, anyone who accepts the existence of such a scale behaves differently than someone who denies it. The poetic act changes with the amount of background reality embraced by the poet's consciousness. In our century that background is, in my opinion, related to the fragility of those things we call civilization or culture. What surrounds us, here and now, is not guaranteed. It could just as well not exist—and so man constructs poetry out of the remnants found in ruins.

ANUS MUNDI

THE CLOACA of the world. A certain German wrote down that definition of Poland in 1942. I spent the war years there and afterward, for years, I attempted to understand what it means to bear such an experience inside oneself. As is well known, the philosopher Adorno said that it would be an abomination to write lyric poetry after Auschwitz, and the philosopher Emmanuel Levinas gave the year 1941 as the date when God "abandoned" us. Whereas I wrote idyllic verses, "The World" and a number of others, in the very center of what was taking place in the *anus mundi*, and not by any means out of ignorance. Do I deserve to be condemned for this? Possibly, it would be just as good to write either a bill of accusation or a defense.

Horror is the law of the world of living creatures, and civilization is concerned with masking that truth. Literature and art refine and beautify, and if they were to depict reality naked, just as everyone suspects it is (although we defend ourselves against that knowledge), no one would be able to stand it. Western Europe can be accused of the deceit of civilization. During the industrial revolution it sacrificed human beings to the Baal of progress; then it engaged in trench warfare. A long time ago, I read a manuscript by one Mr. Ulrich, who fought at Verdun as a German infantry soldier. Those people were captured like the prisoners in Auschwitz, but the waters of oblivion have closed over their torment and death. The habits of civilization have a certain enduring quality and the Germans in occupied Western Europe were obviously embarrassed and concealed their aims, while in Poland they acted completely openly.

It is entirely human and understandable to be stunned by blatant criminality and to cry out, "That's impossible!" and yet, it was possible. But those who proclaim that God "abandoned us in 1941" are acting like conservators of an anodyne civilization. And what about the history of humankind, with its millennia of mutual murder? To say nothing of natural catastrophes, or of the plague, which depopulated Europe in the fourteenth century. Nor of those aspects of human life which do not need a grand public arena to display their subservience to the laws of earth.

Life does not like death. The body, as long as it is able to, sets in opposition to death the heart's contractions and the warmth of circulating blood. Gentle verses written in the midst of horror declare themselves for life; they are the body's rebellion against its destruction. They are *carmina*, or incantations deployed in order that the horror should disappear for a moment and harmony emerge—the harmony of civilization or, what amounts to the same thing, of childish peace. They comfort us, giving us to understand that what takes place in *anus mundi* is transitory, and that harmony is enduring—which is not at all a certainty.

AGAINST
INCOMPREHENSIBLE POETRY

AFTER A LONG LIFE devoted to reflecting and writing, I have been thinking about what is, for me, the core of my reflections. I have reached the conclusion that it is exactly the same as when I was fifteen years old and, reared in the Roman Catholic religion, encountered for the first time the so-called scientific worldview in my biology classes. True, we hear nowadays that we have learned to divide the two fields and that the truth of religion has nothing in common with the truth of science. The religious imagination in our scientific-technological civilization, however, has been eroding inexorably. Those who participate in religious rites, whatever their religion, have a great deal of difficulty maintaining their faith, whether they admit it or not. And those who have received the grace of faith believe differently from their forefathers.

This is a rather peculiar introduction to reflections on poetry. One might ask whether the questions that constrain the mind of a theologian or a philosopher have any significance for the poet today. My response to this is yes, and I shall attempt to explain why.

Literature and art have become separated from Christianity. This was a gradual process which began as early as when the Humanists of the Renaissance discovered the ancient poets and philosophers, which induced them to defend the laws of Reason. This process accelerated dramatically upon the appearance of the scientific worldview in the nineteenth century. At the same time, or, to be more precise, due to the same cause, poetry entered into territory where questions about the meaning of life find no answer, where the mind grapples with an absence of meaning. In this connection, the most representative contemporary poet is Samuel Beckett.

This does not mean that in our century there have been no outstanding works of poetry inspired by religion, as the example of Rainer Maria Rilke's *Duino Elegies* demonstrates. Religious inspiration, however, does not necessarily mean Christian inspiration; exceptions include lengthy poems whose authors speak as members of one of the Christian churches—Paul Claudel's *Odes*, for example, or T. S. Eliot's *Four Quartets*. It is as obvious as can be that they have to overcome a significant resistance, working against both the public's intellectual habits and everything that passes for modern in poetry.

But what is this modernity? Today, postmodernism stands in opposition to modernism; this seems, however, to have as its aim the denial of obvious continuity. We need to return to the time when the family honored traditional beliefs, while the poet felt emancipated from his family and assigned it to a category to which he gave the not very flattering name of bourgeoisie, philistines, and so forth, although what he meant by this was simply ordinary humanity unconcerned with intellectual matters. That situation continues today.

There are still plenty of families devoted to values rooted in religion, and there are countries in which the churches are full. At the same time, he who believes in literature and art chooses a somewhat marginal position, perhaps a sort of distinct religious order following its own collection of fundamental principles.

These principles need not be accepted consciously, because they are inherent in the very form of modern literature and art. Many poets are not even aware of the degree to which they are contributing to the further development of French Symbolism, which in the nineteenth century elaborated patterns of behavior for the rebellious, isolated poet.

What principles? In the first place, Horace's loathing for the crowd was renewed: *"Odi profanum vulgus"*—"I hate the blaspheming (this is also a possible translation) crowd." The poem and every work of art, and thus the creative work of the human mind and the human hand, achieve a superior position, are counted as *sacra*, as opposed to *profana*. Their creator is thereby granted dignity equal to that of a priest. This is the foundation for all sorts of experiments with form, or, in other words, with "incomprehensible" poetry. We might say that the less comprehensible it is, the better, because it shuts the poet off from the wrong people.

Secondly, it is generally accepted that we know nothing, but it is said that man was created in the image and likeness of God, that he fell, and that at a certain moment in his history he was redeemed through incarnation in the Son of God. The evolution of life on earth does not allow us to draw a boundary between man and other mammalian species. History is not a gradual fulfillment of the Divinity's intentions, and good and evil possess no metaphysical foundation. Man rises above himself only in art.

It is sufficient to observe the true cult of art at the present time, at the end of the century, in order to draw a straight line from those early reasons for lauding art to their application. Consider the number of reproductions of works of art in magazines, in books, on the walls of private apartments and hotels. Consider that Baroque music is heard on recordings, on radio broadcasts, in televised concerts. Finally, the greatest temples of our time are the famous art museums visited by millions—the Metropolitan Museum of Art in New York, the Louvre and Musée d'Orsay in Paris, the Prado in Madrid.

Reviewing the events of the century, we also come across the paradox of recognition and nonrecognition. Artists wrote and painted in opposition, and then they were adopted and made to conform. The names of hermetic poets entered the canon of school readings, and the works of painters who died in poverty are sold for millions of dollars.

In 1925 Ortega y Gasset called the retreat from the realistic and melodramatic tastes of the masses "the dehumanization of art." We must admit that artists did not only turn away with disdain but also provoked and stuck out their tongues, and this notion of *pour épater le bourgeois* contained the hope of recognition. Today's entire mass culture, including film, which was realistic and melodramatic when founded, draws upon avant-garde ideas that once seemed crazy.

Here we enter into the sociology of art, which has only marginal significance in relation to the particular laws which modern poetry obeys. Although its earliest practitioners were recognized posthumously, it is doubtful that, for example, Stéphane Mallarmé's fame is equivalent to van Gogh's. The particularly enduring isolation of the poet from his contemporaries seems to be a constant feature of the various schools and tendencies of poetry, which have followed one after the other for well over a hundred years; the discussion of a few names in university seminars has very little impact. If one wanted to define a certain repetitive pattern in the position of poets, from which, of course, there are various exceptions, one would have to compare it with a game of chess. Chess tournaments are of very little interest to those who do not play chess, just as the internal games of poets' clans are of no interest to ordinary bread eaters.

The comparative history of modern poetry in various languages is yet to be written. In general, one can detect a mysterious wandering of creative vigor from country to country, just as in painting first Italy, then Holland, then Spain, and then France were in the forefront. In poetry, France took the lead thanks to her Symbolists, after which there was an explosion of energy around the time of World War I and then a twilight that has lasted to this day. The Russian intelligentsia before 1914 was famous as an unbelievably daring and lively milieu, but it was destroyed shortly after the Revolution. Already before World War I all of European poetry had experienced an American influence thanks to Walt Whitman, who almost caused a revolution in versification by discarding meter and rhyme in favor of free verse. Around 1912 the victorious march of English, and above all of American, poetry begins, and the role played by Ezra Pound explains why he became an almost mythical figure for many people. *Nota bene*: it is not difficult to find echoes of his French predecessors in what he proclaimed when writing as a theorist of poetry.

The mutual fertilization of poetry from various countries does not mean that certain motifs and forms must be repeated, for the different laws of each language, the different pasts and traditions of particular literatures, produce different results. Thus, although the United States dominates today in the number of talented poets and the alacrity with which it swallows everything that is new and different, over the past few decades the poetry of Spanish-speaking countries has been making its presence known, and in addition to Spain, so are Greece and Poland among the European countries.

The isolation of the poet is just a model which helps us gauge more clearly how he diverges from this model. Many poets have rebelled against being locked up in a tower, and this has often pushed them into engagement on the side of revolution, frequently understood in a Marxist fashion, although the most active motivation in this was a post-Christian search for salvation, this time located in time, i.e., in the heaven of the future perfect system. Poetry in the service of social and independence movements has, in a sense, renewed the pact with humanity that it concluded in the Romantic era. However, a contradiction emerged at that time, because it was already, as Ortega y Gasset called it, "dehumanized" poetry—too recherché to appeal to the broad masses. The leaders of political movements barely tolerated it, and this romance of poets with revolution was not devoid of tragicomedy.

I must confess that I did not feel comfortable in the skin of a modern poet and that I was skeptical about "pure poetry" in its various guises (it was put forward under a series of different names) because I detected idol worship in the tributes paid to this poetry. In my youth, however, I did my share of social engagement, and I know that such a way of fleeing the tower leads to no good.

It appears that we are witnesses to the disintegration of this complex of ideas which bears the name "modernity," and in this sense the word "postmodernism" is applicable. Poetry has somehow become more humble, perhaps because faith in the timelessness and eternal endurance of the work of art has been weakened, which, of course, was the foundation of disdain for *profanum vulgus*. In other words, instead of looking at itself alone, poetry began to turn toward the outside. In America, poetry interests me if it observes the situation of man now, in this phase of scientific-technological civilization, with its lack of a foundation on which to base values, with its search for warmth and goodness in bonds of love and in the family, with its fear of transience and of death. I also detect in it the heritage of elevated isolation, and thus of formal complexity, which derives from fear of the friendly judgment of closed milieus. This is even expressed in the lexicon: numerous expressions which the average man does not know, so that even readers who imagine themselves as part of the elite run in secret to consult encyclopedias; also, the many allusions to theories and fantasies fashionable among intellectuals at the moment. Perhaps the very vulgarity of mass culture continues to command a small minority to take refuge in a system of conventional signs; in the past, bohemia has often taken refuge from the bourgeois and the philistine, but in this quarrel of the elect with the insufficiently refined, it is not difficult to side with "the great human family."

The many translations into English of ancient Chinese and Japanese poetry have given me a great deal to think about. They are eagerly read by people who do not like modern poetry and accuse it of being incomprehensible, sterile, tending toward purely formal exercises. It is obvious that at the end of our century these verses by poets of the Far East are closer to what readers want. I asked myself, Why is this the case and what is distinctive about them? Well, their background is a civilization that is different from ours, that is strongly marked by nontheistic religions such as Taoism and Buddhism, which understand man's place in the universe differently. Who knows, perhaps this is what confirms the Buddhists' thesis that the scientific worldview has no quarrel with Buddhism, while it is difficult to reconcile it with the personal God of the Bible. But there is something else as well. The very foundation of Western thought has always been opposition: subject versus object. "I" was opposed to the external world, which had to be known and mastered. And this is precisely the content of Western man's epopees. For a long time, there was equilibrium between subject and object. The arbitrary "I" appears when this equilibrium is disturbed. Painting, which is more and more about the subject, is a good illustration of this.

In ancient China and Japan, subject and object were understood not as categories of opposition but of identification. This is probably the source of the profoundly respectful descriptions of what surrounds us, of flowers, trees, landscapes, for the things we can see are somehow a part of ourselves, but only by virtue of being themselves and preserving their *suchness*, to use a Zen Buddhist term. This is a poetry in which the macrocosm is reflected in each concrete detail, like the sun in a drop of dew.

The example of East Asian poetry inspired me to seek elsewhere, too, for virtues similar to the ones I had found in it. Just as after visiting the art galleries of distant countries we return to our native museums and perceive them in a new light, so the poetry of Europe and America revealed to me a particular current to which I had not paid sufficient attention previously. I began selecting poems in various languages that I found pleasing because they honored the object, not the subject. And thus arose the idea of compiling an anthology of poems which meet my demands and which undermine the widely held opinion that poetry is, inevitably, obscure and inaccessible.

In the beginning I intended to collect examples from various epochs, but in the end I restricted myself to what was chronologically closer to our time. This may be surprising, but to a significant degree it was versification that proved decisive. I had observed that traditional rhymed verse draws attention to its sound structure at the cost (greater or lesser, to be sure) of image. Only the shedding of its fixed meters makes it possible to concentrate on the image. Let me confess to some slight disingenuousness when talking about the selection of East Asian poetry: the originals adhered to strict rules, the number of syllables permitted, and so forth, but we necessarily receive only approximate versions, for their rhythmic structure cannot be discovered, and so we value them according to the expressiveness of their images. These poems have already entered the "free verse" canon, and I have been much too influenced by them to overlook them in my collection.

Thus, profiting from my readings in several languages, I have been preparing an exceedingly capricious selection of modern poetry aimed against modern poetry's chief tendencies: against the floods of artistic metaphors and a linguistic fabric liberated from colloquial meaning. I am searching for purity of line, simplicity, and concision. As, for example, in this short poem by Walt Whitman:

On a flat road runs the well-train'd runner,
He is lean and sinewy with muscular legs,
He is thinly clothed, he leans forward as he runs,
With lightly closed fists and arms partially rais'd.

("THE RUNNER")

Western poetry has recently gone so far down the path of subjectivity that it has stopped acknowledging the laws of the object. It even appears to be proposing that all that exists is perception, and there is no objective world. In which case, one may say anything, for there is no control at all. But the Zen poet advises us to learn about the pine tree from the pine tree, about the bamboo from the bamboo, and this is an entirely different point of view.

There are poems which, following this advice, turn toward the object, even if it does not necessarily agree with the author's views. Sometimes, the same poet will have written some poems which are for, some against. All of modern poetry is torn apart by internal contradictions and temptations.

In a little-known unfinished poem Walt Whitman writes:

I am the poet of reality
I say the earth is not an echo
Nor man an apparition....

     ("I AM THE POET")

He remained faithful to this proclamation by his ceaseless astonishment at the never-exhausted abundance of phenomena. Similarly, D. H. Lawrence, particularly in his late poems, assigns an almost sacral significance to the observed detail. In W. H. Auden, this has a somewhat different appearance, but he makes himself entirely clear:

Poetry can do a hundred and one things, delight, sadden, disturb, amuse, instruct—it may express every possible shade of emotion, and describe every conceivable kind of event, but there is only one thing that all poetry must do; it must praise all it can for being and for happening.

Robinson Jeffers laments in one of his poems that the "wild swan" of the world, which can never be reached by a word, eludes him, the ardent hunter. And Blaise Cendrars, a poet of the triumphant period of French poetry before and immediately after World War I, a traveler in many continents, was such an enthusiastic collector of images of the earth that he called one of his volumes *Kodak*.

In the brief triumphant period of French poetry, which was more or less contemporaneous with Cubism in painting, modernity meant a greedy hunger for the newly discovered elements of objects. What emerged from this later was an almost scientific exploration of a peach, or a thrush, or a snail, that is, of those perceptions of ours which surface when certain objects appear in our field of vision. Often these are dazzlingly intelligent constructions, but I find very little in them for myself. The "suchness" of things is replaced in them by purely intellectual deconstruction into their component parts. This applies, for example, to Francis Ponge and in significant measure to Wallace Stevens too.

My anthology has nothing to do with establishing a literary hierarchy, with dividing names into those who are of greater and of lesser importance. It differs from similar undertakings in that they strive to be fair, at least, according to their editors. When I come upon a poem which meets my criteria, I do not stop to consider whether its author is famous or not. Therefore, I have included poets whom practically no one has heard of. Conversely, I survey the work of very well known figures and am filled with admiration, but very often they are not appropriate to this occasion.

Perhaps the criteria for my choice are not sufficiently clear, yet I proceed like a mute who, unable to explain what he wants, points to it with his finger: "This."

I return to my main point. When W. H. Auden says that poetry "must praise all it can for being and for happening," he is expressing a theological belief. Affirmation of life has a long, distinguished past in Western thought. Thomas Aquinas's placing of an equal sign between God and pure being belongs here, as does the constant identification of evil with an insufficiency of being, by means of which the Devil acts as the power of nothingness. Also in this history is the song of wonder at Nature conceived as the work of the Creator's hands, work which inspired countless painters and supplied a powerful impetus to scholars, at least in the first phase of victoriously ascendant science. "The Metaphysical Sense of the Wondrousness of Being" means, above all, that contemplating a tree or a rock or a man, we suddenly comprehend that it *is*, even though it might not have been.

It is significant that in the poetry of the last few decades, especially in French poetry, the descriptive capacity has been disappearing. To call a table a table is far too simple. But after all, to compare poetry with painting again, Cézanne kept on repositioning his easel and painting the same pine tree, attempting to devour it with his eyes and mind, penetrating its lines and colors, whose multiplicity struck him as inexhaustible.

Description demands intense observation, so intense that the veil of everyday habit falls away and what we paid no attention to, because it struck us as so ordinary, is revealed as miraculous. I do not hide the fact that I seek in poems a revelation of reality, of what is known in Greek as *epifaneia*. This word used to mean, in the first instance, manifestation, the appearance of the Divinity among mortals, and also our recognition of the divine in an ordinary, familiar form, as for example, in the form of a man. Epiphany thus interrupts the everyday flow of time and enters as one privileged moment when we intuitively grasp a deeper, more essential reality hidden in things or persons. A poem-epiphany tells about one moment-event, and this imposes a certain form.

A polytheistic antiquity saw epiphanies at every step, for streams and woods assumed the form of the goddesses, nymphs, and dryads inhabiting them, and it was difficult to distinguish the commanding gods from mortals since they had human features, human customs, and the gift of speech, and often walked around on earth—hence their frequent visits to people's households, where their hosts often recognized them. Even the Book of Genesis tells of God's visit to Abraham in the form of three wanderers. Later, epiphany assumes such an important place in the

Gospels that one of the oldest Christian holidays was given that name. (The name "Three Kings' Day" constricts its original content, which embraced both the birth of Christ and the first miracle in Cana of Galilee.) D. H. Lawrence, a poet of exceptional sensitivity to the rich materiality of things which are accessible to our senses, reveals the ancient imagination in his poem "Maximus" so well that we can almost feel a shudder of recognition, as if the god Hermes had appeared to us. Most likely, Lawrence was thinking of the fourth-century philosopher Maximus, who was the tutor of the emperor Julian, later called the Apostate:

> *God is older than the sun and moon*
> *and the eye cannot behold him*
> *no voice will describe him.*

> *But a naked man, a stranger, leaned on the gate*
> *with his cloak over his arm, waiting to be asked in.*
> *So I called him: Come in, if you will!—*

> *He came in slowly and sat down by the hearth.*
> *I said to him: And what is your name?—*
> *He looked at me without answer, but such a loveliness*
> *entered me, I smiled to myself, saying: He is God!*
> *So he said:* Hermes!

> *God is older than the sun and moon*
> *and the eye cannot behold him*
> *nor the voice describe him:*
> *and still, this is the God Hermes, sitting by my hearth.*

("MAXIMUS")

Obviously, an epiphany of this type, in the sense of communication between people and gods, does not exhaust all the meanings of the word. It can also signify the opening of the senses to reality. The eyes appear to be the privileged organ in this regard, but epiphany can also occur thanks to hearing or touch. It is not worth straining to achieve too precise a definition of what it depends on; that would limit us too much. In general, we are dealing with epiphany when the perceived object in the center of attention and its description achieve greater significance than a character's psychology, the plot line, and so forth. Adam Mickiewicz's *Pan Tadeusz*, for example, independently of its plot and the customs it describes, can be read as a series of revelations of observable detail.

In Japanese haiku, epiphany occurs as a glimmer, as something that is glimpsed unexpectedly and for a very brief time, in the way that a familiar landscape appears different to us in the glare of a lightning flash or a rocket. For example, in the poet Issa (1763–1827):

From the bough
floating down river
insect song.

Related to this are the short verse-perceptions of the poet Miron Białoszewski (1922–1983), perhaps the most "Eastern" of Polish poets. In his case, this was probably connected to his lifestyle, which gave those who knew him pause: carelessness about his own person, an attitude of disengagement, an almost perfect Buddhist monk.

Nothing, perhaps, is simpler and more obvious than what supplied the Brazilian poet Carlos Drummond de Andrade with the theme for his poem. When a thing is truly seen, seen intensely, it remains with us forever and astonishes us, even though it would appear that there is nothing astonishing about it:

In the middle of the road there was a stone
there was a stone in the middle of the road
there was a stone
in the middle of the road there was a stone.

Never should I forget this event
in the life of my fatigued retinas.
Never should I forget that in the middle of the road
there was a stone
there was a stone in the middle of the road
in the middle of the road there was a stone.

("IN THE MIDDLE OF THE ROAD")

Parenthetically speaking, this example can convince us of how little of the thing observed can be captured by a word because, quite simply, language operates with concepts. "Stone" is not precisely this and no other stone, nor a specific shape and color—just a stone in general. In order to paint it as it should be painted, one would have to struggle mightily. Similarly, reading "road," we would like to know what kind of a road—a beaten track, a dirt or an asphalt road? Drummond de Andrade's poem depicts the moment of encounter with the object very well, but it does not satisfy, just as, to tell the truth, any attempt at translating sensory knowledge into words can be only more or less unsatisfying.

Poetry selected in this manner may lead one to believe that it is related to mystical contemplation, although the subject matter honored in it is the world itself. And since the world is often understood in it as the body of the Divinity, perhaps I will be called a pantheist. That would be the truth if a pious attitude toward the physical world had to go hand in hand with a Stoical acceptance of its all-encompassing, unique existence, as in Lucretius. I think, however, that the tragedy of human fate does not permit such a calm acceptance of the splendid, self-sufficient structure of the universe, indifferent to suffering. For this very reason it would be difficult for me to assent to the Buddhist solution. Alas, our fundamental experience is duality: mind and body, freedom and necessity, evil and good, and certainly world and God. It is the same with our protest against pain and death. In the poetry I select I am not seeking an escape from dread but rather proof that dread and reverence can exist within us simultaneously.

My intentions in putting together this anthology extended beyond the realm of literature. Average people feel and think a great deal, but they cannot study philosophy, which would not offer them much in any case. In truth, serious problems reach us by means of creative works, which on the surface appear to have only artistry as their aim, even though they are freighted with questions that everyone poses to himself. And it is here, perhaps, that in the wall surrounding poetry for the elect a gate opens up, leading to poetry for all. I will be satisfied if my attempt at defending poetry against narrowing and dessication will be recognized as one of many attempts that can be made.

REFLECTIONS ON
T. S. ELIOT

1. T. S. Eliot appeared in literature several years before World War I, at a time, that is, when the divorce between poetry and the reading public had already taken place. The model of a bohemia engaged in activities that normal people could not comprehend was a compelling one for poets, who, whatever their nationality, had chosen the French Symbolists as their patrons. It would have been futile to try reducing the stakes and clarifying the aspirations of these poets as "a struggle for a new aesthetics." What was really at stake was an answer to the question "What is man to do in a universe 'emptied of values' by a scientific and positivist worldview?" This dilemma was stated most effectively by Nietzsche. For those poets—Yeats (b. 1865), Rilke (b. 1875), or, in Poland, Bolesław Leśmian (b. 1878)—who were somewhat older than Eliot (b. 1888), the central problem was art as a values-creating act or (and this amounts to the same thing) as a God-creating act and thus a substitute for religion. Eliot's relation to art conceived of in that way (Baron Münchhausen tearing out his hair) defines his entire creative oeuvre.

2. It is significant that among the representatives of so-called modernity, Eliot chose Baudelaire, passing over his French successors, with the exception of Jules Laforgue. Baudelaire was a poet of original sin and therefore a Christian poet. The ironic Laforgue did not declare himself a proponent of the self-sufficient, self-reflexive verbal art whose ascetic priest was the atheist Mallarmé. Laforgue's poems are the intensely personal lament of a man who insists that it is impossible to live with such an *imagination of space* as the scientific worldview has constructed; this is the source of his frequent images of the planets dancing a senseless dance in an endless, protracted void, with neither beginning nor end in time. This is connected with his sense of the meaninglessness of human society as a phantasmagoria unnoticed by the lonely observer. This metaphysical despair is expressed more effectively in Laforgue's poems and songs, which were written in argot, than in the sobs of many another writer, including Stanisław Przybyszewski and Jan Kasprowicz.

Both Baudelaire and Laforgue confirmed Eliot and his friend T. E. Hulme in their cult of Dante as a poet of a lost organic civilization, when people had access to the "living water." Their thoughts thus touched upon phases of a civilization that was turned nostalgically to the past. But as has been the case in Europe since the beginnings of Romanticism, yearning for the past and yearning for the future are interconnected: if industrial and scientific civilization deprived man of his innate, relative equilibrium, this means that an *optimum* exists and can be restored. (The idealization of lost organic ties can also be found among the sources of utopian socialism and in treatises on primitive communism.) Obviously, Eliot and his friends were far removed from the futuristic fantasies of H. G. Wells, which were to be negated by Wells's confession of utter pessimism in his last book. Their ideal was hierarchy, harmony—until a complete restoration, under the threat of annihilation. The subject of *The Waste Land* is the *cité infernale*, which William Blake was the first to describe, followed by Baudelaire—man's situation in the diabolical city grew worse with the passage of time. *The Waste Land* could serve as an illustration of Oswald Spengler's theses about the phase in the development of a civilization when all its life-sustaining powers are exhausted. According to Eliot, the imagination's inability to conceive of a religious ordering of space has its counterpart in the disintegration, chaos, and perceived objects and relations between people, which is conveyed, in fact, by the very structure of the poem—a structure of ruins, rubble, fragments. I say this in order to remind us that Eliot did not join the adherents of art for art's sake, and in contrast to Yeats, he sailed to no Byzantium of perfectly frozen forms. He wanted to be a poet-interpreter and, from time to time, a Christian satirical poet.

3. His poetry was characterized by at least one fundamental internal contradiction. He was "intellectual"; that is, he proposed certain values which will not cease to be such even if they are considered as something other than components of a given artistic whole. At the same time, however, he developed his poetic craft by employing the poetics of the Symbolists. This poetics, beginning from its earliest discoverers back in the orbit of Romanticism, demanded more and more "purity"; it drew an increasingly sharp boundary between poetry_ and colloquial language, so that its end product was "metalanguage" (*zaumnyi iazyk* in Russian). Such a poetics precluded various types of description and discourse. Thus, the dimensions of poetic compositions kept shrinking, until finally not the stanza, but a single line, was the locus of tension and brilliance. Eliot himself, through both his poetic practice and his activity as a theorist, confronted English and American poets with principles that met with considerable opposition, especially in America. Chief among these was the assertion that the poet communicates with his reader not "directly" but by creating "objective correlatives":

instead of saying what he feels and thinks, he portrays objects or groups of objects which correlate with certain life experiences.

It is easy to see that such a poetics, applied to the communication of indefinable states, of thought-feelings or moods, created exceptionally difficult conditions for a poet who was inclined to meditation and who had the temperament, perhaps, of a seventeenth-century Anglican priest. This exceptional resistance, repeatedly mastered by him voluntarily, explains his slight literary output (if we exclude his theatrical pieces). The opposition and resistance that his efforts at mastery met with are, at the same time, the secret of the compactness and energy of every line he wrote; in that, he had no rival in the English language. The reader tries to guess if a given line is all that the poet can offer or if it is but a fraction of the charged load that is lying in wait, "a percentage of the truth." But this also contains the source of the apparition who bears witness to something in the history of culture, and it is in this sense that people ask, "What does he mean?" The growing number of glosses not only on particular works by Eliot but also on individual lines in those works, and the comical despair of critics who cannot for the life of them agree on a unified explication of "what the poet meant to say," demonstrate that we are dealing here with a type of writer who requires different methods of evaluation. Eliot owed the compactness and severity of his form to his oppositional stance, but the poetics he chose made him an "obscure" poet, and some of his digressions, such as those in *Four Quartets*, are indecipherable without resort to the often dubious assistance of his commentators.

4. Whatever his strictly individual vocation may have been, he belonged to his age, and the themes he introduced appeared simultaneously in various countries, independently of literary borrowings. Eliot established his landscape: a landscape of grayness, meaninglessness, futility, fetid sewers, shattered bottles,

blocked drains, London streets in which the people walking past are more like shades of the dead than living human beings. When I became acquainted with his poetry during World War II, I was astonished to realize that this aura, which I would call an aura of man's isolation in relation to objects, was familiar to me from other reading. The French poet Oscar Milosz, who achieved full recognition only posthumously, saturated his "Symphonies" with a similar aura; they were written between 1913 and 1920, precisely at the time when Eliot's long poems were taking shape. The Paris of loners is not a happy place in Milosz's writing: "wastelands of tracks"; mildewed walls; rain pouring down at dawn onto the interior walls of half-destroyed slums with patterns of wallpaper on them; on the street outside his window, the cough of an old garbage collector; the grass in the square "cold and filthy, sleepless like an *idée fixe*"; rust and mold. It is worth recalling that these images visit those poets especially who have a metaphysical orientation, poets of "insatiability," like Eliot and Milosz, although it would be possible to add other examples.

The themes appearing in poetry anticipate by several decades the triumphant march of similar themes in other genres of literature and art. Perhaps this is not a binding rule at all times and in all places, but it has held true in the twentieth century. Without a doubt, Beckett's *Waiting for Godot* is already contained in Eliot's poem "The Hollow Men," and the so-called Theater of the Absurd, entranced by the problem of alienation, cannot in any way shock connoisseurs of a more hermetic form, especially since it repeats the mixture discovered by poets of the grotesque and the macabre: Eliot's *Waste Land* is already a grotesque tragedy. One can, of course, establish the successive stages by which these motifs become universalized and vulgarized. They begin in poetry, then migrate to prose and the theater and from there to film. Certain scenes from the films of Fellini and Antonioni are like translations of poems, often including poems by Eliot; here one can cite, for example, the intellectual's room in

Fellini's *La Dolce Vita* as a borrowing from "The Love Song of J. Alfred Prufrock" ("In the room the women come and go / Talking of Michelangelo"). It is irrelevant whether a given author or director borrows directly or indirectly. Even people who never read poetry receive it in a somewhat more accessible form in the theater and film. Therefore, it can be freely argued that although the number of well-informed readers of Eliot's poetry was never large, people have gradually become acquainted with him indirectly as a new classic whose books one need not ever reach for.

5. Before World War II, Eliot was unknown to Polish poets, although certain similarities could have been found between him and the "Catastrophists." If the then editor of *Criterion*, who was turning established hierarchies upside down, remained at best a name for literary circles in Poland, that means that not much was known there about American and English poetry. The first to write about Eliot was not a poet but a professor, Wacław Borowy; it was his article that moved me to read Eliot in the original, more so, perhaps, than the urgings of my friend, the poet Józef Czechowicz. Czechowicz, "the King of Encyclopedias," was an exception among poets because he was interested in Eliot and had translated three of his poems ("Journey of the Magi," "Triumphal March," "A Song for Simeon"); he also told me, his "Terrible Brother," about the journal *Criterion*, but all this happened right before the war broke out. More important than the date (people were beginning to study English at that time in Poland) is Czechowicz's persona as a representative of a certain poetic technique, different from both the Skamander movement and the First Avant-Garde of the interwar period. Awareness of this distinction led to a regrouping: Czechowicz and Ludwik Fryde founded the journal *Pióro* (The Pen), taking with them also some castaways from the journal *Żagary* (Brushwood). Copies of *Pióro* are a rarity because almost the entire run was consumed by fire in 1939.

So-called literary currents indicate that *attention* is constantly shifting its focus. Both Skamander and the Cracow avant-garde derived from the poetics of the Symbolists, but each emphasized different aspects of that poetics. The Skamander poets' attention was drawn to poetry as melody, as incantation, which accounts for the frequent looseness in their connections between words and sounds. When Tuwim, for example, attempted to impose greater rigor on these connections, he reached for classical models. Such Russian poets as Mandelstam or Pasternak were more concerned than Skamander was with the metaphorical density of a given poem. In Poland, it was the Cracow theorists who took upon themselves the need for metaphorical density, but they rejected almost entirely any incantatory quality, which in turn made them only faintly similar to the Russians; after all, they had a "Galician ear" and did not read the Russian poets. Their program and practice inclined them to focus their attention on what takes place between words, and this schooled them in precision. (Looseness was a disease of Young Poland; Leśmian overcame it, and so did Skamander, to a degree, so the avant-garde's ideas signified a further development of the same tendency.) Nonetheless, by accusing Skamander of murky thinking and a passive acceptance of the dictates of inspiration, the Cracow avant-garde did not take into consideration how very poor and even primitive its own worldview was or that its poems actually narrowed the territory of poetry.

The influence of Czechowicz and the Catastrophists, already visible on the eve of World War II, should be ascribed to their technique of "condensation," which they employed as a means of grappling with the complexities of their worldview. This does not mean that Czechowicz's poems, for example, should be read as philosophy, but his foreboding of immanent destruction and his own death in that destruction, his exploration of dreams, and his personal ties with the circle of young philosophers (Bolesław Miciński's milieu), demonstrate that it would be possible to draw certain parallels between Eliot and the growing "struggle for content" in Poland at the end of the 1930s. The same contradiction as in Eliot encouraged the writing of poems which were encoded messages and which, originally noticed for their dark emotional tone, revealed their layer of meanings only with the passage of time.

The Skamander poets' "household" did not fit with Eliot's, and there is no indication that those among them who later lived for a long time in England or America visited his domain, although language was no longer a barrier. It would seem, though, that the constructivist, rationalist avant-garde would have been at a loss as to what to do among the monsters who, by their very existence, offended the common sense of these progressives. It is no accident, therefore, that Eliot's first translator was Czechowicz, and the second, Czechowicz's friend from *Żagary*.*

Poland during the years 1918–1939 did have a writer, however, who, in his historiosophy, at least, bore a certain resemblance to Eliot. Stanisław Ignacy Witkiewicz, Eliot's contemporary, most likely drew upon rather similar ingredients before World War I, for he noticed a gradual decline in civilization (in religion, philosophy, art). Despite the fact that his understanding moved along different tracks, both he and Eliot share the central motif of "insatiability" and also the grotesqueness of the characters they present, who are like straw dolls, mulches swaying in the wind. It is not for nothing that the Witkiewiczean Theater of Pure Form is, as spectacle, a transition from the theater of the Symbolist playwright Stanisław Wyspiański to contemporary morality plays, whose hero is Everyman, deprived, however, of both heaven and hell, and condemned to Limbo or, as we used to be taught in catechism classes, to the Abyss. One may say, then, that the components of Eliot's poetry were divided in Poland among various authors: Stanisław Ignacy Witkiewicz, in the first

---

*The friend is none other than Czeslaw Miłosz, who was one of the founding editors of this short-lived literary review.

place, and then Józef Czechowicz, Konstanty Ildefons Gałczyński (in his poem "Ball at Solomon's"), and the Catastrophists.

Much was accomplished in Polish literature before Eliot himself became more or less well known. For much of the two decades from 1945 to 1965, his name served as a warning sign at the entrance to territories that had been placed off limits—very large tracts, because they included everything that harbors an anthropological reflection. Today, Polish poetry, through its particular sensibility and the formal transformations appropriate to it, is better prepared to explore those territories; it would be difficult, however, to say what it owes directly to the author of *Four Quartets*.

6. Eliot's influence on American poets and critics was so vast that in the span of several decades he wielded dictatorial power, even though his book-filled office in the publishing firm of Faber and Faber on Russell Square in London did not resemble an autocrat's domain. As could be expected, this did not take place without murmurs of protest, which gradually, around 1950, gathered enough strength to turn into open rebellion. Undoubtedly, Eliot's influence was paralyzing. The native traditions of American poetry are like what Tocqueville foresaw when he analyzed American democracy; his penetrating intelligence is remarkable, for he predicted and defined the characteristics of Walt Whitman before Whitman had even begun to write: a poetry, we could say, that is expressionistic, chatty, expansive, but disdainful of the jeweler's trade. Sandburg was Whitman's successor, but he was not the only one. Distrust of the Symbolist poetics of Europe (which, to be sure, had its American predecessor in Edgar Allan Poe) was thoroughly programmatic in those poets who wanted to chat away about whatever cheered them or depressed them and had no interest in constructing perfectly balanced, concise compositions, ideal objects. The pressure of the content, the theme, was simply too great. True, it was no longer the conquering of a continent, as in Whitman, but an obsession with

contamination, a terror of the separation of nature from man and man from nature, which organized the philosophical naturalism (the "inhumanism") of Robinson Jeffers or the reportorial quality of William Carlos Williams, writing his chronicle of the industrial city of Paterson, New Jersey. One should not simplify the extremely complex penetration of Eliot's influences, but one should also not ascribe to him a role where other factors were at work, especially since it was he, in the first place, who inspired a fundamental reassessment. Compared with poems in which the principle of the "objective correlative" was obligatory, works that simply speak "directly" usually paled as too eloquent and at the same time as incorporating too few layers of meaning. In poetry, multilayered irony, a fluidity of the senses sparked by collisions between words, began to be obligatory. But a strong personality, a connoisseur, imposing muteness and instantaneous comprehension, stood behind Eliot's poetics. Written by skeptics and epicures, and thus devoid of the tension that derives from contradictions, recognized as activity in and of itself, American poetry fell ill; excessive straining for high culture and a fear of simplicity of expression are not, as a rule, healthy for poetry. The range of cultural allusions permitted in American poetry was very broad. Just as elegant suburbs acquire the works of art of all countries and all epochs, so ideas and images taken from beautifully printed albums, from the books of Freud and Jung, from the history of religion, took up their abode in American poetry. So what, if "*panta rhei* [everything is in flux], but nothing is happening," as Gałczyński said. That positioning of the voice, when one wants to howl but screeching is inappropriate, brings to mind a comparison with Polish poetry of the late 1930s and explains the reasons why the first Polish discoverers of Eliot (since the war had taught them to beware such subtle self-censorship) were suspicious and had no desire to be charmed.

The hysterical howls of the Beat poets are the rebellion of a well-brought-up muse, a return to their native tradition, somewhat vulgar but still authentic. They are, it seems, only one of the ways of escaping Eliot's tutelage via experience counter-posed against artistic harmony. Eliot, revered but already academic, congealed during his own lifetime into a chapter of literary history; he has already been accused of stiffness and excessive striving through attacks on his coldly selected devices, such as the use of masks and monologues. His precision also began to appear to be just a structural device concealing his intellectual uncertainty. "Eliot is like a knife, only you can't cut anything with him," said an American student. But every great poet, after a period of recognition, travels to the other shore of the river of forgetting. For schoolchildren, Wordsworth, Coleridge, Shelley, and Eliot all stand on the same shelf, and all the youngsters know is that these men wrote a long time ago.

7. Pessimistic opinions about "a world that has lost its moorings" occasionally have an optimistic finale in literature. Renaissance man lamented the chaos that surrounded and inhabited him, but that is precisely what led to the greatness of Marlowe and Shakespeare. Carried far away by this movement, which begins in the Renaissance, Eliot in turn looked back nostalgically at Dante and his age, when the religious imagination shaped the cosmos without stumbling over obstacles placed there by discursive thought but, on the contrary, finding support in the system of Saint Thomas Aquinas. Eliot's work is an attempt at learning that the imagination, and also religious poetry, can regain its privileges. This is an almost unbelievable undertaking; he built out of impossibility, absence, ruins. If, however, he achieved his aim to some extent, it would mean that people in the twentieth century need not be too pessimistic about their own potency.

ROBERT FROST

I WRITE about him, who is recognized as the greatest American poet of the twentieth century, not with admiration, but rather with amazement that such a figure is possible. Because it is difficult to understand how one country could produce three such different poets as Walt Whitman, Emily Dickinson, and Robert Frost.

Born in 1874, a contemporary, more or less, of Paul Valéry (b. 1871), Leopold Staff (b. 1878), and Bolesław Leśmian (b. 1878), he was already formed intellectually when the twentieth century began. America at that time was far removed from Europe, whose cultural capital was Paris. I can think about Frost comparatively, knowing, as I do, poets who are very different from him—French and Polish poets. Not only Europeans thought of America then as a country of shallow materialism; her citizens did, too, and if they valued culture they looked longingly across the Atlantic. Frost, too, when he was a young man, spent a couple of years in England, where he published *North of Boston* (1914), which also earned him recognition in America. But he built his entire, unusual career after his return to the land of the golden calf. How did he do it?

He changed his clothes and donned a mask. He put himself forward as a rube, a New England farmer, writing in a simple language, full of colloquialisms, about his environs and the people who lived there. A real American, digging in the soil, and not from any big city! A self-made talent, a country sage in daily contact with nature and the seasons! Helped by his acting and declamatory talents, he carefully maintained that image, playing on the appeal of the simple country philosopher. His readings attracted large crowds. I saw that bard with my own eyes when he was already an old man: blue eyes, a white mane, sturdily built, deserving of sympathy and trust with his openness and simplicity.

In fact, he was someone entirely different. His childhood was spent in San Francisco, not in the country outside of Boston. Among his various means of earning his living there were also a couple of years of managing a farm in New England—the oldest part of the American continent to have been colonized by whites. He felt the landscape there, the people, the language; he knew their work because he had done it himself—mower, digger, lumberjack. His readers valued him, however, for his idyllic mood, which was only a disguise. Beneath it was concealed a grim, hopeless vision of man's fate.

A powerful intellect, unusual intelligence, well-read in philosophy, and such enormous deceptiveness that he was capable of hiding his skepticism behind his constant ambivalence, so that his poems deceived with their supposedly wise affability. I am amused by the thought of a French poet reading Frost—for instance, Paul Valéry. He would probably have snorted contemptuously at those little story-plays taken from life and written down with the pen of, you know, a simpleton, a cowboy. At the same time, one should remember that both poets, despite their will and their knowledge, were connected to the language's moment, to its current—descending, in the case of the French, and ascending, in the case of American English.

Frost struggled with the scientific worldview of the nine-teenth century, enthusiastically reading Darwin, who was, *nota bene*, not only a scientist but a thinker, aware of the influence of his discoveries on his contemporaries. For Frost, this meant a break with Emerson, with American faith in the benign power of nature, and acceptance of the ungrounded nature of individual life, which is caused solely by chance. That is to say, he pondered evolution, and also borrowed from his reading of Bergson's *Creative Evolution*, but I won't delve into his philosophy. All I want to say is that Leśmian's poetry has a similar underpinning of skepticism, and that his balladic simplicity is also different from what it appears to be on the surface. His gods and other worlds are a conscious description of the Buddhist veil of maya. Like him in his skeptical worldview, Paul Valéry promoted construc-tions of the self-creating mind which admires its own creations. In Leśmian, however, Nature takes on fairy-tale shapes; it swarms with fantastic creatures, and an almost Christian Heaven opens out into a universe of poetic imagination, redeemed by its own beauty. Constructed out of crystals, the autonomous edifice of in-tellect in Valéry also finds its ultimate realization in the perfec-tion of metric verse, and several lines from *Le Cimetière marin* have always remained with me. Why then, I ask, do I find Frost so disturbing and depressing?

It is not that he dissembled. He decided to become a great poet, mercilessly condemned his rivals, but also knew that he would not achieve greatness pursuing his philosophical bent. Quite simply, he discerned what would be his strengths: rural New England and his superb ear, registering the variants of col-loquial English. He had to limit himself to what he knew well, cling to his seeming provincialness. His poetry is not lyrical but tragic, for his narrative poems about the ties between people are mini-tragedies; or else it is descriptive, or, more accurately, moral-istic. I feel that it is cold.

To think at one and the same time about that poetry and the biography concealed behind it is to descend into a bottomless well. No one will learn about Frost's own wounds and tragedies by reading his poetry; he left no clues. An appalling chain of misfortunes, numerous deaths in the family, madness, suicides, and silence about this, as if confirming his Puritan heritage, which demands that one conceal what is private behind a stoic façade. The worst part of all this is that in concerning oneself with him one is menaced by a sense of one's own particular existence. If the boundaries of the human personality are so fluid that we truly do not know who we are and are constantly trying on different changes of costume, how did Frost manage? It is impossible to grasp who he really was, aside from his unswerving striving toward his goal of fame, in an attempt to exact revenge for his own defeats in life.

I confess that I do not like his poetry and that in calling him great I am only repeating what others, Joseph Brodsky included, have written about him. Brodsky seems to have valued him as a master of metrical poetry. Frost said of free verse that it is like a game of tennis without a net. I, however, am absolutely on Walt Whitman's side.

In Frost's defense, I should add that he did not soften the cruel truth about human life, as he perceived it, and if his readers and listeners did not understand that very well, all the better for them. There is, for example, one poem about how very alone man is in relation to nature, which is absolutely indifferent to him, even though he wishes to receive some sign of understanding. Alone, not only in relation to nature, because each "I" is isolated from all others, as if it were the sole ruler of the universe, and seeks love in vain, while what it takes to be a response is only the echo of his own hope. I cite this poem because it also demonstrates Frost's allegorical and moralistic methods:

THE MOST OF IT

He thought he kept the universe alone;
For all the voice in answer he could wake

Was but the mocking echo of his own
From some tree-hidden cliff across the lake.
Some morning from the boulder-broken beach
He would cry out on life, that what it wants
Is not its own love back in copy speech,
But counter-love, original response.
And nothing ever came of what he cried
Unless it was the embodiment that crashed
In the cliff's talus on the other side,
And then in the far distant water splashed,
But after a time allowed for it to swim,
Instead of proving human when it neared
And someone else additional to him,
As a great buck it powerfully appeared,
Pushing the crumpled water up ahead,
And landed pouring like a waterfall,
And stumbled through the rocks with horny tread,
And forced the underbrush—and that was all.

ON PASTERNAK SOBERLY

FOR THOSE WHO WERE FAMILIAR with the poetry of
Boris Pasternak long before he acquired international
fame, the Nobel Prize given to him in 1958 had something ironic in it. A poet whose equal in Russia was only Akhmatova, and a congenial translator of Shakespeare, had to write a
big novel and that novel had to become a sensation and a best
seller before poets of the Slavic countries were honored for the
first time in his person by the jury of Stockholm. Had the prize
been awarded to Pasternak a few years earlier, no misgivings
would have been possible. As it was, the honor had a bitter taste
and could hardly be considered as proof of genuine interest in
Eastern European literatures on the part of the Western reading
public—this quite apart from the good intentions of the Swedish
academy.

After *Doctor Zhivago* Pasternak found himself entangled in
the kind of ambiguity that would be a nightmare for any author.
While he always stressed the unity of his work, that unity was
broken by circumstances. Abuse was heaped on him in Russia for
a novel nobody had ever read. Praise was lavished on him in the

West for a novel isolated from his lifelong labors: his poetry is nearly untranslatable. No man wishes to be changed into a symbol, whether the symbolic features lent him are those of a valiant knight or of a bugaboo: in such cases he is not judged by what he cherishes as his achievement but becomes a focal point of forces largely external to his will. In the last years of his life Pasternak lost, so to speak, the right to his personality, and his name served to designate a cause. I am far from intending to reduce that cause to momentary political games. Pasternak stood for the individual against whom the huge state apparatus turns in hatred with all its police, armies, and rockets. The emotional response to such a predicament was rooted in deep-seated fears, so justified in our time. The ignominious behavior of Pasternak's Russian colleagues, writers who took the side of power against a man armed only with his pen, created a Shakespearian situation; no wonder if in the West sympathies went to Hamlet and not to the courtiers of Elsinore.

The attention the critics centered on *Doctor Zhivago* delayed, however, an assessment of Pasternak's work as a whole. We are possibly now witnessing only the first gropings in that direction. My attempt here is not so much to make a nearly balanced appraisal as to stress a few aspects of his writings.

I became acquainted with his poetry in the thirties, when he was highly regarded in Polish literary circles. This was the Pasternak of *The Second Birth* (1932); the rhythm of certain "ballads" printed in that volume has been haunting me ever since. Yet Pasternak did not appear to his Polish readers as an exotic animal; it was precisely what was familiar in his poems that created some obstacles to unqualified approval. In spite of the considerable differences between Polish and Russian poetry, those poets who had been shaped by "modernistic" trends victorious at the beginning of the century showed striking similarities due to their cosmopolitan formation. Pasternak, through his very treatment of verse, could be placed within a spiritual family somewhere between Bolesław Leśmian, who achieved maturity when

Pasternak was an adolescent, and Jarosław Iwaszkiewicz or Julian Tuwim, Pasternak's juniors by a few years. Now the fact is that in the thirties the poetics represented by those eminent figures was breaking down. The young poets who claimed the name of "avant-garde" paid lip service to the recognized brilliance of their elders but looked at them with suspicion and often attacked them openly. In spite of all the loose talk proper to so-called literary movements some serious matters were at stake, though veiled by disputes over metaphor and syntax. Those quarrels proved to be fruitful and later gave a new perspective on the writers then in combat. But Pasternak, to the extent that he was used as an argument by the traditionalists, partisans of the "sonorous" verse inherited from Symbolism, had to share the fate of his allies, venerated and mistrusted at the same time by the young.

I say all this in order to show that my approach to Pasternak is colored by developments within Polish poetry of the last decades. My approach is also different, for other reasons, both from that of an American knowing Russian and from that of a Russian. My Slavic ear is sensitive to pulsations of Russian verse, yet I remain on my guard and submit myself with reluctance to the rhythmical spell inherent in the language, which reluctance can be explained by the more subdued accentuation of Western-Slavic tongues like Polish or Czech. Perhaps I lose a good deal that way, but it makes me more resistant to the gestures of a mesmerizer. Of Pasternak's eminence I have never had any doubts. In an article written in 1954 (before *Doctor Zhivago*) I predicted that a statue of Pasternak would stand one day in Moscow.

THE IMAGE OF THE POET

Half a century separates us from the Russian Revolution. When we consider that the Revolution was expected to bring about the end of the alienation of the writer and of the artist, and consequently to inaugurate new poetry of a kind never known before, the place Pasternak occupies today in Russian poetry is astounding. After all, his formative years preceded World War I and his craft retained some habits of that era. Like many of his contemporaries in various countries, he drew upon the heritage of French *poètes maudits*. In every avant-garde movement, the native traditions expressed through the exploration of linguistic possibilities are perhaps more important than any foreign influences. I am not concerned, however, with literary genealogy but with an image which determines the poet's tactics—an image of himself and of his role. A peculiar image was created by French poets of the nineteenth century, not without help from the minor German Romantics and Edgar Allan Poe; this image soon became common property of the international avant-garde. The poet saw himself as a man estranged from a society serving false values, an inhabitant of *la cité infernale*, or, if you prefer, of the wasteland and passionately opposed to it. He was the only man in quest of true values, aware of surrounding falsity, and had to suffer because of his awareness. Whether he chose rebellion or contemplative art for art's sake, his revolutionary technique of writing served a double purpose: to destroy the automatism of opinions and beliefs transmitted through a frozen, inherited style and to mark his distance from the idiom of those who lived false lives. Speculative thought, monopolized by optimistic philistines, was proclaimed taboo: the poet moved in another realm, nearer to the heart of things. Theories of two languages were elaborated: *le langage lyrique* was presented as autonomous, not translatable into any logical terms proper to *le langage scientifique*. Yet the poet had to pay the price: there are limits beyond which he could not go and maintain communication with his readers. Few are connoisseurs. Sophistication, or as Tolstoy called it *utonchenie*, is self-perpetuating, like drug addiction.

This dilemma of the poet is still with us; that is why we tend to project it into the past. Yet great poets of other periods did not know it at all. We saw how in our century poets of the Communist obedience, disgusted by the increasingly narrow scope of modern poetry, turned to the camp of speculative thought, endowed as it was with a new prestige since it dealt in historical optimism (but no longer of the bourgeois variety). And speculative thought, whether incarnated in the police or simply installed in poets' minds, destroyed their art and often also their persons. As for the West, sophistication or *utonchenie* has been destroying poets so successfully that a poem on the page of a magazine is avoided by every self-respecting reader.

The image of the poet that we find in the early poems of Pasternak corresponds to the pattern dear to literary schools at the turn of the century: the poet is a mysterious, elusive creature living in accordance with his own laws, which are not the laws of ordinary mortals. To quote Pasternak: "When a poet is in love, a displaced god falls in love and chaos crawls out into the world again as in the time of fossils." A man born with an ultra-perceptive sensory apparatus gradually discovers that personal destiny which estranges him from the world and transforms a familiar reality into phantasmagoria: "Thus the seas, sudden as a sigh, open up flowing over the fences, to where houses should have stood; thus the iambs start." The weird, incongruous core of things unveils itself to the poet. He is overpowered by elemental forces speaking through him, his words are magical incantation—he is a shaman, a witch doctor.

Here I can refer to my experience. What my generation reproached Polish contemporaries of Pasternak for was less a certain literary technique than a certain philosophy underlying the rocking singsong of their verse. For instance, Julian Tuwim, who shows hallucinating similarities to Pasternak, was shaped by a programmatic scorn for all the programs, by a cult of "life," of an élan vital, by the cultural atmosphere permeated with the direct or indirect influence of Henri Bergson. He evolved from the enthusiastic vitality of his youth toward the horrified screams of a Cassandra tortured by Apollo, but had always been a shaman in trance. Intellectual helplessness, a "sacred naïveté" jealously defended, were typical of him no less than of nearly all his Polish colleagues who started to write about 1912 or 1913. They seemed to elude the dilemma which for my generation was insoluble but oppressive: for us a lyrical stream, a poetic idiom liberated from the chores of discourse, was not enough, the poet should also be a *thinking* creature; yet in our efforts to build a poem as an "act of mind" we encountered an obstacle: speculative thought is vile, cunning, it eats up the internal resources of a poet from inside. In any case, if modern poetry had been moving away from traditional meter and rhyme, it was not because of fads and fashions but in the hope of elaborating a new style which would restore an equilibrium between emotional and intellectual elements.

Pasternak achieved perfection within the framework of traditional meter; one can also say that the wisdom of his maturity grew slowly and organically out of the image of the poet he shared in his youth with many poets. His poetry is written in rhymed stanzas, mostly quatrains. His experimentation consisted in inventing incredible assonances and in weighting every line to the breaking point with metaphors. Such a superabundance should have inclined him, it seems, to search for a principle of construction other than that of pure musicality. Perhaps Pasternak was afraid that his world of flickering bits of colors, of lights and of shadows, would disintegrate if deprived of a unifying singsong. He is often a prestidigitator in a corset, which he wears as if to enhance his skill in the reader's eyes. It so happened that in this attachment to meter he fulfilled, at least outwardly, the official requirements. Strangely enough, in Russia meter and rhyme acceded to political dignity through the rulers' decision to freeze art and literature in their "healthy" stages of the past. Here an analogy between poetry and painting imposes itself. Certain popular notions of the distinctive marks proper to the poet and to the painter have been carefully preserved: the poet is a man who writes columns of rhymed lines, the painter is a man who puts people and landscapes on his canvas "as if they were alive." Those who depart from that rule lack the necessary artistic qualities.

Pasternak's poetry is antispeculative, anti-intellectual. It is poetry of sensory perception. His worship of life meant a fascination with what can be called nature's moods—air, rain, clouds, snow in the streets, a detail changing thanks to the time of the day or night, to the season. Yet this is a very *linguistic* nature. In the Slavic languages words denoting planets, plants, and animals preserve their ancient power, they are loaded with the prestige of their feminity or masculinity. Hence the obsessive desire to identify the word with the object. Julian Tuwim, for instance, wrote a long poem consisting of variations on the word "green." "Greenery," in its double meaning of a quality and of vegetation—together with its retinue of names, adjectives, and verbs stemming from the same root—was for him a sort of vegetable goddess of the dictionary.

Pasternak gradually modified for his peculiar use his image of the poet as an exceptional being in direct contact with the forces of universal life. More and more he stressed passive receptivity as the poet's greatest virtue. The following pronouncement (from 1922) is characteristic:

Contemporary trends conceived art as a fountain, though it is a sponge. They decided it should spring forth, though it should absorb and become saturated. In their estimation it can be decomposed into inventive procedures, though it is made of the organs of reception. Art should always be among the spectators and should look in a purer, more receptive, truer way than any spectator does; yet in our days art got acquainted with powder and the dressing room; it showed itself upon the stage as if there were in the world two arts, and one of them, since the other was always in reserve, could afford the luxury of self-distortion, equal to a suicide. It shows itself off, though it should hide itself up in the gallery, in anonymity.

Did Pasternak when writing these words think of himself in contrast with Vladimir Mayakovsky? Perhaps. Mayakovsky wanted to smash to pieces the image of the poet as a man who withdraws. He wanted to be a Walt Whitman—as the Europeans imagined Walt Whitman. We are not concerned here with his illusions and his tragedy. Let us note only that the instinctive sympathy many of us feel when reading those words of Pasternak can be misleading. We have been trained to identify a poet's purity with his withdrawal up into the gallery seat of a theater, where in addition he wears a mask. Already some hundred years ago poetry had been assigned a kind of reservation for a perishing tribe; having conditioned reflexes we, of course, admire "pure lyricism."

Not all Pasternak's poems are personal notes from his private diary or, to put it differently, "*Les jardins sous la pluie*" of Claude Debussy. As befitted a poet in the Soviet Union, in the twenties he took to vast historical panoramas foreshadowing *Doctor Zhivago*. He enlivened a textbook cliché (I do not pretend to judge that cliché, it can be quite close to reality and be sublime) with all the treasures of detail registered by the eye of an adolescent witness; Pasternak was fifteen when the revolutionary events occurred that are described in the long poems "The Year 1905" and "Lieutenant Schmidt." Compared with his short poems, they seem to me failures; the technique of patches and glimpses does not fit the subject. There is no overall commitment, the intellect is recognized as inferior to the five senses and is refused access to the material. As a result, we have the theme and the embroidery; the theme, however, returns to the quality of a cliché.

Thus I tend to accuse Pasternak, as I accused his contemporaries in Poland, of a programmatic helplessness in the face of the world, of a carefully cultivated irrational attitude. Yet it was exactly this attitude that saved Pasternak's art and perhaps his life in the sad Stalinist era. Pasternak's more intellectually inclined colleagues answered argument by argument, and in consequence they were either liquidated or they accepted the supreme wisdom of the official doctrine. Pasternak eluded all categories;

the "meaning" of his poems was that of lizards or butterflies, and who could pin down such phenomena using Hegelian terms? He did not pluck fruits from the tree of reason, the tree of life was enough for him. Confronted by argument, he replied with his sacred dance.

We can agree that in the given conditions that was the only victory possible. Yet if we assume that those periods when poetry is amputated, forbidden thought, reduced to imagery and musicality, are not the most healthy, then Pasternak's was a Pyrrhic victory. When a poet can preserve his freedom only if he is deemed a harmless fool, a *yurodivy* holy because bereft of reason, his society is sick. Pasternak noticed that he had been maneuvered into Hamlet's position. As a weird being, he was protected from the ruler's anger and had to play the card of his weirdness. But what could he do with his moral indignation at the sight of the crime perpetrated upon millions of people, what could he do with his love for suffering Russia? That was the question.

His mature poetry underwent a serious evolution. He was right, I feel, when at the end of his life he confessed that he did not like his style prior to 1940:

> My hearing was spoiled then by the general freakishness and the breakage of everything customary—procedures which ruled then around me. Anything said in a normal way shocked me. I used to forget that words can contain something and mean something in themselves, apart from the trinkets with which they are adorned. . . . I searched everywhere not for essence but for extraneous pungency.

We can read into that judgment more than a farewell to a technique. He never lost his belief in the redeeming power of art understood as a moral discipline, but his late poems can be called Tolstoyan in their nakedness. He strives to give in them explicitly a certain vision of the human condition.

I did not find in Pasternak's work any hint of his philosophical opposition to the official Soviet doctrine, unless his reluctance to deal with abstractions—so that the terms "abstract" and "false" were for him synonymous—is a proof of his resistance. The life of Soviet citizens was his life, and in his patriotic poems he was not paying mere lip service. He was no more rebellious than any average Russian. *Doctor Zhivago* is a Christian book, yet there is no trace in it of that polemic with the anti-Christian concept of man which makes the strength of Dostoevsky. Pasternak's Christianity is atheological. It is very difficult to analyze a *Weltanschauung* which pretends not to be a *Weltanschauung* at all, but simply "closeness to life," while in fact it blends contradictory ideas borrowed from extensive readings. Perhaps we should not analyze. Pasternak was a man spellbound by reality, which was for him miraculous. He accepted suffering because the very essence of life is suffering, death, and rebirth. And he treated art as a gift of the Holy Spirit.

We would not know, however, of his hidden faith without *Doctor Zhivago*. His poetry—even if we put aside the question of censorship—was too fragile an instrument to express, after all, ideas. To do his Hamlet deed Pasternak had to write a big novel. By that deed he created a new myth of the writer, and we may conjecture that it will endure in Russian literature like other already mythical events: Pushkin's duel, Gogol's struggles with the Devil, Tolstoy's escape from Yasnaya Poliana.

A NOVEL OF ADVENTURES, RECOGNITIONS, HORRORS, AND SECRETS

The success of *Doctor Zhivago* in the West cannot be explained by the scandal accompanying its publication or by political thrills. Western novel readers have been reduced in our times to quite lean fare; the novel, beset by its enemy, psychology, has been moving toward the programmatic leanness of the antinovel. *Doctor Zhivago* satisfied a legitimate yearning for a narrative full of extraordinary happenings, narrow escapes, crisscrossing plots and, contrary to the microscopic analyses of Western novelists, open to huge vistas of space and historical time. The novel reader is a glutton, and he knows immediately whether a writer is one also. In his desire to embrace the unexpectedness and wonderful fluidity of life, Pasternak showed a gluttony equal to that of his nineteenth-century predecessors.

Critics have not been able to agree as to how *Doctor Zhivago* should be classified. The most obvious thing was to speak of a revival of great Russian prose and to invoke the name of Tolstoy. But then the improbable encounters and nearly miraculous interventions Pasternak is so fond of had to be dismissed as mistakes and offenses against realism. Other critics, like Edmund Wilson, treated the novel as a web of symbols, going so far sometimes in this direction that Pasternak in his letters had to deny he ever meant all that. Still others, such as Professor Gleb Struve, tried to mitigate this tendency yet conceded that *Doctor Zhivago* was related to Russian Symbolist prose of the beginning of the century. The suggestion I am going to make has been advanced by no one, as far as I know.

It is appropriate, I feel, to start with a simple fact: Pasternak was a Soviet writer. One may add, to displease his enemies and some of his friends, that he was not an *internal émigré* but shared the joys and sorrows of the writers' community in Moscow. If his community turned against him in a decisive moment, it proves only that every literary confraternity is a nest of vipers and that servile vipers can be particularly nasty. Unavoidably he followed the interminable discussions in the literary press and at meetings—discussions lasting over the years and arising from the zigzags of the political line. He must also have read many theoretical books, and theory of literature in the Soviet Union is not an innocent lotus-eaters' pastime but more like acrobatics on a tightrope with a precipice below. Since of all the literary genres fiction has the widest appeal and can best be used as an ideological weapon, many of these studies were dedicated to prose.

According to the official doctrine, in a class society vigorous literature could be produced only by a vigorous ascending class. The novel, as a new literary genre, swept eighteenth-century England. Thanks to its buoyant realism it was a weapon of the ascending bourgeoisie and served to debunk the receding aristocratic order. Since the proletariat is a victorious class it should have an appropriate literature, namely, a literature as vigorous as the bourgeoisie had in its upsurge. This is the era of Socialist Realism, and Soviet writers should learn from "healthy" novelists of the past centuries while avoiding neurotic writings produced in the West by the bourgeoisie in its decline. This reasoning, which I oversimplify for the sake of clarity, but not too much, explains the enormous prestige of the English eighteenth-century novel in the Soviet Union.

Pasternak did not have to share the official opinions as to the economic causes and literary effects in order to feel pleasure in reading English "classics," as they are called in Russia. A professional translator for many years, mostly from English, he probably had them all in his own library in the original. While the idea of his major work was slowly maturing in his mind he must often have thought of the disquieting trends in modern Western fiction. In the West fiction lived by denying more and more its nature, or even by behaving like the magician whose last trick is to unveil how his tricks were done. Yet in Russia Socialist Realism was an artistic flop and of course nobody heeded the repeated advice to learn from the "classics": an invitation to joyous movement addressed to people in straitjackets is nothing more than a crude joke. And what if somebody, in the spirit of spite, tried to learn?

Doctor Zhivago, a book of hide-and-seek with fate, reminds me irresistibly of one English novel: Fielding's *Tom Jones*. True, we may have to make some effort to connect the horses and inns of a countryside England with the railroads and woods of Russia, yet we are forced to do so by the travel through enigmas in both novels. Were the devices applied mechanically by Pasternak, the parallel with Fielding would be of no consequence. But in *Doctor Zhivago* they become signs which convey his affirmation of the universe, of life, to use his preferred word. They hint at his sly denial of the trim, rationalized, ordered reality of the Marxist philosophers and reclaim another richer subterranean reality. Moreover, the devices correspond perfectly to the experience of Pasternak himself and of all the Russians. Anyone who has lived through wars and revolutions knows that in a human anthill on fire the number of extraordinary meetings, unbelievable coincidences, multiplies tremendously in comparison with periods of peace and everyday routine. One survives because one was five minutes late at a given address where everybody got arrested, or because one did not catch a train that was soon to be blown to pieces. Was that an accident, fate, or providence?

If we assume that Pasternak consciously borrowed his devices from the eighteenth-century novel, his supposed sins against realism will not seem so disquieting. He had his own views on realism. Also we shall be less tempted to hunt for symbols in *Doctor Zhivago* as for raisins in a cake. Pasternak perceived the very texture of life as symbolic, so its description did not call for those protruding and all too obvious allegories. Situations and characters sufficed; to those who do not feel the eighteenth-century flavor in the novel, I can point to the interventions of the enigmatic Yevgraf, the half-Asiatic natural brother of Yuri Zhivago, who emerges from the crowd every time the hero is in extreme danger and, after accomplishing what he has to, returns to anonymity. He is a benevolent lord protector of Yuri; instead of an aristocratic title, he has connections at the top of the Communist Party. Here again the situation is realistic: to secure an ally at the top of the hierarchy is the first rule of behavior in such countries as the Soviet Union.

THE POET AS A HERO

Yuri Zhivago is a poet, a successor to the Western European bohemian, torn asunder by two contradictory urges: withdrawal into himself, the only receptacle or creator of value; movement toward society, which has to be saved. He is also a successor to the Russian "superfluous man." As for virtues, he cannot be said to possess much initiative and manliness. Nevertheless the reader is in deep sympathy with Yuri since he, the author affirms, is a bearer of charisma, a defender of vegetal "inner freedom." A passive witness of bloodshed, of lies and debasement, Yuri must do something to deny the utter insignificance of the individual. Two ways are offered to him: either the way of Eastern Christianity or the way of Hamlet.

Pity and respect for the *yurodivy*—a half-wit in tatters, a being at the very bottom of the social scale—has ancient roots in Russia. The *yurodivy*, protected by his madness, spoke truth in the teeth of the powerful and wealthy. He was outside society and denounced it in the name of God's ideal order. Possibly in many cases his madness was only a mask. In some respects he recalls Shakespeare's fool; in fact Pushkin merges the two figures in his *Boris Godunov*, where the half-wit Nikolka is the only man bold enough to shout the ruler's crimes in the streets.

Yuri Zhivago in the years following the civil war makes a plunge to the bottom of the social pyramid. He forgets his medical diploma and leads a shady existence as the husband of the daughter of his former janitor, doing menial jobs, provided with what in the political slang of Eastern Europe are called "madman's papers." His refusal to become a member of the "new intelligentsia" implies that withdrawal from the world is the only way to preserve integrity in a city ruled by falsehood. Yet in Yuri Zhivago there is another trait. He writes poems on Hamlet and sees himself as Hamlet. Yes, but Hamlet is basically a man with a goal, and action is inseparable from understanding the game. Yuri has an intuitive grasp of good and evil, but is no more able to understand what is going on in Russia than a bee can analyze chemically the glass of a windowpane against which it is beating. Thus the only act left to Yuri is a poetic act, equated with the defense of the language menaced by the totalitarian double-talk or, in other words, with the defense of authenticity. The circle closes; a poet who rushed out of his tower is back in his tower.

Yuri's difficulty is that of Pasternak and of his Soviet contemporaries. Pasternak solved it a little better than his hero by writing not poems but a novel, his Hamletic act; the difficulty persists, though, throughout the book. It is engendered by the acceptance of a view of history so widespread in the Soviet Union that it is a part of the air one breathes. According to this view history proceeds along preordained tracks, it moves forward by "jumps," and the Russian Revolution (together with what followed) was such a jump of cosmic dimension. To be for or against an explosion of historical forces is as ridiculous as to be for or against a tempest or the rotation of the seasons. The human will does not count in such a cataclysm, since even the leaders are but tools of mighty "processes." As many pages of his work testify, Pasternak did not question that view. Did he not say in one of his poems that everything by which this century will live is in Moscow? He seemed to be interpreting Marxism in a religious way. And is not Marxism a secularized biblical faith in the final accomplishment, implying a providential plan? No wonder Pasternak, as he says in his letter to Jacqueline de Proyart, liked the writings of Teilhard de Chardin so much. The French Jesuit also believed in the Christological character of lay history, and curiously combined Christianity with the Bergsonian "creative evolution" as well as with the Hegelian ascending movement.

Let us note that Pasternak was probably the first to read Teilhard de Chardin in Russia. One may be justly puzzled by the influence of that poet-anthropologist, growing in the last decade both in the West and in the countries of the Soviet bloc. Perhaps man in our century is longing for solace at any price, even at the price of sheer Romanticism in theology. Teilhard de Chardin has predecessors, to mention only Alexander Blok's "music of history" or some pages of Berdyaev. The latent "Teilhardism" of *Doctor Zhivago* makes it a Soviet novel in the sense that one might read into it an esoteric interpretation of the Revolution as opposed to the exoteric interpretation offered by official pronouncements. The historical tragedy is endowed with all the trappings of necessity working toward the ultimate good. Perhaps the novel is a tale about the individual versus Caesar, but with a difference: the new Caesar's might has its source not only in his legions.

What could poor Yuri Zhivago do in the face of a system blessed by history and yet repugnant to his notions of good and evil? Intellectually, he was paralyzed. He could only rely on his subliminal self, descend deeper than state-monopolized thought. Being a poet, he clutches at his belief in communion with ever reborn life. Life will take care of itself. Persephone always comes back from the underground, winter's ice is dissolved, dark eras are necessary as stages of preparations, life and history have a hidden Christian meaning. And suffering purifies.

Pasternak overcame his isolation by listening to the silent complaint of the Russian people; we respond strongly to the atmosphere of hope pervading *Doctor Zhivago*. Not without some doubts, however. Life rarely takes care of itself unless human beings decide to take care of themselves. Suffering can either purify or corrupt, and too great a suffering too often corrupts. Of course hope itself, if it is shared by all the nation, may be a powerful factor for change. Yet, when at the end of the novel, friends of the long-dead Yuri Zhivago console themselves with timid expectations, they are counting upon an indefinite something (death of the tyrant?) and their political thinking is not far from the grim Soviet joke about the best constitution in the world being one that grants to every citizen the right to a postmortem rehabilitation.

But Pasternak's weaknesses are dialectically bound up with his great discovery. He conceded so much to his adversary, speculative thought, that what remained was to make a jump into a completely different dimension. *Doctor Zhivago* is not a novel of social criticism, it does not advocate a return to Lenin or to the young Marx. It is profoundly arevisionist. Its message summarizes the experience of Pasternak the poet: whoever engages in a polemic with the thought embodied in the state will destroy himself, for he will become a hollow man. It is impossible to talk to the new Caesar, for then you choose the encounter on his ground. What is needed is a new beginning, new in the present conditions but not new in Russia marked as it is by centuries of Christianity. The literature of Socialist Realism should be shelved and forgotten; the new dimension is that of every man's mysterious destiny, of compassion and faith. In this Pasternak revived the best tradition of Russian literature, and he will have successors. He already has one in Solzhenitsyn.

The paradox of Pasternak lies in his narcissistic art leading him beyond the confines of his ego. Also in his reedlike pliability, so that he often absorbed *les idées reçues* without examining them thoroughly as ideas but without being crushed by them either. Probably no reader of Russian poets resists a temptation to juxtapose the two fates: Pasternak's and Mandelstam's. The survival of the first and the death in a concentration camp of the second may be ascribed to various factors, to good luck and bad luck. And yet there is something in Mandelstam's poetry, intellectually structured, that doomed him in advance. From what I have said about my generation's quarrel with worshippers of "Life," it should be obvious that Mandelstam, not Pasternak, is for me the ideal of a modern classical poet. But he had too few weaknesses, was crystalline, resistant, and therefore fragile. Pasternak—more exuberant, less exacting, uneven—was called to write a novel that, in spite and because of its contradictions, is a great book.

NOTES ABOUT BRODSKY

Brodsky's presence acted as a buttress and a point of reference for many of his fellow poets. Here was a man whose work and life always reminded us that despite what is so often said and written today, a hierarchy does exist. This hierarchy is not deducible through syllogisms, nor can it be decided upon by discussion. Rather, we confirm it anew every day by living and writing. It has something in common with the elementary division into beauty and ugliness, truth and falsehood, kindness and cruelty, freedom and tyranny. Above all, hierarchy signifies respect for that which is elevated, and disdain, rather than contempt, for that which is inferior.

The label "sublime" can be applied to Brodsky's poetry. In his fate as a representative of man there was that loftiness of thought which Pushkin saw in Mickiewicz: "He looked upon life from on high."

In one of his essays Brodsky calls Mandelstam a poet of culture. Brodsky was himself a poet of culture, and most likely that is why he created in harmony with the deepest current of his century, in which man, threatened with extinction, discovered his past as a never-ending labyrinth. Penetrating into the bowels of the labyrinth, we discover that whatever has survived from the past is the result of the principle of differentiation based on hierarchy. Mandelstam in the Gulag, insane and looking for food in a garbage pile, is the reality of tyranny and degradation condemned to extinction. Mandelstam reciting his poetry to a couple of his fellow prisoners is a lofty moment, which endures.

With his poems, Brodsky built a bridge across decades of hackneyed Russian language to the poetry of his predecessors, to Mandelstam, Akhmatova, Tsvetaeva. He was not a political poet, for he did not want to enter into polemics with an opponent that was hardly worthy of him. Instead, he practiced poetry as a particular type of activity which was not subject to any apparent dimensions of time.

To aim directly at a goal, refusing to be deflected by voices demanding one's attention. This means one is capable of distinguishing what is important, and hewing only to this goal. That is precisely what the great Russian writers were able to do, and they deserve to be envied for that.

Brodsky's life and creative work aim straight at fulfillment like an arrow at its target. Of course, this is a delusion, just as with Pushkin or Dostoevsky. So one must conceive of it differently. Fate aims straight for its target, while he who is ruled by fate is able to decipher its main lines and understand, even if only vaguely, what he has been called to.

A collection of interviews with Brodsky, *Reszty nie trzeba* [Keep the Change], in Jerzy Illg's translation, is a constant source of won-

derment for me.* Just to think how much he had to leave out—
what for others was the very essence of the twentieth century:
Marxism-Leninism, Sovietism, nationalism, Nietzscheanism, Freudianism, Surrealism, as well as a dozen or two other isms.

He could have become a dissident, engagé, like his friend Tomas
Venclova. He could have thought about reforming the state. He
could have written avant-garde poems. He could have been a
Freudian. He could have paid homage to structuralism. Nothing
of the sort.

Life as a moral fable. The poet imprisoned and condemned by the
state, then sent into exile by the state, and after his death, the
head of that state kneeling beside his coffin. A fairy tale, yet it
did happen like that, in our hardly fairy-tale-like century.

He spoke as one who has authority. Most likely in his youth he
was unbearable because of that self-assurance, which those
around him must have seen as arrogance. That self-assurance was
a defense mechanism in his relations with people and masked his
inner irresolution when he felt that he had to act that way, and
only that way, even though he did not know why. Were it not for
that arrogance, he would not have quit school. Afterward, he often regretted this, as he himself admitted. During his trial, someone who was less self-assured than he was could probably not
have behaved as he did. He himself did not know how he would
behave, nor did the authorities foresee it; rather, they did not anticipate that, without meaning to, they were making him famous.

When he was fourteen years old, he passed the entrance exam to
the naval academy and was rejected only because of what was

*Reszty nie trzeba: Rozmowy z Josifem Brodskim, selected and edited by Jerzy Illg (Ka-
towice: Książnica, 1993).

recorded in his identity papers under the heading "nationality." I try to imagine him as a cadet. An officer? Lermontov?

Both he and his Petersburg friends behaved in the way Aleksander Wat had wished for Russian literature: that it would "break with the enemy." They did not want to be either Soviets or anti-Soviets; they wanted to be a-Soviet. Certainly, Brodsky was not a political poet. Nonetheless, he wrote a number of occasional poems (on the funeral of Marshal Zhukov, the war in Afghanistan, the Berlin Wall, martial law in Poland), and in a speech at the University of Silesia he thanked Poland for her contribution to overturning a great evil, Communism. In response to the news that the Institute and Academy of Art and Literature in New York had voted in Evgeny Evtushenko as a foreign member, he made his protest known by resigning from the institute.

Submitting to the element of language, or (because this was the same thing for him) to the voice of the Muse, he asserted that a poet must want to please not his contemporaries but his predecessors. The predecessors whose names he mentioned were Lomonosov, Kantemir, Derzhavin, Tsvetaeva, Mandelstam, Pasternak, Akhmatova. His kingdom of Russian poetry endured above and outside of history, in accordance with his conviction that language has its own greatness and selects its own people to serve it.

He was capable of idolizing others. He used to say that he would be satisfied if he were called Auden's epigone. He did not rule out those who wrote in "free verse" but he paid particular homage to metrical poets: Thomas Hardy, Robert Frost, Rainer Maria Rilke. He understood poetry to be a dialogue across the ages, and so he conversed with Horace and Ovid (in Russian translations). As he said, he liked Ovid more, because of his images, even though he was less interesting rhythmically, adhering to the traditional hexameter. Horace, on the other hand, with the immense metrical variety of his stanzas, invited Brodsky to compete with him.

It would be a mistake to imagine Brodsky as a bohemian poet, although if we define bohemia as a milieu on the margins of society and the state, he belonged to it in his youth in Leningrad. He was competent in various trades, and they were by no means mere fictions, useful only as proof of employment. He often "plowed like an ox." He spoke with gratitude of the University of Michigan in Ann Arbor, because it offered employment to "the laziest man under the sun," who did not know English. He treated his obligations as a teacher seriously and it seems his students profited greatly. He made them memorize thousands of lines of poetry in their own language; no other professor would have dared to be so old-fashioned. If a student said something exceptionally stupid in class (for example, from the repertoire of American political naïveté), Brodsky would throw him out of the classroom.

His autodidact's passion allowed him to master English passively while he was still in Russia; afterward, he quite rapidly acquired the ability to use the language freely in speech and writing. His astonishing deftness in the essays he composed in English and in his rhymed translations of his own poems could only have been the result of truly titanic labor.

He considered Polish poetry the most interesting of contemporary European poetries. In Leningrad it reached him only as fragments, but important ones: from Norwid to Gałczyński. His translations include some of my poems, too. When, already an exile, he translated my "Elegy for N.N.," it occurred to me that that poem expressed his view of lyric poetry as preserved autobiography, even if only one-tenth preserved. He understood poets' escaping into prose as the result of pressure from the remaining nine-tenths. He read my *Treatise on Poetry* in Russian, in Natalia Gorbanevskaia's splendid translation. It was published in America in 1982 as *Poeticheskii traktat* by the Ann Arbor publishing house Ardis, which specializes in Russian books.

He had a very strong feeling that he was a part of an estate which was called "Russian language." Since in his opinion poetry is the highest achievement of language, he was conscious of his responsibility. If one were to draw an analogy with the Polish estate, our attachment to Krasicki, Trembecki, Mickiewicz would be understandable. Young Poland, however, is a blank spot (with the exception of Bořeslaw Leśmian) in comparison with what was happening in Russia at that time, and only the poets of the Skamander group can rival the generation of the Russian Acmeists.

Is there anyone among them to whom one could become as attached as to Mandelstam or Akhmatova? For me, that poet was Jarosław Iwaszkiewicz, but the revolution in versification caused the immediate dissipation of that canon.

He used to tell his students that they probably were not terribly familiar with the Decalogue, but it was possible to learn, since there were only seventeen: the Ten Commandments and the seven cardinal sins—taken together, the foundation of our civilization. His Muse, the spirit of language, was, he said, Christian, which explains the Old and New Testament themes in his poetry.

Generosity was one of his traits. His friends always felt showered with gifts. He was ready to help at any moment, to organize, to manage things. But above all, to praise. His generosity is most apparent in his conversation with Volkov about Akhmatova. What praise of her greatness, her wisdom, her kindness, and the magnificence of her heart! For him, the greatness of a poet was inseparable from the poet's greatness as a human being. Perhaps I am mistaken, but I am unaware of a single instance when he praised a poet while admitting at the same time that he was just average as a human being. It was enough, for example, that Robert Frost was great in his poetry to justify not inquiring into his biography. This was consistent with his conviction that aesthetics precedes ethics and is even its source.

The most profound thing he said about Akhmatova, and perhaps the most profound words ever spoken about the so-called creative process in general, is the assertion that she suffered greatly while writing her *Requiem*. Her pain at the imprisonment of her son was genuine, but in writing about it she sensed falsehood precisely because she had to shape her emotions into form. And form makes use of an emotional situation for its own purposes, parasitizing it, as it were.

He wanted to be useful. He came up with the idea of distributing throughout America millions of copies of an anthology of American poetry by placing it in hotels and motels alongside the Bible. He managed to found a Russian Academy in Rome, modeled after the American Academy in that city. He was conscious of Russian literature's ties with Italy (Gogol's *Dead Souls* was written in Rome; the Eternal City is always present in his own poems and in Mandelstam's poetry; he wrote about Venice, which he adored). He had no intention of returning to Russia. It is appropriate, then, that his grave will be in Venice, like Stravinsky's and Diaghilev's.

I would like to extract some pedagogical profit from thinking about Brodsky. Do we have an appreciation of our language such as he had for Russian? That it is the Russians' greatest treasure, right after the icon? Do not I myself rebel against the shushing and hissing sounds of Polish, and even worse, those omnipresent *prze* and *przy* syllables, pronounced "psheh" and "pshih"? And yet Polish is my fatherland, my home, and my glass coffin. Whatever I have accomplished in it—only that will save me.

And do we, as he did, honor our predecessors? Or do we only sneer and bite? And why is it that in the home of literature, whose strength was always poetry, there is suddenly no niche for great poets? Mickiewicz, Słowacki, Norwid are there—but where are the representatives of our century? Will Gombrowicz, Schulz, Witkacy replace the pretty pleiad of the Skamander poets?

A comparative study of Brodsky's poetry and Polish poetry would have to begin with the various laws governing the two languages. What about a comparison of Leśmian's Russian poetry, of his *Pesni premudroi Vasilissy* [Songs of Vasilissa the Wise Woman], with his Polish poetry? But their past is different, their themes are, too, as is the cultural background after 1918.

How far can a poem depart from its original mnemonic function? For Brodsky, phonetics and semantics were inseparable. This is an obvious matter for a Russian, for whom a poem, if it does not insinuate itself into one's memory, is not a poem at all. Despite the Polish language's different laws, one could still memorize the poems of Skamander, and this is true also of Gałczyński's verse.

A departure from metrical norms and from rhymes seems to coincide in time with a vast revolution in the life of societies in the twentieth century, which has something in common with an explosion of quantity. If, as happens to an exaggerated degree in Poland, one were to take France as a model of artistic currents, Paul Valéry, the last poet writing metrical verse, stands on the border beyond which the decline of the meaning of poetry begins, until it disappears entirely from the literary marketplace. Perhaps something similar, in different circumstances, is taking place in other countries. The scattering of the phrase into words and fragments of sentences testifies to the fact that poetry's centuries-old coexistence with the verse of Horace, Virgil, and Ovid has come to an end. It was they who defined meters for poets of various languages. Someone might like to ponder the strange parallels between changes in school and in literature: the revolution in versification coincides in time with high school curricula which no longer include Latin.

Brodsky loved the English language, perhaps because in the face of the revolution in versification English seems to have preserved a greater muscularity, so to speak. For various reasons, which it would be possible to enumerate, the end of the rhymed verse of the Victorian era was the occasion for a new modulation of the phrase, and because rhyme in English did not have the same significance that it had in Italian, for example (Shakespearean iambic pentameter was "blank"), its disappearance was not a glaring departure from the practice of earlier poets. Nevertheless, one is taken aback not only by Brodsky's evaluation of Frost as probably the greatest American poet of the twentieth century but also by his praise of Edward Arlington Robinson (1869–1935), who is known as a name from a bygone era. Walt Whitman's utter lack of influence, in Brodsky's poems and his essays, is also curious.

As is well known, the only elegy on the death of T. S. Eliot in 1965 was written in Russian, by Brodsky. Eliot was already in literary purgatory at the time, which is the usual reaction to a period of peak fame. But in Russia he had only just been discovered. Later, as Brodsky admits, he was disenchanted with *Four Quartets*. In general, he considered the whole current of modernism (in the Anglo-Saxon meaning of that term) as unhealthy for the art of poetry.

He spoke of the politics of his century, employing concepts dating from antiquity: imperium, tyrant, slave. In relation to art, however, he was by no means a democrat. In the first place, he believed that poetry in every society known to history is of interest to little more than one percent of the population. Second, one cannot speak of equality among poets, with the exception of the few who are the very best, to whom it is inappropriate to apply the labels "greater" or "lesser." As egalitarian as could be in his instincts, an opponent of any division into the intelligentsia and the people, in relation to art he was as aristocratic as Nabokov and Gombrowicz.

Thinking about him constantly since his death, I try to name the lesson he bequeathed to us. How did a man who did not complete his high school education, who never studied at a university, become an authority recognized by the luminaries of humanistic knowledge? He was intelligent, and not everyone is granted that gift. But there was also something else that was decisive. The Leningrad milieu of his generation, those a-Soviet young poets and translators, devoured books. Their obsessive drive to read everything they could find in libraries and used bookstores is stunning; they also learned Polish, as Brodsky did, in order to read Western literature that was available to them only in that language. The lesson supplied by his life history is an optimistic one, because it points to the triumph of consciousness over being. But it also cautions us to consider whether among the young generation of Polish writers there exist groups with a similar drive for self-education.

"I permitted myself everything except complaints." This saying of Brodsky's ought to be pondered by every young person who despairs and is thinking about suicide. He accepted imprisonment philosophically, without anger; he considered shoveling manure on a Soviet state farm a positive experience; expelled from Russia, he decided to act as if nothing had changed; he equated the Nobel Prize with the capricious turns of fate he had experienced previously. The wise men of antiquity recommended such behavior, but there are not many people who can behave like that in practice.

PART FOUR

IN CONSTANT AMAZEMENT

THE WORLD was unattainable and there were too many people. I was living in constant naïve amazement. And I was uncertain whether by judging the strangeness surrounding me I was resisting the kernel of madness at the heart of human existence and also the features of a particular civilization. Perhaps vitality itself has always forced me, in the end, to choose the other path.

Energy should encounter resistance; resistance keeps it in practice, rescues it. If, however, energy comes up against a gigantic smooth wall on which there is not a single rough place, not even a crack, this is more than resistance; it is too much. Energy then turns inward, consumes itself, and a person asks himself, "Could it be that there is no wall? Could this be my own delusion? Could it be that all this is my own fault and I should adjust to it?"

A young mathematics teacher whom I befriended showed me one of his poems. It was a poem about a man who tries in vain to climb out of a dark well. In the end, it turns out that this man is the *son* of the one who built the well.

My fascination with Robinson Jeffers derives from the fact that his assumptions were erroneous and blasphemous. He exemplifies the law of the delayed development of two literatures, American and Russian, which, borrowing problems and motifs from Western Europe, gave them greater sharpness and forcefulness. Thus, Jeffers's universe, in which man is negated by infinitely extended Newtonian space and by time deprived of any human meaning but arranged into a cycle of eternal return, is the universe of all the nineteenth-century martyrs. Jeffers also expressed most completely that misery which on rare occasions bears the name of vigorous individualism.

All right, it's a truism, but still, making one's peace with this is impossible—this idea that millions of people sense that their lives are somehow defective and deprived (although what they are deprived of, they do not know), and when they attempt to express something, all that comes out of their mouths is a stammering of blind hatred and aggression. Then they die, and who would dare to weigh their poor souls on the scales of good and evil?

Perhaps my life was triumphant not because it lacked evil and defeats but because I could see with my own eyes how what was just a vague promise is slowly being fulfilled and how that which I suspected of false greatness is disintegrating. The concealed structure of reality is reasonable. To assert this in this terrifying century is a great deal. Nonetheless, almost never, with the exception of a few brief moments, did the conviction abandon me that sooner or later the absurd will fail, and this is what distinguished me from my despairing contemporaries. Impossible to name, accessible only to intuition, the very fabric of movement seemed to me miraculous.

Art against thought, which has been intercepted, separated from the imagination, sentenced to a meager diet of scientific superstitions, shackled with vulgarization. It may well be that this dilemma of the entire nineteenth century attained its most tragic dimensions in the Russian poets who were born around 1890: Anna Akhmatova, Boris Pasternak, Marina Tsvetaeva. They had nothing but a belief in their own powerful, jealous daimonian, who destroyed their human happiness so that their work could be born; this was their Saint George fighting with the dragon. But the dragon, the same one which defeated Baudelaire and Rimbaud, was even more powerful; it had grown heads and fangs.

Modern artists entertain flattering notions about sin, since virtue is the underpinning of the established social order. In this way they try to forget about the moral contradictions of their profession. Art is born out of the desire for good, but concepts and form demand faith in oneself, which derives from infatuation with the agility of one's own mind. Pride, disdain, arrogance, anger are what support an imperiousness that opposes the whole world. People say that we do not deserve to go to hell, because our work redeems our guilt, but perhaps that is just another sentimental misconception.

Atrocity has always lurked just below the surface of our daily hustle and bustle, our habits, social organizations, phrases, smiles; the war years merely brought it to the surface. Afterward, in some other country, in some other city, I used to pause for a moment in the middle of a teeming crowd and say, "Stop this finickiness! If it lasts for even this one more day, that will be good enough."

When we deny the existence of God on the grounds that no one who is good could have thought up a world in which living beings are subjected to such tortures, we treat our denial as an action that has the power to change something; in other words, we hope to shame God.

Right after the war, Kazimierz Wyka, trying to find a label for a certain generation, spoke of those who were "infected with death." But man forgets, even to the extent that he gradually begins to doubt the reality of what he saw with his own eyes. He knows that this forgetting is vile, yet if he were constantly thinking "about that," everything except this one matter would have no meaning for him. That is why ethical poetry and prose arose on that hazy borderline where one is already beginning to forget but one still remembers.

Men and women carry within their imaginations an image of themselves and of others as sexual beings and often that is the only thing that humanizes them. The sexual organs remind us of the transience, the fragility, the insecurity of existence; it is not for nothing that love and death have always been connected. Let us, then, praise guttural intonations, giggles, the lustfulness of eyes. An asexual imagination is the threat of abstraction, mechanical dolls passing each other, an invitation to murder. But the moment when the assembly of men and women appears in their childlike, immature form, with all the sly awkwardness of their evasions, is both possible and necessary. Then the fear of what is referred to as the demonism of sex, that is, of Nature who mocks our values, is tempered by pity and humor, fraternity appears, and a glimmer of paradise lost.

Could it be that another reason why the novel has become impossible is that we are no longer amused by the contrast between behavior prescribed by convention and our corporeality? A hot potato dropping into someone's codpiece during a theological dispute at the dinner table, as in *Tristram Shandy*, is no subject for the demonic inhabitants of the modern city, the *cité infernale*.

We should be grateful for what was given to us in a corner of Europe that was not part of the twentieth, or even the nineteenth, century. We couldn't appreciate it—until later on, observing people who never knew the warmth of organic ties and who try in vain to warm themselves by traveling to the Solomon Islands or to derelict Mexican villages.

Chuckling, I passed by the thick volumes on the library shelves, because on those volumes were the names of people whom I used to know in their corporeality, their vacillations, little games, ridiculous behaviors, downfalls, ravings. But there they were: frozen, preserved, forever. Connected by our *mentalité*, our style (the differences among us are bound to fade), we carved our state in time, a niche or a cavern, which will be overlooked by our immediate heirs and discovered only later, and then evaluated from some new perspective. That was one facet. The other was when I walked around for an hour in a labyrinth of mountain grottoes in Oregon that were discovered by sheer chance at the end of the nineteenth century (a bear that was being hunted suddenly disappeared, "vanished under the earth," along with the dogs running after it). The stalactites and stalagmites bored me, but the wonder of nature acted upon me, transforming itself into a humanistic picture, through its connection with the shelves of a library.

Considering the excessive amount of printed paper, perhaps it is time now to introduce a rule limiting articles, essays, and the like to a single sentence?

If I remain silent for a long time, perhaps it is because I have been overwhelmed by a fear known to everyone who, from an excitation of the blood, has risen to acts of courage out of ignorance of the danger involved, and only later broke out in a cold sweat, his teeth chattering?

———

Why should I not confess to my own stupidity and admit that I have used words to touch upon that which ought not be touched?

Entering the Mission of San José, which was built at the end of the eighteenth century, I knew from the smell of the walls, the old wood, the leather straps, that I had returned home, because where I had spent the happiest years of my childhood, by virtue of provincial wonders, everything had frozen in time in the final years of the old Republic, so how different I was from the other tourists marveling here at a bygone era.

My contemporaries prided themselves on having ceased to persecute artists and writers for being unintelligible, but it never entered their minds that that splendid tolerance referred to yesterday's unintelligibility and that perhaps certain types of simplicity had now become unintelligible to them.

If, despite everything, I would not wish to live in the nineteenth century, because then I would not have the consciousness which I still find difficult to name, but which embraces humanity as a whole, as a unit, as predestination, then let's put an end to this pessimistic chatter about regression or the circle of eternal return.

Since poetry, faced with the setbacks of philosophy, is becoming more and more an organ of knowledge, returning, as it were, to the time of early Greece when there was no other philosophy than poetic philosophy, contemporary graphomania has to assume the appearance of intellectual depth.

In England there is a poet named Philip Larkin, who had the audacity to title his first volume of poetry *The Less Deceived*, not realizing that elegant, genial skepticism is an abomination in poetry, which is possible only as a game in which one bets everything one has.

It is easy to understand why the singer Bob Dylan is so popular among California youth now that I have heard his reply to an interviewer who asked him if he considers himself a poet: "No, I'm *not even* a philosopher. . . ."

A poet's maturation should be evaluated not only on the basis of what he has accomplished, but also on the amount of stupidity he has denied access to himself.

For years I used to think about the indecency of all types of artistry, which, in every country I am familiar with, now or in the past, would have been impossible if the fate of the downtrodden and the humiliated were really felt intensely by others.

The question has been raised in our century how artists could write, compose music, paint pictures knowing that there were concentration camps in their country, but people forget that, for example, charming English Romantic poetry arose in comfortable parishes where the pastor's daughters played the spinet, while in the neighboring industrial city it was normal to see people staggering from hunger or dying in the streets.

Novelists, who once were very concerned with the so-called struggle for existence, have escaped into the regions of deep inner experience, as if it is obvious that their characters have somewhere to live and food to eat, but I find such prose, where no mention is made even of money, to be suspect, and I am grateful to my life experiences for my skepticism.

I am experiencing this second half of the twentieth century so intensely—kinetic sculpture, new music, fashions, the streetscapes of great cities, social mores—that I am constantly amazed by the bond which, in theory, must exist between me and a certain young man in Wilno in the 1930s.

Of necessity, we have grown accustomed to the absurdity that surrounds us and that so clearly contradicts common sense; the endurance of systems based on this absurdity has seemed to us incomprehensible, but since once already, during the last war, we became convinced that people are punished for a lack of reason, we asked ourselves if this new proliferation of absurdity foreshadows something, or if, in expecting punishment, we are making the mistake of thinking by analogy.

It would seem that all human beings should fall into each other's arms, crying out that they cannot live, but no cry escapes from their throat and the one thing they are more or less capable of doing is putting words on paper or paint on canvas, knowing full well that so-called literature and art are instead of.

NOTES

MY INTENTION

1 "My Intention." From *Visions from San Francisco Bay* (New York: Farrar, Straus and Giroux, 1975), translated by Richard Lourie. First published in Polish as "O moim zamiarze" in *Widzenia nad zatoką San Francisco* (Paris: Instytut Literacki, 1969).

WHO WAS I?

7 "Who Was I?" Originally Chapters 1–3 of *The Land of Ulro* (New York: Farrar, Straus and Giroux, 1981), translated by Louis Iribarne. First published in *Ziemia Ulro* (Paris: Instytut Literacki, 1977). The English title has been supplied by the editors of this volume.

9 Bolesław Leśmian (1878–1937): A metaphysical poet who brought to Polish versification melodic and incantatory rhythms and playful linguistic experimentation. Deceptively simple, his often ballad-like poems feature fantastic creatures in bucolic but frightening settings.

9 Skamander: A grouping of Warsaw poets opposed to the symbolist poetics of the preceding era, celebrating vitality in life and in verse. As a group, they were the most popular poets of the interwar period.

9 Karol Irzykowski (1873–1944): The most influential literary critic of the interwar period.

12 "Debraining Machine": The French playwright Alfred Jarry's absurdist satirical drama *Ubu Roi* (1896) concludes with "The Song of the Disembraining," celebrating a machine that slices up people's brains. English translation by Barbara Wright (New York: New Directions, 1961).

NOTES ON EXILE

13 "Notes on Exile." Written in English and first published in *Books Abroad*, Volume 50: Number 2, Spring 1976.

HAPPINESS

20 "Happiness." Written in English and first published under the title "My River" in *Architectural Digest* (May 1998). The author's title for this piece has always been "Happiness."

DICTIONARY OF WILNO STREETS

27 "Dictionary of Wilno Streets." From *Beginning with My Streets: Essays and Recollections* (New York: Farrar, Straus and Giroux, 1991), translated by Madeline G. Levine. Written in 1967. First published in Polish as "Dykcyonarz wileńskich ulic," in *Pamiętnik Wileński* (London: Polska Fundacja Kulturalna, 1972), and reprinted in *Zaczynając od moich ulic* (London: Instytut Literacki, 1985).

27 The poem is "City Without a Name," part 12, translated by Czeslaw Milosz, Robert Hass, Robert Pinsky, and Renata Gorczynski.

32 Zbigniew Pronaszko (1885–1958): Painter, sculptor, graphic artist, and, for a time, a member of the arts faculty at the University of Wilno.

36 *With Fire and Sword* (*Ogniem i mieczem*, 1884): A novel by Henryk Sienkiewicz (1846–1916); an immensely popular book, the first of a trilogy of historical novels about the seventeenth-century Polish *Res Publica*.

37 The "green border" was the fluid, porous boundary dividing Soviet-occupied Poland from German-occupied Poland during the first years of World War II.

37 Pranas Ancewicz: A classmate of Milosz's at the University of Wilno and longtime friend. *Milosz's ABC's* includes an essay memorializing this "atheist, Marxist, socialist, anti-Communist, internationalist" Lithuanian from Samogitia.

43 Leon Petrażycki (1867–1931): A famous Polish scholar (philosophy and sociology of law), he was a professor at Petersburg University and, after 1917, at Warsaw University. Dr. Lande taught at Stefan Batory University in Wilno, then at Jagiellonian University in Cracow. He was a follower of the "Petrażycki school."

43 Henri de Massis's *La Défense de l'Occident* appeared in English under the title *Defense of the West*, in a translation by F. S. Flint (New York: Harcourt, Brace, 1928).

46 Zygmunt Sierakowski (1827–1863): A Polish officer in the Russian Imperial Army in St. Petersburg, he was one of the leaders of the failed 1863 Uprising and was executed by the czarist state.

50 Vsevolod Pudovkin (1893–1953): Russian film director and theorist. Like *Storm Over Asia*, his film *The Mother*, based on Maxim Gorky's novel, is a classic of Soviet film.

51 Maria Rodziewiczówna (1863–1944): A hugely popular novelist and short-story writer whose moralistic works celebrate the gentry society of the Lithuanian/Belorussian borderlands which are Milosz's spiritual home. Having virtually ignored her in his *History of Polish Literature* (New York: Macmillan, 1969), Milosz devoted a sympathetic essay to Rodziewiczówna in his as yet untranslated collection of "borderland essays," *Szukanie ojczyzny* (In Search of a Fatherland, 1992).

51 *Ashes* (*Popioły*, 1904), by Stefan Żeromski (1864–1925): A voluminous neo-Romantic historical novel about the Napoleonic era, based in part on Balzac's novel *Les Chouans*.

AFTER ALL . . .

52 "After All . . ." From *Milosz's ABC's* (New York: Farrar, Straus and Giroux, 2001), translated by Madeline G. Levine. Originally in Polish as "A przecie," the first essay in *Inne abecadło* (Cracow: Wydawnictwo Literackie, 1998).

MISS ANNA AND MISS DORA

55 "Miss Anna and Miss Dora." First published as "Drużyno, Anna i Dorcia" in *Abecadło Miłosza* (Cracow: Wydawnictwo Literackie, 1997); first English publication as "Drużyno, Anna and Dora" in *Milosz's ABC's* (New York: Farrar, Straus and Giroux, 2001), translated by Madeline G. Levine.

JOURNEY TO THE WEST

57 "Journey to the West." From *Native Realm: A Search for Self-Definition* (Garden City, N.Y.: Doubleday, 1968), translated by Catherine S. Leach. First published in Polish in *Rodzinna Europa* (Paris: Instytut Literacki, 1959).

68 Peter Kropotkin (1842–1921): Russian aristocrat and accomplished professional geologist, he is best known as a theorist and proponent of anarchic Communism.

ON OSCAR MILOSZ

77 "On Oscar Milosz." Originally Chapter 31 of *The Land of Ulro* (New York: Farrar, Straus and Giroux, 1981), translated by Louis Iribarne. In Polish, it was Chapter 32 of *Ziemia Ulro* (Paris: Instytut Literacki, 1977). Title added by the editors.

83 Stanisław Brzozowski (1878–1911): A novelist, unorthodox Marxist, and Christian philosopher; also a scathing cultural critic, he places his hopes in the inexorable march of the community of mankind toward freedom and transcendence. Czeslaw Milosz's incisive study of Brzozowski, *Człowiek wśród skorpionów* (A Man Among Scorpions, 1962), remains untranslated except for a portion that appeared as a separate essay, "A Controversial Polish Writer: Stanisław Brzozowski," *California Slavic Studies*, 2 (1963), pp. 53–95.

THE PRIORESS

85 "The Prioress." From *A Year of the Hunter* (New York: Farrar, Straus and Giroux, 1994), translated by Madeline G. Levine, where it appears, untitled, under journal entries dated July 22–July 30, 1988. Originally published in Polish in *Rok myśliwego* (Paris: Instytut Literacki, 1990).

87 Leon Schiller (1887–1954): A stage director who introduced the concept of "monumental theater" during the interwar period; he became—for political as well as artistic reasons—the dominant figure in Polish theatrical art during the postwar years.

87 Stefan Jaracz (1883–1945): An actor and stage director; he died from the effects of imprisonment in Auschwitz, from which he was rescued by the Polish underground, as was Leon Schiller.

87 Edmund Wierciński (1899–1955): Also an actor and director.

87 Bohdan Korzeniewski (1905–1992): After the war, a director and historian of the theater and, in later years, co-editor of a major Polish journal of theater studies, *Pamiętnik Teatralny.*

88 Teofil Trzciński (1878–1952): Managing director of one of Cracow's main theaters for many years; he was also a stage director.

89 Dobiesław Damięcki (1899–1951): A well-known actor and director in prewar Poland.

89 Ferdynand Goetel (1890–1960): A popular novelist, president of the Polish PEN-Club, he was an open defender of fascism before the war and active in the anti-German underground during the war. He left Poland for Great Britain in 1946.

89-90 Jerzy Zagórski (1907–1984): One of the founding members (in 1931), along with Czeslaw Milosz, of the Wilno "Żagary" group of poets. During the war, a collaborator with Milosz and Jerzy Andrzejewski in underground literary activities.

90 Jerzy Andrzejewski (1909–1983): Milosz's closest friend in occupied Warsaw. His novels reveal his evolution from prewar Catholicism to Marxism and collaboration with Poland's Communist regime, to a dissenting position by the mid-1950s and to active collaboration with the democratic opposition after 1970. "Alpha" from *The Captive Mind* (1953) is Milosz's most probing portrait of Andrzejewski.

95 Aleksander Wat (1900–1967): Cofounder of the Polish futurist movement in poetry. He spent many years in prison—as a Communist in prewar Poland, as a Pole in the Soviet Union. His harrowing memoir, *Mój wiek* (*My Century,* translated by Richard Lourie and published in an abridged version by the University of California Press in 1988), is the edited transcript of taped conversations Milosz conducted with him in Berkeley and Paris in 1965. In the 1950s, Wat reemerged as a poet of refined sensibilities; his later poems appeared in English under the title *With the Skin: Poems of Aleksander Wat,* translated and edited by Czeslaw Milosz and Leonard Nathan (New York: Ecco Press, 1989)—an edition that incorporates Milosz's earlier translations of Wat's "Mediterranean Poems."

96 *Dziady* (*Forefathers' Eve*) by Adam Mickiewicz (1798–1855), *Nieboska komedia* (*The Undivine Comedy*) by Zygmunt Krasiński (1812–1859), and *Sen srebrny Salomei* (The Silver Dream of Salomea) by Juliusz Słowacki (1809–1849) are all dramas incorporating mystical elements, written by the "Three Bards" of the Romantic era.

BROGNART: A STORY TOLD OVER A DRINK

102 "Brognart: A Story Told over a Drink." Translated by Lillian Vallee in *Emperor of the Earth: Modes of Eccentric Vision* (Berkeley: University of California Press, 1977). First written in 1960. Originally published in Polish as "Brognart: Moja opowieść przy szklance," in *Prywatne obowiązki* (Paris: Instytut Literacki, 1972).

111 Maurice Thorez (1900–1964): At the time, secretary general of the French Communist Party.

116 "Alpha the Moralist." Chapter 4 of *The Captive Mind* (New York: Random House, 1953), translated by Jane Zielonko. Originally published in Polish in *Zniewolony umysł* (Paris: Instytut Literacki, 1953). "Alpha" is Jerzy Andrzejewski; see note for p. 90.

129 Christopher: Krzysztof Kamil Baczyński (1921–1944), a lyric poet of extraordinary talent, the best of his "lost generation."

142 "Tiger." Originally the first of two chapters devoted to Tiger in *Native Realm: A Search for Self-Definition* (Garden City, N.Y.: Doubleday, 1968), translated by Catherine S. Leach. In Polish, it was the chapter "Tygrys" in *Rodzinna Europa* (Paris: Instytut Literacki, 1959). "Tiger" was Milosz's nickname for Tadeusz Kroński (1907–1958), a philosopher and professor at Warsaw University, author of a book on Hegelian philosophy. The correspondence between the Kroński and Milosz families during the crucial years 1946–1950 reveals the mutual warmth of this intense friendship. Not yet translated into English, the letters have been published in Czeslaw Milosz, *Zaraz po wojnie. Korespondencja z pisarzami, 1945–1950* (Right After the War: Correspondence with Writers, 1945–1950; Cracow: Znak, 1998).

161 Alfred Jodl (1890–1946) and Field Marshal Wilhelm Keitel (1882–1946): Both were sentenced to death by the International War Crimes Tribunal in Nuremberg. It was Keitel who signed the declaration of unconditional surrender on Germany's behalf, May 8, 1945.

162 Vissarion Grigorevich Belinsky (1811–1848): Russia's first professional literary critic, he demanded of literary works a critical, progressive engagement with social reality as well as artistic excellence.

169 "Zygmunt Hertz." From *Beginning with My Streets: Essays and Recollections* (New York: Farrar, Straus and Giroux, 1991), translated by Madeline G. Levine. Original Polish publication under the title "Był raz" in the Paris monthly *Kultura* (March 1980).

171 David Rousset's analytical memoir *L'Univers concentrationnaire* is available in English as *The Other Kingdom*, translated by Ramon Guthrie (New York: Fertig, 1982).

171 *L'Humanité*: Newspaper of the French Communist Party.

174 Boy: Pseudonym of Tadeusz Żeleński (1874–1941), a literary critic, author of popular satirical songs and cabaret scripts; he was also a prolific and accomplished translator and popularizer of French literature. Executed by the Nazis.

174 Antoni Słonimski (1895–1976): A poet, cabaret writer, journalist; his popular feuilletons provided commentary on social and political life throughout the two decades of interwar Poland.

177 Zagłoba: The big-bellied, joke-telling, Falstaffian nobleman in Sienkiewicz's trilogy (1884–1888); see note for p. 36.

177 Marek Hłasko (1934–1969): The author of violent short stories and novels that express the author's profound alienation from society.

180 Dukhobors (literally, "spirit battlers"): A Russian religious sect persecuted by the czars because of their resistance to state authority. Their emigration to North America in the late nineteenth century was financed in part by Leo Tolstoy.

181 Józef Czapski (1896–1993): Trained in Paris in the 1920s, after the war he made his home in France. He and his fellow members of the Paris Committee grouping of Polish painters emphasized the use of color in their landscapes and portraits.

183 Paweł Hertz (b. 1918): Poet, prose writer, literary functionary in Warsaw; not related to Zygmunt Hertz.

PITY

185 "Pity." From *Road-side Dog* (New York: Farrar, Straus and Giroux, 1998), translated by Czeslaw Milosz and Robert Hass. Originally in Polish under the title "Litość," in *Piesek przydrożny* (Cracow: Znak, 1997).

LETTER TO JERZY ANDRZEJEWSKI

189 "Letter to Jerzy Andrzejewski." One of five essays in the form of letters written to Jerzy Andrzejewski in 1942 and 1943 (their correspondence also included four letters by Andrzejewski to Milosz), it was first published in the Warsaw weekly *Tygodnik Literacki* (November 11, 1990) and reprinted as "List III" (Letter III) in *Legendy nowoczesności* (Cracow: Wydawnictwo Literackie, 1996). Translated for this volume by Madeline G. Levine. Regarding Andrzejewski, see note for p. 90.

192 Bruno Jasieński (1901–1939) made his debut as a futurist poet but began writing social protest poetry in the early 1920s; by 1932, having moved to the Soviet Union, he published one of the earliest Socialist Realist novels, which he wrote in Russian. He was arrested during the Terror in 1936 and died in transit in the Gulag system.

193 Hippolyte Adolphe Taine (1828–1893): A French philosopher and historian who emphasized the importance of climate and the environment in human history.

200 Alfred Rosenberg (1893–1946): A Nazi ideologist who in 1941 became minister of the eastern territories occupied by Germany. He was sentenced to death by the International War Crimes Tribunal in Nuremberg and was executed in 1946.

SPEAKING OF A MAMMAL

202 "Speaking of a Mammal." First published in English in the author's own translation in *Confluences* (Cambridge, Mass.: Harvard Summer School, 1956). Polish publication followed the English: "Mówiąc o ssaku" in *Kontynenty* (Paris: Instytut Literacki, 1958).

215 Simone Weil (1909–1943): One of the most important influences on Milosz's development as a religious thinker. See his essay in this volume, "The Importance of Simone Weil."

FACING TOO LARGE AN EXPANSE

218 "Facing Too Large an Expanse." From *Visions from San Francisco Bay* (New York: Farrar, Straus and Giroux, 1975), translated by Richard Lourie. Originally published in Polish as "Co czuję wobec zbyt dużego obszaru" in *Widzenia nad zatoką San Francisco* (Paris: Instytut Literacki, 1969).

RELIGION AND SPACE

221 "Religion and Space." From *Visions from San Francisco Bay* (New York: Farrar, Straus and Giroux, 1975), translated by Richard Lourie. Originally published in Polish as "Religia i przestrzeń" in *Widzenia nad zatoką San Francisco* (Paris: Instytut Literacki, 1969).

CARMEL

226 "Carmel." From *Visions from San Francisco Bay* (New York: Farrar, Straus and Giroux, 1975), translated by Richard Lourie. Originally published in Polish as "Carmel" in *Widzenia nad zatoką San Francisco* (Paris: Instytut Literacki, 1969).

TO ROBINSON JEFFERS

233 "To Robinson Jeffers." From *Visions from San Francisco Bay* (New York: Farrar, Straus and Giroux, 1975), translated by Czeslaw Milosz and Richard Lourie. Originally published in Polish as "Do Robinsona Jeffersa" in *Widzenia nad zatoką San Francisco* (Paris: Instytut Literacki, 1969).

ESSAY IN WHICH THE AUTHOR CONFESSES THAT HE IS ON THE SIDE OF MAN, FOR LACK OF ANYTHING BETTER

235 "Essay in Which the Author Confesses That He is on the Side of Man, for Lack of Anything Better." From *Visions from San Francisco Bay* (New York: Farrar, Straus and Giroux, 1975), translated by Richard Lourie. Originally published in Polish as "Rozdział w którym autor przyznaje się, że jest po stronie ludzi w braku czegoś lepszego," in *Widzenia nad zatoką San Francisco* (Paris: Instytut Literacki, 1969).

243 *The Doll* (*Lalka*) by Bolesław Prus (1847–1912): This large and engaging novel, published in 1890, provides a panoramic view of Warsaw society during the late 1870s, a time of much social change accompanying the development of a modern capitalist economy in Poland.

THE IMPORTANCE OF SIMONE WEIL

246 "The Importance of Simone Weil." Written in English in 1960 and published in *Emperor of the Earth: Modes of Eccentric Vision* (Berkeley: University of California Press, 1977).

247 Leszek Kołakowski (b. 1927): A philosopher and historian of Marxism, since 1968

working outside of Poland, first at Yale, then at Oxford University. The essay referred to here is "The Priest and the Jester," in *Toward a Marxist Humanism: Essays on the Left,* translated by Jane Zielonko Peel (New York: Grove Press, 1968). Kołakowski is also the author of the monumental three-volume history *Main Currents of Marxism* (Oxford: Clarendon Press, 1978), translated by P. S. Falla.

248 Bishop Jacques Bénigne Bossuet (1627–1704): French theologian, defender of the Church as the repository of truth.

SHESTOV, OR THE PURITY OF DESPAIR

260 "Shestov, or the Purity of Despair." Written in 1973 in English and published in *Emperor of the Earth: Modes of Eccentric Vision* (Berkeley: University of California Press, 1977). Later published in Polish as "Szestow, albo czystość rozpaczy" in the London periodical *Zapis* (November 1979).

261 Nikolai Berdyaev (1874–1948): Russian religious philosopher, interested in mysticism and in eschatological elements in human history. He postulated an ethics of freedom and a community of individuals striving toward Godmanhood, which will be achieved at the end of history.

261 Sergei Bulgakov (1871–1944): Russian religious philosopher, co-editor with Berdyaev of the journal *Novyi Put'* (The New Path).

266 Vasily Rozanov (1856–1919): Philosopher, journalist, literary critic. He was the first critic to read "The Legend of the Grand Inquisitor" from *The Brothers Karamazov* as a philosophical statement, which he interpreted as a direct expression of Dostoevsky's own beliefs.

266 Nikolai Strakhov (1828–1896): An influential Russian literary critic and essayist, and proponent of *pochvennichestvo,* a movement advocating the synthesis of Russian Orthodox culture and Western culture as more fertile than either pure conversion to Western ways or self-isolating Slavophilism. A colleague and first biographer of Dostoevsky, he became a trusted intellectual interlocutor of Leo Tolstoy.

272 Vladimir Solovyov (1853–1900): A religious thinker and poet, he introduced the notion of Divine Sophia, the universal feminine element, as the instrument of reconciliation among humans, a necessary step on the path to world harmony. His *Lectures on Godmanhood* were an important influence on Berdyaev's thought.

273 August Cieszkowski (1814–1894): An economist and philosopher, advocate of man's freedom to act and to shape his destiny.

DOSTOEVSKY

281 "Dostoevsky." From *Milosz's ABC's* (New York: Farrar, Straus and Giroux, 2001), translated by Madeline G. Levine. Published in Polish as "Dostojewski" in *Abecadło Miłosza* (Cracow: Wydawnictwo Literackie, 1997).

282 Anatoly Lunacharsky (1875–1933): A Marxist literary critic, he was appointed People's Commissar of Education by Lenin in 1917, a post from which he was removed by Stalin in 1929. Very influential during the "culture wars" of the early Soviet period.

A PHILOSOPHER

284 "A Philosopher." From *Road-side Dog* (New York: Farrar, Straus and Giroux, 1998), translated by Czeslaw Milosz and Robert Hass. Originally published in Polish as "Filozof" in *Piesek przydrożny* (Cracow: Znak, 1997).

SALIGIA

287 "Saligia." From *Beginning with My Streets: Essays and Recollections* (New York: Farrar, Straus and Giroux, 1991), translated by Madeline G. Levine. Written in 1974 and published in Polish under same title in *Ogród nauk* (Paris: Instytut Literacki, 1979).

IF ONLY THIS COULD BE SAID

314 "If Only This Could Be Said." Translated for this volume by Madeline G. Levine. Originally published in Polish in *Res Publica*, 11–12 (1991), under the title "Gdyby to można bylo powiedzieć . . ."; reprinted in Czeslaw Milosz, *Eseje*, edited by Marek Zaleski (Warsaw: Świat Książki, 2000).

316 *The Wedding* (*Wesele*, 1901): A play by Stanisław Wyspiański (1869–1907) that marries techniques of symbolist drama with those of the puppet theater in its merciless portrayal of Polish society as passively awaiting liberation by some unknown external force.

316 *The Marriage* (*Ślub*, 1953): A play by Witold Gombrowicz (1904–1969) that exemplifies the author's concept of the "interhuman church" in which our identities are formed and deformed by the masks, or roles, imposed on us by others.

316 *Tango* (1965): A play by Sławomir Mrożek (b. 1930) that enacts as tragicomedy the disintegration of traditional values and the temptation to reimpose them through authoritarian means.

WHY RELIGION?

329 "Why Religion?" First published in *Road-side Dog* (New York: Farrar, Straus and Giroux, 1998), translated by Czeslaw Milosz and Robert Hass. Originally published in Polish as "Zamiast zostawić" in *Piesek przydrożny* (Cracow: Znak, 1997).

REMEMBRANCE OF A CERTAIN LOVE

333 "Remembrance of a Certain Love." From *Visions from San Francisco Bay* (New York: Farrar, Straus and Giroux, 1975), translated by Richard Lourie. Published in Polish as "Wspomnienie pewnej miłości" in *Widzenia nad zatoką San Francisco* (Paris: Instytut Literacki, 1969).

A SEMI-PRIVATE LETTER ABOUT POETRY

337 "A Semi-Private Letter About Poetry." Translated for this volume by Madeline G. Levine. First published in Polish in the monthly literary journal *Twórczość* (October 1946); reprinted in *Kontynenty* (Paris: Instytut Literacki, 1958).

338 Kazimierz Wyka (1910–1975): Editor of the journal *Twórczość* (Creative Writing) from 1945 to 1950; he was a prolific literary critic whose essays on contemporary

Polish prose and poetry dominated Polish criticism during the first postwar decade.

340 Feliks Topolski (1907–1989): A Polish artist who lived in London from 1935 until his death. His depictions of Russia and Great Britain at war are the product of his service as a war correspondent. Topolski's satirical sketches chronicle contemporary life.

341 Cyprian Kamil Norwid (1821–1883): Virtually unknown during his lifetime, he was rediscovered around the turn of the twentieth century and acknowledged as a major thinker and writer of intellectual poetry and meditations on the philosophy of history.

342 Jan Kochanowski (1530–1584): Poland's great Renaissance poet, he wrote his exquisitely restrained cycle, *Laments* (*Treny*, 1580), on the occasion of his young daughter's death. There is an excellent translation of *Laments* by Stanisław Barańczak and Seamus Heaney (New York: Farrar, Straus and Giroux, 1995).

344 Walenty Wańkowicz (c. 1799–1842): A painter of Romantic scenes and of portraits, including a famous portrait of Mickiewicz.

344 Ignacy Krasicki (1735–1801): The leading writer of the Polish Enlightenment, he also was a bishop (later, archbishop) in the Catholic Church and the prolific author of fables, satires, and mock epics.

345 Józef Weyssenhoff (1860–1932): A conservative aristocrat, author of novels about the rich landowning class in the territories of the former Grand Duchy of Lithuania. In *The History of Polish Literature*, Milosz suggests that Weyssenhoff himself was unclear about what he meant to suggest by the character Podfilipski, whom Milosz dubs "a moron."

347 Maciej Kazimierz Sarbiewski (1595–1640): He wrote mainly Latin odes and was referred to as "the Christian Horace." In his Nobel lecture, Milosz calls attention to his own attraction to double vision, or viewing the earth from above.

347 *Paul et Virginie* (1787): An extremely popular tale of youthful innocence, set against a tropical landscape, written by Jacques-Henri Bernardin de Saint-Pierre (1737–1814). Widely translated, it became an important influence on Romantic literature.

347–48 The quote is from Ovid's *Metamorphoses*, Book I, lines 92–93. Literal translation supplied by Professor Philip A. Stadter.

348 Poem "In Warsaw": From *The Collected Poems, 1931–1987* (New York: Ecco Press, 1988), p. 77.

351 "Will it be a bright butterfly . . . ?": Lines from Mickiewicz's *Ustęp* (Digression), a part of *Forefathers' Eve* (*Dziady*). It is a well-known reference to the uncertain future of czarist Russia. The translation is by Milosz, from *The History of Polish Literature*, p. 224.

RUINS AND POETRY

352 "Ruins and Poetry." The fifth of the Charles Eliot Norton lectures Milosz delivered at Harvard University in 1981 and 1982, published under the title *The Witness of Poetry* (Cambridge, Mass.: Harvard University Press, 1983).

353 Michał Borwicz (b. 1911): A Polish Jew who survived the war working with the

Polish cultural underground, he is the author of a seminal study of the messages left by people condemned to death by the German occupying forces—*Écrits des condamnés à mort sous l'occupation allemande (1939–1945)* (Paris: Presses Universitaires de France, 1954). .

355 *Akropolis* by Stanisław Wyspiański (see note for p. 316): In this Symbolist drama, tapestries and statues in Cracow's Wawel Castle come to life, enabling mythological and classical Greek figures to communicate with dead Polish heroes and to enact their faith in action and resurrection.

355 Jerzy Grotowski (1933–1999) gained international recognition for his innovative theatrical productions and his theory of a "poor theater."

355 Tadeusz Różewicz (b. 1921): Playwright, short-story writer, and poet; his writings confront the moral dilemmas posed by the war and by contemporary society. Castigated by Wyka and others in the late 1940s for being "obsessed with death," he was also recognized as an authentic voice of his generation.

357 Anna Świrszczyńska, or Anna Swir (1909–1984): Milosz values her poetry, which is "about not being identical with one's body, about sharing its joys and pains and still rebelling against its laws" (from his introduction to Anna Swir, *Talking to My Body*, translated by Czeslaw Milosz and Leonard Nathan; Port Townsend, Wash.: Copper Canyon Press, 1996). Milosz has also written an appreciative critical study about Świrszczyńska, *Jakiegoż to gościa mieliśmy* (What a Guest We Had!; Cracow: Znak, 1996). Quotations from *Building the Barricade* are from the translation by Magnus J. Krynski and Robert A. Maguire (Cracow: Wydawnictwo Literackie, 1979).

360 *A Memoir of the Warsaw Uprising* (*Pamiętnik z powstania warszawskiego*, 1970) by Miron Białoszewski (1928–1983). English translation by Madeline G. Levine (Ann Arbor, Mich.: Ardis, 1977; Evanston, Ill.: Northwestern University Press, 1991).

362 Zbigniew Herbert (1924–1998): Milosz introduced Herbert's severe, intellectually and morally challenging poetry to English-language readers in *Selected Poems*, translated by Czeslaw Milosz and Peter Dale Scott (Harmondsworth, England: Penguin, 1968). Since 1977, when their collection of *Selected Poems* (Oxford: Oxford University Press, 1977) appeared, Herbert's poetry has been translated exclusively by John and Bogdana Carpenter.

365 *Lucifer Unemployed* by Aleksander Wat (see note for p. 95) was translated by Lillian Vallee (Evanston, Ill.: Northwestern University Press, 1990).

ANUS MUNDI

371 "*Anus Mundi.*" From *Milosz's ABC's* (New York: Farrar, Straus and Giroux, 2001); translated by Madeline G. Levine. First published in Polish in *Abecadło Miłosza* (Cracow: Wydawnictwo Literackie, 1997).

AGAINST INCOMPREHENSIBLE POETRY

373 "Against Incomprehensible Poetry." Translated for this volume by Madeline G. Levine. Originally planned as the introduction to Milosz's anthology, *A Book of Luminous Things* (Orlando, Fla.: Harcourt Brace, 1996), this essay was delivered as

a lecture (in Polish) at the Jagiellonian University in Cracow on May 10, 1990, and published for the first time under the title "Przeciw poezji niezrozumiałej" in the Catholic weekly *Tygodnik Powszechny* (1990, no. 21). Also published in *Eseje*, edited by Marek Zaleski (Warsaw: Świat Książki, 2000). The discussion of epiphany, beginning on p. 383, appeared as a separate piece in *A Book of Luminous Things*, p. 3.

381 Auden quote is from "Making, Knowing and Judging" in *The Dyer's Hand and Other Essays* (New York: Random House, 1962), p. 60.

384 Lawrence quote is from *Complete Poems of D. H. Lawrence*, edited by Vivian de Sola and Warren Roberts (Harmondsworth, England: Penguin, 1977).

385 Issa poem was translated by Lucien Stryk and Takashi Ikemoto.

385 Drummond de Andrade poem was translated by Elizabeth Bishop.

REFLECTIONS ON T. S. ELIOT

388 "Reflections on T. S. Eliot." Translated for this volume by Madeline G. Levine. "Myśli o T. S. Eliocie" was originally published in the Paris monthly *Kultura* (March 1965) and reprinted in *Prywatne obowiązki* (Paris: Instytut Literacki, 1972).

388 Bolesław Leśmian: See note for p. 9.

389 Stanisław Przybyszewski (1868–1927): A bohemian writer, a cultural figure, and an Expressionist with ties to Young Scandinavia, he declared that art is the sole absolute value, the only avenue of expression for the "naked soul." He saw man as in thrall to instinct, whose aim is the perpetuation of the human species; man only imagines he is free. Author of novels, essays, prose poems, and memoirs.

389 Jan Kasprowicz (1860–1926): A poet who moved from Positivism through Symbolism to Expressionism; his "hymns" express terror in the face of universally present evil.

393 "Catastrophists": Czeslaw Milosz was himself dubbed a Catastrophist, a label he accepted.

393 Józef Czechowicz (1903–1939): His ballad-like poems borrow their deceptive naïveté and simplicity of content and form from folk songs and madrigals, but this masks a darker vision that justified his being included among the Catastrophist poets.

393 Skamander: See note for pp. 89–90.

393 Ludwik Fryde (1912–1942): A Jewish literary critic who died in the Holocaust.

393 *Żagary*: See note for pp. 89–90.

394 Julian Tuwim (1894–1953): Like Jarosław Iwaszkiewicz (see note for p. 406) a member of the Skamander group of poets, he was probably the most popular poet in interwar Poland, admired for his dazzling rhythms and verbal ingenuity. Tuwim was also an admirer and translator of Russian poetry.

394 "Galician ear": Because in partitioned Poland (before 1918) Cracow was part of Galicia, the easternmost province of the Austro-Hungarian Empire, its writers were attuned to Austrian and West European, rather than Russian, literary currents and language.

394 Bolesław Miciński (1911–1943): Essayist, poet, and friend of Milosz.

395 Stanisław Ignacy Witkiewicz, also known as Witkacy (1885–1939): Playwright, professional portrait painter, essayist, and novelist. He espoused the Theater of Pure Form, renouncing realism and logic as unsuited for portraying the horrifying reality of an increasingly mechanistic, soulless society.

396 Konstanty Ildefons Gałczyński (1905–1953): Author of genuinely humorous and whimsical poems and miniature plays and also of grotesque fantasies in verse, like his wildly imaginative, ominous long poem "Ball at Solomon's."

ROBERT FROST

399 "Robert Frost." Published as "Frost, Robert" in *Milosz's ABC's* (New York: Farrar, Straus and Giroux, 2001), translated by Madeline G. Levine. Originally in *Inne abecadło* (Cracow: Wydawnictwo Literackie, 1998).

399 Leopold Staff (1878–1957): A superb craftsman as poet and translator; his humanistic poetry evolved from its Symbolist beginnings to a haiku-like purity by the end of his life.

399 Bolesław Leśmian: See note for p. 9.

ON PASTERNAK SOBERLY

404 "On Pasternak Soberly." Written in English in 1963 and published in *Books Abroad* (1970); reprinted in *Emperor of the Earth: Modes of Eccentric Vision* (Berkeley: University of California Press, 1977).

406 Jarosław Iwaszkiewicz (1894–1980): Better known as a novelist and short-story writer, his metrically innovative, sensual, vivid poems made a strong impression on the young Czeslaw Milosz.

408 Julian Tuwim: See note for p. 394.

NOTES ABOUT BRODSKY

421 "Notes About Brodsky." Translated for this volume by Madeline G. Levine. First published as "Noty o Brodskim" in *Tygodnik Powszechny* (no. 11, 1996) and reprinted in *Życie na wyspach* (Cracow: Wydawnictwo Znak, 1997).

423 Tomas Venclova (b. 1937): A Lithuanian poet, literary critic, and translator born in Milosz's beloved Wilno (Vilnius), he has been a professor of Slavic literature at Yale University since 1977. Venclova has translated Milosz's poetry into Lithuanian and is the author of the first major English-language study of Aleksander Wat, *Aleksander Wat: Life and Art of an Iconoclast* (New Haven, Conn.: Yale University Press, 1996).

424 Mikhail Lomonosov, Antiokh Kantemir, and Gavrila Derzhavin were all poets of eighteenth-century Russia. Modern Russian poetry rests upon their transformative versification. Marina Tsvetaeva, Osip Mandelstam, Boris Pasternak, and Anna Akhmatova—the great Russian poets of the twentieth century—were Brodsky's immediate predecessors, since he recognized no intermediate generation. Akhmatova was his patron and protector until he was expelled from the Soviet Union.

425 Norwid: See note for p. 341.

425 Gałczyński: See note for p. 396.

426 Krasicki: See note for p. 344.

426 Stanisław Trembecki (1735–1812): Creator of sensual, vibrant poems and of fables written in colloquial language.

428 Bruno Schulz (1892–1942): Often referred to as "the Polish Kafka," though his prose is far more lyrical and metaphorically rich, this provincial art teacher and engraver was the author of two slim volumes of dreamlike tales, *Sklepy cynamonowe* (1934) and *Sanatorium pod klepsydrą* (1937). The first, literally "Cinnamon Shops," was published in English under the title *The Street of Crocodiles,* in a translation by Celina Wieniewska (New York: Walker, 1963), and the second as *Sanatorium Under the Sign of the Hourglass,* by the same translator (New York: Walker, 1978).

FROM "NOTEBOOK"

433 Excerpts from "Notatnik" translated for this volume by Madeline G. Levine. Written between 1964 and 1966 and published in *Kultura* (1966, nos. 5 and 6); reprinted in *Prywatne obowiązki* (Paris: Instytut Literacki, 1972).

INDEX

Note: Works by Czeslaw Milosz are listed by title. All other works appear as subentries under their authors' names.